GEORGE BOWYER

COMMENTARIES

ON THE

MODERN CIVIL LAW

Elibron Classics
www.elibron.com

Elibron Classics series.

ISBN 1-4212-1351-6 (paperback)
ISBN 1-4212-1350-8 (hardcover)

This Elibron Classics Replica Edition is an unabridged facsimile of the edition published in 1848 by V. & R. Stevens and G. S. Norton, London.

COMMENTARIES

ON THE

MODERN CIVIL LAW.

BY

GEORGE BOWYER, ESQ., D.C.L.

BARRISTER-AT-LAW,

AUTHOR OF "COMMENTARIES ON THE CONSTITUTIONAL LAW OF ENGLAND."

LONDON:
V. & R. STEVENS AND G. S. NORTON,
Law Booksellers and Publishers,
(Successors to the late J. & W. T. CLARKE, of Portugal Street,)
26, BELL YARD, LINCOLN'S INN,
AND 194, FLEET STREET.
MDCCCXLVIII.

TO THE MOST NOBLE

THE MARQUIS OF LANSDOWNE, K.G.

&c. &c. &c.

LORD PRESIDENT OF HER MAJESTY'S MOST HONOURABLE PRIVY COUNCIL.

My Lord,

These Commentaries were written by the advice, and at the desire of, several learned persons, who repeatedly gave me their opinion that a Treatise, containing within a small space the most important doctrines and rules of the Roman Civil Law, clothed in an English garb, and rendered accessible even to persons unversed in legal science, would be in many ways useful and valuable.

But to compose such a work was an undertaking so novel and difficult that I should scarcely have persevered in it but for certain fortunate circumstances, which materially assisted me. And among them I am in no slight degree indebted to the encouraging manner in which your Lordship was pleased to accept the Dedication of this book.

For a work on the Civil Law to appear under the auspices of the Lord President of the Council, the Supreme Civil Law Court of the Empire, might well satisfy the wishes and surpass the hopes of its author. But above all I could desire nothing more fortunate than that my book should bear the name of a statesman engaged both by high office and by personal zeal in the general promotion of knowledge, and eminent as a patron, not only of art and letters, but of every branch of learning.

I however should feel great anxiety in submitting this Treatise to your Lordship's judgment, if I did not know that those who have passed their lives in the cultivation of learning and in great functions and offices of state, are usually most indulgent towards others; and willing to look favourably on every well-meant endeavour for the advancement of knowledge.

My hopes for the success of these Commentaries with the world at large, are chiefly founded on the nature of the objects for which they are designed. Those objects may, by their utility, in some measure compensate for the defective execution of my work. They are as follow :—

I have endeavoured to condense within a moderate number of pages all, or almóst all, the Civil Law learning that English readers will probably desire, but which few have the leisure or the inclination to seek in the Corpus Juris and its Commentators.

For this purpose I have as much as possible left out everything technical and historical, and reduced the law to its scientific elements, having regard especially to the *Modern Civil Law*,—that is to say, the Civil Law augmented and polished by the great Masters of Jurisprudence, since the commencement of the School of Bologna.

The use of the Roman Law as *written reason* has been here kept chiefly in view. As *written reason* it has long been considered throughout the Continent of Europe on the footing of a practical branch of philosophy, affording not only rules for the decision of a multitude of questions of right and wrong occurring in public and private life, but also a means of mental discipline and exercise not inferior in any respect, and in some superior, to mathematics.

I need not dwell on its use in matters of public Law. Grotius and D'Aguessau, among many other great men, have pointed out the Roman Law as the most important source of equitable rules to determine questions in the Law of Nations. All nations have admitted its authority, *non ratione imperii sed rationis imperio.* And for the same reasons it is of great authority in Ecclesiastical questions, where scrupulous equity is especially required.

These considerations have led me above all things to

explain principles and deduce them to their consequences (distinguishing what is technical or arbitrary from the equity of the Law) and to give rules and maxims, which are the pillars and keystones of the science of Justice. I have carefully explained the reasons and grounds of the Law, remembering that in the opinion of Lord Hale, they are nowhere so well given as in the Corpus Juris Civilis, and that Lord Mansfield looked upon Justinian's compilation not only as "a venerable monument of antient wisdom," but as "containing the sublimest notions both in philosophy and religion."

So careful have I been to put every doctrine in a familiar and easy form, that some readers will perhaps be offended at finding positions resembling mere truisms, which however on further inspection will prove to be necessary links in a chain of equitable deductions from fundamental principles of reason and justice.

By studying the Roman Law in this manner, as a branch of practical philosophy, the highest uses are obtained from it. Thereby the equity, the *written reason* of that system, is separated from what is arbitrary, and readily applied to the decision of doubtful questions in public and private law; and a habit of distinguishing and applying rules to facts is acquired, which is necessary to constitute a legal and a judicial mind.

The same views have led me to make this book an introduction to Grotius, Pufendorf, and Vattel, the study of which cannot be pursued with full benefit, unless it be preceded by the acquisition of a competent knowledge of the Civil Law.

The utility of the Civil Law to English Lawyers has not been absent from my mind. It is a position recognized by high authority.

The Benchers of the Middle Temple have publicly asserted it by founding a Civil Law readership for the members of that house; and it is supported by the great names of Hale, Holt, Mansfield, Hardwicke, Brougham, Grant, and Bruce.

I have therefore endeavoured to provide, what English Lawyers have often desired in vain, namely, an easy and a practical Commentary on such parts of the Civil Law as may probably be serviceable to them.

The study of the Civil Law might at one period of our history have exercised a prejudicial influence over the growing and still incomplete constitution of the realm. But no such dangers can now be apprehended in the advanced maturity of our institutions. And the cultivation of the Roman Law is eminently adapted to assist the improvement of our own, which, having been gradually created by the course of events and practice, rather than by the scientific construction of a system, must be benefited by the influence of a complete theoretical body of jurisprudence formed on philosophical principles.

I have therefore carefully noted such analogies between the English and the Imperial Law as are not trite nor accidental nor obvious, but are calculated to suggest how the former science may be illustrated, explained, and improved by the latter.

And with a view to all these objects, I have selected the best authorities on every successive point, preferring especially the great classical writers whose works constitute the Digest or Pandects of Justinian, and those commentators and text writers who are generally received as authority in the courts and the schools.

In the execution of my plan I have, for several reasons, followed the method of Justinian's Institutes, translating the more useful portions of the text, but omitting even whole Titles or Chapters where the matter contained in them seemed ill adapted to the purposes explained above. And by constantly resorting to the Pandects and the Code for authorities and principles of law, I have rendered these Commentaries an easy introduction to the great mass of learning and legal wisdom contained in those celebrated works of antiquity.

The result of these labours I now dedicate to your Lordship, trusting that, as in some costly but imperfect work of Eastern art, the beauty and richness of the materials will cause the unskilfulness of the artificer to be forgotten.

I remain, my Lord,

Your Lordship's obedient servant,

George Bowyer.

EXPLANATION

OF

REFERENCES TO THE CORPUS JURIS CIVILIS IN THIS BOOK.

REFERENCES to the Pandects or Digest are indicated by the letters Pand., followed by the Book, the Title, the Rubric of the Title, and the Number of the Law.

Thus, Pand. lib. iv. tit. i. De in Integrum Restitutionibus, L. 1, means the first law of the first title of the fourth book of the Pandects,—the title being rubricked, De in Integrum Restitutionibus. References to the Code are the same, but indicated by the word Cod. instead of Pand.

The mark § signifies a paragraph of a law: and the letters princip. or princ. mean the commencement of a law.

The famous title of the Pandects, De Regulis Juris, is referred to thus: Pand. lib. l. tit. ult. L. 4.

The 30th, 31st, and 32nd books of the Pandects are not divided into titles, but form three treatises, De Legatis and Fideicommissis. They are therefore referred to thus: Pand. lib. xxxi. lib. ii. De Legatis et Fideicommissis, L. 2.

The references to the Institutes are indicated by the letters Inst. followed by the book, the title, and the paragraph—thus: Instit. lib. iii. tit. xxv. § 4. The letters princip. signify the opening paragraph of a title.

The Novellæ Constitutiones are referred to by their numbers, preceded by the word Novell.

MODE OF REFERENCE FOLLOWED BY SOME OTHER WRITERS.

PANDECTS.

The Pandects are indicated by the letters Pand. Dig. II. D. or ff.

The most usual way of citing is thus: L. 49, § 1. ff. De Act. Empti, which signifies law 49, parag. 1, in the Pandects; title, De Actione Empti. The title is easily found by reference to its name in the table of rubrics. Some writers give the first words of the law cited, and some omit the letters ff. Another mode of reference is thus: D. De Jure Dotium, L. profectitia, § si pater, which means Digest, title De Jure Dotium; Law, commencing with the word *profectitia*; parag. commencing with the word pater.

Sometimes the letter or letters indicating the Pandects, followed by the rubric of the title, are placed last—thus :

L. profectitia, § si pater, D. De Jure Dotium.

Or the numbers of the law and paragraph are given instead of their commencing word—thus :

L. 5, § 6, D. De Jure Dotium.

The law cited is sometimes indicated by the letters Fr. instead of L.

It is not unusual to cite the Pandects by the numbers of the book, title, law, and paragraph only—thus : D. 23. 3. 5. 6.

The three books De Legatis and Fideicommissis are indicated by their numbers.

The Code.

The Code is cited in the same way as the Pandects, excepting that it is indicated by the letters Cod. or C. And some writers use the letters *Const.* (Constitutio) instead of L.

The Institutes.

The Institutes are indicated by the letters Inst. Instit. or I.

The most usual mode of citation is by the number of the paragraph, followed by the rubric or heading of the title—thus : § 3, I. (or Inst.) De Nuptiis, which signifies, parag. 3 in the Institutes ; title, De Nuptiis. The title is readily found by reference to the table of rubrics.

Sometimes the reference is made by the numbers of the paragraph, book, and title—thus :

§ 3, Inst. 1. 10.

The letters, *princ. pr.* or *princip.* designate the commencing paragraph of a title, the numbers only beginning at the second paragraph, which is § 1.

TABLE OF CONTENTS.

CHAPTER XI.

THE LAW OF THINGS.

CHAPTER XII.

THE LAW OF THINGS.

CHAPTER XIII.

THE LAW OF THINGS.

CHAPTER XIV.

THE LAW OF THINGS.

CHAPTER XV.

THE LAW OF THINGS.

CHAPTER XVI.

THE LAW OF THINGS.

CHAPTER XVII.

THE LAW OF THINGS.—INCORPOREAL THINGS.

CHAPTER XVIII.

THE LAW OF THINGS.—ACQUISITIONS BY MUNICIPAL LAW.

CHAPTER XIX.

THE LAW OF THINGS.—ACQUISITION BY MUNICIPAL LAW.—DONATIONS.

CHAPTER XX.

THE LAW OF THINGS.—POWERS OF, AND RESTRAINTS UPON, ALIENATION.

CHAPTER XXI.

THE LAW OF THINGS.—ACQUISITION OF THINGS PER UNIVERSUM.—TESTAMENTS.

CHAPTER XXII.

THE LAW OF THINGS.—TESTAMENTS.

CHAPTER XXIII.

THE LAW OF THINGS.—LEGACIES.

CHAPTER XXIV.

OF THE FALCIDIAN LAW.

CHAPTER XXV.

THE LAW OF THINGS.—FIDEICOMMISSARY INHERITANCES AND LEGACIES.

CHAPTER XXVI.

THE LAW OF THINGS.—CODICILS.

CHAPTER XXVII.

THE LAW OF THINGS.—INHERITANCE AB INTESTATO.

CHAPTER XXVIII.

THE LAW OF THINGS.—OBLIGATIONS.

CHAPTER XXIX.

THE LAW OF THINGS.—REAL CONTRACTS.

CHAPTER XXX.

THE LAW OF THINGS.—OBLIGATIONS BY WORDS.

CHAPTER XXXI.

OF CONDITIONAL CONTRACTS.

CHAPTER XXXII.

OF JOINT CONTRACTS, OR OBLIGATIONS IN SOLIDUM.

CHAPTER XXXIII.

OF VOID CONTRACTS.

CHAPTER XLII.

OF THE EXTINCTION OF OBLIGATIONS.

CHAPTER XLIII.

THE LAW OF THINGS.—OBLIGATIONS ARISING EX MALEFICIO.—THEFT.

CHAPTER XLIV.

OBLIGATIONS EX MALEFICIO.—OF RAPINE.—DAMAGE TO PROPERTY.—INJURY TO PERSONS.—OBLIGATIONS QUASI EX DELICTO.

CHAPTER XLV.

OF ACTIONS.

CHAPTER XLVI.

OF ACTIONS.

CHAPTER XLVII.

OF ACTIONS.

CHAPTER XLVIII.

OF ACTIONS.

CHAPTER XLIX.

THE LAW OF ACTIONS.—OF THE EXTINCTION AND PERPETUATION OF RIGHTS OF ACTION.

CHAPTER L.

THE LAW OF ACTIONS.—OF EXCEPTIONS AND REPLICATIONS.

CHAPTER LI.

THE LAW OF ACTIONS.—OF INTERDICTS.

CHAPTER LII.

THE LAW OF ACTIONS.—OF THE OFFICE OF THE JUDGE.—OF PARTITIONS AND BOUNDARIES.

COMMENTARIES

ON

THE MODERN CIVIL LAW.

CHAPTER I.

INTRODUCTION.

THE HISTORY OF THE ROMAN LAW DOWN TO THE REIGN OF JUSTINIAN.

The Comitia Curiata.—The Comitia Centuriata.—The Papyrian Civil Law.—The Decemviri.—The Law of the Twelve Tables —Debates of the Forum.—Actiones Legis.—The Flavian Civil Law.—The Ælian Law.—Plebiscita.—Senatus Consulta.—The Edicts of the Magistrates.—The Cornelian Law.—The Perpetual Edict.—Imperial Constitutions.—Gregorian Code.—The Hermogenean Code.—The Theodosian Code.—Enumeration of the Sources of the Roman Law. P. 6.

The elements of the Roman law cannot be learned without a previous knowledge of the sources from whence that law is derived. To understand the details of a great system of law, and to conceive a notion of it as a whole, without previously knowing how its parts arose, would be almost impossible.

We will, therefore, take a view of the rise and progress of the Roman law, before we proceed to explain the principles of that system of jurisprudence.

In the beginning (says the Jurisconsult Pomponius [a]) Rome was governed without any fixed law, and without any legal science; and all things were ruled by the discretionary power of the kings.

When the city had afterwards considerably increased, Romulus divided the people into thirty parts, which he named Curiæ, because to them belonged the care of the republic, which they governed by laws called Leges Curiatæ.

Servius Tullius introduced the Comitia Centuriata, for the purpose of giving a preponderance to the richer classes; and the Comitia Curiata afterwards fell into disuse, except for comparatively unim-

[a] Pand. lib. i. tit. i. De Origine Juris. See on this law the Commentary of Cujacius—Cujac. Op. tom. i. col. 775 (edit. Venet.).

portant purposes.[b] He divided the people into 390 centuriæ, each containing a number of citizens, who, taken together, were taxed to a certain amount, and as each centuria had one vote, riches in those assemblies greatly preponderated over numbers,—for a multitude of poor men classed together enjoyed but a single vote.[c]

Servius Tullius was the principal legislator among the Roman kings, and, according to Tacitus, even the limits of the royal authority were defined by his laws. But his successors also were the authors of many laws. The laws of all the kings were compiled together by Sextus Papirius, under the reign of Tarquinius Priscus.[d]

This compilation is called the Papirian Civil Law, but though it appears from the words of Pomponius[e] that it existed in his time, few fragments of its enactments have come down to us.

After the expulsion of the kings, their authority was abolished by the *Lex Junia de Imperio Consulari*, proposed by Junius Brutus, and their laws fell into disuse, except as customary law. Thus the Roman people were again, during nearly twenty years, governed by customary law, and the discretionary power of their magistrates,[f] the power of making laws being vested in the body of the people or nation.

Virginius, the Tribune of the People, put an end to this arbitrary authority of the consuls, by proposing a law whereby ten magistrates, entitled *Decemviri*, were invested with supreme power, that they might draw up a body of laws, and both interpret and correct them.[g]

Three legates were then appointed to proceed throughout Italy and Greece, but particularly to Lacedemon and Athens, to collect laws; and that mass of legislation was digested with the assistance of Hermodorus, a Greek exile, a native of Ephesus, and finally promulgated and inscribed on twelve tables of oak.[h] This was the celebrated code of the Twelve Tables, so highly eulogized by Cicero, who patriotically preferred their wisdom and equity to all the books of the philosophers, and which Tacitus asserts to have been the last law of those times not dictated by ambition and faction.[i]

Disjointed portions of this celebrated piece of legislation are pre-

[b] Heinecc. Antiqu. lib. i. c. i. 44.

[c] Gravina, Orig. Jur. xi.

[d] Tacit. Annal. lib. iii. c. 26.

[e] Pandect. eod. tit. § 2. Gravina, Orig. Jur. § xxxi. Gibbon, Decl. and Fall, ch. 44.

[f] Heinecc. Antiquit. Procem. 3, not. *e*. Pand. eod. tit. § 4.

[g] Pothier, Pandectæ Justinianeæ, Præf. de LL. Antiqu. Pand. eod. loc. Gravina, Orig. Jur. § xxxi.

[h] Pand. eod. loc.

[i] Cic. de Legib. ii. 23; De Orat. i. 43, 44. Tacit. An. lib. iii. § 27.

served, and they have been collected by learned men, so as to give a tolerable notion of its contents and their arrangement.

[k] The forms of judicial proceedings were regulated in the first two Tables. The third regarded the law of usury, depositum, and the execution of judgments. In the fourth, the law of marriage, and of parent and child was contained. The fifth regulated testaments, successions, and wardships. Sales, acquisition by length of possession, the rules touching the insertion of beams into the walls of neighbouring houses, and the law of divorce, were the subjects embraced by the sixth. The punishments for offences were provided by the seventh. The eighth contained the law regulating the rights which may be annexed to property over that of neighbours, and the vicinity of buildings; and gave to the corporate bodies of Rome the power of making bye laws. But this power was subject to the limitation that such bye laws should contain that main arbitrary to the public or general law.

The tent Table was the chief source of public law. It forbade objection by way of privelege from the operation of the general low prohibited noeturnal assemblies, and punished sedition. It also secured pardon to rebels returning to their allegiance, threatened a corrupt judge with capital punishment,—that is to say, loss of citizenship or liberty,—and enacted that no Roman citizen should be liable to so severe a penalty without a trial in the Centuriata Comitia.

The rites of religious worship, sepulchres, oaths, ceremonies, and things consecrated, were subjected to regulation by the tenth Table.[l]

The eleventh and twelfth Tables, which were promulgated a year after the others, are shewn by Pothier to have been a sort of supplement to them. The former commences by enacting, that when two laws do not agree, the last shall be preferred; it forbids marriages between Patricians and Plebeians; and declares detestable all sacred rites partaken with foreigners.

The last Table contained a few enactments respecting pawned goods, false and calumnious judgments, and the surrender of a slave as compensation for an injury committed by him.[m]

Such are the chief heads of the Twelve Tables which the researches of the learned have brought to light.

After the enactment of these laws, the debates of the Forum became necessary to interpret them by the authority of the learned. We are told by Heineccius that the Jurisconsulti met, for the purpose of debating and deciding disputed points, near the temple of Apollo, who is therefore called by Juvenal "*juris peritus Apollo.*"[n] There is a

[k] Gravin. Orig. Jur. xxxii.

[l] Vid. XII. Tab. apud Pothier, Pandectæ Justinianeæ. [m] Ibid.

[n] Pand. De Orig. Jur. § 5. Heinecc. Antiqu. lib. i. tit. ii. § 35. Juvenal, Sat. i. v. 128.

remarkable instance of this species of proceeding in the Institutes, where it is related,[o] that Augustus, having a doubt respecting the legality of codicils, convoked an assembly of the learned to debate and decide the question.

The law produced by the opinions of those assemblies had no specific name, but was confounded with the Civil Law. Cujacius informs us that the Patricians, who in the early times of the republic alone could enter the legal profession, made law by means of these opinions, for their own purposes.[p]

At about the same period forms of action were constructed out of those laws for the use of suitors in asserting their claims and disputing those of others before the courts.[q] All the most important civil acts, such as adoption, emancipation, the acceptation of an inheritance, and, in fact, every act having legal effects, were subjected by the Jurisconsulti to certain formulæ of a strict and technical nature.[r] They were called *actus legitimi*, or generally *actiones legis.*

The technicality of these formulæ, which, like the original writs in the English Law, became the very key of the whole law, is described by Cicero in his oration *pro Murœna*,[s] with a keen wit which drew from the learned Cato the exclamation *Quam ridiculum habemus consulem!*

That the people might not be enabled to perform those legal acts, and bring actions in whatever manner they pleased, the formulæ were solemnly and strictly defined, and committed to the custody of the College of Pontiffs. To them belonged the interpretation, and the sole privilege of granting those formulæ. These functions were performed by one among them annually elected from the body of Pontiffs, to preside over the private Law, while the others devoted themselves to the public law and to sacred matters.[t]

That state of the Roman law, consisting of the Twelve Tables, the decisions of the learned assemblies of the Patricians, and the formulæ invented by them, and strictly preserved from divulgation by their interpreters the College or Corporation of Pontiffs, continued for a century.[u]

We are told by Cicero that in his time the Pontiffs had jurisdiction only over matters connected with religion, though they kept a control over all judicial proceedings by virtue of their power of fixing the *feriœ*, or days when no court could sit.[x]

[o] Inst. lib. ii. tit. xxv. in princip.

[p] Cujac. Observ. ad loc. cit. sup.

[q] Pand. De Orig. Jur. § 6.

[r] Heinecc. Antiqu. Prooem. § 7. Gravina, Orig. Jur. § xxxii.

[s] Cic. Pro Muræn. c. ix. 13.

[t] Pand. loc. cit. Pothier, Pand. Præfat. De Leg. Antiqu. § 3.

[u] Pand. eod. tit.

[x] Cicero de Leg. ii. 19.

The formulæ were made known to the people by Gnæus Flavius, secretary of Appius Claudius, who had drawn them up in a body; and the book in which they were contained received the name of the Flavian Civil Law.[y]

The people were deprived of the fruits of this publication of the legal mysteries of the Patricians. New formulæ were invented, and jealously kept secret; but they were divulged by Sextus Ælius, and received the name of Ælian Law.[z]

After this there arose serious differences between the Patricians and Plebeians. The latter retired to the Aventinum, and afterwards to the Janiculum: and the Hortensian Law gave an universal extension to the enactments of their assemblies, under the name of *Plebiscita*, which before were binding only on their own order.[a]

The difficulty of convoking the whole body of the people or the Plebeians, necessarity threw the care of the republic into the hands of Plebistists, and the enactments of that assembly were obeyed under the name of senatus Consolta.[b] But this Senate did not acquire a legislative power equal to that formerly enjoyed by the people or by the Plebeian order until the time of the empire; and their legislative functions were circumscribed within the limits of the public administration of government.[c]

Cujacius makes use of this part of the law of Pomponius, *De Origine Juris*, relating to this matter, to explain a law of Modestinus, in which the latter Jurisconsult says that all law is created by consent, constituted by necessity, or formed by custom. The great commentator shows that Modestinus derived that law from a verse of Menander, and argues that a species of necessity has in all countries transferred the authority of the people, which the increase of numbers renders it difficult for them to exercise, from the multitude to a select body or a single person. Hence the term *jus necessarium* under which the Senatus Consulta and the Imperial Constitutions were included.[d]

The magistrates also issued law, and that the people might know what law would be followed in each species of case, they promulgated an edict at the commencement of their official duties, containing the law which they proposed to observe in the administration of justice. These edicts were called perpetual when they were intended to last the whole year, and *repentina* when issued on particular cases.[e]

The magistrates entrusted with this important authority were the

[y] Pand. lib. i. tit. ii. De Orig. Jur. § 7.

[z] Heinecc. Hist. Procem, 8.

[a] Pand. ubi sup. § 8. Pothier, Pand. tit. De Orig. Jur. § 6, not. 13.

[b] Pothier, Pand. eod. tit. § 7.

[c] Pothier, Pand. eod. tit. § 7, not. 2.

[d] Cujac. Recitat. Solemn. ad L. 7, Pand. lib. i. tit. i. De Justitia et Jure.

[e] Pothier, Pand. Præf. cap. 3, per tot.

Prætors, to whom belonged the judicial functions of the Consuls, and the Curule Ædiles in Rome, and the Proconsuls and Legates in the provinces. Their law was called *Jus Honorarium.*

The Edicts of the Prætors were by far the most important portion of the honorary law. They were commented upon by Servius Sulpicius during the lifetime of Cicero, and compiled by Ofilius under Augustus; but the Cornelian Law, whereby, about the year 686, the Prætors were bound to observe their own edicts, did not settle the Prætorian jurisprudence.

This was accomplished by the great Jurisconsult, Salvius Julianus, who filled the Prætorian office under the Emperor Hadrian. His compilation of the edicts of his predecessors was ratified by the Emperor and the Senate under the name of the *Perpetual Edict.* Julianus commented on his own code, and his commentary was followed by those of many other Jurisconsulti. At a later period of Roman history the state of parties inevitably led to the government of the commonwealth being thrown into the hands of a single person, as the power of making laws had before been transferred from the body of the people to a select assembly. Thus the legislative power became vested in the Emperor.[f]

The Imperial Constitutions became very numerous, and they were successively collected into four different bodies.[g] The first of these, the Gregorian Code, is believed by Gothofredus to have been compiled by a jurisconsult named Gregorius, who was Præfect of the Prætorium, under the Emperor Constantine, and it contained the Imperial Constitutions, from the reign of Hadrian to that of Diocletian and Maximian. The second, the Hermogenean Code, is attributed to the Jurisconsult Hermogenes, by Baronius. This opinion Pothier appears to favour, but Gothofredus ascribes it to Hermogenes, who was Præfect of the Prætorium under Diocletian. It was probably a supplement to the Gregorian Code; but fragments only of these works have reached modern times.[h]

The third code, the Theodosian, was composed under the authority of the Emperor Theodosius the younger. It contains the constitutions of the Christian Emperors, including those of Theodosius himself. It was in sixteen books, of which nine only remain entire.

The fourth code, that of Justinian, will be considered in a subsequent chapter.

We may conclude with the following enumeration of the sources of the Roman law explained in this chapter.—1. The Law enacted by the People. 2. The Civil Law, strictly so called, which proceeded from the

[f] Pand. De Orig. Jur. § 11. [g] Pothier, Pand. Præf. cap. 11, § 3.

[h] Heinecc. Hist. Procem. § xviii. § 9. Pothier, Pand. Præf. cap. 11, § 3.

interpretation of the learned. 3. The Legal Formulæ. 4. The Plebiscita, enacted by the Plebeian order, or the people, without the concurrence of the Patricians. 5. The Edicts of the Magistrates, constituting the Honorary Law. 6. The enactments of the Senate alone, or Senatus Consulta. 7. The Constitutions of the Emperors.[i]

CHAPTER II.

INTRODUCTION.

OF THE WRITINGS OF THE JURISCONSULTI; OR, RESPONSA ET INTERPRETATIO PRUDENTUM.

Origin of this branch of the Civil Law.—Quintus Mucius Scævola.—Servius Sulpicius.—**Connection of Jurisprudence with Greek Philosophy.**—The Sabinians **and Proculeans.—The Distinctions between the Method of those two Schools or Sects.—The Union of the two Schools under Hadrian.—Salvius Julianus.—The Ecclectici or Misculiones.—Gajus, Papinianus, and Ulpian.**—Decline of the **Roman Schools of Jurisprudence.**—The Constitution of Valentinian and Theodosius respecting the Authority of the Jurisconsulti. P. 10.

One branch of the Civil Law remains for consideration, namely, the writings of the Jurisconsulti to whose decisions during a thousand years, as well as to the equity of the Prætors must be attributed the preponderance of substantial justice over the technical formalities, and solemn frivolities of the antient law.

We are told by Gravina[k] that the high character and reputation for learning of the public men who professed the law first gave them authority to decide questions in consultation with their clients.

Such persons must have existed in very early times, but the first who publicly taught and professed the law was Tiberius Coruncanus. He was succeeded by Sextus Ælius, who was Censor about the year 555, Cato, Mucius, Manlius, Brutus, and Drusus. But neither these fathers of the law, nor their scholars, did more than give detached answers on particular points, and those were often of a strictly technical nature.[l]

Servius Sulpicius, who was considered the greatest orator in Rome after his friend Cicero, introduced a more scientific mode of deciding questions of law.[m]

[i] Pand. lib. i. tit. ii. De Origine Juris, § 12.

[k] Gravina, de Orig. Jur. xli.

[l] Pand. lib. i. tit. ii. De Origine Juris, § 35, 38. Pothier, Pand. Præf. pars 2da.

[m] Pand. ibid. § 43.

It is related that he had occasion to consult the most learned lawyer of the time, Quintus Mucius Scævola, and he was reproved severely by that jurisconsult for being unable to understand his opinion. It is disgraceful, said Scævola, to a patrician and an orator of causes to be ignorant of that law with which he has so much concern.[n]

This reproach so strongly impressed Sulpicius with the sense of his deficiencies that he devoted himself to legal studies; and applying his logical and philosophical learning to jurisprudence, he raised it from a technical art to an abstract science resting on principles of ethics. His works amounted to 180 volumes, in which he arranged, and explained on theoretical principles, and with dialectical method, all the decisions of his predecessors as well as his own.[o]

From that time jurisprudence became closely bound up with Greek philosophy, and the doctrines of the Jurisconsulti differed according as they were Stoics or Epicureans.

We may see throughout the treatise of Cicero respecting illustrious orators, that the public men of his time passed many of the best years of their youth in Greece under the tuition of Greek philosophers, orators, and dialecticians. Thus Greece partakes with Rome the glory of having formed the Civil Law.

The severe and mathematical logic of the Stoics forms the chief distinctive feature of the writing of the Roman lawyers; but they differed greatly as to the dogmatical principles of abstract jurisprudence.

In the reign of Augustus, the power of giving answers in consultation was restricted to those on whom the Emperor conferred that privilege; and with that innovation commenced the division of the Jurisconsulti into two sects or schools,—the *Sabinians* and the *Proculeans.*

[p] The founder of the Sabinians, Ateius Capito, whose immediate successor, Sabinus, gave his name to that school, was a constant follower of antient tradition and established practice.

Antistius Labeo, the chief of the sect to whom Proculus afterwards gave the name of Proculeans, was deeply imbued with the writings of the Greek Stoics, and, proceeding on more abstract principles, he attempted numerous innovations.

Such were the distinctive features of the doctrines professed by the two sects of Jurisconsulti, which remained unaltered after the Sabinians, under the auspices of Cassius, and the Proculeans, under those of Pegasus, had assumed the names of Cassians and Pegaseans: the

[n] Pand. eod. loc.

[o] Gravin. xlii.

[p] Pand. eod. tit. § 47. Tacit. Annal. lib. iii. § 78.

former in the reign of Nero, and the latter during that of Vespasian.[q]

The Proculeans, with more subtile and abstract dialectics, scrutinized the very nature and derivation of the principles on which a case was to be decided, and sought out legal origins in the etymology of words; but the Sabinians, when not compelled by their respect for authority to follow the doctrines of the antients, were often more equitable in their decisions than the inflexible logic and rigorous conclusions of the Proculeans would permit the latter to be.

We may deduce from the examples given in the admirable chapter of Pothier's preface to his Pandects on the Sects of the Jurisconsulti, that the fault of the Proculeans was, that when their abstract principles led to a manifestly harsh conclusion, they yet adhered to the rule, instead of doubting either its accuracy or the universality of its application. They became too strictly pragmatical, while the Sabinians, though ready to surrender their own opinions to the authority of the antients, decided more on the principle of avoiding harshness, and of seeking the most equitable decision in each case, than by the strict and rigorous application of doctrines drawn from invariable premises.

The separation of the two schools did not survive the reign of Hadrian. That Emperor restored the freedom of the legal profession by a rescript granting to all Roman citizens his permission to give legal opinions. He entrusted to Salvius Julianus, chief of the Sabinians, the task of compiling into a digest the equitable law of the Prætors, and this body of Prætorian law, known as the Perpetual Edict, the laws framed by the advice of Julianus, as well as the candid discussions of the Jurisconsulti themselves, led to the termination of their division into sects.

The succeeding lawyers drew their learning impartially from the writings of both schools, and are therefore distinguished by the title of Ecclectics or Misculiones.[r]

The most illustrious among them were Gajus, the author of the Institutes on which those of Justinian are modelled; Æmilius Papinianus, the greatest of all the Jurisconsulti;[s] Ulpian, whose works constitute a large portion of the Pandects; Julianus, Paulus, and Modestinus.

After the reign of Gordian, the successor of Maximin, the schools of Rome produced no great masters of jurisprudence. Valentinian III. and Theodosius II. attempted to remedy the inconvenience resulting from the conflict of opinions contained in the writings of preceding lawyers, by ordering the judges to follow implicitly the

[q] Pothier, Pand. Præf. pars 2, cap. 2; *De Sectis Jurisc.*

[r] Ibid.

[s] Vid. Cujac. Op. tom. iv. in Papin. princip.

decisions of the majority of five Jurisconsulti—Papinian, Paulus, Gajus, Ulpian, and Modestinus.[t]

Whether this constitution of Valentinian and Theodosius was the first law commanding the judges to follow implicitly the decisions of the Jurisconsulti is a question on which high authorities differ.

Pomponius, in the law *De Origine Juris*, writes that Augustus restricted the power of giving legal opinions to those who were privileged to do so by himself, in order that the authority of the law might be greater. He says nothing of any command to the judges to obey the Jurisconsulti, and Pothier concludes, upon strong grounds, contrary to the opinion of Heineccius and Gibbon, that the authority of the *responsa prudentum* was not positive and invariable, but obtained only when their opinions were confirmed by general reception. This view of the question is supported by Gravina, who justly remarks that force of positive law could not have been given to the opinions of a number of living men, who might frequently differ among themselves.

But he observes that where the Jurisconsulti were unanimous, or one opinion was held by the greater number, their authority, as emanating from that of the Emperor, must have been conclusive. Thus they possessed a legislative power, though not unqualified.[u]

CHAPTER III.

INTRODUCTION.

THE LEGISLATIVE WORKS OF JUSTINIAN.

First Code of Justinian.—The Commission for Compiling the Pandects.—The Labours of the Commissioners.—The Imperial Institutes.—Publication of the Pandects.—The Opinions of the Learned on the Arrangement of that Work.—Strictures on Trebonian.—The Fifty Decisions.—The New Code Published.—The Novellæ Constitutiones, or Novels.—Their Compilation.—The Thirteen Edicts.—Enumeration of the Parts of the Corpus Juris. P. 14.

THE rise and progress of the Roman Law have now been traced down to the lower Empire, and nothing remains for the completion of the historical and preliminary portion of this treatise, but to consider the change wrought in that body of jurisprudence by the authority of Justinian.

[t] Poth. Pand. Præf. pars 1, c. 4. Terrasson, Hist. de la Jurisp. Rom. p. 225. Savigny, Hist. vol. i. ch. 1.

[u] Pand. lib. i. tit. ii. De Orig. Jur. § 47. Poth. Pand. Præf. par. 1, c. 4. Heinecc. Antiqu. lib. i. tit. xi. Gibbon, chap. 44. Gravin. De Or. Jur. Civ. xli.

In the first year of his reign, A. D. 520—he issued an Imperial letter announcing to the Senate of Constantinople that he had commanded ten commissioners to draw up into one body the constitutions of all the Emperors, expunging repetitions, contradictions, and all unnecessary recitals and enactments.[x] This first code was promulgated in the third year of Justinian's reign.

In the following year the Emperor issued a commission empowering Trebonian, his celebrated minister, to choose among the learned professors of the law, as well as among the magistrates and advocates of the supreme courts, a sufficient number of persons, and with them to consolidate the most valuable portions of the writing of the sages of the law into a single volume. The authority conferred on these commissioners by the Imperial Constitution was most unbounded, and the instructions contained in that document, though clothed in pompous and prolix language, are deserving the attention of modern law reformers.

Trebonian and his seventeen colleagues completed in four years the enormous task for which ten had been allowed by Justinian; they condensed into the fifty books of the Pandects the most valuable portions of two thousand volumes of legal writings, containing three millions of verses; and those select extracts, consisting of a hundred and fifty thousand verses, were classed according to the method of the perpetual edict.[y]

But the laws of the Pandects rest upon the authority of forty writers, in whose works the entire legal science of those times was probably summed up. One month before the promulgation of the Pandects, the four books of the Institutes drawn up by three commissioners, Trebonian, Dorotheus, and Theophilus, received force of law.[z]

They were moulded upon the Institutes of Gajus, Ulpian, and Marcian, and are very superior in point of method to the Pandects, of which they contain the elements, arranged in a manner which has not yet been successfully rivalled.

In the month of December, in the year 533, an Imperial constitution was addressed by Justinian to the Senate and all the nations under his dominion, in which he gives a narrative of his legislative labours, announces the completion of the Pandects, explains the method of that volume, commands all his subjects to obey the laws therein

[x] Cod. Constit. De Novo Codice Faciendo. Cod. Const. De Justin. Cod. Confirmando. Gravin. de Orig. Jur. cxxxi.

[y] Gravin. Orig. cxxxii. Pand. Constit. *Tanta* § 19, § 1. Pothier, Pand. Præf. 3ª pars, De Op. Justin.

[z] Inst. Procem. § 3.

contained, and abrogates all those not comprised either in his Code, his Institutes, or his Pandects.

The acrimony of the Anti-Trebonian sect of modern civilians, and the zeal of their opponents, have sometimes rendered the discussion of the arrangement or method of the Pandects a party debate, rather than a useful and scientific examination of the subject.

The violence of Hotmannus drew forth from Cujacius a somewhat too zealous and uncompromising defence of the classification adopted in the Digest. That classification is explicitly condemned by Pothier; the German Vigilius failed in an attempt to rearrange its laws; the Chancellor L'Hopital completed a similar work, which has never appeared; and Cujacius himself showed his disesteem for the compilation of Trebonian, by taking it to pieces, and commenting separately on each of the ancient Jurisconsulti.[a]

The Pandects are divided into seven parts, after the method of the Perpetual Edict. The first part, composed of four books, is called *πρωτα*. After certain prolegomena upon justice and law, upon the rise and progress of the Roman law, and on each of its sources, the legal diversities in the status of persons, and the classifications of and introduction to the law of things, are expounded.

The offices of the different magistrates, the treatise on jurisdiction, and other matters of a judicial nature, prepare the way for the second part, which is entitled *De Judiciis.*[b] Here we find the celebrated classification of law, according to its objects, under the heads of *Persons*, *Things*, and *Actions*. At this part of the work, the systematic arrangement of the law, upon a comprehensive plan, comes to an end. The remainder of the Pandects is under the head of Actions; and though there is a certain concatenation of one part with another, as well as with the digressions by which various treatises, not reducible to that head, are introduced, yet no distinct scheme and broad arrangement of parts are visible.[c]

Trebonian and his associates are reproached with other defects in the execution of their work.

A digest of the enormous mass of legal rules and doctrines accumulated during more than a thousand years could not but present inconsistencies and conflicting laws; a collection of fragments could scarcely be rendered as clear as the complete theories of the original writers. Many laws became obscure by being estranged from the antient customs, events, and traditions with which they were originally connected; and the hasty completion of the gigantic task,

[a] Pothier, Pand. Præf. Cap. de Vitiis Pand.; and see the Strictures of Donellus on the Method of Trebonian, Comment. lib. i. cap. 1, princ.

[b] Constitution, *Tanta*, § 3.

[c] Pothier, Pand. Præf. pars 3, cap. 1, § 2.

for which ten years seemed insufficient to the Emperor,[d] must have in some degree aggravated those inconveniences.

The most strenuous apologists of Trebonian have failed to defend him from the imputation of having hastily executed a work for which half a century would not have been too long a period ; and the interpolations of the eighteen commissioners have met with condemnation from the greatest modern civilians.

But the great scientific attainments of Trebonian are confirmed by the testimony of the caustic Procopius ; his legal and legislative greatness has been strenuously defended by the powerful authority of Cujacius ; and a candid, conscientious, but favourable judgment has been pronounced upon his memory by the impartial Gravina.

Fifty important points of law upon which the antient Jurisconsulti differed, were singled out by the eighteen commissioners, and decided under their advice by as many Imperial Constitutions, called the Fifty Decisions. Those laws were distributed among the different titles of the code, which was subjected to the revision of four commissioners,—Dorotheus, Questor of the Sacred Palace, and three others. This new code was then promulgated and the old one abrogated, by a constitution dated on the 16th of December, in the year 534.[e]

The Code of Justinian is divided into twelve books, and its subject-matter is arranged in a method similar to that of the Pandects, but the Constitutions are arranged in each title in chronological order.

The legislative activity of Justinian was not exhausted by these labours. Numerous laws under the name of Novellæ Constitutiones, were promulgated in the Greek language, translated into Latin by the Imperial authority, and published under the name of Authentica. They were compiled together under the reign of Justin II., by a professor of Constantinople, from whom that collection acquired the name of the Authentica of Julian.[f]

An epitomized compilation of the Novels was prepared by Irnerius the second professor of the school of Bologna; but the authentic Novels of Justinian, which are to be found at the end of the Corpus Juris, were collected to the number of 168, and distributed into nine parts or collations by a law doctor, of the name of Burguntius in the year 1040.[g]

The Thirteen Edicts of Justinian and the Constitutions of his successors, Justin I., Tiberius II., and Leo Sophus, are of greater curiosity than legal authority. The former regard matters of a confined nature, and the latter never obtained a general reception.[h]

[d] Const. *Tanta*, § 12. [e] Cod. Const. *Cordi Nobis*, § 1, 2.
[f] Pothier, Pand. Præf. pars 3, c. 1, § 4. Cod. Const. *Cordi Nobis*, § 5.
[g] Poth. ubi sup. Gravin. Orig. cxxxvi. [h] Ubi sup.

The inconsistent enactments and proneness to change of Justinian are severely reflected on by Pothier; he vainly forbade all comments on his laws, boasting of having converted brass into gold; and a suspicion of venality has attached to the frequent and trifling alterations effected by the Novels. But Cujacius attributes great intrinsic merit to many of the laws prepared under the advice of Trebonian.[1]

We have now seen the origin of the several parts of which what is called the Corpus Juris Civilis is composed, namely, the Institutes, the Pandects, the Code, and the Novels.

CHAPTER IV.

GENERAL VIEW OF THE INSTITUTES AND OF LAW.

General View of the Institutes, Inst. lib. i. tit. i. De Justitia et Jure.—Of Justice and Law.—Justice.—Jurisprudence.—Precepts of Law.—Public and Private Law. P. 18.

JUSTINIAN'S Institutes, though in four bocks, are divided into three parts; 1st of Persons; 2nd of Things; and 3rd of Actions. The first part relates to the legal capacity of persons according to the natural or social circumstances in which they are placed. It does not teach their obligations and rights, otherwise it would comprehend the whole law; but it is confined to their natural, legal, and social capacity to be bound by those obligations, and to acquire and hold those rights.

The second part, entitled of things, includes within that denomination both the right *of* property or *dominium*, or the right *to* property, which is right without possession, and also the other legal rights which have not the right of property for their direct object. In the first of these classifications it is easy to recognize the English division of property in possession and property in action.

These various classes of rights are considered with reference to the manner in which they and their corresponding obligations are created and transferred from one person to another, their nature, effects, and extinction.

The third part, entitled of actions, relates to the mode in which municipal law enables men to vindicate their legal rights by calling on the civil magistrate, who wields the power of society for that purpose, to compel the fulfilment of the obligations corresponding with those rights.

[1] Cujac. Comm. in Cod. *De Legat.*

Such is the general scheme of the Institutes of Justinian, which will be our guide in the following explanation of the Civil Law.

There are two modes in which every system of law may be contemplated. It may be considered first in the abstract, and secondly with regard to its provisions or enactments. The first of these modes is the object of the two introductory titles of the Institutes—*De Justitia et Jure*, and *De Jure Naturali, Gentium et Civili*. The remainder of the Institutes regards the law with reference to its enactments.

The first of these titles will be the subject of the present chapter. It opens with a definition of justice.

Justice is a constant and perpetual will to give to every man what is his.

It has been observed that this is rather a definition of justice, as a quality of a person, than in itself abstractedly considered. To obtain more accurate notions on this subject, reference must be made to the jurists of modern times. It results from the works of Grotius and Pufendorf and their commentators, that justice, taken in its most general sense, means no more than conformity with natural law or the rules of duty. But duty may be of three species according to its different objects: 1, God; 2, ourselves; and 3, other men.

Our duty to God is regulated by natural religion and by revealed religion, for there is a portion of religion which would be binding on the conscience, even if it were not revealed in the strict sense of the word. The theory of our duty to God is the science of theology in its strictest sense, and the performance of that duty is piety. But theology in its widest sense includes all the duties of man, considering them as derived from the express or implied will of the Deity.

Our duty to ourselves is that part of moral law which does not regard others, and the conformity of our actions and thoughts to it constitutes temperance and moderation in those things, the effects of which are confined to our own mind or body.

Our duty to others consists in the conformity of our actions to their rights, or to what they have a right to expect of us.

This conformity is justice. Where it is a quality of the mind, it may be defined to be a constant and perpetual will to give to every man that which he has a right to. *Justitia* (as Ulpian says) *est constans et perpetua voluntas jus suum cuique tribuendi.*

It follows that when justice is a quality of men's actions it should be defined—the performance or fulfilment of our obligations towards others.

The definition of justice is followed by that of jurisprudence in the words of Ulpian.

Jurisprudence is the knowledge of things, human and divine, the science of justice and injustice.[k]

Ulpian here considers jurisprudence with reference to its objects. Those objects are the actions of men as they regard things human and divine. This is the true sense of the words *rerum divinarum et humanarum notitia*,—that is, the knowledge of those affairs with reference to the law.

But it may be asked,—why should things divine be included in the definition? Vinnius, in his comment on this part of the Institutes, explains this difficulty, by showing, that among the antients sacred things were under the cognizance of the Jurisconsulti, who therefore reckoned them as part of the science of jurisprudence.

The next paragraph contains three precepts of law.

The precepts of law are these: to live honourably, not to hurt any man, and to give to every one that which is his due.[l]

The first of these precepts properly regards morality, or that species of moral duty which is not enforced by civil law, and which even sometimes engenders an obligation not to do things which are permitted by the civil or municipal law.

The two other precepts are laws of negative and positive justice. Not to hurt any man is the prohibition of actions at variance with the rights of others; and the abstinence from such actions may be called negative justice. To give to every one that which is his due, on the contrary, is the fulfilment of obligations towards others which may be called positive justice.

Justinian next passes to the division of law into two parts.

This science (Jurisprudence) *has two distinct branches—Public and Private. Public law is that which regards the constitution of the Roman commonwealth; private law is touching the welfare of private men.*[m]

These two definitions of Ulpian apply only to municipal law. But public law, which regards the constitution of the Roman state, is no more than a part of public law. Thus jurists of modern times have divided public law into *internal* and *external*. The former is that which regulates the constitution and government of each community or commonwealth within itself, and the latter is that which concerns the intercourse of different commonwealths with each other. This is properly known by the name of *international law*, which is divided by Grotius into two parts, the Law of War and the Law of Peace.

[k] Instit. lib. i. tit. i. § 1. Pand. lib. i. tit. i. De Justitia et Jure, L. 10, § 2.
[l] Instit. ibid. § 3.
[m] Instit. ibid. § 4. Pand. lib. i. tit. i. De Justitia et Jure, L. 1, § 2.

Upon the affairs of War and Peace, says that illustrious writer, turn all the differences among those who acknowledge no common civil law by which those differences may be determined, such as a multitude of people not formed into a community, or persons belonging to different nations in a place where there is no civil law, or persons invested with sovereign authority.[n]

All the best writers on internal public law agree that it springs from the necessity of the social state for the welfare of man. Apart from the institution of society, man is born responsible only to God for his conduct, and therefore free in his actions so far as those actions are not restrained by natural law. But by the institution of civil society that natural law is enforced so far as it regards the actions which affect the rights or welfare of others. Thus far internal public law has for its object the enforcing of natural law. But there is another branch of internal public law, which has for its object the remaining purpose of civil society, which is the greatest possible moral and physical welfare of the whole community,[o] and here the reader must be reminded that in public as well as in private law, two sorts of laws are to be distinguished. One consists of the rules which are of the law of nature, and which being necessary consequences of the principles of justice and equity are unchangeable, and the same in all times and all places. The other is composed of the rules which are established by those who have the authority to make laws, and are called arbitrary laws, which may be established, abolished, or changed, according as occasion requires, and at the will and pleasure of the lawgiver. Arbitrary internal public law has for its principle not justice but expediency, policy, or the *salus populi*. But it is limited by its very principle; for every law of this species, as it forbids or commands something not forbidden nor commanded by natural law, is a restraint on the natural freedom of man.

It follows that any positive or arbitrary law which is not useful for the furtherance of the purposes of society is to be condemned as an encroachment on the right of men to do all those things which are not directly or indirectly prejudicial to the welfare of others. The consequence deducible from these principles is, that when a man is restrained in his natural liberty by no municipal laws but those which are requisite to prevent his violating the natural law, and to promote the greatest moral and physical welfare of the community, he is legally possessed of the fullest enjoyment of his civil rights of individual liberty.

But it must not be inferred that individuals are to judge for them-

[n] Grot. Dr. de la Guerre et de la Paix, liv. i. chap. i. § 1.

[o] Lampredi Diritto Publ. Univers. tom. 3, cap. 1.

selves how far the law may justifiably restrict their individual liberty; for it is necessary to the welfare of the commonwealth that the law should be obeyed; and thence is derived the English legal maxim, that *no man may be wiser than the law.*

Private law is defined by the Emperor to be *quod ad singulorum utilitatem pertinet.* The word utilitatem is liable to objection, as it may convey an inaccurate notion of private law. But it must be understood to mean the lawful interests or rights of individuals. Justinian then divides private law into three branches.

Private law is tripartite, for it is composed either of natural precepts, or of those of Jus Gentium, or of Civil Laws.[p]

These three divisions are the subject of the next title of the Institutes, which will be explained in the following chapter.

CHAPTER V.

OF NATURAL LAW: JUS GENTIUM.

Natural Law: Jus Gentium.—Instit. lib. i. tit. ii. De Jure Naturali, Gentium et Civili. —Doctrine of a Natural Law common to all Living Creatures.—Civil Law distinguished from *Jus Gentium.*—The Nature of the Jus Gentium of the Antients.—The Modern Doctrine respecting the Natural Law.—Its obligatory force.—Separation of Natural Law into Branches.—External Public or International Law.—Internal Public Law.—Private Law. P. 22.

The second title of the Institutes (wherein Justinian proceeds to explain the three branches of private law before enumerated) commences with the singular doctrine of a natural law common to all living beings.

Natural law is that which nature has implanted in all living things. For this law is not proper to men exclusively, but belongs to all animals, whether produced in the earth, in the air, or in the water. Thence proceeds the conjunction of the male and the female, which, in our species, we call matrimony. From thence proceeds the procreation of children, and our care in bringing them up. We perceive also that the rest of the animal creation are regarded as having a knowledge of this law.

In one sense this doctrine is correct. It is true that all living things are moved to certain actions according to and by certain invariable rules and motives, and those rules may be called natural laws, as we apply the term of the laws of nature even to those which govern

[p] Instit. lib. i. tit. i. § 4. Pand. lib. i. tit. i. De Justitia et Jure, L. 1, § 2.

inanimate matter. But except in this improper sense the definition of natural law by the Roman jurists and philosophers is erroneous, for nothing can be properly called law excepting a rule of conduct addressed to and binding on creatures capable of feeling an obligation by means of reason.[q] Pufendorf conjectures that this error of the antients sprung from the hypothesis of some philosophers respecting a certain soul of the universe, of which all others were portions, all having the same nature, but producing different effects, according to the bodies with which they were united.[r] But it is unnecessary to pursue the subject further.

Justinian proceeds to distinguish *Jus Gentium* from Civil Law, as follows:—

Civil Law is distinguished from the law of nations (Jus Gentium) because all nations who are ruled by laws and by customs are governed partly by their own particular laws, and partly by those laws which are common to all mankind. The law which a people enacts is called the civil law of that people, but that law which natural reason appoints for all mankind is called the law of nations, because all nations use it. The people of Rome are governed partly by their own laws, and partly by the laws which are common to all men.[s]

The distinction between purely municipal law and universal law is here well set forth by Gajus, whose words the Emperor adopts, but the *Jus Gentium* of the antients answers to the correct definition of natural law, and is not what modern jurists designate as the law of nations.

The antients included under the name of Jus Gentium all those rules which "*naturalis ratio inter omnes homines constituit.*" This definition included not only all those transactions among the citizens of the same nations which were governed by rules of natural equity and forms common to all men, but the very institution of civil society, which springs from the social nature of man, the institution of property, wars among different communities, and all the different consequences of the division of mankind into separate nations or commonwealths.[t]

But the more mature science of the modern civilians has rejected this classification, which includes, under the head of Jus Gentium, all that remains of the whole law, if the arbitrary law, which is peculiar to, and different in each commonwealth, be excepted.

[q] On this subject see Lampredi Diritto Publ. Univ. tom. 1, cap. 2.

[r] Pufend. Dr. des Gens. liv. ii. ch. iii. § 2.

[s] Instit. lib. i. tit. ii. § 1. Pand. lib. i. tit. i. De Justitia et Jure, L. 9.

[t] Ex hoc jure Gentium introducta bella; dicretæ gentes: regna condita: dominia distincta: agris termini positi: ædificia collocata: commercium emptiones venditiones locationes conductiones obligationes institutæ, exceptis quibusdam quæ a jure civili introductæ sunt. *Hermogenianus,* Pand. lib. i. tit. i. L. 5.

The Romans give the reason of the universality of what they call the law of nations in these words—quod *naturalis ratio* inter omnes homines constituit. But the civilians of modern times have drawn their classification from the reason of the alleged universality of the law, and not from that universality itself, which, owing to the ignorance of some nations, does not, in point of fact, exist. That reason is, because the obligatory force of the law is pointed out by the mental faculties of man.

This universally obligatory law (though not universally observed) is called *natural law*, and is thus defined by Grotius. Natural law consists in certain principles of rectitude of reason, which enable us to know that a certain action is morally right or wrong, according to its congruity or incompatibility with a reasonable and social nature, and consequently that God, who is the Author of Nature, commands or forbids that action.[u]

Natural law is considered in this definition under two aspects, that is to say, with regard to, 1st, its nature and essential qualities, and 2ndly, its obligatory force.[x]

The interest of man, and his total inability to live in a manner worthy of the superiority of his nature over that of animals, without mutual assistance, as well as the great power of human creatures to hurt each other, produced natural law, considered independently of its obligatory force. The same causes produced the social state, and from the social state and its consequences sprung the most extensive branches of natural law.

Suppose a number of men, living without any social order, and each independent of the others, like some kinds of animals. Their reason would probably induce them to see the necessity of assisting, and being on good terms with each other. This necessity would produce a sort of natural law. But if those men, finding their insulated condition inadequate to enable them to satisfy their wants, mental as well as physical, formed themselves into a community (according to the sociable or gregarious nature of mankind), those primitive rules would be totally insufficient to regulate their more complicated relations with each other. This supposed case exemplifies the distinction between pure and simple or primary natural law, and that which regards a certain state of things out of which it arises, and which is called secondary natural law.

Thus the natural law forbidding men to wantonly injure and destroy each other is independent of any particular state of things; but the

[u] Grot. Droit de la Guerre et de la Paix, liv. i. chap. i. § 10.

[x] Pufend. Dr. de la Nat. liv. xi. chap. iii.

rights of property are to a certain extent artificial, for if mankind did not acquiesce in the appropriation of things to individuals, and if that acquiescence were not required for the welfare of the human species, no man could be expected to forego a thing which he desires or of which he stands in need if he can take it from another.

But the institution of property once granted, its consequences follow from the nature of man and of that institution which is necessary for the welfare and peace of society.

Thus Paulus says that theft is forbidden by natural law, and Ulpian calls it a thing naturally wrong.[y] They refer to secondary natural law.

We may conclude that secondary natural law springs from necessity acting on the reason and the gregarious or social nature of man.

It remains to be considered what is the source or reason of the obligatory force of natural law.

The existence of natural law is a fact which we feel in our own minds, which forces upon us the sense of the truth of what is right, and the falseness and deformity of wrong or evil. We must perceive (as Cicero has shown) that it is our true interest always to obey the rules of rectitude and justice. But does it follow from the congruity of the laws of nature with the nature of things that we are bound to obey them? Does it follow from the utility to ourselves of obedience to those laws that we are under an obligation to obey them? Philanthropy and justice may be natural to some men, and in acting rightly they may act only according to their nature, but a man of a contrary disposition may argue that in seeking his own interests alone he acts according to *his* nature, and that though he may admire the self denial of those who forego their own immediate interests when incompatible with the interests of society or of others, yet he cannot see that the mere moral beauty of their actions renders those actions duties incumbent upon him. He might add that as for the argument that virtue is in the end more advantageous to those who practise it than vice, it is a calculation of interest which every man must, therefore, have a right to appreciate, and to judge of according as his reason convinces him of its correctness or incorrectness.[z]

There is but one answer to be made to this argument. It is grounded on the Divine authority. The will of God is directly or indirectly the source of all obligation.

If we look upon the nature of things and consequently the natural law arising from it as the work of a Creator, and if we believe that

[y] Pand. lib. l. tit. xvi. De Significatione Verborum, L. 47. Pand. lib. xlvii. tit. ii. De Furtis, L. 1. § 3.

[z] Barbeyrac ad Epist. Anon. Libnitz.

our conscience (that is to say, our sense and perception of the natural law) was given to us by the Creator that we might know and obey His laws, the difficulty of perceiving the source of moral obligation vanishes.

It is evident that a conscience which enables us to discriminate between good and evil, and which produces in us a sense of guilt when we have violated the natural law, could not have been given to us with any other intention than that of binding us by an obligation to observe the natural law, and of making us responsible for our transgressions against that law.

As the law of nature is the foundation of every branch of law, the Roman Jurisconsult Hermogeneanus enumerates every branch of law as partaking of the principles of Jus Gentium. The laws of war, the separation of men into nations, their governments, the institution of property, boundaries and the divisions of the earth, and transactions respecting property between man and man.[a]

This enumeration shows the separation of natural law into branches with reference to its objects; 1st, When it regards the relations of different communities with each other it is external public law, or international law; 2ndly, Where it regards the government of each community within itself, it is internal public law; 3rdly, When it regulates the rights of property of individuals and their transactions among themselves, whether they are members of the same or of different communities, it is private law.

But in the two last of these branches natural law is intermingled with arbitrary law, which is made obligatory by the express or tacit command of a human superior. Now as there is no common human superior authority over independent nations, it is evident that there can be no such thing as an arbitrary international law in the strict sense of the term, and that it must consequently consist of, or at least (as is the case with treaties) derive its force from natural law, which all men are equally bound to observe.[b]

It also follows from the same principles that there are only two modes of deciding differences between sovereign states in as far as they are sovereign, negotiations and war, both of which have for their object the conclusion of a treaty by which the differences between the sovereign powers are settled.

[a] Pand. lib. i. tit. i. De Justitia et Jure, L. 5.

[b] Pufendorf, Droit de la Nature et des Gens, liv. ii. chap. iii. § 23, not. Barbeyrac.

CHAPTER VI.

MUNICIPAL LAW.—WRITTEN LAW.

Municipal Law.—Written Law.—Instit. lib. i. tit. ii. De Jure Naturali, Gentium et Civili, § iii. § iv. § v. § vi. 1. Division of Law into Written and Unwritten, and Sub-Division of Written Law.—Privilegia or Private Laws.—Written Law. 2. Effects or Operation of Laws.—The Extinction of Laws.—Interpretation of Laws. 3. Constitutions.—The rule *Quod principi placuit legis habet vigorem.* P. 30.

After separately considering Justice and Law, and distinguishing the different branches of law one from the other, the Emperor proceeds in the third paragraph of the second title of the Institutes to the subject of municipal law.

Our law is composed, as among the Greeks, partly of written law, and partly of unwritten law. The written comprises,—Laws—Plebiscites—Decrees of the Senate—Acts of the Sovereigns—Edicts of the Magistrates, and Answers of the Learned in the Law.[c]

Law is defined by Erskine to be the command of a sovereign, containing a common rule of life for his subjects.[d]

That law which the legislator promulgates by an express command is called written law; because it is usually written in the express words of the legislator: and that which is introduced by custom, and acquires forcibly the tacit consent of the legislator, is called unwritten law; for though it is to be read in books of law, yet the words in which it is explained are not obligatory, as they contain only the assertion of the existence of the custom.[e]

The Roman Jurisconsulti describe law as a general command enacted regarding that which occurs ordinarily, and not in particular and specific cases.[f]

There are, however, a species of laws which form an exception to these principles, so far that they are intended to apply only to certain specific and insulated cases and persons. They are called in the Roman law *privilegia*, or private laws,—as contra-distinguished from leges, or public laws. But even these private laws, such as are private Acts of Parliament, may properly be defined as general commands of the legislator, because they are binding on all his subjects, so far that they must submit to those laws. Thus if a man be authorized by a

[c] Instit. lib. i. tit. ii. § 3.

[d] Erskine, Instit. book i. tit. i. § 2.

[e] Vinnii Comment. ad Instit. lib. i. tit. ii. § 3.

[f] Voet, Comm. ad Pand. lib. i. tit. iii. Pand. lib. i. tit. iii. De Legibus, L. 1, L. 3. L. 4, L. 8.

special law to do what by the general law he may not do, all the subjects of the legislative power whence that law emanates are so far bound by this private law, that they must not molest or obstruct him in the enjoyment of his privilege.[g]

The purposes of laws are thus distinguished by Modestinus. "The purpose of laws is—to command, to forbid, to permit, or to punish."[h]

Even a law which permits, is obligatory; not indeed on the person who receives the permission, but on others who are commanded not to violate the right which it vests in him. In this sense every law is a command, though they are divisible into three classes:—laws commanding,—forbidding or prohibitive, and permissive. As for the fourth class referred to by Modestinus,—those that punish,—they may belong to any of the other three classes, for any species of law may be enforced or guarded by the fear of punishment.

With regard to the effect or operation of laws on affairs between man and man, they may either permit that which is done contrary to their provisions to subsist, or they may render it null and void. In the former case, the law can only be rendered effectual by rewards,[i] or by punishments.

The laws rendered effectual by rewards are of two species:—1, Those the object of which is to induce men to do something which all men are not able to do. Such are those which offer rewards for scientific inventions. 2, Those laws, the object of which is to make men more vigilant in the performance of legal duties, or the enforcing of other laws, than they could, without oppressive rigour, be compelled to do. Such are laws offering rewards for the detection of offenders.

As for the laws enforced by punishment, they are all intended to oblige men to do their duty, or to deter them from committing wrong, and in some instances to produce their moral amendment. These are criminal laws.

It is important to distinguish in what cases the law does, and in what it does not, by implication, render void what it forbids. Voet thus determines this question.[k] Where the law forbids an act, or a certain mode of performing it, there is a presumption that, if done contrary to the prohibition, it is null and void by law. But where

[g] See the Constit. of Valentinian and Theodosius, *De Privilegiis*, Cod. lib. i. tit. xiv. L. 2.

[h] Pand. lib. i. tit. iii. De Legibus, L. 7.

[i] Pand. lib. i. tit. i. De Justitia et Jure, L. 1, § 1.

[k] Voet ad Pand. Comm. lib. i. tit. iii. De Legib. § 16. Grotius, Droit de la Guerre, liv. ii. chap. v. § 14, num. 5.

there is a penalty provided by the law, that presumption ceases, and the act is valid though punishable.[l]

But what is the effect of laws which are not directly prohibitory, but prescribe a certain act or a certain mode of performing an act? Is that which is done contrary to or not in accordance with those laws necessarily void?

The leading authority on this subject, is the following law of Papinian in the Pandects.[m] "The public law may not be changed by the pactions of private persons." But Ulpian lays it down that pactions may be made contrary to the edict of the Prætor, provided they do not tend to the public detriment.[n] He elsewhere gives a case bearing on this point of law. A man gave a dotation or marriage portion to a woman, on condition that in case of her death her husband should not pay her funeral expenses, which he was bound by law to do, out of the portion. That paction was held to be void, as contrary to what the customs of the Romans made them consider a law of public importance.[o]

Another case is given in another part of the Pandects.[p] By law, when several municipal magistrates appointed a guardian to a minor, they were all jointly responsible for his good administration. Two magistrates agreed that this liability should be on one of them only. But the Emperor Hadrian decided by his rescript that such an agreement was void, because it was contrary to a law provided to prevent a public evil, namely, the appointment of unfit guardians, or the insufficiency of the magistrates.

The Jurisconsult Julian, on the same principle, decides that a clause in a will whereby the testator desired that a guardian whom he appointed for his son should render no account, is void. That clause in the will is contrary to the policy of the law provided to prevent frauds on infants by their guardians.[q] It may be concluded from these authorities, that whenever the law requires a thing to be done, or to be done in a certain manner for the purpose of preventing a mischief, or something which is contrary to the policy of the law, in those cases the law is not merely directory, and whatever is done contrary to its provisions comes under the operation of an implied prohibition

[l] See Code, lib. i. tit. iv. De Legibus, L. 5, *De eo quod est contra legem.* Pand. lib. xlviii. tit. xix. De Pœnis, L. 41. Ulpiani Fragmenta, tit. i. § 2.

[m] Pand. lib. ii. tit. xiv. De Pactis, L. 38, *Jus publicum privatorum pactis mutari non potest.*

[n] Pand. lib. ii. tit. xiv. De Pactis, L. 7, § 14.

[o] Pand. lib. xi. tit. vii. De Religiosis, L. 20.

[p] Pand. lib. xxvii. tit. viii. De Magistratibus Conveniendis, L. 1, § 9.

[q] Pand. lib. xxvi. tit. iv. De Admin. et Peric. Tutor. L. 5, § 7.

and is therefore void. This rule, however, is subject to the exception above-mentioned, that if the law provides a penalty in case of its not being observed, the nullity is not to be presumed.

Another rule respecting the effect of laws is, that they regulate acts done after their enactment, and are not retroactive, that is to say, they do not apply to any thing anterior, unless it be so expressly provided.[r] The reason of this rule is, that the subject cannot be bound to obey the law until it is made known to him.

It follows from this principle that no law is, by the Roman jurisprudence, obligatory until made known by promulgation or publication.[s] But it is otherwise in the English law.

Laws may be extinguished entirely by dispensation, by abrogation, by subrogation, by obrogation, and by derogation. Of these terms the following explanation is given by Voet in his Commentary on the Pandects.[t]

Dispensation is where certain persons or things are in some particular instance withdrawn from the operation of the law. Dispensations can only proceed from the legislative power. This last principle is also laid down by Grotius.[u]

Abrogation is where a law is repealed by another. For later constitutions are to be followed in preference to those enacted before them.[x]

Subrogation is where any thing is added; *obrogation* where any thing is changed; and *derogation* where any thing is excluded or taken out of a law by subsequent legislation.

One more, and that a very important part of the theory of written law in general, remains to be considered. It is the interpretation of laws.[y]

"Laws;" says Julian, "cannot be so drawn up as to provide for every case that may occur: but it is sufficient that they should comprehend expressly those cases which are most frequent. Therefore it is necessary that the meaning of laws should be settled by interpretation and by imperial constitutions. Every case cannot be

[r] Cod. lib. i. tit. xiv. De Legibus, L. 7. Novel. 19, in Præfat. Novel. 73, in fin. cap. ix.

[s] Cod. lib. i. tit. xiv. De Legibus et Constit. L. 9. Ibid. tit. xviii. De Juris et Facti Ignorantia, L. 12. And see Novell. 2; Nov. 66, cap. i. Vinnii Comm. ad Instit. lib. i. tit. ii. § 3, num. 2.

[t] Voet ad Pand. lib. i. tit. iii. De Legibus, § 38.

[u] Grot. Droit de la Guerre, liv. ii. chap. xx. parag. 24. Voet, ubi sup. 25.

[x] Pand. lib. i. tit. iv. De Constitutionibus Principum, L. ult.

[y] On this subject see Domat, Loix Civiles—Traité (préliminaire) des Loix, chap. xii.; and Loix Civiles, tit. i. § 2. Burlamaqui, Principes du Droit de la Nature et des Gens, part iv. chap. xvi. vol. 3, p. 468.

expressly provided for by law: it is therefore necessary that where the intention of the law is clear, the Judge should extend it to cases of like nature in law, as those expressly provided for."[z]

But the law may comprehend within its words more as well as less than is comprised within its intention. Thus Paulus decides that it is unlawful to do a thing which though not contrary to the letter of the law is contrary to its intention. A third species of law where interpretation is requisite, is where the meaning of the law is ambiguous or otherwise doubtful.

The law is to be interpreted either by the judicial or by the legislative power; and Domat shows that the legislative power should be called upon to interpret the law only in those cases where the rules of construction which the courts are bound to follow prove insufficient to remove the difficulty. This was the original and sound doctrine of the Roman law, though after the legislative power became vested in the Emperors, legislative interpretation far exceeded those limits.[a]

The Pandects and Code contain many valuable rules of construction or interpretation, most of which are followed even in our English jurisprudence.

Paulus gives the rule that where the terms of the law have a certain settled meaning they should be so understood, and that meaning should not be changed by construction.[b] But in the last title of the Pandects there is a law of Marcellus qualifying and explaining the principle of that of Paulus, as follows:—Though nothing should be lightly changed in the meaning of settled legal forms, yet where evident equity requires it, relief should be given.[c] And thus Paulus says:—In all things, but especially in law, equity must be observed.[d]

It follows that the law should be understood according to the usual meaning of its terms, where that usual meaning does not lead to consequences manifestly contrary to equity.

The meaning of the law must be drawn from its entire context,[e] and the intention, not the mere letter, ought to be followed. *Lex interpretatione adjuvanda est. Voluntatem potiusquam verba spectari oportet.*[f]

[z] Pand. lib. i. tit. iii. De Legibus, L. 10, 11, 12.

[a] Domat, Loix Civiles, tit. i. § 2, § 12; as for the interpretation of Canons, see Cod. lib. i. tit. ii. De Sacrosanctis Ecclesiis, L. 6. Cod. lib. i. tit. xiv. De Legibus, L. ult.

[b] Pand. lib. i. tit. iii. De Legibus, L. 23.

[c] Pand. lib. l. tit. ult. De Reg. Jur. L. 183.

[d] Pand. eod. tit. L. 90.

[e] Pand. lib. i. tit. iii. De Legibus, L. 24.

[f] Pand. tit. De Conditionibus et Demonstrationibus, L. 64; lib. l. tit. penult. De Verborum Significatione, L. 219.

But a reason must not be sought for every law, because otherwise many things which are settled would be made uncertain.[g]

Laws must be construed not only according to their entire context, but in some instances by each other. Paulus says that subsequent laws regard anterior laws to which they are not contrary,[h] but where two laws disagree, the last is to be obeyed. The disagreement of a law with another or with itself may be only apparent. In most of those cases the rule of Papinian is applicable:—*Generi per speciem derogatur, et illud potissimum habitur quod ad speciem directum est.* But a general expression includes all the species of the same genus.[i] The converse of this rule is also to be observed.

One species of laws are never resorted to for the interpretation of other laws, namely, those which have been received contrary to the rules of law, and those which have been made *propter necessitatem*, that is to say for a particular exigency.[k] These laws are not to be extended by argument or inference.

The least harsh interpretation of the law should always be preferred, provided it be consistent with the intention of the legislature,[l] and in cases of ambiguity or obscurity, that meaning should be preferred which is without objection, most usual, or most probable.[m] But in case of doubt where the rules will not serve, it is safest to follow the letter of the law.[n] And where the intention of the law is clear, it must be followed, though it be harsh, according to the common saying of Ulpian, *Dura lex est sed servanda.*

Callistratus calls custom *optima legum interpres*, and he gives a rescript of the Emperor Alexander Severus, prescribing the observance of custom, and a train of uniform judicial determinations in the decision of doubtful points of law.[o] Custom will be more properly treated of hereafter. As for the observance of precedents, it is restricted by a remarkable constitution of Justinian, as follows:—"Let no judge or arbiter believe himself bound to follow official opinions which he holds not to be correct, nor even the judgments of the Prefects, or other Magnates, nor those of the Supreme Court of Prefecture, and of the other supreme courts; but we command all our judges to follow truth, justice, and the law. It does not seem good to

g Pand. lib. i. tit. iii. De Legibus, L. 20, 21.

h Pand. eod. tit. L. 26.

i Pand. lib. l. tit. ult. De Reg. Jur. L. 113. Ibid. lib. l. tit. penult. De Significatione Verborum, L. 1; ibid. L. 11.

k Pand. lib. i. tit. iii. De Legibus, L. 14. Ibid. lib. l. tit. ult. De Reg. Jur. L. 162.

l Pand. lib. i. tit. iii. De Legib. L. 18.

m Pand. ibid. L. 19. Pand. lib. l. tit. ult. L. 114.

n Pand. lib. xiv. tit. i. De Exercitoria Actione, L. 1, § 20.

o Pand. lib. i. tit. iii. De Legib. L. 37, 38.

us that if one judge decides wrong, his error should be extended to others. The decisions of the judges should be founded on law and not on precedents."—*Legibus non exemplis judicandum est.*[p]

The doctrine of the Civil Law on this subject is, that precedents must indeed be presumed to be according to law, for as Ulpian says, *Res judicata pro veritate accipitur*,[q] and the presumption is strong in proportion to the number of precedents, and the eminence of the judges from whom they emanate, but this is to be appreciated by the judge, who is to decide on his own conviction and not by a blind adherence to precedents.[r]

Laws, Plebiscita, and Senatus Consulta, require no further explanation than they have already received in a former chapter, but a few observations are necessary on *Constitutions*, which are thus described by Justinian:—

That which seems good to the Emperor has force of law, for by the Lex Regia which was enacted respecting his power, the people transferred and granted to him all their authority and power. Therefore whatever the Emperor enacted by an epistle, decreed on an inquiry made before him, or ordained by edict, is law. These are called constitutions. But some of them are personal, and are not considered as precedents, for such was not the intention of the Emperor: for that which he granted to an individual on account of particular claims, or if he inflicted a penalty, or if he granted relief to any one contrary to the ordinary course of law, all these things do not extend beyond the person. But the other constitutions are general, and they therefore extend to all men.[s]

This paragraph contains the famous maxim, *Quod principi placuit legis habet vigorem*, so much stigmatised by our English lawyers as an assertion of arbitrary power. It is, however, immediately followed by an equally explicit profession of the delegation of sovereign power to the prince by the people: *cum populus ei, et in eum omne suum imperium et potestatem conferat.* This transfer is asserted to have been made by the apochryphal[t] Lex Regia, and there are few instances in history where such a delegation by the people can be shown,[u] but it is evident that the Roman law does not attribute to the royal authority a Divine origin. The doctrine of the Divine right of Kings commenced with the Ecclesiastical, not with

[p] Cod. lib. vii. tit. xlv. De Sententiis, L. 13; and see Cujacius, Recitationes Solemnes ad Lib. vii. Pandectar. tit. De Justitia et Jure.

[q] Pand. lib. l. tit. ult. De Regul. Juris, L. 207.

[r] And see Erskine, Inst. book i. tit. i. § 16. Instit. lib. i. tit. ii. § 6.

[t] Noodt, Op. Dissert. 3, De Jure Summi Imperii.

[u] Pufendorf, Droit de la Nat. et des Gens, liv. vii. chap. xi. § 8, not. 2, Barbeyrac.

the Roman law, and is based on analogies, real or supposed, with the Jewish monarchy.[x] It is also remarkable that though the Emperor was by the Roman law *legibus solutus*, or above the law, yet the Imperial Constitutions declare that it is most worthy of his majesty to profess himself bound by the law, and to submit the regal dignity to the law.[y]

CHAPTER VII.

MUNICIPAL LAW CONTINUED.

Municipal Law.—Instit. lib. i. tit. ii. § 7, 8, 9, 11, 12.—The Edicts of the Magistrates. —The Answers of the Learned.—Customary Law: its three Requisites.—How it is Proved.—Immutable and Mutable Laws.—Explanation of the Nature of both. P. 38.

Three of the sources of Roman law remain to be considered: namely, the edicts of the magistrates; the answers or opinions of the learned; and custom.

The edicts of the Prætor were of great authority in law, and with those of the Curule Ædiles, which exclusively regarded the contract of sale, constituted what was called *Jus Honorarium*.[a] But the most important part of the honorary law flowed from the jurisdiction of the Prætors, the consolidation of whose edicts into the Perpetual Edict under Hadrian, has already been related.[b]

The[c] Prætorian Law is that which the Prætors introduced to assist, to supply the deficiency of, and to correct the Civil Law for the public good, and Marcian calls it the living voice of the Civil Law. Such is the general description of the Prætorian Law, the analogy of which to our equitable jurisprudence has been shown by Lord Chief Baron Gilbert in his learned book called Forum Romanum and Lex Prætoria.

The jurisdiction of the Prætor was divided into three parts, which were expressed by the three words—*Do*, *Dico*, *Addico*.[d] It is in

[x] Allen on Royal Prerogative (1830), p. 23. Blackst. Comm. book i. chap. iii. (edit. 16), p. 191.

[y] Voet, Comm. ad Pandect. lib. i. tit. iii. § 15. Cod. lib. i. tit. xiv. De Legib. L. 4. Digna vox est majestate regnantis legibus alligatum se principem profiteri. . . . . Et revera magis imperio submittere legibus principatum. (Theodos. et Valent. Impp.)

[a] Instit. book i. tit. ii. § 7. Pand. lib. xxi. tit. i. L. 1.

[b] Vide chap. i. supra.

[c] Pand. lib. i. tit. i. De Just. et Jur. L. 7, 8.

[d] Heinecc. Antiqu. Jur. Rom. lib. i. tit. ii. parag. 22, 23. Voet ad Pand. Comm. lib. i. tit. xiv. De Offic. Prætor.

allusion to these formulæ, that Ovid says, speaking of the days on which the judges could sit—

Licet omnia fari,
Verbaque honoratus libera Prætor habet.[e]

The word *Do* represented that part of the Prætorian jurisdiction by which the magistrate gave judges to the parties who had a right of action. By the word *Do* the Prætor also gave arbiters and *recuperatorës*. The former were commissioners having an equitable arbitrary authority, whereas judges were confined to certain points by the commission or formula of action issued to them by the Prætor.[f] Recuperators were judges appointed to decide a question of possession, and of this we have an example in Cicero's oration, *pro Cecinna*.[g] They resembled the recognitors of assize in our law. By the same formula the Prætor granted *an action*, which was the commission, without which the judges could not proceed, as our courts could not without an original writ issued from the officina justiciæ in Chancery. In the same manner the Prætor gave *an exception* or plea to the defendant, which he was then at liberty to plead before the judges, whose power was restricted to the questions submitted to them in the *actio*, and who had not, therefore, the power to determine any new allegation unless their commission was extended by the Prætor. These technical formulæ were abolished by the Emperor Constantine.[h]

Lastly, the Prætor by the word *Do* gave guardians to minors by virtue of the Atilian Law.

We come now to the word *Dico*. By that formula he issued *interdicta*, which bore an analogy to the injunctions of our courts of equity: and he ordered parties to possessory actions to go through the form of taking possession of the thing in litigation.[i]

The word *Addico* was uttered by the Prætor when he adjudged the estate of a debtor who made *cessio bonorum* to his creditors.

Though the Prætors (like our courts of equity) professed to observe the laws, they in reality changed or modified the law by their edicts under the plea of equity. They even gave relief by *restitutio in integrum* against judgments obtained by fraudulent law, and they enforced a discovery on oath by a defendant by means of an interrogatory action analogous to a bill of discovery.

These things are required to be known for the purpose of under-

[e] Ovid. Fast. lib. i. v. 47.

[f] Heinecc. Antiqu. ubi supr. and lib. iv. tit. vi.

[g] And see Plautus, Baccid. act ii. scen. 3, v. 37.
Chrysalus.—Postquam quidem Prætor recuperatores dedit.

[h] Cod. lib. ii. tit. lviii. De Formul. et Impetr. Action. Subl.

[i] Heinecc. Antiqu. ubi supr. lib. iv. tit. vi.

standing many passages in the antient classics, as well as in the Civil Law writers; but by the consolidation of the law under Justinian, the distinction between the Prætorian and the Civil Law became extinct.

The *Responsa Prudentum* are next briefly defined by Justinian.

Responsa Prudentum are the decisions and opinions of those who had the privilege of giving legal opinions upon being consulted: for in former times persons were appointed to give public interpretations of the laws, to whom Cæsar gave the power of deciding questions of law upon consultations. They were called Jurisconsulti. Their opinions and decisions were of so great authority that the judges were bound not to decide contrary to them.[k]

The last sentence refers to the celebrated constitution of Valentinian, but on the subject of the Responsa Prudentum enough has already been said.[l]

The second branch of the municipal law: namely, unwritten law, remains to be considered.

That which long use sanctioned became law without being written; for long prevailing customs become of the same nature as law by the consent of those who follow them.[m]

In the Roman law the authority of custom springs from the consent of the legislature; for what, says Julian, is the difference between the consent of the people given by their votes, and their will signified by their acts?[n] This principle is sanctioned by Grotius, who holds that on general principles any nation, however completely under subjection, may introduce a custom by virtue of the acquiescence of the legislative power.[o]

There is no general rule of public law fixing the limits of the time requisite to constitute a valid and binding custom, but the period of time during which the usage has existed must be sufficient to raise the presumption of acquiescence on the part of the sovereign.[p]

Such is the origin of the law of custom. We will now briefly examine, 1st, its effect; 2ndly, its requisites; and 3rdly, the evidence by which its existence must be supported.

I. The Emperor Constantine declares that though the authority of custom is great, yet it cannot prevail against law.[q] But this constitution refers not to the general custom, which is unwritten law, but to particular customs, which are not valid if contrary to law.[r] And in

[k] Instit. lib. i. tit. ii. § 8.

[l] Vid. chap. i. sup.

[m] Inst. lib. i. tit. ii. § 9.

[n] Pand. lib. i. tit. iii. De Legib. L. 32, L. 33.

[o] Grot. Droit de la Guerre et de la Paix, liv. ii. c. x. § 5. And see Voet ad Pand. lib. i. tit. iii. § 27.

[p] Grot. ibid.

[q] Cod. lib. viii. tit. liii. Quæ sit longa Consuetudo, L. 2.

[r] Hugonis Donelli Comment. De Jur. Civ. lib. i. cap. x. § 6.

the Roman jurisprudence, written as well as unwritten laws may be abrogated, not only by being repealed, but by becoming obsolete by custom;[s] that is to say, not by mere non use, but by contrary usage.[t]

The reason of this legal doctrine is admirably given by the great French lawyer, Cochin, as follows:—"The public authority is established for the purpose of maintaining good government and the tranquillity of society: therefore, where a too rigid adherence to, and enforcement of, the laws which it has enacted would, on the contrary, throw families into disorder and cause mischief, it is then indispensably necessary that that same authority should take into consideration the circumstances of the case. Thus, when laws have remained without execution, and where a contrary usage has prevailed, their authority can no longer be appealed to. The legislature may revive them for the future, and stop the course of their violation by a rigid attention to their execution; but all that was done before their revival must remain in full force and validity."[u]

This opinion is in accordance with a letter of the Emperor Trajan to Pliny, who had consulted him respecting the propriety and legality of enforcing an obsolete law, the *Lex Pompeia*, in Bithinia, where Pliny was Proconsul. The Emperor answered that long custom ought to prevail against the law, which should, however, be put in force for the future; but that it ought not to be revived with a retroactive effect, because such retroactive revival would produce confusion and inconvenience.[x]

This is according to justice, for obsolete law is *jus incognitum*, and Lord Bacon lays it down that the law to be just must give warning before it strikes.[y]

It must, however, be admitted that it is far better for the legislator to abrogate his laws himself than to let them lose their authority.

This is implied by the 94th Novell of the Emperor Leo, wherein he declares that the reformation of the law has for its object not only the abrogation of those which are contrary to the public good, but also to cancel those which are useless and have been forgotten and are become obsolete through disuse.

But until the law has become obsolete no custom can prevail against it. This is the meaning of Julian where he says, *De quibus causis jure scripto non utimur, id custodire oportet quod moribus et consuetudine inductum est.*[z] Now custom could only be observed

[s] Pand. lib. i. tit. iii. L. 32, § 1, in fin. So it is in the Scotch Law, Erskine, Inst. book i. tit. i. § 45; but it is otherwise in the English Law.

[t] Donellus, Comment. De Jur. Civ. lib. i. cap. x. § 5.

[u] Cochin, Op. tom. 3, Consult. 52.

[x] Plin. Epist. lib. x. epist. cxvi.

[y] Bac. Aphor. 8, sect. 1.

[z] Pand. lib. i. tit. iii. L. 32 and L. 33, ibid.

where written law was not followed, but the words *non utimur* apply as well to cases where the written law had fallen into disuse as to those in which there was no written law. This is the only construction to be put on the text of Julian, since he in the subsequent part of the same law expressly says that custom may abrogate written law, which would be a gross inconsistency if we were to follow the interpretation adopted by Blackstone, who understood Julian to say that written law excluded custom entirely, and that the Romans only adopted custom where the written law was deficient.[a]

It appears then that the meaning of the text is this:—Where we do not follow written law, we observe custom—or, in other words, we obey either written law or custom.

Custom, which has the power even to abrogate written law, must necessarily have that of controlling its interpretation. *Optima est legum interpres consuetudo.*[b] And interpretation by custom is similar in principle to interpretation by declaratory written law.[c]

One species of customary law has a more restricted effect than customary law in general. It is that usage which is introduced *non ratione sed errore*, and afterwards obtains by custom. This species of custom is not to be extended by induction and applied to other similar cases.[d]

II. We have next to consider what are the requisites of customary law. Custom to have force of law must possess three qualities. It must be—1st, not contrary to reason and justice; 2ndly, antient; and 3rdly, uniformly observed.

1st. It is not necessary that a custom should be founded on a known and sufficient reason, for, as Julian says, a reason cannot be given for all that our ancestors constituted; and Neratius adds, therefore the reason of those things must not be required, otherwise many things which are settled would be overthrown.[e] But no custom can become law that is positively unreasonable or contrary to reason and justice.[f] Such a usage is an abuse, and *malus usus abolendus non servandus.*

2nd. The second requisite of customary law is length of duration. What that duration ought to be in the Civil Law is a question much

[a] Blackst. Comm. book i. Introd. Chap. of the L. of England, p. 73, § 1.

[b] Pand. lib. i. tit. iii. L. 37 and L. 23.

[c] Voet ad Pand. Comm. lib. i. tit. iii. § 19. But note the difference explained by Voet.

[d] Pand. lib. i. tit. iii. L. 39, and vide L. 14, eod. tit. Voet understands the former law to refer to *abusus non usus*, which is void. But it seems to apply not to what is contrary to reason, but to an anomalous custom.

[e] Pand. lib. i. tit. iii. L. 20, L. 21.

[f] Cod. lib. viii. tit. liii. Quæ sit longa Consuetudo, L. 2. Pand. lib. xlvii. tit. x. De Injur. L. 13, § 7.

contested and not settled by any text in the Corpus Juris. Hotoman and Connanus in their comments on the title *De Legibus* of the Pandects, hold the duration of human life to be the standard, and that custom has force of law when it has existed beyond memory of living man. The Glossators refer the duration of custom to the standard of the period of prescription. But Vinnius argues that there is no analogy between prescription, which affects the rights only of certain individuals, and customary law binding on every man within a certain territory;[g] and he concludes, citing Cujacius, that each case must be considered separately, and that no positive limitation of time can be defined for the establishment of custom. And so it is in the law of Scotland.[h] But Donellus holds custom to be introduced in the space of ten years, which is the time limited by the law of prescription. He, however, specifies that ten years are not sufficient unless there be a frequency of acts,[i] which, however, is not precisely defined in the Civil Law, though all the authorities agree that two acts cannot induce a custom.

3rd. The third and last requisite of custom is this:—it must have been uniformly observed, that is to say, the acts constituting the custom must be uniform in all essentials; for a custom can only be established by a succession of similar acts not intermixed with contrary acts, or acts discordant with the custom.[k]

III. Nothing now remains but to consider how the existence of a custom is proved. A distinction is drawn by the Civil Law in this matter, between notorious and general custom, and mere local and not unquestionable custom. The former requires no more proof than the written law, for judicial notice of its existence is taken by the courts. It is analogous to our common law. But the latter must be proved by the party asserting and relying on it.[l]

Judicial determinations are strong evidence to prove the existence of a custom,[m] but it may be established by documentary evidence and by witnesses.

A few witnesses, however, are not sufficient. As a custom must be generally known where it prevails, it must be supported by the evidence of many witnesses, who must depose not only to some fact among those

[g] Vinn. ad Instit. Comment. lib. i. tit. iii. § 9, num. 4.
[h] Cujac. Observ. lib. xx. obs. i. tom. 3, p. 526. Erskine, Inst. book i. tit. i. § 43.
[i] Hug. Donell. Comm. lib. i. cap. x. § 2, 3.
[k] Voet ad Pand. Comm. lib. i. tit. iii. § 31.
[l] Voet ad Pand. Comm. lib. i. tit. iii. §. 32. Pand. lib. i. tit. iii. De Legib. L. 36.
[m] Pand. ibid. L. 34.

which establish the custom, but to their own knowledge that the custom exists.[n]

The reason of this is that the repetition of an act does not produce a custom, unless there be evidence of a general consent, and that the custom was generally understood to exist. This is a consequence of the very nature of custom.

As to the question what communities, and what portions of the community, may have peculiar customs, it is to be decided by the municipal law of each country.[o]

We will now proceed to the eleventh paragraph of this title of the Institutes, where the Emperor divides laws into two classes—immutable and mutable.

Natural law, which is observed equally among all men, being constituted by Divine Providence, always must remain firm and immutable. But those laws which each community enacts, peculiar to itself, are often changed, either by other laws or by tacit consent.[p]

All laws, whether public or private, human or divine, of religion or of civil government, may be reduced to two classes, which comprehend all possible descriptions of laws. Those two classes are *immutable laws*, and *mutable or arbitrary laws*.[q]

The former are those which, being principles of the law of nature, cannot be changed without violating the natural obligations upon which the order of society is founded.

The latter are those laws which are not principles of natural law, and which, as they are not essential to the obligations on which society is founded, may be changed without violating those obligations.

Arbitrary laws are of two different species, as there are two different causes which render them necessary. The first of these causes is the necessity of regulating certain cases of difficulty which arise in the application of the immutable laws, where those cases are not provided for by the immutable laws themselves. For instance :—It is a natural or immutable law, that persons who have not a sufficiently full use of their reason and discretion, from defect of maturity, or experience, or knowledge, should not have the management of their affairs : and on the other hand that they should be entrusted with the management of their property so soon as the maturity of their minds renders legal disability unnecessary for their protection.

Thus it is of natural right and an immutable law, that no man

[n] Voet ad Pand. Comm. lib. i. tit. iii. § 33, 34, 35.

[o] See on this subject Co. Litt. § 165 and note, Hargr.

[p] Inst. lib. i. tit. ii. § 11.

[q] Domat, Loix Civiles, Traité des Loix, chap. xi. per tot.

should take advantage of the necessities or the simplicity of another, to buy any thing of him at an injuriously low price. But as it would occasion great inconvenience to trade, if every unfairness in the price of a thing sold should be sufficient ground to annul the sale; and on the other hand, if the principle of natural law above referred to be enforced, a limit must be drawn somewhere; the arbitrary law of many countries has provided that a sale shall not be annulled for the lowness of the price, unless it be less than a certain proportion of the just price.

It is important to observe that each of these arbitrary laws has two distinct aspects or characters. A portion of them is immutable law, and the remainder is arbitrary law. Thus the law that regulates the annulling of sales for the wrongfulness of the price, contains two distinct provisions. One of these enacts that no one shall obtain from another his property at a wrongful price, and the other that no contract of sale shall be valid, which was entered into in consideration of a price less (for instance) than half of the just price. The former is a natural and immutable law, but the latter is an arbitrary law, for it might without injustice have fixed the limit at six-tenths or five-eighths, instead of half of the just price.

The second cause of arbitrary law is the invention of certain institutions which are believed to be beneficial to society. These laws rest chiefly on the rules of policy.

Even these matters, however, are partly regulated by immutable laws, for good faith and justice must be observed in all the transactions of life; but the number of arbitrary laws here preponderates over that of the immutable laws, whereby they are regulated. On the contrary, in matters unconnected with these arbitrary institutions, natural law predominates over arbitrary law, which is subsidiary to the former.

But immutable laws are not all similar in respect of the extent of their operation. For instance, the immutable law which makes fraud illicit, and commands good faith and honesty is universal. But the immutable law that a vendor should secure to a purchaser the possession of the thing in consideration of which the purchaser has given his money, is not universal and without exception, for the parties may agree that no warranty shall be attached to the sale.

It is of great importance to distinguish between the two different species of arbitrary laws, that the reason on which each is founded may be kept in view. It is also necessary to distinguish between those immutable laws which are universal, and those which are not so.

All questions in which there is an apparent opposition between arbitrary and immutable laws, or between different immutable laws, should be decided with reference to the respective nature of those conflicting laws, that each may be applied to the extent demanded by its nature.

Unless these distinctions be carefully attended to, it may happen that by giving the preference to an immutable law in a particular case, over an arbitrary law which regulates the application of the former, some other immutable law may be violated which was the reason and object of the arbitrary law. There is also a danger that by confounding together the two species of immutable laws, and by therefore not giving to each its proper extent according to its nature, an immutable law may be extended beyond its province, and thus some other immutable law may be violated.

The jurisprudence of immutable law is a vast and complicated system, composed of a multitude of rules, which are however all in the most perfect harmony with each other; but that harmony can only be maintained in the application of those rules, by the nicest discrimination of the nature of each law.

The application of immutable law, and the wants of human society, have created a multitude of arbitrary laws, and each of these must be applied in such a manner as to serve the purpose for which it is intended, so as not to wound any one of the immutable laws, unless the injustice of the legislator renders such a violation of equity compulsory on the Judge.

These important objects can only be attained by an accurate discrimination between arbitrary laws regulating arbitrary matters, and arbitrary laws solving difficulties arising from the application of immutable laws; as well as by carefully distinguishing the equitable from the arbitrary character of the latter species of arbitrary laws.[q]

[q] Domat, Loix Civiles, Traité des Loix, chap xi. per tot.

CHAPTER VIII.

THE OBJECTS OF LAW.

The Objects of Law.—Instit. lib. i. tit. ii. § 12.—Explanation of the Classification of Persons.—Instit. lib. i. tit. iii. princip.—Division of Persons into Freemen and Slaves: Definition of Freedom and Servitude, § 1.—Law of Marriage: Impediments Dirimant and Prohibitive.—Consanguinity and Affinity explained.—The Degrees of Collateral Consanguinity.—Restriction of the Prohibited Degrees by the Laws of the Church.—Marriages between Natural Relations. P. 47.

LAW has in the preceding pages been considered in its own abstract intrinsic nature as law. It will henceforth be considered in its rules and provisions.

Justinian introduces this part of his Institutes by the following classification of law with reference to its objects.

All law which prevails among us, is touching persons, or things, or actions. And first we will consider that law which regards persons: for it is impossible to know the law unless that which regards persons, for whom all law is constituted, is previously understood.[r]

An eminent civilian[s] has neatly expressed this classification by the following words:—Omne jus redditur personis, *de* rebus, *per* actiones et judicia. But to understand the full value of this classification, it is requisite to return to natural law.

The fundamental principle and starting point of natural law, and therefore of all law, is the natural equality of the rights of all men considered simply as such.[t] It follows that the natural duties of all men, simply as men, are equal. These are called by jurists the *absolute* rights and duties of man.

But this perfect equality of rights among men is destroyed by the diversity of their respective and reciprocal duties and rights springing from their different relations to each other; 1st, as members of families; 2ndly, as reasonable creatures living under the social state; and 3rdly, as having voluntarily entered into and contracted obligations with each other by express or tacit consent.

These are called hypothetical rights and hypothetical duties, because they assume and spring from certain relations between men, and not from human nature alone.

[r] Inst. lib. i. tit. ii. § 12, et ult.

[s] Weisembechii Comment. ad Pand. lib. i. tit. v. num. 1, not.

[t] Pand. lib. l. tit. ult. De Reg. Jur. L. 32. Ulpian . . . Quod ad jus naturale attinit, omnes homines æquales sunt.

Now the exposition of the absolute rights of men, (their rights simply as such men,) evidently requires no classification of persons. But it is otherwise with the hypothetical rights of men.

First, where those rights and the obligations correlative to them spring from the relation in which a man has placed himself with regard to other men, either as a community or as individuals, by a deliberate act, he must be capable of discrimination to perform that act in such a manner as to bind himself by those duties, and to exercise the rights springing from that act.

On this principle is founded the classification of men by nature, according as they are capable or incapable of perceiving the obligatory force of certain duties, or of exercising certain rights. This classification of persons does not extend to the absolute rights of men; for instance, an idiot has the same rights considered simply as a human creature, that belong to a wise man, but, on the other hand, it does extend to the absolute duties of men, for no man can be bound by the *vinculum juris* of a duty who is not capable of distinguishing right from wrong.

The next and sole remaining principle by which persons are classified, extends no further than the hypothetical duties and rights of men.

The relations in which persons stand with respect to each other, either as members of a community, or as members of a family, render them either by the social law, or by the natural family or patriarchal law, capable or incapable of entering into certain obligations which spring from the transactions of men with each other.

Thus persons standing in the relation of husband and wife are incapable of entering into engagements contrary to the obligations which the social law has annexed to their situation as members of a community standing in that relation towards each other. For instance, where the social law of the community gives the husband a power over the property of his wife, she is thereby disabled from entering into transactions in violation of that power.[u]

Upon a similar principle a son living in his father's family is by the natural patriarchal law, and as a member of the family, under a disability to enter into any otherwise not unlawful transaction which is incompatible with his obligations as member of the family.

These doctrines may be summed up as follow. Men are bound by four distinct species of obligations; 1st, as men simply; 2ndly, as men placed under certain obligations by natural relations with others; 3rdly, as members of a community; and 4thly, as having bound themselves by various acts and transactions of social life.

[u] Grotius, Droit de la Guerre, liv. xi. ch. v.

Now the municipal law must distinguish and classify persons, with reference to their natural and their social capacity, to be bound by those four species of obligations, or to possess and enjoy the four species of rights of which those obligations are counterparts.

It follows that persons must be legally classified with reference—1st, to nature; 2ndly, to the family; and 3rdly, to the community; and according as they are capable or incapable under those three aspects of being bound by, or of entering into those four enumerated species of obligations—of men—of members of a family—of members of society—or of contracting parties.

They must also be classified in law according as they are capable or incapable of the possession or exercise of three species of rights correlative to the three last of the four species of obligations, that is to say, the rights of members of a family—of members of society, and of contracting parties, or persons taking on themselves obligations by their own act.

This enumeration includes every legal classification of persons whether by public or by private law. The public law classifies persons according as they possess, or are capable or incapable of acquiring or exercising portions of the civil power of government, including Ecclesiastical functions when the church is established by law, and all the remaining classifications with reference to other legal capacities and incapacities of persons belong to private law.[x]

As for the classification of things it is easily understood. They are classified according to diversities in their nature: for instance, moveable or immoveable, and according to the nature of the rights by which they are held as property by persons. The jurisprudence of the rights of things relates to the mode of acquiring, holding, and transferring them by natural law, and by means peculiar to the Civil or Municipal Law.

The third great division, *of Actions*, relates to the remedies provided by the Municipal Law to enable persons to enforce their rights, or for the purpose of restraining wrongs by the infliction of punishment on wrong doers.

Justinian commences his classification of persons according to the Civil Law by dividing them into two parts,—freemen, and slaves,[y] and then he defines freedom and slavery as follows, according to Florentinus and Ulpian in the Pandects.

[x] These legal doctrines are taken from the great works of Grotius and Pufendorf, but so much condensed that particular references would be too numerous.

[y] Instit. lib. i. tit. iii. De Jure Personarum, princip.

Freedom is the natural faculty of doing what each man pleases except that which is forbidden by force or law.[z]

Servitude is an institution of the Law of Nations, whereby a man is subjected to the right of property by another, contrary to nature.[a]

These two definitions are so celebrated that they could not be omitted here, but the law of slaves is happily so obsolete as to be mere matter of curiosity. It occupies the portion of the first book of the Institutes, from the third to the eighth title, where persons in bondage are sub-divided into slaves, and unemancipated children who, according to the Roman Law, were in a species of bondage to their fathers. The ninth title regards the paternal power by the Roman Law, a subject which has no practical value in our times and country. The paternal power could only arise by the procreation of children in lawful marriage or by adoption, and thus the ninth title forms a natural transition to the tenth, which is entitled *De Nuptiis.*

This part of the Civil Law deserves attention, because the law of marriage is in all Christian countries founded on the rules of the Canon Law, which are in a great degree derived from the Roman jurisprudence.

The following general principles on the subject of the marriage contract should in the first place be understood.

Marriage is defined by Pothier to be an engagement, clothed with the forms prescribed by law, whereby a man and a woman who are both capable of entering together into that engagement, bind themselves towards each other to live together during their lives in the manner prescribed by the duties of husband and wife, principally for the purpose of procreating children.

But though that purpose of marriage be the most essential and natural, yet marriage is fully completed, so far as its obligatory force is concerned, by lawful consent.[b]

Among Roman citizens there were two species of marriage; one was called *Justæ Nuptiæ*, and the other Concubinatus.

The latter was as lawful a marriage as the former, and subject to the same legal restrictions, except those respecting difference of rank. Thus no man could marry as a concubine the wife or the concubine of another, nor a woman so nearly related to him that he could not make her his wife. The difference between *Justæ Nuptiæ* and Concubinatus

[z] Inst. lib. i. tit. iii. De Jure Personarum, § 1. Pand. lib. i. tit. v. De Statu Homin. L. 4.

[a] Inst. ibid. § 2. Pand. lib. i. tit. v. De Statu Homin. L. 4, § 1. Pand. lib. l. tit. ult. De Reg. Jur. L. 32.

[b] Pand. lib. l. tit. ult. De Reg. Jur. L. 30. Ulp. *Nuptias non concubitus sed consensus facit.*

consisted in the intention with which the marriage was contracted. In the latter case that intention was not to elevate the woman to the rank of a wife, (*justa uxor*,) and consequently the children proceeding from such an union, though not *spurii*, nor *nothi*, were not *justi liberi*. The father had not the full paternal power over them. He had them not in bondage, and consequently they were not his heirs by the antient Civil Law. Such children were called *liberi naturales*. This inferior species of marriage was instituted for the purpose of enabling Roman citizens to marry such women as they could not by law, or according to the rules of social rank, make their wives. That indulgent legislation was acquiesced in by the Christian church. The 17th Canon of the Council of Toledo, held in the year 400, sanctions the union of a Christian with a single concubine where both parties were free from previous bonds; and this species of connection has been continued in Germany, under the names of Morganatic or left-handed marriage.

These distinctions did not exist among those who were not Roman citizens. Their marriages were distinguished by the name of *Matrimonium*, and the less honourable name of *Contubernium* belonged to the marriages of slaves.

Marriage is a contract which, according to the doctrine of the Roman Catholic Church, has been elevated by the Christian religion to the dignity of a sacrament, and to which the Established Anglican Church attributes a sacramental character. But it is here to be considered as a contract in a legal or civil, and not in a religious view.

Of marriage, considered in this light, Justinian says:—*Those contract lawful matrimony who, being Roman citizens, unite according to the precepts of the law, both parties being of the age of puberty, provided that if they are under paternal power they have the consent of their father.*[c]

The expression *contract matrimony* in this text implies, and all the authorities agree, that matrimony is a contract, and thus Ulpian lays it down that *nuptias non concubitus sed consensus facit*. It ollows then that wherever consent is wanting the marriage is void, and this the contract of marriage has in common with other contracts. Consent is wanting whenever the acquiescence or apparent consent of one or both of the parties was obtained or given through error, force, or fraud.

Ulpian defines consent to be where persons *ex diversis animi motibus in unum concurrunt, id est, in unam sententiam decurrunt*,[d] and else-

[c] Instit. lib. i. tit. x. De Nuptiis, princip.

[d] Pand. lib. ii. tit. xiv. De Pactis, L. 1, § 3.

where he decides that a person acting under the influence of error does not consent.[e]

But by the Canon Law no error can make a marriage null that does not fall upon the identity of the person.[f] Thus an error respecting some quality of the person does not render the marriage void. A Novel of Justinian[g] makes an exception to this rule, by enacting that a marriage, with a slave who the other party believed to be a free person, is void.

It is evident that the employment of force or intimidation is incompatible with consent properly so called.[h] But a marriage cannot be dissolved as being brought about by intimidation or force, unless that intimidation or force were such as might have determined a person of ordinary firmness, nor unless the compulsion were *contra bonos mores*, as Ulpian expresses it.[i]

The effect of fraud is to produce error; and fraud is as incompatible with lawful consent as error itself. But the effect of fraud upon the validity of marriage is more extensive than that of error without fraud, for the Civil Law applies to this matter the maxim, no man shall take advantage of his own wrong.[k] These principles matrimony has in common with all other contracts, but the text of Justinian given above points out three requisites for lawful matrimony, the first general, and the other two specific. They are—1st, Conformity with the Law; 2ndly, Puberty; and 3rdly, the Consent of the Parent.

Pothier observes that it is competent to the authority of the state to regulate all contracts and restrict their use according as may seem requisite for the welfare of the community, and that matrimony is more particularly subject to this control. It is exercised in two modes:—1st, by making marriage void in which the provisions of the law were not observed or were violated; and 2ndly, by punishing disobedience to those provisions by a penalty. The facts producing nullity are called by the Canonists *dirimant impediments*, and those which are only followed by a punishment, civil or spiritual, are denominated *prohibitive impediments*.[l] Some of both these classes are called *absolute* impediments, because they prevent the person subject to them from marrying at all without either the nullity of the mar-

[e] Pand. lib. l. tit. ult. L. 116, § 2.

[f] Decret. Gratian. 2da pars, Causa xxix. Quæst. i.

[g] Novel. 22.

[h] Pand lib. l. tit. ult. De Reg. Jur. L. 116.

[i] Pothier, Traité du Mariage, part 4, ch. 1, art. 11. Lancelot, Instit. Jur. Canon. lib. ii. tit. xii. § 19. Pand. lib. iv. tit. ii. Quod Metus Causa, L. 3.

[k] Pand. lib. l. tit. ult. L. 134, § 1. *Nemo ex suo delicto meliorem suam conditionem facere potest.*

[l] Lancelot, Instit. Jur. Canon. tit. *De Nuptiis.*

riage or its being punishable, and others are called relative, because they regard only certain persons with respect to each other.[m]

Under these two classifications are included all the facts the effect of which is to make a marriage either void or unlawful. Dirimant impediments are derived either from Natural Law, or from Civil Law, or from Ecclesiastical Law sanctioned by the Municipal Law.

Of the former of these three classes are those which have been already explained under the head of defect of consent. To the law of nature also must be referred want of lawful age, which the Roman Law limited at twelve years in females, and fourteen in males; and provided that either of the parties married below that age should be at liberty to disagree from and declare void their premature union upon reaching the age of consent.[n]

But the Canon Law judges of puberty from physical capacity rather than age (according to the doctrine of the Sabinian school of Roman Jurisconsulti), looking chiefly to the procreation of children as the purpose of marriage.[o]

On the same principle is founded the dirimant impediment of impotency.

Defect of reason (from whatever cause it may proceed) is also a dirimant impediment, because it implies want of consent.[p]

A subsisting marriage is a dirimant impediment, and, according to Grotius, a natural impediment also.[q] But the former engagement must be an actual marriage by words *de presenti*, and not an engagement by words *de futuro*, which by the Canon Law is no more than a promise of marriage.[r]

Grotius also refers to natural law the dirimant impediment arising from the prohibition of marriages between ancestors and descendants and between the children of the same parents.[s]

We come now to dirimant impediments arising from the Civil Law, and from Ecclesiastical Law sanctioned by the temporal law. These will best be considered together, though the distinction between their respective origins cannot, as matter of history, be omitted.

[m] Pothier, Traité du Mar. part 3, ch. 1, § 90. Lancelot, Instit. Jur. Canon. lib. xi. tit. xii. not.

[n] Pand. lib. xxiii. tit. ii. De Ritu Nupt. L. 4. Constitut. Imp. Leonis, Constit. cix. And see the Comm[s]. of Vinnius and Heineccius on this tit. of the Institutes.

[o] Cap. *Puberes;* Extra. (Decretals), De Spons. Impuber.

[p] Pothier, Traité du Mar. part 3, ch. 2, art. 1. Pothier, Traité des Obligations, part 1, chap. 1. art. 4.

[q] Grotius, Droit de la Guerre et de la Paix, liv. xi. chap. v. § xi.

[r] Poth. Tr. du Mar. part 3, ch. 2, art. 1. Lancelot, Inst. Jur. Can. tit. De Nupt. § 6, tit. De Sponsal. § 22.

[s] Grot. ubi sup. § 12, et seq.

The Canon Law reckons eleven distinct impediments of these two classes, but we will confine our attention to those which are most important.

The most remarkable is relationship within the prohibited degrees.

Relationship is of two species—1, Consanguinity; and 2, Affinity.

Consanguinity is direct or collateral. The former is the relationship which exists between an ancestor and a descendant; and the latter is the relationship between persons descended from a common ancestor. The degrees of direct consanguinity are reckoned by counting the number of descents between the two. Thus father and son are related in the first degree, and grandfather and grandson in the second degree.

The degrees of collateral consanguinity are differently reckoned in the Canon and in the Civil Law. The Canon Law counts the number of descents between the common ancestor of the two persons and the one of them who is most distant from that common ancestor. Thus brothers are in the first degree to each other, and a child of one of them is in the second degree to his uncle and aunt. But the Civil Law reckons the number of descents between the persons on both sides from the common ancestor. Thus brothers are, by the Civil Law, in the second degree.

In the law of marriage, consanguinity is reckoned according to the Canon Law. This was established by the Council of Lateran under Pope Alexander II. in the year 1065. The prohibited degrees, which had been more extended under the Imperial Law, were restricted to the fourth degree among collaterals, by the Council of Lateran, held under Innocent III. in the year 1215. The prohibition of marriage between ancestors and descendants, however, still remains without limit.

Pothier lays it down that natural consanguinity, not arising from marriage, is subject to the same prohibitions as legitimate consanguinity, and this the Roman Scævola decides in express words.[t]

Affinity is relationship by marriage,[u] and by the Roman Law it did not depend on consummation. The Canon Law decided the contrary, and holding the husband and wife to be one flesh, has laid down the rule that the relations of each are related in the same degree to the other. Thus the brother of the wife is brother to the husband.[x]

The Council of Lateran limited the prohibited degrees of affinity in

[t] Pothier, Tr. du Mari. part 3, chap. 3, § 149. Pand. lib. iii. tit. ii. De Ritu Nupt. L. 54. *Et nihil interest ex justis nuptiis cognatio descendat an vero non: nam et vulgo quæsitam sororem quis vetatur uxorem ducere.*

[u] Pand. lib. xxxviii. tit. x. De Grad. et adfinibus, L. 4, § 3.

[x] Pothier, Tr. du Mari. part 3, chap. 3, art. 2.

the same manner as those of consanguinity: consequently a widow or widower cannot, by the Ecclesiastical Law, marry any relation within the fourth degree of the deceased husband or wife.[y]

Clandestinity, or the want of celebration in the face of the church, is also a dirimant impediment by the Ecclesiastical Law,[z] but this subject is very differently regulated in different countries.

We come now to prohibitory impediments which make marriage not void but punishable, or at least unlawful or sinful. In the first place, circumstances which, had they existed at the time of celebration, would have been dirimant, if they supervene subsequently are prohibitory impediments to the use of matrimonial rights.[a]

Precontract is by Ecclesiastical Law a prohibitive impediment.[b]

There are other impediments of this class, but the regulations of different countries vary so greatly on this subject, and are so incapable of being reduced to general principles, that it would not be profitable to enter into an account of them according to the Civil and Canon Law.

The Law of Adoption naturally follows that of Marriage, but it is a subject on which it is unnecessary to enter in a treatise such as this.

CHAPTER IX.

OF WARDSHIPS.

Of Wardships.—Instit. lib. i. tit. xiii. De Tutelis; tit. xv. xvi. xx. xxi. xxii.—Subdivision of Persons *Sui Juris*.—Guardianship, by Will, by Law, and by Appointment of the Magistrate.—Authority of Guardians.—Capacity and Liability of Infants.—Termination of Guardianship.—Puberty. P. 54.

A SUBDIVISION of persons *sui juris*, that is to say, neither in servitude nor under the paternal power (which by the Roman Law was a species of bondage), next requires our attention. It is this. Persons *sui juris* are either under guardianship, or under curatorship, or under neither. And first, of those who are under guardianship.

By the Roman Law, in the times of Justinian, infants were under

[y] Pothier, Tr. du Mari. part 3, chap. 3, art. 2. And see Co. Litt. § 20, n.

[z] Hericourt, Loix Eccles. part 3, chap. 5. art. 3, num. 71.

[a] Ibid. num. 8.

[b] *Ne quis.* Extra. (Decretals), De Sponsal.

the authority of guardians until the age of puberty, but by the modern Civil Law, guardianship does not finish until full majority.[c]

Guardianship is defined by Justinian, in the words of Sulpicius, to be a lawful power and authority over a free citizen to protect him who, by reason of his immature age, cannot protect himself.[d] The latter part of the definition is intended to exclude curatorship, by which those were governed who were under incapacities not proceeding from childhood, such as adolescents below twenty-five years of age, prodigals, persons insane, and persons labouring under incapacity arising from incurable diseases.

Vinnius enumerates three species of guardianship—1st, by will; 2nd, by the law; and 3rd, by appointment of the magistrate.

With regard to the first of these (guardianship by will), three cases are distinguished by the Roman Law:—1st, that of children in bondage; 2ndly, that of posthumous children; and 3rdly, that of children emancipated.

The Law of the Twelve Tables gave to fathers the power of appointing guardians by will to their children, being subject to the *patria potestas*.[e] This species of testamentary guardianship arises entirely from the obsolete law of the paternal power. We will therefore proceed to the testamentary guardianship of posthumous children.

The Roman Law considering (as in many other cases) posthumous children as born before their father's death, allows him to assign guardians to them by will, provided they would have been under his bondage if they had been born in his lifetime.[f]

The important doctrine on which this species of guardianship is founded—that children *in utero*, or *en ventre sa mere*, are to be considered as actually born in all matters affecting their interest—has been partially admitted into our law,[g] and it is carried to the fullest extent by the Roman Law.[h] We come now to the third species of guardianship by will, that applicable to emancipated children.

The Twelve Tables only allowed the father to appoint guardians by will for his children under his *patria potestas*. It follows that after their emancipation, which extinguished his power over them, he could

[c] Vinnii Comment. ad Instit. lib. i. tit. xxii. Proem, n. 5. See on the subject of Wardship, Domat, Loix Civiles, tit. Des Tutelles, liv. ii., tit. i.; Burge, Comment. vol. 3, p. 930. See Blackst. Com. book i. chap. xvii. [d] Inst. lib. i. tit. xiii. § 2.

[e] Pand. lib. xxvi. tit. ii. De Testamentaria Tutela, L. 1, princip. § 2. Voet, Comm. ad Pand. lib. xxvi. tit. ii. [f] Instit. lib. i. tit. xiii. De Tutelis, § 4.

[g] Blackst. Com. book ii. chap. xi. § 3, p. 169, note by Coleridge. Stat. 10 and 11 Will. III. cap. 16.

[h] Pand. lib. i. tit. iii. De Statu Hom. L. 7, L. 26. Voet, Com. ad Pand. lib. i. tit. iii. Pand. lib. l. tit. penult. De Verbor. Signif. L. 231.

no longer assign guardians to them by will. But in this species of case, and in others where the assignment of a guardian by will was not valid at Civil Law, the magistrate in whom was vested the jurisdiction to appoint guardians confirmed the appointment and thus supplied the defect.[i] This confirmation was, however, not in every case decreed in the same way. The general rule was that before the confirmation was decreed, an enquiry was made into the fitness of the guardian for the office, and security taken for his due administration. This rule was observed where the appointment was by the will of the mother (except as to giving security) or of any other ancestor, but not in general where it was by the will of the father, because he was held to be the best judge of the fitness of the guardian.[k]

This privilege of the guardian appointed by the father's will was, however, not allowed where circumstances could be shown to have arisen since the date of the testament, raising a presumption that if the father had been aware of them he would not have wished the confirmation to be decreed. This presumption is particularly cogent where the will was made by the father a short time before his death, and so as to render it probable that he did not know, or had not time to deliberate and act upon, the circumstances in question.[l] The general principle of the Roman Law in this matter is, that the Prætor must consider the welfare of the infant rather than the words of the testament or codicil.[m]

Upon the same important principle is grounded a celebrated law of Pomponius, where a distinction is drawn between those parts of a will which produce an obligation to execute them, and those which rest only on the *auctoritas scribentis*, that is to say, upon the respect due to the intentions of the deceased. Thus, when a testator provided as follows—"let my children remain where their mother thinks fit," Scævola held that that part of the will rested in the discretion of the Prætor. The reason is that though respect is due to the expressed intentions of the testator, yet the Prætor may have grounds for holding that it is inexpedient for the infants to remain where the mother wishes, or even where the father by his will expressly desires them to be: and it must be presumed that the father had nothing in view but the welfare of his children.[n]

[i] Vinnii Comment. ad Inst. lib. i. tit. xiii. De Tutelis, § 5. Pand. lib. xxvi. tit. iii. De Confirmando Tutore, L. 1, § 1.

[k] Pand. lib. xxvi. tit. iii. De Confirmando Tutore, L. 3, L. 6.

[l] Pand. ibid. L. 8.

[m] Pand. ibid. L. 10. *Utilitatem pupillorum Prætor sequitur, non scripturam testamenti vel codicillorum.*

[n] Pand. lib. xxxiii. tit. i. De Annuis Legatis, L. 7. *In testamentis quædam scribuntur*

In the case of a natural child, that is to say, the child of a concubine, the appointment of a guardian by the father's will was not confirmed without an inquiry, unless accompanied by the bequest of a competent provision;[o] and the appointment of a guardian by any other person, except the father, is not capable of confirmation, unless with such provision.[p]

As for bastards, *spurii*, born out of both marriage and concubinage, they by the Roman Law follow the condition of their mother, and therefore cannot receive guardians except with an inheritance by will, or by the appointment of the magistrate.[q]

The second kind of guardianship, that is to say, Guardianship by Law, or succession, is of four species:—1st, that of the agnati or relatives by consanguinity; 2nd, that of patrons over their enfranchised slaves; 3rd, that of fathers over their emancipated children; and 4thly, fiduciary guardianship, which is that of the father over his nephews and nieces, emancipated by their deceased father. These are all called *legitimæ tutelæ*, or guardianships by law, because they took place by law in default of appointment by will.

The first only of them requires explanation here, as the other three spring from the obsolete Civil Law of servitude and paternal power.

Guardianship by affinity of blood was restricted by the Law of the Twelve Tables to *agnati*, that is to say, relatives in the male line to the exclusion of the *cognati*, or relatives through females.[r] But the law on this subject in the Institutes was altered by the 118th Novell of Justinian.[s]

That celebrated law from which the English Statute of Distributions is believed to have been derived, admitted relations in the female as well as the male line, equally to succeed to the guardianship in the same order of line and degree in which they would succeed to an inheritance: that is to say, ascendants excluding collaterals, collaterals of the whole blood excluding those of the half blood, and the nearest in degree of affinity in each line excluding the others. It was however provided that no female should succeed to the guardianship except the mother or grandmother of the infant, and that those relatives who were disqualified by law should be passed over. But where there was

quæ ad auctoritatem duntaxat scribentis referuntur, nec obligationem pariunt . . . . Et in omnibus ubi auctoritas sola testatoris est, neque omnimodo spernenda neque omnimodo observanda est, sed interventu judicis hæc omnia debent, si non ad turpem causam feruntur, ad effectum perduci.

[o] Pand. lib. xxvi. tit. iii. De Confirm. Tutor, L. 7.

[p] Vinnii Comment. ad Instit. lib. i. tit. xiii.

[q] Pand. lib. i. tit. v. De Statu Hominum, L. 25, L. 24, L. 19.

[r] Instit. lib. i. tit. xv.

[s] Novel. 118, cap. 15.

more than one qualified person in the same degree and line, it was enacted that the Judge should appoint one or more persons out of the number at his discretion, and that the property of the persons so appointed should be liable for their administration in the same manner as if they had taken the guardianship by legal succession.

The *jus agnationis*, or right of consanguinity, was extinguished by loss of liberty, loss of citizenship, or of status or legal capacity as a person *sui juris*.[t] These changes in the legal situation of a person were called *capitis diminutiones*. The first was called *maxima*, in which a citizen became a slave; *media*, by which a man lost citizenship, as for instance, if he was banished for ever; and the third was called *minima capitis diminutio*, in which a man in his own power placed himself under the paternal bondage of another by adoption, or where a father emancipated his son; for in the latter case the son lost the quality of *suus hæres* of his father, and being forisfamiliated could not inherit under the Law of the Twelve Tables, nor indeed by the Civil Law, as contra-distinguished from the Prætorian Law.

We come now to the third species of guardianship. It is guardianship by appointment of the magistrate, which the Romans called *tutela dativa*. This jurisdiction of the Roman magistrate to appoint guardians and curators, bears some analogy with that of the Court of Chancery in England. Both were assumed originally as a sort of usurpation.[u] Both exercised that authority as a branch of jurisdiction distinct from all others.[x] And guardians and committees of the person and estate are appointed upon petition by the Court of Chancery, as they were by the Roman magistrates, and by the same mode of proceeding.[y]

Guardians were appointed in the Roman Law by virtue of the Atilian Law, by the Prætor of Rome, and the Tribunes of the people, and in the Provinces by the Præsides, by virtue of the Julian and Titian Law.[z] And during the suspension of the appointment of a guardian by will, as by a condition or a term, the magistrate could appoint.[a]

[t] Instit. lib. i. tit. xvi.

[u] Co. Litt. book ii. chap. v. § 123, note 13. *The second is guardian. . . .*

[x] Cujacii Op. tom. vii. col. 72 (edit. Mutinæ), Recitationes Solemnes ad Leg. 1. Pand. tit. De Jurisdictione. Blackst. Com. book i. chap. xvii. § 1; and see Blackst. Com. book iii. chap. xxvii. § 1. Co. Litt. ubi supr. Blackst. Com. book i. chap. xvii. § 1, note, Coleridge.

[y] Coke, Litt. book ii. chap. v. note 13. Pand. lib. xxvi. tit. vi. Qui Petunt Tutor. vel Curat. Voet ad eundem tit. Pand. Comment.

[z] Inst. lib. i. tit. xx. princip.

[a] Instit. ibid. § 1.

But the Atilian, and the Julian and Titian Laws, fell into disuse after the Consuls under the Emperor Claudius commenced appointing guardians upon inquiry, and the Prætors alone did the same by virtue of a constitution of Antoninus; for by the antient law there was no provision for either obliging guardians to give security for their due administration, or compelling them to execute the office.[b]

This jurisdiction was probably usurped by the Consuls before it was authorized by law.[c] In the reign of Justinian, the Præfect of the City, or the Prætor at Rome, and the Præsides in the provinces, appointed guardians on inquiry. The municipal magistrates, or the Juridicus of Alexandria, or the Defensor and Bishop of each town, also exercised this function, when the estate of the infant was small.[d]

The law respecting the authority of a guardian may be arranged under three heads: 1, Cases where authorization by the guardian is requisite for the validity of the acts of the ward; 2, At what time the authorization must be given; and 3, What is required by law where it cannot be given, but some authorization is requisite.[e] The authorization of the guardian is necessary for the ward to bind himself in any obligation, but not for him to stipulate for something to be due to him. The reason of this is that the law permits the infant to improve his condition by acquiring rights or property, but not to bind himself without his guardian's authority.[f]

The authorization of the guardian was more particularly important in the Roman Law, because he was technically held, with respect to the management of the infant's estate, to be *in loco domini*.[g] But immoveable property of infants cannot be sold, hypothecated, or in any way alienated, without a decree of the Court, which is pronounced when such hypothecation or alienation is expedient for the payment of debts.[h] And it was provided by Justinian that no payment except annual payments below a certain amount, and in arrear for more than two years, should be made to a ward without the authority of a decree, because it might be for the advantage of the infant to leave the money out at interest.[i]

But where the execution of an invalid engagement with an infant has benefited the infant, he is bound to execute his part so far as he has derived advantage; and he is bound wherever he has received any thing

[b] Instit. lib. i. tit. xx. § 3.
[c] Vinnii Comment. ad loc. cit.
[d] Inst. ibid. § 5, 6.
[e] Vinnii Comment. ad Instit. lib. i. tit. xxi. in princip.
[f] Instit. lib. i. tit. xxi. princip.
[g] Pand. lib. xxvi. tit. vii. De Administratione et Periculo Tutorum, L. 27.
[h] Pand. lib. xxvii. tit. ix. De Rebus eorum qui Sub Tutela.
[i] Cod. lib. v. tit. xxxvii. De Administratione Tutorum, L. 25.

which in equity is due to another.[k] The reason of this is, that the object of the law is to protect infants, but not to enable them to commit fraud or wrong.

The contract of an infant without the authorization of his guardians, is not absolutely void, for if he ratify it after reaching majority, it becomes binding upon him in law.[l]

As to the effect of the authorization of the guardian, it is subject to the rule *Dolus tutorum puero neque nocere neque prodesse debet.*[m] Therefore when the authorization is given in a case in which it ought not to be given, it is the same in law as if the infant had acted without authorization.[n] The doctrine of the Roman Law is, that while the infant may not retain any gain wrongfully acquired for him by the guardian,—he is on the other hand not bound or made liable by the wrongful act of the guardian towards others, nor by the guardian's breach of duty towards his ward, in authorizing transactions which it was the object of his appointment to prevent.[o]

There is another important qualification of the power of the guardian to enable the infant to bind himself. No guardian can give valid authorization to his ward in transactions to which the guardian himself is a party: consequently, when it is necessary that a question be judicially settled between guardian and ward, a curator *ad litem* is appointed to act for the latter.[p] But where there are several guardians with authority distinct one from the other, one of them may authorize transactions between the infant and any or all of his colleagues.[q]

If this limitation of the powers of guardians were carried beyond what is necessary for the security of infants, inconvenience would arise to them in the management of their affairs. The Roman Law, therefore, does not hold a mere interest of the guardian in a transaction to be sufficient to disable him from authorizing his ward therein, but restricts the disability of the guardian to cases where he would acquire a right as against the infant, either by himself or through others.[r]

Guardianship terminates in six different modes by the Roman Law, that is to say: 1, by the ward attaining puberty, that is to say, the age

[k] Pand, lib. xxvi. tit. viii. De Auctoritate et Consensu Tutorum, L. 5. Pand. lib. l. tit. ult. L. 206. Pand. lib. xx. tit. v. De Distractione Pignorum, L. 12, § 1.

[l] Pand. lib. xxvi. tit. viii. De Auctoritate et Consensu. Tutorum, L. 5, § 2.

[m] Pand. lib. xxvi. tit. ix. Quando ex Facto Tutorum Minores agere vel conveniri possunt, L. 3.

[n] Pand. lib. xxvi. tit. viii. De Auctoritate Tutorum, L. 2.

[o] Instit. lib. i. tit. xxi. § 3.

[p] Instit. ibid. § 3.

[q] Pand. lib. xxvi. tit. viii. de Auctor. et Consensu Tutor. L. 5. *Pupillus obligari tutori eo auctore non potest.* Ulpian.

[r] Pand. lib. xxvi. tit. viii. De Auctoritate et Consensu Tutorum, L. 7, L. 1, princip.

of twelve years, if a female, and fourteen if a male; 2, by his suffering *capitis diminutio;* 3, by the accomplishment of a condition, whereby the duration of a testamentary guardianship is limited; 4, by the death of the guardian or ward; 5, by the *diminutio capitis* of the guardian; and 6, by his removal from office by decree.[s]

In France, Holland, and all over Germany, guardianship lasts beyond the age of puberty, and until the infant has attained majority; and it is the same in the English Law except with respect to guardianship in socage and for nurture.[t] The ages of puberty by the Roman Law are three, namely,—simple (*simplex*), full (*plena*), and complete (*plenissima*). The first is twelve years in females, and fourteen in males; the second fourteen in females, and eighteen in males; and the third is twenty-five, that is to say, the age of majority in both.[u]

CHAPTER X.

OF CURATORS.

Of Curators.—Instit. lib. i. tit. xiii. De Curatoribus.—Difference between the Office of Curator and that of Guardian.—Causes of the Appointment of Curators.—Curators of Persons of Unsound Mind and of Prodigals.—Observations on the Law of England compared with that of Scotland and the Civil Law as to the Interdiction of Prodigals.—Effect of Interdiction.—The Removal of Guardians and Curators.—Diligence required by the Law from them.—Grounds of Removal. P. 59.

At the commencement of the preceding chapter, persons *sui juris*, that is to say, neither in servitude nor under the paternal power, were divided into three classes, that is to say: 1, those under guardianship; 2, those under curatorship; and 3, persons subject to neither of those restraints.

The first of these classes has been considered, and the second only remains to be examined, after which the first of the three general divisions or parts of the Institutes, that of Persons, will have been concluded; for the third class, consisting of persons in the unrestrained use of their respective legal capacity, requires no especial notice.

[s] Instit. lib. i. tit. xxii.

[t] Vinnii Comment. ad Inst. lib. i. tit. xxii. Domat, Loix Civiles, tit. Des tutelles, liv. ii. tit. i. The edition of 1835 contains references to the French code, with cases, &c. Blackst. Comm. book i. chap. xvii.

[u] Vinnii Comm. ad Pandect, lib. iv. tit. iv. § 1.

A difference between the office of a curator and that of a guardian is, that the former is given principally to the estate, and the latter principally to the person, but the duties of both are similar.[x]

Curators (who are appointed by the same magistrates that appoint guardians)[y] are generally divided by the Roman Law into two classes; 1st, those who are appointed for the care of a thing; and 2nd, those appointed for the government of the affairs of a person. The former are no more than mere trustees or receivers, while the latter have full powers of administration.[z]

Curators to persons are appointed for two species of causes—on account of immaturity of age, or by reason of a serious infirmity of body or mind. Adults of both sexes, by the old Roman Law, receive curators until majority, that is to say, until they have completed twenty-five years, because, after the cessation of guardianship by their attaining puberty, they still remain incapable of administering their own affairs.[a] For this reason the modern Civil Law, as modified by the laws of different countries of Europe, prolongs the duration of wardship to the age of complete majority.[b] Thus the law of curatorship over minors is now of little importance. We will, therefore, proceed to other sort of curators.

Persons of unsound mind and prodigals, though above the age of twenty-five years, are placed under the governance of their relatives by the Law of the Twelve Tables. But, by the law of Justinian's reign, curators are required to be appointed for them, after inquiry by the Prætor or Præfect in Rome, and the Præses in the provinces.[c]

The interdiction of prodigals is part of the law of Scotland,[d] and prevails generally in the countries whose law is based on the Roman Law; but it is rejected by that of England, and combated by Blackstone as inconsistent with the liberty of the subject in the disposal of his property.[e] The Roman Law, however, lays down the general principle, *expedit Reipublicæ ne sua re quis male utatur*,[f] which seems founded on sound legal reason; for much of the internal good government of the state depends on restrictions of the rights of property, framed to prevent their abuse, contrary to the general good; and in all countries some limitation of those rights have been considered ex-

[x] Vinnii Comment. ad Instit. lib. i. tit. xxiii. in princip. Voet, Comment. ad Pand. lib. xxvii. tit. x. num. 2.

[y] Instit. lib. i. tit. xxiii. § 1.

[z] Pand. lib. xxvi. tit. vii. De Administratione et Periculo Tutorum et Curatorum, *per tot*, et L. 48, ibid.

[a] Inst. lib. i. tit. xxiii. princip.

[b] Voet, Comment. ad Pand. lib. xxvii. tit. x. num. 1.

[c] Instit. ibid. § 4. Pand. lib. xxvii. tit. x. De Curatoribus Furioso vel aliis Personis extra Minores Dandis, L. 7.

[d] Erskine, Instit. book i. tit. vii. § 53.

[e] Blackst. Com. book i. chap. viii. § 18.

[f] Instit. lib. i. tit. viii. § 2.

pedient or necessary. Thus in our own law we have strict settlements and trusts to preserve property for various purposes, and not only bodies corporate,[g] but the Crown itself is prevented from exercising the power of alienation, except under certain restrictions. It may, indeed, be argued with abundant reason, that the absence, in this country, of all remedy by interdiction against prodigality and wanton waste, renders the restraints of settlements and trusts especially requisite here for the preservation of families.

If the interdiction of a prodigal be contrary to principles of right, it will be difficult to justify that of a person of unsound mind. Thus Ulpian and Antoninus Pius compare the former to the latter, and hold that both are reduced to pupillage by the law for the same reasons.[h] And it is questionable whether prodigality be not a species of mental unsoundness.

By the Roman Law an interdicted prodigal can alienate nothing, and is legally incapable of any act diminishing his estate.[i] But the law of Scotland has qualified that rule by providing that his rational acts shall not in all cases be subject to reduction.[k]

The general principle of the Civil Law is, that the magistrate should appoint curators to all those persons who are incapable of managing their own affairs, though not without the fullest previous enquiry.[l] Thus curators are appointed not only to persons of insane mind, but to persons deaf and dumb.[m]

A lunatic is held in law to be *in loco absentis*, and the same principle applies to those who have not sufficient use of their faculties to act with that discernment which the law requires. And thus it is laid down that lunatics and persons interdicted *have no will*.[n]

Here a distinction must be drawn between persons *in fact* incapable of discernment and persons interdicted for prodigality.

To persons of the former class the rule of Ulpian is applicable—*non videtur qui errat consentire*[o]—because there is no substantial difference in principle between a man acting under the influence of error or de-

[g] Thus, in several respects, corporate bodies are invested with the privileges of infants. Pothier, Traité des Personnes, tit. vii. art. 2.

[h] Pand. lib. xxvii. tit. x. De Curatore Furios. L. 1. Pand. lib. xxvi. tit. v. De Tutor. et Curator. datis ab his qui Jus dandi habent, L. 12, § 2.

[i] Pand. lib. xxvii. tit. x. De Curat. Furios. et Aliis, L. 10, princip.

[k] Erskine Instit. book i. tit. vii. § 58.

[l] Pand. lib. xxvi. tit. v. De Tutor. et Curat. datis, L. 12. Pand. lib. xxvii. tit. x. De Curator. Furios. vel Aliis, L. 6, princip.

[m] Instit. lib. i. tit. xxiii. § 4.

[n] Pand. lib. l. tit. ult. De Reg. Jur. L. 124, § 1. Pand. lib. l. tit. penult, De signif. Verb. L. 246. Pand. lib. l. tit. ult. L. 40.

[o] Pand. lib. l. tit. ult. L. 116, § 2.

lusion, and one who is incapable of discriminating between error and truth. If the latter act rightly, it is by what is commonly called accident, and not from rational will and choice. Both are equally incapable of consent, and may therefore be correctly said to *have no will.*

As for those who, though not in point of fact incapable of discrimination, are restrained by law and incapacitated from acting, they are said to have no will, because their will cannot have any legal effect, and is therefore a nonentity in law.[p] This is the case with regard to adults under guardianship and prodigals interdicted.

It follows from these principles that persons under natural incapacity, or incapacity *in fact,* such as insane persons, can execute no act that is not vitious, even before their incapacity is declared by decree, provided it be proved that the act was performed during the incapacity.[q] And even after a person *non compos* has been placed by decree under curators, an act done by him during a lucid interval is valid,[r] but the presumption is that it was not so done.

As for minors and prodigals the case is different, because they are under an incapacity amounting to a legal prohibition to do certain acts, and their incapacity is without intervals, and determinable only by decree.[s]

The duty of the curator of an insane person extends as well to the person as to the estate, but the Prætor sometimes granted these two functions to separate persons according to the practice of the English law.[t]

We will now proceed to the twenty-fourth title of the Institutes. That and the two subsequent titles contain matters relating both to guardians and to curators.

The first of those three titles regards the sureties taken for the good administration of guardians and curators.[u] But the law of sureties will be explained in another part of this treatise.

The next title specifies the circumstances under which persons were excused from serving the office of guardian or curator, which was

[p] Grotius, Droit de la Guerre et de la Paix, liv. ii. chap. xi. § v. 2, 4, and chap. xiii. § xx.

[q] Cod. lib. vi. tit. xxxvi. De Codicillis, L. 5.

[r] Cod. lib. v. tit. lxx. De Curatore Furios. vel. Prodig. L. 6 (De Lucidis Intervallis). Voet Comm. ad Pand. lib. xxvii. tit. x. § 4.

[s] Voet Comm. ad Pand. lib. xxvii. tit. x. num. 7. Pand. lib. l. tit. ult. De Reg. Jur. L. 35. Pand. lib. xxvii. tit. x. De Curat. Furios. L. 1 is shown by Voet not to be an authority against this position. As to the distinctions between *Furiosi* and *Mente Capti,* &c., see Vinnii Comment. ad Instit. lib. i. tit. xxiii. § 4, and Cod. lib. v. tit. lxx. L. 6. And see Lord Nottingham's note to Co. Litt. § 405, p. 246.

[t] Pand. lib. xxvii. tit. x. De Curat. Furios. vel Aliis, L. 7, L. 13.

[u] Inst. lib. i. tit. xxiv. De Satisdatione Tutorum vel Curatorum.

otherwise compulsory.[x] The third is a more important title, where the law respecting the removal of guardians and curators by the magistrate is propounded.[y]

Their accusation and judicial removal, to which they were all liable, however appointed, commenced from the Law of the Twelve Tables; and by the law set forth in the Institutes, this jurisdiction belonged to the Prætor in Rome, and the Præses and Proconsular Legate in the provinces.[z]

Any person is, by the Roman Law, permitted to be the accuser, including women, who are admitted to this function by the rescript of Alexander Severus, and that of Antoninus Pius, provided they be near relations of the infant or other person under curatorship, or his nurse. And the Prætor may also admit any other woman whom he believes to be influenced only by a sense of duty.[a]

This is a judicious exception to the rule of the Roman Law, which excluded women from the performance of any public function.[b]

That exclusion was founded on reasons of policy, but in one instance Ulpian assigns to it a rather amusing origin. He relates that a certain Cafrania, whom he stigmatises as *improbissima femina*, so tormented and persecuted the judges with her continual and clamorous arguments in Court, that they issued an edict forbidding all women to appear before them as advocates.[c]

The general principles, with reference to which petitions for the removal of guardians and curators are adjudicated upon, will best be understood from the limits assigned to the duty of those functionaries by the Civil Law.

The same diligence is required of them in their administration which a father of a family ought to use in the management of his own affairs. They must do *quod quivis paterfamilias idoneus facit*:[d] and Alexander Severus decides that in accusations against guardians and curators, the judge must principally consider whether the accused was guilty of any fraud or neglect.[e]

A great commentator reduces to sixteen heads the legal grounds

[x] Instit. lib. i. tit. xxv. De Excusationibus Tutorum vel Curatorum.

[y] Inst. lib. i. tit. xxvi. De Suspectis Tutoribus et Curatoribus.

[z] Pand. lib. v. tit. xliii. De Suspect. Tutor. et Curat. L. 1, § 2, L. 3, § 2, 3. Inst. ubi sup. princip. § 1, 2.

[a] Instit. ibid. § 3. Pand. ubi. sup. L. 1, § 6, 7.

[b] Pand. lib. l. tit. ult. De Reg. Jur. L. 2.

[c] Pand. lib. iii. tit. i. De Postulando, L. 1, § 5. Bynkershock holds, after learnedly discussing the subject, that a woman may be lawfully sent as an ambassador. Questiones Juris Publici, lib. i. chap. v. *Qui recte* legati mittantur.

[d] Pand. lib. xxvi. tit. vii. De Admin. et Peric. Tutor. L. 33, L. 10.

[e] Cod. lib. v. tit. xliii. De Suspect. Tutor. L. 5.

for removing a guardian or curator. The most important of these heads are as follow.[f]

1st. Where the guardian or curator is at enmity with the father of the ward.[g]

2nd. Where he is discovered to be stained with some vice or depravity.[h]

3rd. Where he becomes unfit or unable to administer his own affairs.

4th. Where he either fraudulently, or from neglect or want of consideration, prevented the infant or other person under his charge from accepting an inheritance.[i] And the principle of this rule is applicable whenever the fraud or fault of the guardian or curator deprived his charge of any considerable advantage.[k]

5th. Where the guardian or curator obtained his office unlawfully, as by purchase, or without legal title.

6th. Where he neglected to make an inventory.

7th. This head includes all kinds of malversation and peculation.

8th. Where the guardian or curator alienates immoveable property of the person under his charge without a decree.

The 9th, 10th, and 11th are—where he conceals himself, does not appear on judicial summons, or refuses to communicate with his colleague in the administration.

One effect of removal of a guardian or curator for fraud is legal infamy, and such is the care of the Roman Law to protect persons under incapacity, that as soon as the guardian or curator is accused, the Prætor is to interdict him from administering until the proceedings are concluded.[l]

[f] Voet, Comment. ad Pand. lib. xxvi. tit. x. § 2. He cites Montanus, *Tractatus de Tutelis*, Lugd. Batav. 1697.

[g] Pand. lib. xxvi. tit. iii. De Confirmando Tutore vel Curatore, L. 8. [h] Ibid.

[i] Pand. lib. xxvi. tit. x. De Suspectis Tutoribus et Curatoribus, L. 3, § 17.

[k] Cod. lib. v. tit. xliii. De Suspect. Tutor. L. 5.

[l] Instit. lib. i. tit. xxvi. § 6, 7.

CHAPTER XI.

THE LAW OF THINGS.

The Law of Things.—Instit. lib. ii. tit. i.—De Rerum Divisione et Acquirendo ipsarum Dominio, princip. § 1, 2, 3, 4, 5.—Jus *in Re* and Jus *ad Rem*.—Jus *ad Rem* or *in Personam*.—Things common to all Mankind.—Running Waters.—Rivers.—High Seas.—The Shores of the Sea.—Banks of Rivers. P. 67.

THE chief features of the Law of Persons have now been sketched out, and with this chapter commences the second great division of Justinian's Institutes,—namely, the LAW OF THINGS.

The Law of Things may be divided into two parts—first, *dominion*, that is to say, the proprietorship of a thing, or the right whereby it is ours, at least in certain respects; and secondly, the right which we have, not over the thing, but with regard to it against the person who has bound himself to deliver it to us. The former species of right is *dominion*, and the latter springs from obligations.

Where the right is a right directly to a thing which the possessor is bound to deliver because it is not his, and because it is the property of the other party, that right is called *jus in re:* but where the person is bound to give or to do something for the benefit of another, the right corresponding to that obligation is called *jus ad rem*, or *jus in personam*.[m]

Having thus divided the Law of Things into dominion over things, and rights to things; or in other words, rights to obtain a thing, and rights to compel a person to the execution of an obligation, independently of any right of ownership over a thing, we will proceed to the first title of the second book of Justinian's Institutes, which is headed, "Of the classification of things and the modes of acquiring them."

Things are first classified with reference to the nature of their appropriation. *They are either in the patrimony of some one* (*in nostro patrimonio*) *or not in the patrimony of any one* (*extra patrimonium nostrum*). *For some things are common to all men by Natural Law, some are public, some belong to corporate or politic bodies, some belong to no one, many to individuals: and these are acquired by each person in divers modes.*[n]

Thus Justinian first divides things into private property (*res in patrimonio*), and things which are not private property (*res extra patrimonium*)—after which he again divides them into five classes, the first

[m] Pothier, Traité du Droit de Domaine, chap. Préliminaire.

[n] Instit. lib. ii. tit. i. princip.

of which is composed of things incapable, except in a qualified manner, while the other four classes are capable, by natural law, of exclusive appropriation.

And first of those which are by nature common to all men.

These things are common to mankind by natural right—air, running waters, the sea, and therefore the shores of the sea. Therefore, no one is forbidden to approach the shores of the sea, provided he abstain from the villas, and monuments and buildings, for these are not of common right, as the sea is.[o]

Both Grotius and Pufendorf deduce the appropriation of things which must probably have originally been common to all men, from the very constitution and organic rules and necessities of the social state, as well as from the objects for the furtherance of which that state is intended.[p]

But it follows from the same principles, that those things, the exclusive appropriation of which, either to a portion of mankind or to certain individuals or purposes, is unnecessary for the objects of the social state (that is, for the furtherance of the welfare of mankind), must remain by Natural Law common to all men.

Thus air and light cannot be brought under the power of any one person. Their use is common to all, and indeed no kind of exclusive appropriation is requisite for their full enjoyment.

Upon these principles running waters are held by the Roman Jurisconsulti to be common to all men. But it also follows that this decision does not apply to waters, the appropriation of which (to the exclusion of common enjoyment) is necessary for a certain purpose, such as water included in a pipe or other vessel for certain uses. The common right to the use of running water, therefore, applies only to those cases where the quantity of water is so great that its entire exclusive appropriation is not necessary, having regard to the general objects of the institution of property.[q]

In such cases as these, to prevent any man from making use of and appropriating to himself any portion of the water, without injuring the right of other men to do the same, would be contrary to natural law.[r]

But Grotius holds rivers to be capable of being subject to a qualified right of property. He argues that liquids have no boundaries of their own nature, for a liquid must be limited in its extent by something

[o] Instit. lib. ii. tit. i. § 1.

[p] Grot. Droit de la Guerre et de la Paix, liv. ii. chap. ii. § 2. Pufendorf, Droit de la Nature et des Gens. liv. iv. chap. iv.

[q] Grot. Droit de la Guerre et de la Paix, liv. ii. chap. ii. § 3. See the whole of chap. v. of the 6th book of Pufendorf's Droit de la Nature et des Gens.

[r] Grot. ibid. § 12.

differing from it in nature. Consequently liquids can be possessed only so far as they are included and restrained within bounds differing from them.[s] It is on these principles that Coke lays it down that water is not demandable in a real action at law except together with land, and Blackstone writes that "water is a moveable wandering thing, and must of necessity continue common by the laws of nature."[t] But these principles are manifestly applicable to running water only, and not to water included on all sides within limits, which is not "a wandering thing."

Now a river is bounded in its breadth, though not in its length, so far that the water is always in motion; therefore, though it may be considered as one body of water, yet the particles of which that body is composed remain the property of whoever is owner of the banks and bed, only while they are within those bounds.[u] This is what in the English Law, and in the writings of jurists, is called transient or qualified property; and it is not only transient in point of duration, but also qualified by the rule of natural law—that no man can without injustice prevent another from making use of that which is the property of the former, when he cannot suffer any inconvenience or other injury thereby, and still more if it be of such a nature as to be susceptible of being made use of by all men with equal advantage to each.[x]

Thus running water is capable, indeed, of a qualified appropriation, as property, but subject to a common right by natural law, where it is capable of being fully enjoyed without exclusive possession.

These principles serve to explain the maxim *cujus est solum ejus est usque ad cœlum*, adopted by our Law from the Civil Law.[y] It was observed by Lord Ellenborough that if it were trespass to interfere with the column of air superincumbent upon a close, an action of trespass might be brought against an aeronaut by the owner of every field over which he passed in his balloon, and he held that if damage arise from an object that overhangs the close, the remedy must be by action on the case, and not by action of trespass.[z]

This decision is precisely in accordance with the principles of Barbeyrac, in his notes on Grotius, where he shows that air is susceptible of being subjected to a right of property analogous to that over running

[s] Grot. liv. ii. chap. ii. § 3, num. 2.

[t] Co. Litt. 4, a. Blackst. Com. book ii. chap. ii. p. 18, edit. Coleridge.

[u] Grot. ubi supra; and see liv. ii. ch. iii. § 7. &c.

[x] Grot. Droit de la Guerre et de la Paix, liv. ii. chap. ii. § 11.

[y] Pand. lib. xliii. tit. xxiv. Quod Vi aut Clam. L. 21, § 2. Erskine, Instit. book ii. tit. ix. § 5.

[z] Pickering *v.* Rudd, 4 Campb. 219.

water, so far as that exclusive appropriation is essential to the enjoyment of rights of property over solid things.[a]

The same doctrines hold good as to light, portions of which may be subjected to a transient right of property as accessory to other property.

On these principles has been decided the great and celebrated question of the nature of the common rights of mankind over the high seas.

Ulpian and Celsus distinctly hold that the sea is common to all mankind, and a declaration of the Emperor Antoninus that "Though he was the Lord of the world, the Law only was ruler of the sea, has been held to convey the same doctrine."[b] But the contrary was powerfully maintained by our illustrious Selden, while the freedom and community of the seas was vindicated by Grotius.[c]

Grotius distinguishes between the right of jurisdiction and that of property, which may be asserted over the seas. But Barbeyrac correctly argues,[d] that with respect to the sea that distinction could not exist unless several persons had taken possession of the sea, and one of them had been invested with jurisdiction over the other proprietors, therefore with regard to the sea jurisdiction and property are the same, such an arrangement never having existed, though it is not upon legal principles impossible.[e] We will therefore consider the question of dominion without following the distinction of Grotius. The exclusive appropriation of the things of the world which are intended for the use of mankind, springs from the necessities and from the very objects of the social state. The things of the world must be subjected to exclusive appropriation to persons or bodies of men, wherever that appropriation is necessary for the tranquillity of society, or for the purpose of rendering them as beneficial and valuable as their nature admits of their being made.

Now the high seas are of so great an extent that the fullest benefit may be derived from them without any exclusive appropriation, and

[a] Grot. Droit de la G. et de la Paix, liv. ii. chap. ii. § 3, note 3, 4; and see Pufend. Devoir de l'Homme et du Citoyen, liv. i. chap. xii. § 6, note 2, Barbeyrac, and § 4, note 2.

[b] Pand lib. viii. tit. iv. Communia Prædiorum, L. 13. Pand. lib. xliii. tit. viii. Ne quid in Loco Publico, L. 3, § 1. Pand. lib. xiv. tit. ii. ad Leg. Rhodiam, L. 9. Gothofredus in his Opusc. De Imperio Maris explains this law somewhat differently.

[c] The treatises of these two great men, entitled *Mare Clausum* and *Mare Liberum*, on this subject, are well known. See Wheaton Hist. of the Law of Nat. p. 153.

[d] Grot. Droit de la Guerre et de la Paix, liv. ii. chap. iii. § 13, note *Barbeyrac*.

[e] Bynkershock, De Dominio Maris Dissertatio, cap. 3, 4.

such appropriation is not necessary for the purposes of society or the advantage of mankind. Moreover, the use of the seas may be said to be matter of necessity to all those nations who have any part of their territories bounded by it; and as no nation can possibly assert that they are unable to enjoy the fullest use of the sea without the exclusion of others, so no nation can have any just ground for excluding others from an advantage which all may enjoy, together with equally full utility to each.[f] This legal doctrine is thus admirably summed up by a German civilian. "The great sea is a thing the use of which is inexhaustible, consequently as no one can acquire the dominion of things the utility of which is unbounded and inexhaustible, no one (even were it possible in fact) can subject the great sea to his dominion without violating natural law. And the same must be understood with respect to several nations, who cannot, for the same reasons, divide the dominion of the great seas among them. Consequently no nation can, without infringing natural law, subject to its dominion either the great sea or any considerable part of it." [g]

It remains to be considered how far the common right of mankind to the use of the seas extends. The legal doctrines upon which that common right is founded, imply that it extends only to the high or open seas. Thus there are passages in the Pandects showing that portions of the sea may become private property.[h] And Grotius argues that a portion of the sea may become the property of an individual in the same manner as a river, that is to say, by being partly included within his ground.[i]

It is evident that such enclosed portions of the sea are not "*res usus inexhausti*" when they are in the nature of a pond or lake enclosed within the private property of any one. In such cases the dominion of those portions of the sea rests upon the same legal principles as other rights of property, subject to the general limitation laid down by Grotius and Pufendorf, that no man can, without violating natural

[f] Grot. liv. ii. chap. ii. § 3. Pufendorf, Droit de la Nature et des Gens, liv. iv. chap. v. Grot. liv. ii. chap. iii. § 13, note; and see Vattel, Droit des Gens. liv. i. chap. xxiii.; and Bynkershock, Dissertatio de Dominio Maris. His argument is singular. He says: Mare in dominium redigi posse, ut quod maxime, neque tamen hodie ullum mare imperio alicujus Principis teneri, nisi qua forte in illud terra dominetur.

[g] Wolf, Jus Gent[m]. § 121, 127. See on this subject Co. Litt. § 440, note 1, Hargrave. As to renunciations by treaty, see Grotius, liv. ii. chap. iii. § 15 and the rule in Pand. lib. iv. tit. iv. De Minoribus, 25 Ann. L. 41.

[h] Pand. lib. xlvii. tit. x. De Injuriis et Famosis Libellis, L. 14.

[i] Grot. ibid. liv. ii. chap. iii. § 10. See the Treaty of the Dardanelles, 1841. Wheaton Hist. of the Law of Nat. p. 585.

right, exclude others from deriving a benefit from his property, which will not hinder his full and complete enjoyment of it.[k]

These doctrines are equally applicable to nations in their aggregate capacity. It is requisite for the welfare of a nation that it should have the power of excluding other nations from the immediate vicinity of its shores and from the parts of the sea enclosed in its territories, as well as from the territories themselves.[l]

And so it is with regard to a fishery, which is not *res inexhaustæ utilitatis*, unless it be a general common right of fishing in the high seas, or in any part of them not belonging to any territory.[m]

Grotius argues that no nation has a right to refuse a passage to other nations through the rivers, estuaries, or portions of the sea which belong to it, without some especial and just cause of refusal. This, however, must be understood with the limitation contained in the rule of Wolfius—that "no nation is bound to prefer the interests of another nation to its own."[n]

On this principle, as well as because foreigners who have the advantage of the protection of a government may be expected to contribute towards its support, Wolfius argues that foreign persons and goods passing through a territory may be subjected to a toll or tax.[o]

Grotius and Vinnius extend the right of requiring a reasonable toll to every case where a nation has rendered the navigation more secure by works, such as lighthouses, breakwaters, &c.[p]

By the Roman Law, rivers and ports are public property, therefore all men have a right to fish there.[q] The distinction is here shown between running waters (*aqua profluens*) which we have seen to be common to all men, and the whole body of water, with its bed and banks, which is public property of a state, as being within its territories. But it has been shown that an individual may have a qualified right over a river so far as is compatible with the common right.

The right of fishing in ports and rivers is, however, regulated and disposed of by the law of each country, which may also prevent the running waters from being common to all mankind, by excluding foreigners from its territories. Thus the common right of mankind

[k] Grot. liv. ii. chap. iii. § 11. Pufend. Devoir de l'Homme et du Cit. liv. i. chap. viii. § 4.

[l] Grot. liv. ii. chap. iii. § 10, num. 2. Wolf. Jus Gent. § 128, 132.

[m] Wolf. § 122.

[n] Grot. liv. ii. chap. ii. § 13, n. 1. Wolf. § 206; and see the correction of the doctrine of Grotius as to the supposed right of passage, in Pufendorf, Droit de la Nat. et des Gens, liv. iii. chap. iii. § 5, and notes of Barbeyrac.

[o] Wolf. Jus Gent. § 214.

[p] Grot. liv. ii. tit. iii. § 14. Vinnii Com. ad Instit. lib. ii. tit. i. § 1.

[q] Instit. lib. ii. tit. i. § 2.

takes place where it is not excluded by the dominion of each country over its own territories.[r] The same principle applies to the shore of the sea, which is defined in the Civil Law to extend *quatenus hybernus fluctus maximus excurrit.*[s] Thus Justinian lays it down that *the use of the shores of the sea is public and common to all men in the same manner as the sea itself, therefore it is lawful for all men to build there, and to dry nets, as well as to draw up anything from the sea upon the shore. But the property of the shore may be understood to be in no one, and partaking of the same legal nature as the sea and the soil or sand under the sea.*[t]

This decision is subject to the same qualifications as the law respecting dominion of the sea itself. "Littorum usus publicus est et juris gentium *sicut et ipsius maris.*" Thus Scævola says that it is lawful to build on the sea shore so far as the public utility will permit, and Celsus declares the shores of the Roman territory to belong to the Roman people.[u] But by the Roman Law the sea shore is not vested in the state, as in the Feudal and English Law, which places the shore *inter jura regalia;*[x] for Neratius compares it as somewhat analogous to things *feræ naturæ*, which may be acquired as private property, by being taken possession of.[y]

In the same way Justinian distinguishes between the public use and the private property of the banks of rivers.

The use of the banks is public by natural law, in the same manner as that of the river. Thus all have *a right as well to touch upon them with vessels, to tie ropes to the trees that grow there, and to place any thing upon the banks, as to navigate the river. But the property of the banks is vested in those who are proprietors of the land whereof they form part; for which reason the trees that grow upon the banks belong to those proprietors.*[z]

It appears by this law that the public use of the banks of rivers is a consequence of the public right over the river itself. But because the

[r] See an analogous distinction in Co. Litt. § 440, n. 1.

[s] Instit. lib. ii. tit. i. § 3. Pand. lib. l. tit. penult. De Verbor. Signif. L. 96; *Littus est quousque maximus fluctus a mari pervenit.* And see Cicero, Topic. cap. vii.

[t] Instit. ibid. § 5. Virgil Æneid. vii. v. 229:

. . . . litusque rogamus
Innocuum et cunctis undamque auramque patentem.

[u] Pand. lib. xliii. tit. viii. Ne Quid in Loco Publico, L. 4. Pand. ibid. L. 3.

[x] Liber Feudorum, lib. ii. tit. lvi. Co. Litt. § 440, note 1.

[y] Pand. lib. xli. tit. i. De Acquirendo Rerum Dominio, L. 14. Quod in litore quis edificaverit, ejus erit: nam litora publica non ita sunt ut ea quæ in patrimonio sunt populi sed ut ea quæ primum a natura prodita sunt et in nullius adhuc dominium pervenerunt: nec dissimilis conditio eorum atque piscium et ferarum. . . .

[z] Instit. ibid. § 4.

river, considered as a mass of water included within its bed and banks, is public though the running water is common to all men, the banks must also be public and not common to all men.

There may, however, be private streams or rivers, and the general rule is that a public river is one which is navigable. Thus the public right to the use of navigable rivers is analogous to the right to the use of public highways.[a]

CHAPTER XII.

THE LAW OF THINGS.

Of Things belonging to Aggregate Bodies, and of Things belonging to no one, but appropriated.—Instit. lib. ii. tit. i. De Rerum Divisione et Adquir. ipsarum Domin. § 6.—*Res Universitatis.*—Explanation of the term Universitas.—Of Bodies Politic.—*Res Nullius.*—Abeyance of the Freehold.—Division of *Res Nullius.*—Classification of Things by the Canon Law. P. 70.

A SKETCH has now been given of the first two classes into which Justinian divides things, that is to say, things common to all men,—and things public. We come next to *res universitatis*, or things belonging to corporations or bodies politic.

By the Roman Law the word *universitas* includes every lawful aggregate body composed of persons, and such bodies are considered in law in the light of persons.[b] Bodies aggregate are also called *corpora*. Pomponius distinguishes three species of bodies: 1st, *corpus unicum*, which consists of but one thing, such as a man or a stone; 2ndly, *corpus connexum*, which consists of several parts joined together, though having been originally separate, such as a ship or a building; and 3rdly, *corpus ex distantibus*, or composed of things not joined, but yet forming a whole together. Under this last head, Pomponius enumerates as examples, a nation, a legion, and a flock.[c] And although the parts composing these bodies be constantly changed, yet the identity of the whole remains.[d]

[a] Voet, Comm. ad Pandect. lib. xliii. tit. xiv. Co. Litt. § 475, et n. Pand. lib. xliii. tit. xii. De Fluminibus ne quid in Flum. Pand. lib. lii. tit. xiii. Ne quid in Flumine Publico fiat.

[b] Voet, Comm. ad Pand. lib. iii. tit. iv. § 1. Pand. lib. xlvi. tit. i. De Fidejussoribus, L. 22. And see on this subject Domat, Droit Public, liv. i. tit. xv.

[c] Pand. lib. xli. tit. iii. De Usurpationibus et Usucapionibus, L. 30.

[d] Pand. lib. v. tit. i. De Judiciis et ubi, L. 76. Pand. lib. iii. tit. iv. Quod cujuscumque Universitatis Nomine, L. 7, § 2.

The property of bodies aggregate (says Justinian) *was sometimes called public, but this was only as contra-distinguished from the property of private individuals, for Ulpian expressly says that nothing is public but what belongs to the Roman people.*[e]

In this section of the Institutes, the Emperor speaks of those things only which belong indeed to the whole body as an aggregate being, but are used by every individual composing it. Thus he enumerates as examples, theatres, and stadia, to which Vinnius adds basilicæ, porticoes, market-places, common pastures, and public gardens.[f]

Nothing is said here of the patrimony of cities and other aggregate bodies, which are subservient to their corporate uses, because as Gajus lays it down, *civitates privatorum loco habentur.*[g] Bodies politic, considered as persons, are governed by the same law in their dealings with others as natural persons, and they are subjected to certain restraints as some natural private persons are, such as minors, because experience has shown that men who are provident in their private individual character are often extravagant in their corporate capacity. Thus the patrimony of a body politic does not differ in point of legal principle from that of a body natural or individual, but it is subjected to certain legal regulations to prevent its misuse: consequently the only portion of the *res universitatis* which has a legal nature differing from the property of a natural person, is that which belongs to the aggregate body, but is in the actual use of its component members in their individual capacities.

The same distinction exists with regard to the property of the state; for Neratius says, "We do not call the shores of the sea *public*, in the same sense of the word as when we speak of public property, meaning the patrimony of the state."[h] Thus Labeo mentions roads, ways, and common fields as public.[i] Ulpian writes that public places are used by private persons, not as the property of each individual, but as that of the body of which they are members.[k] But the same Jurisconsult adds, that *res fiscales* are *in fisci patrimonio*, and are *quasi propriæ et privatæ principis.*[l] It is to be observed that Ulpian says, not *privatæ* but *quasi privatæ*, for those things are for public purposes; and accordingly he enumerates as public in another part of the Pandects,

[e] Instit. lib. ii. tit. i. § 6. Pand. lib. l. tit. penult. De Verborum Significatione, L. 15.

[f] Vinnii Com. ad Instit. lib. ii. tit. i. § 6. Cod. lib. ii. tit. lx. De Pascuis Publicis et Privatis.

[g] Pand. lib. l. tit. penult. De Verborum Significatione, L. 16.

[h] Pand. lib. xli. tit. i. De Acquirendo Rerum Dominio, L. 14.

[i] Pand. lib. xliii. tit. viii. Ne quid in Loco Publico vel Itinere fiat, L. 2, § 3.

[k] Pand. eod. tit. L. 2, § 2.

[l] Ibid. § 4.

various articles of revenue which are to be found among the *Regalia* in the Book of Fiefs.[m]

We come now to the last class of things which are not private, that is to say, *res nullius.*

Those things are the property of no one which are consecrated, or religious, or sacred: for things that are of divine right belong to no one.[n]

The doctrine that a thing may be actually appropriated, and yet not be the property of any person, deserves to be examined.

Notwithstanding the jealous eye with which our Common Law looks upon the suspense or abeyance of the inheritance, we find it laid down by Littleton, that "if a parson of a church dieth, now the freehold of the glebe of the parsonage is in none during the time that the parsonage is void, but in abeyance."[o] This is an example of *res nullius*, which is nevertheless property.

By our law, the freehold of the church is in the parson.[p] But the property which he has in the church is of a different nature from his right over his private property, and even that which he has over the glebe and the parsonage house. The property of the parson in the church and churchyard is only for the technical purpose of enabling him to bring actions for injuries to them.[q]

We may therefore conclude that the actual property in the church, in its strictest sense, is vested in no one, though the technical freehold is vested in the parson, who is a body corporate, to protect the rights of the church which he personates.

In truth, both in this case, and in that of the vacancy of a benefice, the church or other ecclesiastical thing is not the property of any one in the strict sense of the term, but it is neither unappropriated nor vacant, because it is appropriated to a purpose, though not to any person.

The Roman Law divides things *nullius*, that is to say, *divini juris*, into three classes:—1st, things consecrated (*sacræ*), which were those dedicated to sacred purposes by the pontiffs; 2ndly, things religious (*religiosæ*), which were connected in their use with religious rites, such as tombs; and 3rdly, things sacred (*sanctæ*), which only enjoyed a certain inviolability, such as the walls of cities. This part of the Roman Law is important, as having been followed in the classification of things by the Canon Law.

Ecclesiastical things are first generally divided by the Canon Law into, 1st, things spiritual, which belong immediately to divine worship

[m] Pand. lib. l. tit. penult. L. 17, § 1. Lib. Feudor. lib. ii. tit. lvi.

[n] Instit. lib. ii. tit. i. § 7.

[o] Co. Litt. § 646, note Hargr. Litt. § 647.

[p] Co. Litt. § 12, p. 18 b.

[q] Blackst. Com. book i. chap. xi. § 5, 7.

or ecclesiastical duties; and, 2ndly, things temporal, which are requisite for the maintenance of the clergy.[r]

Things spiritual are subdivided into incorporeal things, which belong to the province of theology, and corporeal things, such as sacraments, altars, and sacred utensils.[s]

The remaining member of the first and general division, that is to say, things temporal, is subject to the same classification as secular or lay property.

Corporeal things are sub-divided, after the example of the *res divini juris* of the Roman Law, into things consecrated and sacred, or *sacrosanctæ*, and things *religiosæ*.

Things consecrated are churches, altars, and other things dedicated to divine service; but as these are made inviolable, they are also called sacred, and thus the tripartite classification of the Roman Law is condensed into two members: *sacræ res*, or *sanctæ res*, which are sometimes called *sacrosanctæ*, and things *religiosæ*, which are those that have a connection with divine rites, or the duties and functions of the clergy,—such as cemeteries, tombs, and houses of refuge for old and infirm persons, and other objects of charity, which may be under the government of the clergy.[t]

All the classes of things except *res singulorum*, or the private property of individuals, have now been considered.

CHAPTER XIII.

THE LAW OF THINGS.

The Law of Things.—Inst. lib. ii. tit. i. De Rerum Divisione et Acquirendo ipsarum Dominio, § 11—17.—*Res Singulorum.*—Two Modes of acquiring: 1, by Natural Law; 2, by Municipal Law.—Modes of acquiring by Natural Law, or Jus Gentium.—Occupancy.—Creatures *Feræ Naturæ.*—Creatures not *Feræ Naturæ.*—Capture in War, or Acquisition *Jure Belli.*—Its Limits.—Jus Postliminii.—Complete Capture. P. 81.

Justinian, as we have seen, classifies things with reference to the nature of their appropriation, first under two heads, *i. e.* things, 1st, *In nostro patrimonio;* and 2ndly, *Extra nostrum patrimonium.* He then enumerates specifically things, as, 1, *Naturali jure communia omnium;* 2, *Publica;* 3, *Universitatis;* 4, *Nullius;* all of which are

[r] Lancelotti Instit. Juris Canon. lib. ii. tit. i. princip.

[s] Ibid. § 1.

[t] Ibid. tit. xxii. xxiii.

extra nostrum patrimonium, or not private property.[u] The legal nature of these has been explained. The fifth class, *res singulorum*, or private property, remains to be examined. The Emperor divides the modes in which this last-mentioned class of things are acquired into two species, that is to say, 1st, modes of acquiring by natural law, called by the old Roman civilians *jus gentium*; and 2ndly, modes of acquiring by the Civil or Municipal Law. And first of the more antient of the two, that is to say, modes of acquiring by natural law.[x]

The natural law referred to by Justinian in this part of the Institutes is *secondary natural law*, that is to say, the natural law which arises not from the mere nature of man by itself, but from the institution of the rights of property.[y]

Grotius divides modes of acquiring things into two classes; 1, *original;* and 2, *derived.*[z] The first are where something that was the property of no one becomes that of some one, and the second are those modes whereby a right of property which was vested in one person is transferred to another from the former.

Original acquisition is reducible to the single head of occupancy, for if a number of persons take possession of a country and divide it among themselves, each of them acquires by occupancy, though by the division his share is defined and limited. Now this is the only case in which Grotius conceives a doubt whether an original acquisition should be referred to occupancy.[a]

Occupancy is sub-divided into two kinds; 1, *simple*, or mere occupancy; and 2, consequent occupancy. The former is where a man takes possession as proprietor of a thing which is the property of no one, and the latter is where, 1st, our property produces fruit, such as the young of our female animals; or 2ndly, anything adheres to and becomes part of our property.[b]

There is this important distinction between the effect of original and that of derived acquisition. Wherever an acquisition is original, the right acquired to the thing thus becoming property must be unlimited and unqualified, since as no one but the occupant has any right to the thing, he must have the whole right of disposing of it. But with regard to derived acquisition it may be otherwise, for the person from whom the thing is acquired may not have an unlimited right to it, or he may transfer or convey it with certain reservations of right.

[u] Instit. lib. ii. tit. i. princip.

[x] Instit. lib. ii. tit. i. § 11.

[y] Grotius, Droit de la Guerre et de la Paix, liv. ii. chap. viii. § 1, n. 3.

[z] Grot. liv. ii. chap. iii. § 1.

[a] Grot. ibid. and Notes of Barbeyrac, and liv. ii. chap. ii. § 3, note ad num. 12.

[b] Pufendorf, Droit de la Nature et des Gens, liv. iv. chap. vi. Vinnii Comm. ad Instit. lib. ii. tit. i. § 19. Pand. lib. vi. tit. i. De Rei Vindic. L. 5, § 2.

These preliminary classifications having been explained, we will proceed to Justinian's exposition of the modes of acquiring by natural law.

Wild animals, therefore, and birds, and fish, and all animals that are produced in the sea, the heavens, and the earth become the property by natural law of whoever takes possession of them. The reason of this is that whatever is the property of no man becomes by natural reason the property of whoever occupies it.

It is the same whether the animals or birds be caught on the premises of the catcher or on those of another. But if any one enters the land of another to sport or hunt, he may be warned off by the owner of the land. When you have caught any of these animals it remains yours so long as it is under the restraint of your custody. But as soon as it has escaped from your keeping and has restored itself to natural liberty, it ceases to be yours, and again becomes the property of whoever occupies it. The animal is understood to recover its natural liberty when it has vanished from your sight, or is before your eyes under such circumstances that pursuit would be difficult.[c]

Here we find the celebrated maxim of Gajus—*Quod nullius est id ratione naturali occupanti conceditur.*[d] It is founded on the following doctrine:—Granting the institution of the rights of property among mankind, those things are each man's property which no other man has a right to take from him. Now no one has a right to that which is *res nullius*, consequently whoever possesses *rem nullius* possesses that which no one has a right to take from him. It is therefore his property.

But this general right of acquiring things by occupancy is subject to an important qualification.[e] Grotius justly argues that it is not an absolute right, for though it is indeed founded on natural law it is matter of permissive law, and not one which requires that full liberty should be left to men to avail themselves of it, since such liberty is unnecessary in many cases for the welfare of mankind, and may even, as Blackstone observes, be prejudicial to the peace of society if it be not limited by positive law.[f] Barbeyrac also argues that where a country is taken possession of by a body of men, it becomes the property of that body or of the person who represents them, and that therefore the right of the individual members to take possession of portions of it or any of the things therein contained, may be restricted or taken away according as the welfare of the community may

[c] Instit. lib. ii. tit. i. § 12.

[d] Pand. lib. xli. tit. i. De Acquirendo Rerum Dominio, L. 3.

[e] Grot. liv. ii. chap. iii. § 5.

[f] Blackst. Com. book ii. chap. xxvi. princip.; book ii. chap. xxvii.

demand.[g] These principles are applicable to the whole jurisprudence of acquisition by occupancy.

The acquisition of things tangible must be made *corpore et animo*,[h] that is to say, by an outward act signifying an intention to possess. The necessity of an outward act to commence holding a thing in dominion is founded on the principle that a will or intention cannot have legal effect without an outward act declaring that intention, and on the other hand no man can be said to have the dominion over a thing which he has no intention of possessing as his.[i] Thus, a man cannot deprive others of their right to take possession of vacant property by merely considering it as his, without actually appropriating it to himself; and if he possess it without any will of appropriating it to himself, it cannot be held to have ceased to be *res nullius*.

The intention to possess is to be presumed wherever the outward act shows such an intention, for that is to be presumed which is most probable.

The outward act or possession need not, however, be manual, for any species of possession, or, as the antients expressed it, *Custodia*, is a sufficient appropriation.[j]

The general principle respecting the acquisition of animals *feræ naturæ* is, that it is absurd to hold anything to be a man's property which is entirely out of his power. But Grotius limits the application of that principle to the *acquisition* of things, and therefore justly dissents from the doctrine of Gajus given above, that the animal becomes again *res nullius*, immediately on recovering its liberty, if it be difficult for the first occupant to retake it.[k] He argues that when a thing has become the property of any one, whether it be afterwards taken from him by the act of man, or whether he lose it from a natural cause, he does not necessarily lose his right to it together with the possession; but that it is reasonable to presume that the proprietor of a wild animal must have renounced his right to it when the animal is gone beyond hope of recovery, and where it could not be identified. He therefore argues that the right of ownership to a wild animal may be rendered lasting notwithstanding its flight, by a mark or other artificial sign by which the creature may be recognised.

With regard to fish, Voet argues that when they are included within artificial boundaries they are private property, but that when they are in a lake or other large piece of natural water, though the proprietor of the land may have a right of fishery there, yet the fish

[g] Pufendorf, Droit de la Nat. et des Gens, liv. iv. chap. vi. § 3, note.

[h] Pand. lib. xli. tit. ii. De Acquir. et Omittenda Possessione, L. 3, § 1, 3.

[i] Grot. liv. ii. chap. iv. § 3.

[j] Grot. liv. ii. chap viii. § 11, note 1, Barbeyrac.

[k] Pand. lib. xli. tit. i. De Acquirendo Rerum Dominio, L. 3, § 2.

are in their natural state of liberty, and consequently they cannot be his property until he has brought them within his power by catching them.[l]

It was disputed among the antient Roman Jurisconsulti, whether a wild animal becomes immediately the property of whoever wounds it so that it can be secured, or whether it becomes the property of him only who actually secures it. And Justinian confirmed the latter opinion, because many circumstances might occur to prevent the wounded animal being taken by him who wounded it.[m]

Bees, also, are of a wild nature, and, therefore, they no more become the property of the owner of the soil by swarming in his trees than do the birds which build in them; and they are not his unless he enclose them in a hive. Consequently whoever hives them makes them his own. And while they are wild any one may cut off the honeycombs, though the owner of the land may prevent this by warning off trespassers. And a swarm flying from a hive belongs to the owner of the hive so long as it is within his sight, but otherwise it is the property of whoever takes possession of it.[n]

With regard to creatures which have the habit of going and returning, such as pigeons, they remain the property of those to whom they belong, so long as they retain the *animus revertendi*, or disposition to return. But when they lose that disposition they become the property of whosoever secures them. And they must be held to have lost the *animus revertendi* as soon as they have lost the habit of returning.[o] Such are the doctrines of the Roman Law, which are conformable to the English Law, with the qualification of Grotius, which is applicable to the case of all animals *feræ naturæ*, that is to say, that a mark or collar prevents the rights of the proprietor of a wild animal being extinguished by its escape from his sight and pursuit.[p]

We come now to animals not of a wild nature, which are called in the English Law animals *domitæ naturæ*, in which a man may have an absolute property as in any other thing.[q] On this subject, Justinian says:—

But fowls and geese are not of a wild nature; and this we may perceive from the fact that there are particular species of fowls and

[l] Voet, Comm. ad Pandectas, lib. xli. tit. i. De Acquir. Rer. Domin. num. 5.

[m] Instit. lib. ii. tit. i. § 13. Grotius, Droit de la Guerre et de la Paix, liv. ii. chap. viii. § 3, num. 3.

[n] Instit. lib. ii. tit. i. § 14; and see the same principles in Blackst. Com. book ii. chap. xxvi. p. 393, edit. by Coleridge.

[o] Instit. ibid. § 15.

[p] Blackst. Com. book ii. chap. xxv. Grotius, Droit de la Guerre et de la Paix, liv. ii. chap. viii. § 3.

[q] First Rep. of the Commission on Crim. Law, 1834, p. 13.

geese, called wild. Therefore if your geese or fowls escape, they remain yours; though out of your sight, and in whatever place they may be, and whoever takes possession of them with intent to appropriate them, is guilty of theft.[r]

It is indeed clear that whoever finds that which must be the property of some one, since it is never found in a natural state and common to all men, is bound to restore it to the proprietor, or at least not to take it for himself.[s]

We come now to a more important mode of acquisition, also referable to the head of occupancy, namely, acquisition by right of war.

Also those things (says Justinian) *that we take from an enemy become instantly our own by the Law of Nations: so far even that freemen are in that manner reduced to servitude under us. But as soon as they escape from our power and return to their own party, they recover their former state.*[t]

The acquisition of property by right of war is referred in the Pandects[u] to the principle *res nullius naturaliter fit primi occupantis.* It has been argued that law is suspended during war, and therefore the rights of property are suspended; but, as Grotius justly observes, Civil Law only is suspended by war; and the rights of property are part of secondary natural law.[v] However, Grotius, Pothier, Theophilus (the colleague of Trebonian), Vinnius, and Voet, all refer the right in question to the head of occupancy.[x] And acquisition *jure belli* is acquisition by occupancy in the following sense. Assuming the right of war by which a belligerent may lawfully acquire the property of the enemy, that property is *res nullius,* not generally, but only with regard to those who possess that right, so far as that right extends. So this *jus belli* does not arise from the property of the enemy being *res nullius,* but the property of the enemy is *res nullius* with regard to the other belligerent, so far as the latter has a a right to take it.[y] The foundation of this right remains to be considered.

Grotius lays it down that by natural law a belligerent lawfully

[r] Instit. lib. ii. tit. i. § 16.

[s] Pand. lib. xli. tit. i. De Acquirendo Rerum Dominio, L. 44; and see Vinnii Comment. ad Instit. lib. ii. tit. i. § 16.

[t] Instit. lib. ii. tit. i. § 17. Pand. lib. xli. tit. i. De Acquirendo Rerum Dominio, L. 5, § 7, L. 7, princ. Pand. lib. xlix. tit. xv. De Captivis et Postliminio, L. 19, princ.

[u] Pand. lib. xli. tit. ii. De Acquir. ed Omitt. Possess. L. 1, § 1.

[v] Grot. Droit de la Guerre et de la Paix, prélim. § 27.

[x] Grot. liv. iii. chap. vi. § 8, num. 3. Pothier, Traité du Domaine de Proprieté, part 1, chap. 2, § 2. Theophilis Parafras. ad Instit. hoc tit. Vinnii Comm. ad Inst. lib. ii. tit. i. § 17. Voet, Comm. ad Pand. lib. xli. tit. i. num. 8.

[y] And see Pothier, Traité du Domaine de la Proprieté, part 1, chap. 2, § 2, num. 86.

acquires in a just war so much of the enemy's property as amounts in value to what is due to him, or so much as is sufficient to punish the enemy for the injuries received.[z]

But this doctrine, though satisfactory with respect to the acquisition of public property by right of war, is not equally conclusive when applied to private property.

But Grotius holds that the property of the members of a community is, as it were, hypothecated for the obligations of the aggregate body; and Barbeyrac argues that the liability of private property is a necessary consequence of the constitution of civil societies acting as bodies politic, and that without that remedy to obtain redress of an injury (which must above all be repaired) it would often be impossible to compel a state to do justice to those who have demands against it. He however, shows that every state is bound to indemnify its subjects for any losses which they may suffer individually in consequence of the fault or injustice of their superiors.[a]

The right of war, by virtue of which all things taken from an enemy in any war are acquired as property by the state or by the individual captors,[b] is what is called by Modestinus, *jus quod necessitas constituit*, and that law which Justinian referred to, *humanæ necessitates.*[c] The question must be considered, 1st, with regard to third parties; and 2ndly, with regard to the belligerents themselves.

And 1st, with regard to third parties:—Grotius argues that a state that takes no share in the contest between the belligerents must not assume the authority of judging which side has the juster cause, nor of deciding how far the acts of hostility, not affecting itself, are justifiable on either side in the course of the war. Neutrals must therefore leave those questions to the parties who have appealed to arms for the purpose of deciding them, and should consequently (while they remain neutral) hold all those things to be lawful which are done on both sides, so far as regards the legal effects of those acts.

This doctrine is a consequence of a fundamental doctrine of international law, that all nations are naturally equal in point of right, as having no common superior, and are therefore in the situation of men living in a state of nature; for Ulpian lays it down that *quoad jus naturale omnes homines equales sunt.*[d]

Barbeyrac confirms the argument of Grotius, by showing that it is necessary for the tranquillity of mankind, that those who remain

[z] Grot. liv. iii. chap. vi. § 2.

[a] Grot. liv. iii. chap. ii. § 2, note 1, Barbeyrac.

[b] Grot. liv. iii. chap. vi. § 2.

[c] Pand. lib. i. tit. iii. De Legibus, L. 40. Instit. lib. i. tit. ii. § 2.

[d] Vattel, Droit des Gens, préliminaires, § 18. Pand. lib. l. tit. ult. De Reg. Jur. L. 32.

neutral during a war should not afterwards dispute the legality of the results of the war, or the facts arising therefrom, on grounds of justice and right.

We come now to the question of the legal validity of the results of the war, as between the belligerents themselves.

War is considered in international law as the last resort of those who have no common superior to whom they can refer for the decision of their differences. While the war lasts, the differences of the belligerents remain unsettled, and whatever is acquired by one party *jure belli*, may be retaken and recovered by the other.

The recovery of things and persons from the enemy, and their return *in pristinum statum*, is called *postliminium*, which is defined by Servius Sulpicius to mean the return of a thing or person within the boundaries or *limina* of a country, after that thing or person had been taken in war.[e] But the sense of the word was extended to every species of recovery or deliverance from the enemy, which had the effect of restoring the thing or person to its former state.

It is decided in a celebrated law of Tryphoninus, that, except in a particular case, the conclusion of a war by a treaty of peace deprived the prisoners who were not restored by the treaty of the right of Postliminium.[f] Grotius argues that the true legal reason of this determination is, that if what has been acquired in war were not to be considered as lawfully and finally acquired, after the conclusion of a treaty of peace, not providing for its restitution, one war would lead to another, and there would be no end to hostilities.[g]

Upon the same principles Grotius argues in another place, that when a treaty has been concluded at the end of a public war, the justice of the cause of the war, and that consequently of the settlement by treaty, ought not to be called in question by the parties, who must be at any rate bound by that settlement.[h] Those rules of international law are absolutely necessary for the tranquillity of mankind, precisely on the same ground upon which, among persons living under municipal law, the judgment of a supreme court must be final, though it may be neither just nor even according to law.[i] Thus the principles of universal legal policy invest, for the welfare of mankind, with a species of inevitable legality, many acts which are not agreeable to the dictates

[e] Instit. lib. ii. tit. i. § 17. Instit. lib. i. tit. xii. Quibus Modis Jus Patr. Potest. solvit. § 5. Pand. lib. xlix. tit. xv. De Captiv. et Postlimin. per tot.

[f] Pand. lib. xlix. tit. xv. De Captiv. et Postlimin. L. 12. Grot. liv. iii. chap. ix. § 4.

[g] Grot. ubi cit. num. 4.

[h] Grot. liv. iii. chap. xix. § 11.

[i] Pand. lib. l. tit. ult. De Reg. Jur. L. 207. Pand. lib. i. tit. i. De Justit. et Jure, L. 11. *Prætor quoque jus reddere dicitur etiam cum inique decernit.*

of natural law. But it is necessary here to remember the maxim of Paulus—*Non omne quod licet honestum est,*[k] for the acquiescence of the law in such cases is only a species of impunity granted for the sake of the greater welfare of the greatest number of mankind, and to avoid more serious evils; and the acts in question are no more really just than the unlawful decision of a supreme tribunal, which however has force of law in the particular case decided.

Such are the doctrines on which the right of capturing the enemy's property in war is grounded. We have next to consider the limits of that right.

It is evident that though the property of the citizens is liable for the acts of the state, yet the property of the state is primarily liable, and should bear the liability in preference to that of private individuals, according to the equitable rule of the Canon Law, *Non debet aliquis alterius odio prægravari.*[l]

Grotius argues that if the property of individuals were not liable, the impunity of the state to which they belong might often be the consequence of that inviolability of private property. But it follows from this very principle that where it is in the power of a belligerent to indemnify himself, *jus suum consequi*, out of the public property of the enemy, it is not justifiable to take the property of private persons.

On this principle the equitable usages of modern war exempt from confiscation all private property on land, with the exception of such as may become booty in special cases when taken from the enemy in the field or in besieged towns, and of military contributions levied on the inhabitants of the hostile territory. This exemption extends even to the case of an absolute and unqualified conquest of an enemy's country.[m] But the property belonging to the government of the vanquished nation passes to the victorious state, which also takes the place of the former sovereign in respect of eminent domain. The effect of acquisition by conquest is to transfer the sovereignty and dominion of the conquered country from its former sovereign to the conqueror.[n]

With respect to maritime war the case is different, for the capture of the enemy's merchant ships may be the only effectual remedy against him, because his public property on the sea may be totally inadequate for that purpose. And the capture of the private shipping

[k] Pand. lib. l. tit. ult. De Regulis Juris, L. 144.

[l] Sext. Decretal. tit. ult. De Reg. Jur. Reg. 22.

[m] Wheaton, Elem. of International Law, vol. ii. p. 80, 81.

[n] Vatel, Droit des Gens, liv. iii. chap. xiii. Hall *v.* Campbell, Cowper's Reports, 210. Blackst. Com. book i. chap. iii. p. 199, edit Coleridge.

of a commercial country is likely to prove an effectual means of bringing the war to a speedy termination.

The question whether the enemy's property taken in war belongs to the state or to the captors depends in each case on the municipal laws of the particular country. But on this subject the following general principles may be laid down. Lawful belligerents are those only who act under the authority of a sovereign power by virtue of public law.[o] It is therefore the permission or command of the public power that renders legal the hostile acts of individuals. They act in the name of that power, and on the principle, *qui facit per alium facit per se,* all things taken from an enemy by a person acting in the execution of a public duty, are acquired for and by the state.[p]

But moveables captured by individuals not in the service of the state, or taken by persons in the public service, but at a time when they are not acting as public servants, are acquired by the individual captors, subject to the regulations of the law of the state to which they belong.[q]

With respect to immoveables, they become the property of the state, because land is taken possession of by military occupation, which is a public act of the state.[r]

The question when things taken from an enemy become legally vested in the captor or the state, as the case may be, or in other words, when the capture is legally complete, remains to be considered. This question is necessary to be settled for the decision of two species of cases:—1. Cases of recapture, and 2. Those in which captured property has passed into the hands of neutrals.

Grotius lays it down that whenever a territory is reconquered or taken by the original sovereign from the conqueror during a war, the property of land confiscated returns to its former proprietors by *jus postliminii.*[s] It follows that nothing can give a good title to land held by right of war, except a treaty of peace, and those who purchase conquered land during the war do so at their peril.

But moveables do not in all cases return *jure postliminii* to their former owners upon ceasing to be in the power of the enemy during

[o] See the celebrated definition of Ulpian, Pand. lib. l. tit. penult. De Signif. Verbor. L. 118. *Hostes hi sunt qui nobis vel quibus nos publice bellum decrevimus: cæteri latrones aut prædones sunt;* and Pand. lib. xlix. tit. xv. De Captivis et Postliminio Reversis, L. 24.

[p] Sext. Decretal. tit. ult. Reg. 73. Grotius, liv. iii. chap. vi. § 9, 12.

[q] Pothier, Traité du Domaine de la Proprieté, part 1, chap. 2, num. 88, 89, 90, 91; and see Abbot on Shipping, part 1, chap. 1, § 7.

[r] Pand. lib. xlix. tit. xv. De Captiv. et Postliminio Reversis, L. 20. Grot. liv. iii. chap. vi. § 11.

[s] Grot. liv. iii. chap. ix. § 13.

war.[t] If they have passed during the war from the enemy to neutrals or to subjects of the state to whose citizens they originally belonged, they cannot be claimed even during the war by their original proprietors.

And Grotius decides in the same manner the question whether a person who had lost a thing by fate of war could reclaim it in the hands of a third party who had captured it from the first captor.[u]

These principles are followed among nations with regard to their own subjects, to encourage recaptures, and with respect to neutrals to avoid difficulties and contests which might compromise their neutrality, as well as for the sake of general convenience in disposing of prizes.

The general principle is, that things are not completely captured so as to exclude the right of *Postliminium* of the former proprietor unless, as Grotius expresses it, they are so captured that the proprietor must have lost all immediate hope of recovering them.[x] This principle is drawn by analogy from a law in the Pandects respecting things taken by wild beasts.[y]

But there is much difference of opinion as to the exact time or circumstances that constitute complete capture so as to exclude the original proprietor from his *jus postliminii.*

In the Pandects it is defined that the captured property must be brought *intra præsidia.* Grotius holds the capture to be complete when the property has been brought to a place of which the capturing state is master.[z]

When this last decision is applied to a country occupied in war, the expression "a place of which the capturing state is master," must be construed to mean only that tract of country which is actually occupied, in fact, according to that celebrated rule of Celsus, *Si cum magnâ vi ingressus est exercitus : eam tantummodo partem quam intravit obtinet.*[a]

In the *Consolato del Mare*, which contains the antient maritime customs of the Mediterranean, it is laid down with respect to ships, that when the capturer has placed them in security, "*in luogo sicuro,*" if they be recaptured, the former owner does not recover his right, but that it is otherwise if they be recaptured when they are still in a place where they are not in security.[b]

[t] Grot. liv. iii. chap. ix. § 14.

[u] Grot. liv. iii. chap. vi. § 7.

[x] Grot. liv. iii. chap. vi. But see a distinction drawn by Barbeyrac, note 1.

[y] Pand. lib. xli. tit. i. De Acquirendo Rerum Dominio, L. 44.

[z] Pand. lib. xlix. tit. xv. De Captivis et Postliminio Reversis, L. 5, § 1, and vide ibid. L. 19, § 3. Grot. liv. iii. chap. vi. § 3, num. 2.

[a] Pand. lib. xli. tit. ii. De Acquirenda et Omittenda Possessione, L. 18, § ult.; and see Bynkershock, Quæstiones Juris Publici, lib. i. cap. vi.

[b] Consolato del Mare, cap. 287. Casaregi Spiegazione, ibid.

By the established usage of maritime nations, ships and goods captured at sea are not generally considered as completely divested from their owners until carried *infra præsidia*, and regularly condemned in a competent court of prize.[c] By some writers, however, twenty-four hours' possession is held to complete the capture, and Voet informs us that forty-eight hours were required by the law of the United Provinces.[d]

With regard to the recapture of property of a state or its citizens by the state itself or its subjects, the municipal law of each nation may freely regulate the questions which may arise, but in every other case in which rules have not been settled by treaty, these authorities are of great importance.

CHAPTER XIV.

THE LAW OF THINGS.

The Law of Things.—Instit. lib. ii. tit. i. § 18—24.—Consequent Occupancy.—Fœtura, or Procreation.—Accessio.—Alluvion.—Boundaries.—Three Classes of Lands with reference to Boundaries.—Sudden Additions to Land.—Islands in the Sea and in Rivers.—Changes of the Course of Rivers.—Return of Rivers to their former Beds.—Inundations. P. 86.

One more instance of simple or mere occupancy is given by Justinian, namely, that of stones and gems and other things found on the shores of the sea, which are *res nullius*, and become the property of whoever takes possession of them.[e]

He then proceeds to *consequent* occupancy, which occurs—1st, where our property produces fruit; and 2ndly, where anything adheres to and becomes part of our property.[f] He gives as an instance of the former kind the offspring produced by female animals, which by the law of nature belong to the owner of those animals.[g] This mode of acquiring is called by the civilians *fœtura*, which indeed Vinnius denies to be a species of occupancy.

[c] Wheaton, Elem. of Internat. Law, vol. ii. ch. ii. § 11, p. 89. Robinson, Admir. Reports, vol. i. p. 50, *The Santa Cruz*. Abbot on Shipping, part i. chap. i. § 9.

[d] Voet ad Pand. lib. xlix. tit. xv. De Captivis et Postliminio Reversis, num. 4.

[e] Instit. lib. ii. tit. i. § 18. Pand. lib. xli. tit. ii. De Acquir. vel Omit. Possess. L. 1, § 1.

[f] Vinnii Comm. ad Instit. lib. ii. tit. i. § 11, num. 4.

[g] Instit. ibid. § 19. Pand. lib. vi. tit. i. De Rei Vindicatione, L. 5, § 2.

We have next to examine the second kind of consequent occupancy, which Vinnius calls *accessio.* And first of *alluvion.*

Also (says Justinian) *whatever a river adds to your estate by alluvion becomes yours by natural law. Alluvion is an imperceptible augmentation.*

That is held to be added by alluvion which is gradually joined on, so that it is impossible to distinguish how much is added in each moment of time.[h]

Grotius divides lands, with reference to their boundaries, into three classes,[i] as follow :—

1st, Those lands which are specifically assigned, and which Florentinus denominates *limited,* because they are included within artificial boundaries.[k]

2ndly, Those that are limited in extent without any specified and defined boundaries.[l]

3rdly, Those which are bounded by natural limits, such as rivers or mountains. These are called *arcifinite* lands, or *agri arcifinii.*

Florentinus decides that *in agris limitatis, jus alluvionis locum non habere constat,* and he cites a law of Antoninus Pius to that effect.[m] It is, indeed, evident that upon the most accurate legal principles, when land is possessed within certain boundaries, whatever is added to the land is out of those boundaries, and therefore not the property of the owner of that land.

The same principles apply to land limited in quantity or extent though without any specific boundaries. Thus, for instance, if a man have conveyed to him four acres of a certain piece of land, he can have title to no more than four acres, whatever additions the land may receive from alluvion.

But where land is limited by water, it is evident that if the water add something to the land, the boundaries of the land are at the same time enlarged by their own nature ; and as the additions made by the water by alluvion are so small within each small period of time, or so gradual that the portions newly incorporated cannot be identified as parts of any other person's property, they must naturally belong to

[h] Instit. lib. ii. tit. i. § 20. *Est autem Alluvio incrementum latens.* Pand. lib. xli. tit. i. De Acquirend. Rerum Dominio, L. 7, § 1, *Per alluvionem autem id videtur adjici, quod ita paulatim adjicitur ut intelligere non possimus quantum quoquo momento temporis adjiciatur.*

[i] Grot. Droit de la Guerre, liv. ii. chap. iii. § 16.

[k] Pand. lib. xli. tit. i. De Acquir. Rer. Domin. L. 16 ; and see Littleton, § 36.

[l] Littleton, § 44.

[m] Pand. lib. xli. tit. i. De Acquirendo Rerum Dominio ; and see Vattel, Droit des Gens, liv. i. chap. xii. § 267.

the person with whose property they become identified and incorporated.

Now where the proprietor of the adjoining land has not the right of alluvion by the nature of the boundaries of his property, the alluvial deposits are by natural law *res nullius*, and may be acquired by the first person who takes possession of them. But Grotius observes that where the rights of property of individuals are an exception to the general rule that the whole territory is possessed by the commonwealth or its representative, so that whatever is not appropriated to some person is the property of the state, in that case whenever the right of alluvion is not a legal accessory to an already acquired right of property of some person, it is vested in the state.[n]

The next paragraph of the Institutes relates to a more sudden and considerable species of addition by water to the volume or extent of land.

But if the force of a river detached a part of your land, and drove it to the land of another person, it evidently still remains yours. But if it adhered to his estate for a considerable space of time, and the trees which were carried with it struck their roots into his land, it from that time is acquired as an integral part of the estate to which it is joined.[o]

This paragraph is founded upon the rule of Pomponius, *Id quod nostrum est, sine nostro facto ad alium transferri non potest.*[p] Grotius observes that this axiom applies only to those cases where a transfer of right is not effected by the sole operation of the law.[q] Now according to that rule, as the property detached from the land of one man and driven to that of another is capable of being identified, its change of locality without the participation of the proprietor cannot affect his right to it. Therefore it remains his.

But an omission is in law an act, and thus Paulus says that a person alienates his property when he permits another to acquire it by long usage or prescription.[r]

Upon these principles Justinian here decides that when a proprietor has permitted a detached portion of his land to become an integral part of that of another, he cannot reclaim it after having so long neglected to assert his right.[s]

It follows from the same principles that if a piece of land slip over

[n] Grot. liv. ii. chap. iii. § 19. [o] Inst. ibid. § 21.
[p] Pand. lib. l. tit. ult. De Divers. Regul. Juris, L. 2.
[q] Grot. liv. ii. chap. viii. § 10, num. 3.
[r] Pand. lib. l. tit. penult. De Verbor. Signif. L. 28.
[s] Vinnii Comm. ad Instit. lib. ii. tit. i. § 21. Voet, Comm. ad Pand. lib. xli. tit. i. num. 16.

the land of another proprietor, the owner of the former will not lose his right. The destruction of the lower property is a misfortune imputable to no one, and it must therefore be borne by the person whose property is destroyed, since that destruction cannot divest the right of another who is in the possession of his own property. *Potior est in re pari causa possessoris.*[t]

We come now to the case of islands formed in a river, or in the sea.

An island formed in the sea (which rarely occurs) is the property of whoever occupies it, for it is held to belong to no one. But an island formed in a river (which is a more frequent occurrence) if it be in the middle of the river is the common property of those who have land on each side of it next to the water, in proportion to the extent of their respective possessions. But if the island be nearest to one bank, it belongs to the owner or owners of that bank. If the river be divided into branches in one place, and those branches unite in another, the land thus enclosed, which becomes a sort of island, remains the property of its former owner.[u]

The Law of England gives an island rising in the sea to the King,[x] but this must be understood of an island within the Maritime Jurisdiction of the Crown, or one taken possession of by subjects of the Crown, for if an island rise in the sea out of the bounds of that portion of the sea, it is *juris gentium,* and must belong to the first nation that takes possession of it.

As for islands rising in rivers, the owners of the banks have no claim to them when the lands of such owners are artificially bounded, and this observation applies also to the case of a piece of land detached from one estate and joined on to another *vi fluminis.* This and the preceding paragraph of Justinian therefore apply only to *agri arcifinii,* which have no boundaries but water.

Grotius holds that when the territories of two states are separated by a river, those territories must be presumed not to be confined within measurements, nor within artificial limits, but to be bounded by the river. In that case he holds that the true limit is a line passing in the middle of the stream.[y] He, however, observes that the whole river may belong to the territory on one side, or may be unequally divided between the two.[z] In both the last-mentioned cases the property in the island should be adjudged to one or each of

[t] Pand. lib. xxix. tit. i. De Testam. Militari, L. 36, § 3.

[u] Instit. lib. ii. tit. i. § 22. Pand. lib. xli. tit. i. De Acquir. Rer. Domin. L. 7, § 3. Pand. lib. xliii. tit. xii. De Fluminibus, L. 1, § 6, § 4. Ibid. § 10.

[x] Blackst. Comm. book ii. chap. xvi. p. 261. edit. Coleridge.

[y] Grot. liv. ii. chap. iii. 17.

[z] Grot. ubi sup. § 18.

the adjoining states according as it is included entirely or partly within the line that forms the real boundary of their territories.[a]

If the proprietors of the banks of the river have not the right of alluvion, or in other words, if their land be within artificial bounds or admeasurements, the island is by the Roman Law *res nullius*.[b] But Grotius justly qualifies this decision, and argues that the bed of the river, if not appropriated to any person, must belong to the commonwealth or its representative unless the state have left it unappropriated and vacant, in which last case it is *res nullius*, and may be acquired by occupancy.[c]

The next paragraph of the Institutes relates to considerable changes in the course of rivers.

If a river leaving entirely its natural bed should flow in another place; the former bed is the property of those who possess the shores in proportion to the extent of their possessions along the banks: but the new bed becomes the same in law as the river, that is to say, public. But if the river subsequently return to its former bed, the new bed becomes again the property of those who are owners of the shores.[d]

This paragraph must be understood to be limited to the case of rivers the lands adjoining which have the right of alluvion, or are not within artificial boundaries, nor within metes and bounds not including the river; for if the adjoining lands are within invariable limits, the bed of the river when left dry becomes *res nullius*,[e] unless it belongs to the state.[f]

This decision of Justinian only applies to total changes of the course of a river (*naturali alveo in universum derelicto*), for gradual or partial changes are analogous upon principle to alluvion. Thus Grotius decides that a river separating two territories changes their boundaries by gradually altering its course.[g]

But he argues that where a river totally changes its course, by a sudden and violent flood or other hasty means, it loses its identity, and the boundaries of the adjoining territories are therefore no longer limited by it, but remain as they were before the vacant bed was dried up.[h] The middle of the relinquished bed must, therefore, after such change, remain the boundary of the two adjoining territories, according to the intention of the parties when the boundaries were originally fixed.

[a] Pand. lib. xli. tit. i. De Acquir. Rer. Domin. L. 29.

[b] Pand. lib. xliii. tit. xii. De Flumin. L. 1, § 6.

[c] Grot. liv. ii. ch. viii. § 9, num. 3.

[d] Instit. lib. ii. tit. i. § 23.

[e] Pand. lib. xli. tit. i. De Acquirend. Rer. Domin. L. 7, § 5. Pand. lib. xliii. tit. xii. De Flumin. L. 1, § 7.

[f] See Grotius, ubi sup.

[g] Grot. liv. ii. chap. iii. § 16, num. 4.

[h] Grot. ibid. § 17.

It follows from the principles already laid down that if the river subsequently return to its former bed, the new bed thereby relinquished becomes again the property of those who formerly owned it.[i] The law, indeed, in all cases of temporary loss of the possession of land by changes in the course of rivers, restores the land to its former owners as soon as the water has ceased to flow over it.

But if the river change its new bed by alluvion and not *eodem impetu*, in that case the alluvial deposits belong to the owners of the lands to which they are added.[k]

With regard to inundations, they do not alter the ownership of the inundated land, and on the water receding, the land remains the property of its former owners.[l] Thus Ulpian distinguishes an inundation from the formation of a new course by the force of a river, and he says—*si* (*flumen*) *vel imbribus, vel mari, vel qua alia ratione ad tempus excrevit: ripas non mutat,* exemplifying his position by reference to the inundations of the Nile, which in no respect change the rights of property in land.[m] It is the excavation or longitudinal depression of the land that distinguishes the new course of a river from an inundation.[n]

The Law of England agrees with the Code of Napoleon in holding that if a man lose his ground by a sudden change of the course of a river, he shall have what the river left dry as compensation for his loss.[o]

CHAPTER XV.

THE LAW OF THINGS.

The Law of Things,—Instit. lib. ii. tit. i. § 26—34.—Acquisitions by Consequent Occupancy continued.—Acquisition by *Specification.*—By *Accession.*—*Confusion.*—*Commixio.*—Classification of Bodies.—Law of *Accession* continued. —Building with the Materials of another.—Building on the Soil of another. —Plants and Seeds.—Writings.—Pictures.—What Things are Accessories. P. 91.

Having given an outline of the law regarding alluvion, new islands, and the effects of water on the boundaries of land, Justinian proceeds

[i] Pand. liv. xli. tit. i. De Acquir. Rerum Domin. L. 7, § 5. [k] Pand. ibid. L. 36.

[l] Instit. lib. ii. tit. i. § 24. Pand. lib. xliii. tit. xii. De Flumin. L. 1, § 9.

[m] Pand. lib. xliii. tit. xii. Le Flumin. L. 1, § 9, § 5.

[n] Vinnii Comm. ad Instit. lib. ii. tit. i. § 24; and see the very interesting Law of Ulpian, Pand. lib. xliii. tit. xii. De Fluminibus, L. 1.

[o] Blackst. Comm. lib. ii. chap. xvi. in fin. Cod. Napol. art. 565.

to another species of consequent occupancy, called *specification*, or the production, by one man, of a new species out of materials belonging to another.

It was a debated point (says the Emperor) *between the Proculeans and the Sabinians, to whom a thing should belong which is composed by one man out of materials the property of another man—whether to the author of the new species, or to the owner of the materials. For instance, if out of another person's grapes wine be made; or, if one man make a vase out of another man's metal. It seemed good to us to adopt a middle opinion or compromise between the opinions of the conflicting authorities, and to decide that where the thing could be reduced to its former nature, the proprietor of the materials or substance, and where that was impossible, then the artificer should be adjudged proprietor of the thing. But if any one make a new species out of materials partly his own, and partly belonging to another, the maker of the thing is its proprietor, because he contributed the labour and part of the materials.*[p]

Cujacius shows that in these cases the proprietor of the materials has, by the Roman Law, an action against the person who acquired them, by forming a new species, to be indemnified for the loss.[q] And it is the same in the Common Law of England.[r] But in the Civil Law, no man acquires materials by the production of a new species, unless he do so, 1st, believing the materials to be his own, and 2ndly, on his own account, and not for another person.[s]

Grotius dissents from this decision of Justinian, and argues that by natural law, a thing, the matter composing which belongs to one man, while it owes its form to another, must in every case be the common property of both.[t]

We come next to acquisition by accession, which is a mode of acquiring *vi et potestate rei nostræ*, while *specification* is referrible to occupation, but is in fact anomalous and arbitrary.

If any man wove the purple of another man into his own cloth, though the purple be more valuable than the cloth, yet it belongs to the cloth as an accessory.[u] It does not appear that the good or bad faith of the person possessing the thing, whereof the other becomes an accessory, makes any difference in law, except that a larger indemnity might be

[p] Instit. lib. ii. tit. i. § 25.

[q] Cujac. Comm. ad tit. De Rei Vindicatione, lib. vi. Pand. L. 5. Cujac. Op. tom. vii. col. 236, 7, 8. edit. Mutinæ.

[r] Blackst. Comm. book ii. chap. xxvi. § 6.

[s] Vinnii Comm. ad Instit. lib. ii. tit. i. § 25. Pothier, Traité de la Proprieté, num. 186. But Voet differs, Comment. ad Pand. lib. xli. tit. i. De Acquir. Rer. Domin. § 21.

[t] Grot. liv. ii. chap. viii. § 19, 20; et ibid. cit. Pufendorf, note Barbeyrac; and see the French Code Civil, art. 570, 571, 572.

[u] Instit. lib. ii. tit. i. § 26. Blackst. Comm. book ii. chap. xxvi. § 6.

demanded from a person thus appropriating to himself the property of another. Grotius observes that this paragraph does not contain a principle of natural law, but a rule of positive or arbitrary law for the division of common property.[x]

We come now to the effect of the mixing of things which by their nature become incorporated with each other, such as liquids, whether in their natural state or rendered liquid by fusion. This species of mixture is called *confusion.*

The effect of this *confusion* of substances (such as wines or melted metals) whether brought about by chance or by consent, is, that the body so formed is the common property of both owners.[y]

With regard to the mixture of things which are not fluid and do not become confounded together, it is called *commixio;* it is thus explained by Justinian.

If your corn has been mixed with that of Titius, the whole will be common to you both, if it was done by consent; because each body, that is, each grain of corn, which was the separate property of either, is made common property by your will and consent. But if the mixture was the effect of chance, or produced without your participation, by Titius, it does not appear that the mixed corn is common, for each body preserves its own separate identity. In that case the corn is no more common than a flock of sheep would be, if your sheep were mingled with those of Titius. But if the mixed corn be detained by either party, the other has an action in rem against him who detains his corn; but it is in the power of the judge to assess the amount of the damages in proportion to the value of the corn.[z]

The distinction between *confusion* and *commixio* is, that in the first it is impossible, and in the second it is possible, to effect a separation of the mingled substances.

When two liquids are mixed together, the particles of each in reality remain distinct, as is the case with the grains of corn mentioned above, though the identity of each particle of the liquids is not perceptible to our senses. But where, from the similarity of the species of corn, a separation of the identical grains belonging to each is impossible, such a mixture should be considered in point of law as similar to the mixture of liquids, or *confusio.* Indeed, it is by no means impossible in every instance to separate fluids, and where this can be done, the mixture of such fluids is similar in point of legal reason to that of things consisting of distinct grains, or *commixio.* The legal reason of the distinction between *commixio* and *confusio* is to be found in a law in the Pandects

[x] Grot. ubi sup.

[y] Instit. ibid. § 27, and so in the English law. Blackst. Comm. book ii. chap. xxvi. § 7.

[z] Instit. ibid. § 28.

already cited, which distinguishes bodies into three classes. The first includes those which are formed of one substance, and not of separate parts joined together. These are said to be contained *uno spiritu.* The second class of bodies are called *corpora ex pluribus inter se cohærentibus*, and are formed of separate bodies, united together, such as a ship or a house. The third class are *corpora ex distantibus*, and are formed of separate bodies subjected to a collective form, such as a nation, a flock, or a legion.[a] *Ex distantibus capitibus sed uno nomini subjecta.* Now, liquids are of the first class—*uno spiritu continentur*—and therefore it is held by the Roman Jurisconsulti that, as a mixture of two liquids constituted a body contained *uno spiritu*, there must be held to be a confusion of substances between the two liquids. But corn or a flock of sheep is a body of the third class, or *ex distantibus*, composed of *corpora plura non soluta sed uni nomini subjecta;* and when different aggregate bodies of this nature are mingled together, the separate bodies (*corpora plura*) whereof they are composed still remain distinct. Each of the separate bodies—as the sheep or the grains of corn—remains the property of its owner, notwithstanding the mixture, unless it be effected by consent, which implies an intention to possess that mixture in common, whereby each individual grain or sheep becomes the property of both the persons so consenting to unite their property. Without such consent the parties are on an equality in point of right, and whoever has the possession must therefore pay to the other the value of his share.

Our English law gives the entire property to the person without whose consent the things were mixed, as a punishment to him who interfered with the property of another, but in other respects it agrees with the Roman Law.[b]

The law of accessories, or acquisition by *accession*, already treated of in the instance of the purple, which was adjudged to belong as an accessory to the cloth with which it was interwoven, is next further explained.

If any one build upon his own ground with materials belonging to another, the former is the owner of the building, because all that is built on the ground follows the ground. But the owner of the materials does not thereby cease to be so: he is, however, prevented from claiming them, and from demanding them, by the Law of the Twelve Tables, which provides that no one shall be compelled to remove a beam from his house

[a] Pand. lib. xli. tit. iii. De Usurpationibus et Usucap. L. 30; and see the Comment. of Cujacius, Cujac. Op. tom. i. col. 983, 984, edit. Venet. sive Veneto Mutinæ.

[b] Blackst. Comm. book ii. chap. xxvi. § 7. Blackstone somewhat misunderstood the Roman law on this head.

which belongs to another man, though he must pay twice the value if sued by the action de tigno juncto. The law so provided, that buildings might not be demolished.[c]

The maxim, *omne quod solo inedificatur solo cedit*, is in conformity with the Law of England.[d]

In the next paragraph of the Institutes, the converse of the case explained in the preceding one, is decided upon similar principles; but as the doubt in these cases could only arise from the Law of the Twelve Tables prohibiting the demolition of buildings, the subject is not one of much legal interest.[e]

The principle *quidquid solo cedit pars fundi est* is then applied to plants growing, or seeds sown in another person's ground. In every case the plant is adjudged to belong as an accessory to him from whose land the plant derives nourishment. In this our law agrees with that of Rome, except as to *emblements*.[f]

The ownership of trees, and other vegetables, *ratione soli*, is the subject of two paragraphs of the Institutes, in which the following three general rules are laid down:—[g]

I. Trees and other vegetables do not become accessories to the soil and consequently their ownership does not pass to the proprietor of the soil until they have cast roots into the ground.

Upon the same principle it was before decided that the ownership of a piece of ground detached by the force of a river from the land of one man, and carried to that of another, did not become vested in the latter until the trees had struck their roots into his soil.[h]

II. Vegetable productions, when they have struck their roots into the earth, become the sole property of the person, or the common property of those persons, from whose soil they derive nourishment.

III. But the proprietor of the vegetable is entitled to receive its value, unless he knowingly placed it in another man's ground.

He who sowed another man's land *bonâ fide* (*i. e.* believing it to be his own), is entitled to the value of the crop.[i]

Writings also are by the Roman Law accessories of the substances on which they are inscribed, and therefore follow the ownership of those substances by *accession*. But the owner of that upon which the writing

[c] Instit. lib. ii. tit. i. § 29.

[d] Co. Litt. § 1, p. 3 b; and see Pand. lib. l. tit. penult. De Verbor. Signif. L. 115. *Fundus est omne quidquid solo tenetur*. Pand. eod. tit. L. 211.

[e] Instit. lib. ii. tit. i. § 30.

[f] Instit. ibid. § 31. Blackst. Comm. book ii. chap. xxvi. § 6; and see Sugden, Vendors and Purchasers, vol. i. chap. iii. § 2, p. 142, et seq. edit. 10.

[g] Instit. ibid. § 31, 32. [h] Instit. lib. ii. tit. i. § 21. [i] Ibid. § 32.

was inscribed, cannot claim his property without paying the expense of the writing (*impensas scripturæ*) to the writer, provided he acquired the paper or other substance *bonâ fide*.[k]

The reverse is held by the Scottish Law, on the ground of the superior value of writings, in most instances, to that of the substances on which they are inscribed.[l]

This principle is followed by the Roman Law in the case of a picture.

If (says Justinian) *any one painted on another man's board, some hold that the board is an accessory to the painting; while others are of opinion that the painting is an accessory of the board. And the former seems to us the better opinion. It would, indeed, be ridiculous that a picture by Appelles and Parrasius should follow a valueless board as an accessory. Thus, if the painter claim the picture, being in the possession of the owner of the board, he must first pay the value of the board (pretium tabulæ). But if the painter possess the picture, the proprietor of the board may sue him, in which case the plaintiff must first pay the expense of the painting (impensam picturæ) before he succeeds in his action: provided the defendant was* bonâ fide *possessor of the board.*[m]

The rule of the Roman Law is, that one of two things should be considered the accessory which cannot exist without the other. Thus Paulus says—"*Necesse est ei rei cedi quod sine illa esse non potest.*" But he adds that an exception, according to the opinion of some, was made in the case of a picture on account of the value of the art.[n] That opinion was confirmed by Justinian, and the painter may retain the picture, of which the law holds him to be the owner, paying the value of the board or canvas.[o]

Here concludes the subject of acquisition by right of accession.

[k] Instit. lib. ii. tit. i. § 33.

[l] Erskine, Instit. lib. ii. tit. i. § 15, 16.

[m] Instit. lib. ii. tit. i. § 34. Pand. lib. xli. tit. i. De Acquir. Rer. Domin. L. 9, § 2.

[n] Pand. lib. vi. tit. i. De Rei Vindicatione, L. 23, § 3.

[o] Vinnii Comment. ad Instit. lib. ii. tit. i. § 34, num. 4.

CHAPTER XVI.

THE LAW OF THINGS.

The Law of Things.—Instit. lib. ii. tit. i. § 35, 37, 39—41, 44—48.—Acquisition of Fruits by *bonâ fide* Possession.—Cessation of *Bona Fides*.—Treasure Trove. —Derivative Modes of Acquisition. — Difference between Derivative and Original Modes.—Distinction between *Modus Acquirendi* and *Causa Possidendi*. —Acquisition by Delivery.—Effect of Sale and Delivery.—Quasi Delivery.— Symbolical Delivery.—Delivery to Uncertain Person.—Dereliction or Abandonment.—Wreck. P. 99.

Acquisitions *vi et potestate rei nostræ*, which are the subject of the preceding chapter, are a legal consequence of an already acquired right of property. They therefore do not require our knowledge and participation to take full legal effect. Thus, if my animals produce offspring, or my field increase by alluvion without my knowledge, I acquire the young and the alluvial deposits as fully as if I had taken possession of them by a separate act.

But these are not exceptions to the rule that property must be acquired *corpore et animo*, for the reason of that rule is, 1st, the necessity of an intention of acquiring to produce a legal right of property; and 2ndly, the necessity of an outward act of appropriation to give effect to that intention, since as Grotius says, a mere mental movement cannot produce any legal effects obligatory upon others. Now this reason is applicable to acquisitions *vi et potestate rei nostræ*, since the intention to acquire is in that case naturally presumable, and must, therefore, be presumed to exist, and that intention is sufficiently declared by the possession of the thing by means of which the other property is acquired.

From acquisitions *vi et potestate rei nostræ*, the Emperor passes to the rule of the Roman Law which allows the acquisition by a *bonâ fide* possessor of the fruits of a thing which he erroneously believed to be his.[p] But Grotius justly observes that such a rule of law, though it may be grounded upon sound legal policy, is not of natural law.[q] It is indeed an exception to the rule of natural law, *suum cuique tribuere*, for no man can acquire by natural law the fruits of a thing which belongs to another man, to which that other man has a right, and to the fruits of which he consequently has a right.

It is evident then that a *bonâ fide* possessor (that is to say, one who

[p] Instit. lib. ii. tit. i. § 35.

[q] Grot. liv. ii. chap. viii. § 23.

on probable and just grounds believed the property to be his),[r] so soon as he discovers that he has been in possession of the property of another, should according to the strictness of natural law restore to the real proprietor not only the thing but the clear profits of its enjoyment. Positive law, however, has in most countries derogated from this *summum jus*, which in many cases might become *summa injuria* from the difficulty of so modifying the rule of natural law as to exclude hardship.

The acquisition of the profits of a thing by *bonâ fide* possession is therefore a mode of acquiring by positive, and not by natural law, though the Roman Law contains an equitable reason, permitting the *bonâ fide* possessor to retain the fruits of the property, or *mesne profits* as they are called in the English Law, (which, however, does not allow this privilege to *bonâ fide* possessors,) in consideration of his care of the estate. But the Civil Law allows no man to profit by his own wrong, and therefore the rightful owner recovering his property from a *malæ fidei* possessor, that is to say, one who knows that he possesses what is not his, may also recover the fruits or mesne profits from the time when the *mala fides* or knowledge of the rightful title by the possessor commenced.[s]

The general rule is that *bona fides* ceases with litiscontestation,[t] that is to say, from the time when the rightful owner has made his claim and demand before a competent court, and the wrongful possessor has put in his defence. Then each party may form a probable estimate of the event of the cause, or at least the possessor should see that the property is not his, and he may reasonably be expected to reserve the fruits of the property to abide the result of the adjudication. But facts coming to the knowledge of the possessor may be soc lear as to put an end to his *bona fides* without litiscontestation. And so it is also in the case of a possessor *pro hærede*, or a *bonâ fide* possessor of an inheritance.[u] Even a *bonâ fide* possessor must restore the fruits existing, that is to say, not consumed at the time when the property is taken from him.[x]

We now return to the law of occupancy. The Emperor Hadrian granted treasures to the finder according to natural equity, provided the finder be the owner of the land where the treasure is discovered,

[r] Pand. lib. l. tit. penult. L. 109.

[s] Cod. lib. iii. tit. xxxii. De Rei Vindicatione, L. 22. Pand. lib. v. tit. iii. De Heredit. Petit. L. 20, § 12.

[t] Cod. lib. iii. tit. xxxii. De Rei Vindic. L. 22.

[u] Pand. lib. xli. tit. i. De Acquir. Rer. Domin. L. 23, § 1, L. 48, § 1. Pand. lib. v. tit. iii. De Hæred. Petit. L. 20, § 11.

[x] Cod. lib. iii. tit. xxxii. De Rei Vindicatione, L. 22.

and he enacted that when a treasure is found by one man in the land of another, they shall share equally.[t] These rules he extended to the cases of treasures found in lands of the Emperor, of the fisc, of the public, and of a city.

The acquisition of treasures by the finder is evidently grounded on the rule *res nullius naturaliter fit primi occupantis.* They are among the things which have no owner, because the owner is unknown, and cannot be discovered; for that which does not appear is the same in law as that which does not exist.[u]

But our English Law gives treasures to the Crown.

Derivative modes of acquisition by natural law, or acquisitions by transfer from one man to another, remain to be considered. The most simple of these is delivery.

Things are also acquired by virtue of natural law by means of delivery; for nothing can be more in accordance with natural law, than to give effect to the will of a proprietor who transfers his property to another. Consequently, whatever may be the nature of any corporeal thing, it may be delivered, and being delivered, it is alienated by the proprietor.[x]

The power of transferring property is by natural law essential to the very nature of a full right of proprietorship. But no transfer can have effect in law, unless it be declared by some outward act. The delivery of the thing is, however, necessary only by arbitrary and not by natural law to complete the transfer.[y] This theory is in accordance with a celebrated law in the Pandects, which decides that as no possession is acquired, except by intention of the mind, or an outward act of the body (*animo et corpore*), so none is lost, unless both concur to the contrary effect.[z] And so Paulus says, *quibus modis adquirimus, iisdem in contrarium actis amittimus.*[a]

Upon abstract principles, any manifestation of a transfer of right would have effect, unless contrary to law; but the law of most countries has principally attached legal consequences to one particular outward act of transfer, that is to say, *delivery*. So it is with livery of

[t] Instit. lib. ii. tit. i. § 39.

[u] Grot. liv. ii. chap. viii. § 7. *Thesaurus est vetus depositio pecuniæ cujus non extat memoria, ut jam dominum non habeat. Sic enim fit ejus qui invenit quod non alterius sit.*—Pand. lib. xli. tit i. L. 31, § 1. Here the word *Pecunia* must be understood to mean every species of valuable thing. See Pand. lib. l. tit. penult. De Verb. Signif. L. 5, 88, 97, 178, 222.

[x] Instit. lib. ii. tit. i. § 40.

[y] Grot. liv. ii. chap. vi. § 1.

[z] Pand. lib. xli. tit. ii. De Acquirenda vel Omittenda Possessione, L. 8; and see Pand. lib. l. tit. ult. De Reg. Jur. L. 35.

[a] Pand. lib. l. tit. ult. De Reg. Jur. L. 153.

seisin in our Common Law, which, however, is derived from feudal principles and not from the Roman Law.

Vinnius makes a valuable observation on the difference in the Civil Law between original and derivative acquisition.[b] He distinguishes the title to a thing from the mode of acquiring the thing. The title to the thing is the right to possess it. Coke, in the words of the Civil Law, defines title to be *justa causa possidendi quod nostrum est.*[c] Now, in original acquisition, the *modus acquirendi* is identical with the *causa possidendi,* or title. Thus in occupancy, the act of taking possession is the cause of acquisition, and it is also the mode of acquiring. But it is otherwise with regard to derivative acquisitions. In these the title is the cause of the transfer, or the intention with which the transfer is made, and the mode of acquiring is the delivery or other act equivalent in law to delivery. Thus, for instance, if the title to a thing is gift, or sale, or exchange, or loan, those are the respective causes of possession of the thing transferred. But the *modus acquirendi* is delivery and acceptation.

Where an unlimited right, or *plenum dominum,* is not transferred, the title, or *causa possidendi*, limits the mode of possessing; and the extent of the right of a possessor must always be judged and measured by the cause or title of his possession. Thus the *modus acquirendi* gives effect to the title.[d]

Justinian thus qualifies the general rule, *per traditionem jure naturali res nobis acquiritur.*

But things properly sold and delivered do not become the property of the purchaser, unless he either pay the price, or otherwise satisfy the vendor; for instance, by giving him security either real or personal. Such are the provisions of the Twelve Tables; but this is also natural law. If, however, the vendor give credit to the purchaser for the price, the property in the thing sold is transferred before payment of the price.[e]

This paragraph illustrates the importance of the distinction drawn above, between the *modus acquirendi* and the *causa possidendi,* or title. The *modus acquirendi*, that is, delivery, would by itself have the effect of transferring the property entirely and irrevocably, by virtue of the legal principles laid down in the preceding paragraph of the Institutes. It would be a gift if it were a deliberate act. But where the delivery of a thing is by virtue of a sale, there, as a sale is the

[b] Vinnii Comment. ad Instit. lib. ii. tit. i. § 40.

[c] Co. Litt. § 650.

[d] See as instances, Livery of seisin, *secundem formam Chartæ,* Co. Litt. 48 a; and also deeds *to lead the uses* of other more direct conveyances, Blackst. Com. book ii. chap. xx. § 15.

[e] Instit. lib. ii. tit. i. § 41.

transfer of a thing in consideration of a price, it is to be presumed that the vendor intended to transfer his rights over the thing only in the event of the price being paid. The payment of the price, therefore, has a retrospective effect upon the delivery.[f] The whole of this theory depends upon the principle that the intention of the proprietor transferring his rights is to be observed.[g]

If, however, the sale be upon credit, then the intention of the parties is different, and the property of the thing sold is transferred before payment of the price for which the vendor has his remedy by action.[h]

There are three species of delivery of possession; 1st, actual delivery, which requires no further observation; 2nd, *quasi* delivery; and 3rd, symbolical delivery. *Quasi* delivery is when the person to whom delivery is to be made has the thing already in his possession. So it would be if A lent something to B and delivered it to him, and subsequently sold or gave it to B. In such cases the mere will of the owner is equivalent to delivery, and is called in the Civil Law *quasi traditio*.[i]

This is an illustration of the important rule of law laid down by Salvius Julianus, *Nemo sibi ipsi causam possessionis mutare potest*.[k] Paulus says that there are as many species of possession as there are causes of acquiring that which is not ours.[l]

Now as that which is ours cannot without our own act be transferred to another person, it follows that when a thing has been transferred to be possessed under a certain title, there, if the title do not give an unlimited right, the possessor cannot of his own authority change his title or cause of possession so as to destroy the right reserved by the qualified nature of the title. Thus a lessee can only acquire the full ownership by the act of the person in whom that ownership is vested subject to the lease. *This quasi tradition of the* Roman Law, whereby the right of a person in possession is enlarged without any distinct act of delivery, is analogous to the conveyance called release in our law, especially releases which enure to enlarge the estate. So Littleton says, "If I let certain land to one for term of years, by force whereof he is in possession, and after I release to him all the right which I have, &c., then hath he an estate for term

[f] See the principle, Pand. lib. xii. tit. i. De Rebus Creditis, L. 8.

[g] Instit. lib. ii. tit. i. § 40. *Nihil tam conveniens est naturali æquitati quam voluntatem Domini volentis rem suam transferre ratam habere*; and see Pand. lib. l. tit. ult. De Reg. Jur. L. 11.

[h] Instit. lib. ii. tit. i. § 41, et Vinnii Comment. ibid. num. 3.

[i] Instit. ibid. § 43.

[k] Pand. lib. xli. tit. iii. De Usurpationibus et Usucapionibus, L. 33, § 1; and see the Comment of Cujacius, Cujac. Op. tom. i. fol. 985, tom. vi. fol. 311, edit. Venet. Mutin.

[l] Pand. ibid. § 21.

of his life." Here the releasee without livery of seisin acquires as large an estate as the rules of law will permit him to acquire by the words of the deed of release.[m]

Symbolical delivery is thus described by Justinian: *If any one sell merchandise in a warehouse, as soon as he has delivered the key of the warehouse to the purchaser, the property in the goods is transferred to the latter.*[n]

This paragraph gives only an instance of symbolical delivery, which may be made in various modes. Thus Neratius Priscus says: "*Non est corpore et actu necesse apprehendere possessionem, sed etiam oculis et affectu.*"[o] This is similar to the *seisina per effectum et aspectum* of Bracton, which is called by Coke livery in law.[p] It is indeed probable that the word *effectum* ought to be read *affectum*, as the expression was probably taken by Bracton from the Civil Law.

A right of property may be transferred by delivery, though that delivery be not made to any specified person. Of this Justinian gives us an example, that the Prætors and Consuls throw money and other things among the crowd without intending them for any individual. Yet the intention being that each man should have whatever he could catch, each becomes the owner, by delivery of what he catches.[q]

An important consequence of the rule *res nullius fit primi occupantis* remains to be considered, it is this. A thing abandoned by its owner being as much *res nullius* as if it never had had an owner may be acquired by occupancy. And those things are held to be abandoned, the possession of which was relinquished by their owner with the intention that they should no longer be his property. By reason of that intention he immediately ceases to be the proprietor.[r]

Pomponius says, in whatever modes we acquire property, we lose it by contrary modes.[s] Thus it appears that for dereliction and abandonment, an outward act of relinquishing the possession, together with an intention to give up the right are requisite.

Upon these principles, things cast out to lighten a ship in a storm remain the property of their owners, for they were forsaken not because the owner intended that they should no longer be his, but to enable him to escape the perils of the sea. Thus by the Civil Law, any one appropriating to himself such things, either in the sea or after they are thrown ashore by the waves, is guilty of theft. The

[m] Litt. § 465.

[n] Instit. lib. ii. tit. i. § 44.

[o] Pand. lib. xli. tit. ii. De Acquirenda vel Omittenda Possessione, L. 1, § 21.

[p] Co. Litt. 48 b.

[q] Instit. ibid. § 45; and see Pand. lib. xliv. tit. vii. De Obligationibus et Actionibus, L. 55.

[r] Instit. ibid. § 46.

[s] Pand. lib. l. tit. ult. De Reg. Jur. L. 153.

case of things that fall out of a cart or carriage is similar in point of principle.[t]

Paulus says, *Retinere animo possessionem possumus, apisci non possumus;* we can *retain* possession by intention alone, but not *obtain* it without a corporeal act also.[u] So Papinian holds that a man who buries money in the ground and goes abroad intending to return and take it, retains possession (that is to say, legal though not corporeal possession) of the treasure though he forgot where he had put it, and though it be buried in another man's land.[x]

Thus a mere relinquishment of corporeal possession by the owner, without an intention to abandon the right to the thing, gives no right to others to make the thing theirs.

And so Salvius Julianus explains the law regarding wrecks, by comparing things thrown overboard in a storm to things left upon a road while the owner goes to seek assistance to carry them away, for he observes that if the owner afterwards found his property which he cast into the sea, he would certainly take it again.[y] And Paulus thus neatly sums up the law on this subject: *Res jacta domini manet, nec fit adprehendentis, quia pro derelicto non habetur.*[z]

The antiquity of this just law, which has been so cruelly violated in modern times, is shown by a curious passage in Plautus, where a dispute takes place between Gripus a fisherman and Trachilio a slave, about their claims to a trunk fished up by the former after a storm. Gripus argues

> Ubi dimisi retem atque hamum, quidquid hæsit extraho,
> Meum quod rete atque hami nacti sunt meum potissimum'st.

But Trachilio urges that to take the property is theft, and threatens that unless half of it be given to him, he will divulge the fact, and he moreover claims a share even if there be no owner, on the ground that they were partners in the prize. After a violent dispute they agree to refer the matter to Dæmones who lived in a villa near the shore. He comes down to the shore with two young women who had been wrecked in the storm, and to whom he had given hospitality. One of them, Palæstra, claims the property, and Dæmones decides that it is hers on her describing the contents, from which she is proved to be the daughter of Dæmones.[a] The whole conversation is very curious and amusing.

[t] Instit. lib. ii. tit. i. § 47.

[u] Pand. lib. xli. tit. ii. De Adquir. vel Omitt. Possess. L. 30, § 5.

[x] Pand. ibid. L. 44.

[y] Pand. lib. xiv. tit. ii. Ad Legem Rhodiam, L. 8.

[z] Pand. lib. xiv. tit. ii. Ad Legem Rhodiam, L. 2, § 7.

[a] Plaut. Rudens, act iv. scen. iii. 44.

Here terminates the subject of modes of acquiring by natural law, or *Jure Gentium.* Modes of acquiring by Civil or Municipal Law remain to be considered.

CHAPTER XVII.

THE LAW OF THINGS.—INCORPOREAL THINGS.

Incorporeal Property.—Instit. lib. ii. tit. ii. De Rebus Corporalibus et Incorporalibus.—Distinction between Corporeal and Incorporeal Things.—Dominion and Obligations.—*Jus in Re* and *Jus ad Rem.*—Distinction between Natural and Civil or Legal Possession.—Servitudes.—Personal Servitudes.—Real or Prædial Servitudes.—Rural Servitudes.—Urban Servitudes.—General Principles respecting Servitudes.—Personal Servitudes.—Usufruct.—Reference to the English Law of Uses.—Rights of the Usufructuary.—Law of Waste.—How Usufruct terminates.—Comparison with the English Law.—Consolidation and Confusion or Merger.—Reference to the English Law.—Use.—Habitation. P. 109.

Under the general denomination of *Things,* not only visible and tangible things, but *Rights* also are comprehended.

Vinnius very acutely observes that the modes of acquisition by virtue of the natural law are applicable only to corporeal things.[b] Acquisition by occupation, and by accession and by delivery are evidently applicable to things corporeal, and not to rights to things as distinguished from their possession as property or *jure dominii.* But the municipal law of property has sanctioned a more complex division of the rights to things, which differs in different countries. They are acquired in divers modes, which are called modes of acquisition by Civil Law, because the forms of those modes arise from the modifications of property under municipal law. But these modes of acquiring by Civil Law are grounded on secondary natural law.

It follows that before entering on the subject of acquisition by Civil Law, it is necessary to distinguish between corporeal and incorporeal things which are subjects of that species of acquisition.

Some things (says Justinian) *are corporeal, and some things are incorporeal.*

Corporeal things are those which are tangible by their nature, such as land, gold, silver, and other things innumerable.

Incorporeal things are those which are not tangible, but consist in right, such as a right of inheritance, usufruct, use, and rights and

[b] Vinnii Comm. ad hunc. tit. princip.

obligations in whatever mode they may be contracted. It is not to the purpose that the inheritance contains corporeal things, for the fruits which are received by the usufructuary are corporeal, and that which is due to us by virtue of an obligation is generally corporeal; but the very right of inheritance, and right of usufruct, and the right and the obligation are incorporeal.

Among incorporeal things are also those rights of urban and rustic estates which are called servitudes.[c]

It has already been shown[d] that the law of things may be divided into two parts, *Dominium* or property strictly so called, and *Obligations.* The former is the subject of *jus in re* defined by Pothier to be a right which we have over a thing, by virtue of which it belongs to us at least in certain respects. The latter are the objects of the *jus ad rem* which the same great civilian defines to be a right which we have, not to the thing, but with respect to the things, and against the person who has contracted the obligation to give us that thing.[e]

Now it is evident that if a man have either the *jus in re* without the possession of the thing, or the mere *jus ad rem*, he possesses in both cases no more than a right or incorporeal thing. But if he possess a thing *jure dominii*, though he possesses the right to the thing which is incorporeal, he also possesses the thing itself which is corporeal, and this is called corporeal property. Thus it appears that corporeal things are the objects of rights, and incorporeal things are rights. And rights arise either from dominion, or from obligations. The former species of rights are *jura in re*, and the latter are *jura ad rem.* But if a man hold a corporeal thing not *jure dominii* or as his property, but as the property of another which he has a right to hold for a certain purpose, there he does not possess the thing itself as his, though he holds it, but he possesses the right to use or hold it for a certain purpose. He therefore does not possess as his the thing which is corporeal, but the right to the thing which is incorporeal. The reason of this is that his possession of the corporeal thing is the possession of the owner. It is what is called natural possession as contradistinguished from civil possession, which is the possession of the owner.[f]

Thus he who has a right over the property of another without the

[c] Instit. lib. ii. tit. ii. princip. § 1, 2, 3. Pand. lib. i. tit. viii. De Rerum Divisione et Qualitate, L. 1, § 1. This distinction was in use among the ancient philosophers. See Seneca, Epist. 58 and 106; and Lucretius (lib. i. v. 305) says, *Tangere enim et tangi nisi corpus nulla potest res.*

[d] See Chap. xi.

[e] Pothier, Traité du Droit de Domaine de Proprieté, chap. prélimin.

[f] Cujacii Comment. seu Recitationes Solemnes ad Pand. Leg. 9. tit. De Rei Vindicatione. Cujac. Op. tom. vii. col. 249, 250, &c. edit. Mutinæ, seu Venet. Mutin.

natural possession of that property, possesses only the right, which is an incorporeal thing. These rights over the property of another are called by Pothier *dismemberments of the rights of dominion.*[g] One species of such dismemberments of the right of *dominium* are very specially defined and regulated by the Roman Law. They are called servitudes. A servitude is a burthen affecting lands, whereby the proprietor is either restrained from the full use of that which is his own, or is obliged to suffer another to do something upon it.[h] Servitudes are also defined by Voet to be rights, constituted in favour of one man over the property of another, whereby some one other than the owner derives a benefit from that property, contrary to the nature of *dominium.*[i] Thus if one man have the *dominium* or ownership of property, and another the right of taking the fruits and using it, or the usufruct, that right is a servitude. And so is a right of way which a man has over the land of another.

Servitudes are of two species in the Civil Law, that is to say; 1, *Personal;* and 2, *Real* or *Prædial.*[k]

Personal sevitudes are called *jura personalia,* because they belong to men in their personal capacity, and not in right of, and as in appendage to their estates. Thus a right of usufruct cannot be appendant to an estate, so that the proprietor of that estate should have a right as such, to the usufruct of another estate. But real or prædial servitudes are those rights, whereby one estate serves or is subject to another, and they are appendant and appertaining to an estate. Thus the right of restraining a neighbour from building a wall, may be appendant and appertaining to an estate so as to belong to whoever is proprietor of that estate.[l]

To be *prædial* or *real* a servitude must be for the benefit of an estate, though Papinian decides that its use may be confined to a particular person.[m]

We will now proceed to the consideration of real or prædial servitudes.[n] They are divided into two classes; 1, servitudes of rural estates, that is to say, of lands exclusive of buildings; and 2, servitudes of urban estates, that is to say, of houses or other buildings.

[g] Pothier, ubi cit. Grot. liv. i. chap. i. § 5; liv. ii. chap. iii. § 2; and see Co. Litt. p. 19 b, 20 a.

[h] Erskine, Instit. book ii. tit. ix. See, on the subject of Servitudes, that useful book of Cæpola, Tractatus de Servitutibus, edit. 1686, 4to. and 1759, 4to.

[i] Voet, Comm. ad Pand. lib. vii. tit. i. De Usufructu et quemadmodum quis utatur fruatur, princip.

[k] Pand. lib. viii. tit. i. De Servitutibus, L. 1.

[l] Instit. lib. ii. tit. iii. De Servitutibus Prædiorum, § 3.

[m] Pand. lib. viii. tit. iii. De Servitutibus Prædiorum Rusticorum, L. 4.

[n] Instit. lib. ii. tit. iii. De Servitutibus Prædiorum Rusticorum et Urbanorum.

The leading principle of both species of real servitudes is that the obligations produced by them are negative or passive and not active. So Pomponius says, *Servitutum non ea natura est ut aliquid faciat quis sed ut aliquid patiatur aut non faciat.*[o] Thus Bartholus the glossator says, *Qui debet servitutem cogitur pati, non agere,* and this rule is followed by our English Law, with regard to rights of way.[p] And an obligation on the proprietor of an estate *to do* something, would not produce a real right or servitude, but a personal right to be enforced by a personal action.[q]

RURAL SERVITUDES.

Servitudes of rural estates are these: footpath, horse road, cart road, and aqueducts. The first (iter) is the right of way for human creatures, but not for driving a beast or cart. The second (actus) is the right of way for driving a beast or cart; consequently, he who has the second has the first also, and can use it without a beast; but he who has the first has not the second. The third (Via) is the right of way with beasts and vehicles, such as carts, and it comprehends iter and actus. The fourth (aquæductus) is the right of carrying running water through the ground of another.[r]

There are in the Civil Law five other rural servitudes, namely, 1. The right of drawing water; 2. That of watering cattle; 3. Pasture; 4. The right of burning lime; and 5. That of digging sand or gravel.[s] But these may be *personal.*

It is only necessary here to explain the difference between *actus* and *via.* It consists in this: *actus* may only comprehend the right to drive beasts or to ride, but *via* necessarily comprehends the right of driving a cart or other vehicle also; besides, the width of a *via* or road is defined by law to be a width sufficient for a cart to turn round in. As for the decision that *via* comprehends the other two species of rights, and that *actus* comprehends *iter,* it is founded on the rule of Ulpian, *Non debet cui plus licet, quod minus est non licere.*[t]

Aquæductus is defined by Ulpian to be *jus aquam ducendi per alienum fundum.*[u]

[o] Pand. lib. viii. tit. i. De Servitutibus, L. 13, § 1.

[p] Taylor *v.* Whitehead, Dougl. 745.

[q] Cujacii Recitat. Solemn. ad tit. Pand. De Servitut. L. 15, § 1. Cujac. Op. tom. vii. col. 389, 390, edit. Venet. Mutin.

[r] Instit. lib. ii. tit. iii. princip. Co. Litt. 56 a.

[s] Ibid. § 2. Vide Vinnii Comment. in Instit. lib. ii. tit. iii. § 2; and Pand. lib. xxxiv. tit. i. De Aliment. Legat. L. 10.

[t] Pand. lib. l. tit. ult. De Reg. Jur. L. 21.

[u] Pand. lib. viii. tit. iii. De Servit. Rust. L. 1.

URBAN SERVITUDES.

Servitudes of urban estates are those which are proper to buildings, and they are therefore called by that designation, for all buildings are called urban messuages, though they be situated in the country. The following are the servitudes of urban property: The right of resting the weight of a house upon a neighbour's building; the right of fixing a beam or joist in the wall of a neighbouring house; the right of allowing water to drip or flow upon a neighbour's tenement, or upon his area, or his drain, or of not receiving it; and the right of restraining the neighbour from building higher, or from injuring the light or prospect of the neighbouring messuage.[x]

Servitudes are *contra naturam dominii*, that is to say, they are exceptions to the right which men have over that which is theirs, to exclude all others from the use of it.[y] It follows, that being restraints on the rights of proprietors, they are *stricti juris;* they are, therefore, not presumed, if the acts on which they are claimed can be explained consistently with freedom; and when servitudes are constituted, they ought to be used in the way least burthensome to the servient messuage.[z]

Servitudes may be constituted not only by the express will of the person who has the power to burthen the property therewith,[a] but by length of time or prescription. But the length of time during which a proprietor did not exercise a right, does not of itself suffice to establish a servitude against him. Thus the fact of a man not having raised his buildings for any length of time, cannot preclude him from doing so if he thinks fit, for that is what is called *res meræ facultatis*, which is not subject to prescription.[b] It follows that those servitudes which are negative, that is to say, which consist in a restraint upon a proprietor, depriving him of some portion of the free disposal or management of his property, cannot be produced by prescription; while those, on the contrary, which consist in a right to do something with or upon

[x] Cæpola, in his Tractatus De Servitutibus, explains this part of the subject very fully and practically. The urban servitudes in the Roman Law are six:—1, *Altius tollendi et officiendi luminibus vicini;* 2, *Aut non extollendi;* 3, *Stillicidium avertendi in tectum vel aream vicini;* 4, *Vel non avertendi;* 5, *immittendi tigni;* 6, *Projiciendi protegendive.* Pand. lib. viii. tit. ii. De Servitutibus Prædiorum Urbanorum, L. 2.

[y] Voet, Comment. ad Pand. lib. vii. tit. i. De Usufruct. princip.

[z] Erskine, Instit. book ii. tit. ix. Of Servitudes, § 33, 34. Pand. lib. viii. tit. i. De Servitut. L. 9.

[a] Instit. ibid. § 4.

[b] Voet, Comm. ad Pand. lib. viii. tit. iv. Communia Prædiorum tam Urban. quam Rustic. num. 5. Cod. lib. iii. tit. xxxiv. De Servitutibus et Aqua, L. 8, 9.

the property of another, may be constituted by prescription. Thus the French code enacts[c] that apparent or positive servitudes may be acquired by a title or by possession during thirty years; that non apparent or negative servitudes cannot be acquired otherwise than by some title other than prescription or long possession.

We come now to personal servitudes, which are so called because they are those whereby the property of a person is burthened, not in favour of an estate or messuage, but in favour of a person.[d] They are *jura personæ in aliena re constituta;* but though that definition shows that their variety may be infinite, three only are specially defined by the Civil Law as essentially personal servitudes. They are, *Usufruct, Use,* and *Habitation.* Usufruct first claims our attention.

Usufruct is the right of using and enjoying the property of another, the substance thereof being preserved. It is a right over a thing, which thing ceasing to exist, the right is necessarily extinguished.[e]

The separation of the use from the ownership, or property in land, was originally introduced by the clergy into the English Law, for the purpose of avoiding the provisions of the Statutes of Mortmain; but uses soon became very different from usufruct, because no limits were placed to the duration of the dismemberment of the *jura dominii* by the English law of uses; consequently, the right of property or estate of the *terre tenant,* or person seised to uses, became absolutely illusory, and, indeed, existed only for technical purposes. And so it is with regard to trusts and uses, after the Statute of Uses, which are not executed by force of that statute. This was contrary to the Roman Law.

But usufruct most resembles estates for life in our law, both with respect to its duration and with respect to the extent of the right vested in the usufructuary. Thus the rights of enjoyment of the tenant for life are restricted by the obligation of not committing waste, and waste is any *destruction . . . to the disherison of him in the reversion or remainder.*[f] Now, Ulpian says, *Usufructuarius causam proprietatis deteriorem facere non debet.*[g] These two principles are the same, which renders it not surprising that the English Law respecting the question what is and what is not waste, should be the same as the Roman Law on that subject. This similarity is more particularly striking with respect to the principles on which the equitable remedy

[c] Code Civil, art. 690, 691.

[d] Erskine, Instit. book ii. tit. ix. Of Servitudes, § 39.

[e] Instit. lib. ii. tit. iv. De Usufructu. Pand. lib. vii. tit. i. De Usufructu, L. 1, *Ususfructus est jus alienis rebus utendi fruendi salva rerum substantia.* Pand. ibid. L. 2, *Est ususfructus jus in corpore quo sublato, et ipsum tolli necesse est.*

[f] Co. Litt. 52 b, 53 a.

[g] Pand. lib. vii. tit. i. De Usufruc. L. 13, § 4.

by injunction is afforded by the Court of Chancery, in cases of waste, committed by tenants of estates less than freeholds of inheritance, and by tenants in tail. The whole of that law is founded on the principle that the tenant has the right, like the usufructuary, *utendi fruendi salva rerum substantia.*

In the Scottish law *usufruct* and *liferent* are convertible terms, and estates by *curtesy* and the *tierce*, or estate of a tenant in dower, are enumerated among the species of liferents or usufruct.[h] This confirms the argument, that estates for life in our law were in many respects moulded upon the principles of the Roman usufruct.

The right of the usufructuary is defined to be *jus utendi fruendi.* The first (*jus utendi*) entitles him to use the thing for his own benefit and convenience, provided he does so according to the nature of the thing, and for such uses as it is appropriated to either by its nature or by its proprietor. The second (*jus fruendi*) entitles the fructuary to appropriate to himself all the fruits, or produce of the thing, both natural produce and legal or civil profits, such as rents, or the price of the sale of the usufruct.

But this he must do *salva rerum substantia;* that is to say, he must not consume the thing from which he is entitled to derive use and profit, nor injure the rights and interests of the proprietor, nor change the form of the thing.

He must not consume nor destroy the thing; thus, if he have the usufruct of an estate with a house, he must not pull down the house.[i]

Secondly, he must not injure the rights of the proprietor.[k] Thus he must not cut down fruit trees, nor remove parts of the house, such as partition walls, though he may ornament them.[l] The usufructuary must keep the property, and restore it in as good a state as that in which he received it. Therefore, he must not let it want necessary repairs, but must keep up the buildings and plantations.[m] He however is not bound to rebuild that which is totally destroyed or has fallen down. Thus the usufructuary is bound to no more than *modicam refectionem,* which is incident to the use of the thing.[n] Upon this principle, that the usufructuary must not suffer the interest of the proprietor to be injured in his hands, Ulpian decides that he is bound to keep up the number of the animals the usufruct of which he has, by supplying the place of those which die from the young.[o]

The usufructuary must not change the nature or form of the thing.

[h] Erskine, Instit. ubi sup. tit. Of Servit. § 40, &c.

[i] Pand. lib. vii. tit. i. De Usufructu, L. 13, § 4. Co. Litt. 52 b, 53 a, 53 b.

[k] Pand. ibid. L. 13, § 4. [l] Pand. ibid. § 7. [m] Pand. ibid. L. 44.

[n] Voet, Comm. ad Pand. tit. de Usufruct. num. 36.

[o] Pand. ibid. L. 68, § 2. Instit. lib. ii. tit. i. § 38.

Thus he must not cut down ornamental timber, and convert pleasure grounds into cultivated land, such as vineyards:[p] but he may open quarries or mines, if it can be done without injury to agriculture, as in waste places, or if the change is undoubtedly for the benefit of the estate.[q] This last decision is a judicious qualification of the rule of the English Law, that no new mines or pits can be opened.[r]

It is the duty of the usufructuary to cultivate rightly, and to use the property as a good farmer should, and *non debet uti nisi secundum conditionem rei;* whereas a proprietor has the right not only *utendi,* but *abutendi et negligendi rem suam.*[s]

The servitude of usufruct, or the separation of the usufruct from the property, may be constituted either by property being conveyed *inter vivos,* or by will, so as to vest the usufruct in one man and the property in another, or by the proprietor alienating it and retaining the usufruct, or the contrary.[t]

It may be constituted not only in lands and other immoveables, but in slaves, and horses, and all other things, excepting those which are consumed by use. For in these the separation of the usufruct is incompatible with natural and legal reason.[u]

Usufruct terminates by the death of the usufructuary, and by his suffering the greater or middle capitis minutio, and also by non use during a certain space of time defined by our Constitution. Also it finishes when the usufruct is surrendered by the usufructuary to the proprietor (for surrender to a stranger has no such effect), or if, on the contrary, the usufructuary acquired the property of the thing of which he has the usufruct. These extinctions of usufruct by the union of the usufruct with the property, are called consolidation. And it is evident that the usufruct of a house is extinguished by its being burnt or otherwise destroyed, and that the usufructuary has no right to the usufruct of the site.[x]

A perpetual separation of the usufruct from the property is contrary to the policy of the Roman Law.[y] For this reason usufruct is a personal right, which finishes by the death, natural or civil, of the person in whom it is vested, and becomes consolidated with the property.

But by a special limitation to that effect, a usufruct might be made to descend to the heir of the usufructuary. Justinian, however, by one of the fifty decisions, determined that the usufruct should end in

[p] Pand. ibid. L. 13, § 4. [q] Pand. ibid. L. 13, § 5. [r] Co. Litt. 53 a, b.

[s] Pand. lib. vii. tit. ix. Usufructuarius quemadmod. Caveat, L. 1, § 3. Pand. lib. vii. tit. i. De Usufructu, L. 15, § 1. Pand. lib. v. tit. iii. De Hæreditatis Petitione, L. 25, § 11. Pand. ibid. L. 31, § 3. But see the rule, *Expedit reipub. re sua ne quis male utatur,* Instit. lib. i. tit. viii. § 2. [t] Instit. lib. ii. tit. iv. § 1.

[u] Ibid. § 3. [x] Inst. ibid. § 3. [y] Instit. ibid. § 1, in fin.

the person of the first heir of the usufructuary, though limited to his heirs.[z] Upon the same principle, it was doubted by the ancients, whether an usufruct could be held by a city or body of municipes; for *periculum esse videbatur ne perpetuus fieret*, because those bodies could not suffer natural, and would probably not suffer civil death, and thus the *dominium*, or property, would become illusory. But the law in the Pandects allows a body politic to enjoy the usufruct for 100 years, being the utmost limit of human life.[a] And this limitation of time extends to all churches, ecclesiastical bodies, and pious foundations and purposes.

It seems then that the device contrived in this country to avoid the operation of the law of mortmain would have been rendered ineffectual if the principles of the Civil Law, which does not permit the perpetual separation of the use from the possession, had been appealed to.

The evils enumerated by Lord Bacon,[b] as resulting from that permanent separation, were foreseen and prevented by the wisdom of the antient Jurisconsulti; and if their limitations of the duration of usufruct had been adopted together with the invention of uses, there would have been no need for the statute for transferring uses into possession.

As for the position that the *terre tenant* was bound to account to the *cestui que use* for its profits, that obligation could not be perpetual by the Civil Law contrary to the rules of law, which no private disposition can alter or affect.[c] The union of the usufruct with the naked property (*nuda proprietas*) is called in the Civil Law *consolidatio*, because it vests in the proprietor the *solidum dominium*;[d] also *confusio*, because the dominion is dismembered by the usufruct being vested in one person and the property in another, consequently the union of the two rights in one person merges or confuses the servitude with the dominion of which it is a part.[e]

It is indeed a general principle, applicable to all servitudes, prædial as well as personal, that they become extinguished by being merged in the dominion, from the moment that they are due to and from the same person. Thus prædial servitudes are extinguished by merger

[z] Voet, Comm. ad Pand. lib. vii. tit. iv. Quibus Modis Ususfr. Amitt. num. 1.

[a] Pand. lib. vii. tit. i. De Usufruct. L. 56. Pand. lib. vii. tit. iv. Quibus Modis Ususfruc. Amitt. L. 21. Cod. lib. i. tit. ii. De Sacrosanctis Ecclesiis, L. 23.

[b] Blackst. Comm. book ii. chap. xx. p. 331-2.

[c] Pand. lib. ii. tit. xiv. De Pactis, L. 38. Pand. lib. l. tit. ult. De Reg. Jur. L. 45, § 1.

[d] Pand. lib. xxxix. tit. iii. De Aqua et Aqua Pluvia Arcenda, L. 9, § 2.

[e] Pand. lib. vii. tit. iv. Quibus Mod. Ususfruct. Amitt. L. 27. Vinnii Comm. ad Instit. De Servitut. Rust. et Urb. princip.

or confusion, if the same person become at the same time proprietor of both estates.[f]

The theory of confusion, or merger, is grounded on the legal principle that a right and its corresponding obligation cannot coexist in the one person as such, or in the same character or right.[g] Thus no man can owe a servitude to himself. A man's rights can be limited, not by his own rights, but by the rights of others. And thus in the English Law, if there be tenant for years, and the reversion in fee-simple descend to, or be purchased by him, the term of years is merged in the inheritance. But they must come to one and the same person in one right, else if he hath the freehold in his own right, and the term be in right of another, there is no merger.[h]

Merger, or consolidation, may take place by act of the parties, as where the usufructuary surrenders to the proprietor. Thus, in our English Law, surrender is a yielding up of an estate for life or years, to him who hath an immediate estate in reversion, wherein the estate for life or years may drowne.[i]

Justinian adds: *Cedendo extraneo nil agit*, that is to say, he does not extinguish the usufruct, but effects an alienation and not a surrender.

Consolidation may also be by the proprietor conveying his dominion to the usufructuary. This agrees with the definition of a release in the English law, which operates by the greater estate descending upon the less.[k]

Usufruct is extinguished not only by the extinction of the thing, but by the thing being so totally changed that the usufruct of it, or of what remains of it, is totally different from that which was originally granted to the usufructuary.[l]

Lastly, usufruct is lost by abandonment and non-use. When the whole right of usufruct has terminated, it returns to the proprietor, who thereby no longer has the naked property, but acquires the full power over the thing: but if there be more than one joint usufructuaries, they have *jus accrescendi*, or the right of survivorship, as joint-tenants have in the English Law, and they succeed to each other by survivorship.[m]

[f] Pand. lib. viii. tit. vi. Quemadmodum Servitutes Amittantur, L. 1.

[g] Pand. lib. iv. tit. viii. De Receptis et qui Arbitrium Recipiunt, L. 51.

[h] Blackst. Com. book ii. chap. ii. p. 176, edit. Coleridge.

[i] Instit. lib. ii. tit. iv. § 3. Co. Litt. 337 b.

[k] Instit. ibid. Blackst. Comm. book ii. chap. xx. p. 323, 324. Co. Litt. 337, note 1.

[l] Instit. ibid. Pand. lib. vii. tit. iv. Quibus Modis Ususfr. Amitt. L. 4. Pand. ibid. L. 23, and L. 24.

[m] Instit. ibid. § 4. Pand. lib. vii. tit. ii. De Usufruct. Accrescendo, L. 1, and L. 3.

The two remaining personal servitudes are *usus* and *habitatio.*[n]

Use is thus described by Vinnius: *Usus quotidiana utentis sufficientia et consumptione terminatur.* Thus he who has the use of an orchard, may take what fruit he requires for his consumption; but he must not take fruit to sell for profit. Use is of the same nature as usufruct, but of less extent, and in the last respect it resembles common of estovers in the English Law, but is applicable to everything to which the right of usufruct is applicable.[o]

Habitation is said by Justinian to be *proprium aliquod jus;* but in effect it is similar to use, being the use peculiar to houses.[p] Here ends the explanation of the nature of things incorporeal, except inheritances and obligations, of which more hereafter.

CHAPTER XVIII.

THE LAW OF THINGS.—ACQUISITIONS BY MUNICIPAL LAW.

Instit. lib. ii. tit. vi. princip. § 1—8.—Acquisitions by Municipal Law.—Prescription. Its Foundation.—Antient Differences between Usucapion and Prescription.—Usucapion and Prescription assimilated by Justinian.—Distinction between Moveables and Immoveables.—Land, Houses, &c.—Their Accessories.—Trees and other Vegetables.—Incorporeal Moveables and Immoveables.—Definition of Usucapion.—Limitation of Actions.—Requisites for Usucapion.—Bona Fides: Sufficiency of Title.—A Possessor not required to produce his Title.—Ignorance of Law.—Effect thereof.—Error in Fact.—Duration of Possession requisite for Usucapion.—Continuance of Possession.—Interruptions, in Law and in Fact.—Conjunction of the Possession of the Heir and the Deceased and of Alienor and Purchasor.—Things incapable of being acquired by Prescription. —Prescription by Thirty and Forty Years' Possession, or *Præscriptio longissimi Temporis.* P. 119.

HAVING explained servitudes personal and prædial, it might be expected that Justinian would proceed at once to the two remaining species of incorporeal things which he had enumerated, namely, inheritances (*hæreditates*) and obligations; but these he defers for future explanation,—the first because it is reasonable previously to explain how *jura in re* are acquired *inter vivos*, and how individual things are acquired; and the latter, because having commenced expounding the law of

[n] Instit. lib. ii. tit. v. De Usu et Habitatione.

[o] Vinnii Com. ad Instit. ibid.

[p] Inst. ibid. § 5. Pand. lib. vii. tit. viii. De Usu et Habitat. L. 10.

jura in re and *dominium*, it seemed consistent with good arrangement to conclude that subject before treating of *jura ad rem*, which spring from obligations.

Justinian now explains two modes whereby individual things are acquired, namely: *prescription* and *donation;* and with the last paragraph of the 9th title of the 2nd book, he commences *universal* modes of acquiring, that is to say, *inheritance*, whereby all the property or estate of one man passes to another.

Having explained the modes of acquiring things by natural law or *jure gentium*, the Emperor now proceeds to the exposition of the modes of acquiring by municipal law. *Quibus modis legitimo et Civili Jure res acquiruntur.*

And first of *prescription*, which is perhaps the most artificial of all.

Prescription (says Grotius) is established by municipal law, for time alone has no power in nature to produce anything, and nothing is done by time, though everything is done with time.[q] In truth, by natural law, that which is ours cannot without our act be transferred from us to another.

But the municipal law, upon grounds of policy, deprives men of their property and transfers it to others by lapse of time and duration of adverse possession. Grotius argues that an omission is as much a manifestation of an intention in many cases as a positive action; and that consequently when any one, knowing his property to be in the hands of another, permits a long period of time to elapse without claiming it, there is ground for believing that he neglected to assert his claim because he no longer considered the thing as his property; unless there be other reasons excluding that inference.[r]

But in the greater number of cases, men lose their rights by lapse of time, not because they have willingly abandoned them, but through error, ignorance, or negligence. *Sed Jus Civile vigilantibus scriptum est;* and assuming that a limitation of time within which men may assert their rights is expedient and necessary, the rule of Paulus applies, *Propter privatorum commodum non debet communi utilitati prejudicari*, and prescription is established *ne rerum dominia in incerto essent*, and because it is useful for the commonwealth that there should be some limit to litigation.[s] It follows that though prescription is not

[q] Grot. liv. ii. chap. iv. princip.

[r] Grot. liv. ii. chap. ix. § 5. Pand. lib. xxxix. tit. ii. De Damno Infecto, L. 15, § 21. Pand. lib. xxii. tit. i. De Usuris et Fructibus, L. 17, § 1.

[s] Inst. lib. ii. tit. vi. princip. Pand. lib. xli. tit. iii. De Usurp. et Usucap. L. 1. *Bono publico usucapio introducta est, ne scilicet quarundam rerum diu et fere semper incerta dominia essent; cum sufficeret dominis ad inquirendas res suas statuti temporis spatium.* Hugon. Donelli Comment. Jur. Civil. lib. v. chap. v. § 4.

without a foundation in natural law, it is in truth a mode of acquiring by municipal law, and indeed the limitation of the precise time requisite for prescription must necessarily be matter of arbitrary or positive law.

The rubric of this title of the Institutes, *De Usucapionibus et Longi Temporis Præscriptionibus*, naturally suggests the inquiry, What is the difference between usucapion and prescription? The ancient Roman Law distinguished one from the other by many marked features of diversity, with respect to the things which were their objects, the lapse of time which they required, and their effects.[t]

Usucapion was not applicable to all moveables but to such immoveables only as were *Juris Italici;* while prescription was proper (though not exclusively so) to provincial estates or not *Juris Italici.*[u] Usucapion was derived from the Law of the Twelve Tables, and therefore applied only to the Italian territory of the Romans or to those to which the *Jus Italicum* extended. It was also the peculiar privilege of Roman citizens, for the Law of the Twelve Tables enacted *adversus hostem eterna auctoritas esto;* but the harshness of this rule was subjected to successive modifications. Usucapion was limited to two years in immoveables, and one in moveables; while to acquire by prescription, ten years were necessary when the former proprietor was present, and twenty when he was absent. In the third place, usucapion gave to him who had the benefit of it the *dominium* of that which he acquired by possession; which prescription did not. Usucapion gave the *dominium Quiritarium*, or *dominium* κατ'ἐξοχην; but by prescription *dominium bonitarium* only was acquired, which was called *dominium non optimo jure*, because it had not certain privileges and it was subject to disadvantages, by which it was distinguished from the first-mentioned *dominium*, called *dominium optimo jure.*[x]

But this distinction, which arose from the provinces having been acquired by the Roman people by right of conquest, and being therefore subject to a species of paramount right or *jus summi dominii*, together with a permanent land-tax, was totally done away by Justinian in a constitution which shows that the distinction had become merely nominal and technical.[y]

Justinian also totally abolished what remained in his time of the differences between usucapion and prescription, making the two convertible terms; but he preserved the distinction between moveable and immoveable things, and enacted that the first should be acquired by a

[t] Vinnii Comm. ad Instit. hoc tit. princip.

[u] Heineccii Antiquitates, ad hunc tit. § 2.

[x] Ibid. lib. ii. tit. ii. § 29.

[y] Vinnii Com. ad Instit. hoc tit. ad princ. num. 4. Cod. lib. vii. tit. xxv. De Nudo Jure Quirit. Tollendo.

possession of three years, and the second by a possession during ten years *inter præsentes*, and twenty years *inter absentes*, providing also that usucapion should extend to incorporeal things, to which it was before not applicable, because by the antient law usucapion could not be acquired without possession, and incorporeal things were not the subjects of possession in the strict acceptation of the term, but only of quasi possession.[z]

Before entering on the explanation of the law of usucapion, it is necessary to explain the rules by which the distinction between moveables and immoveables is governed. Moveables are defined by Pothier to be those things which are capable of being transported from one place to another.[a] Immoveables are land, houses, and all those things which are parts of either. All things which are accessories of and joined to or parts of immoveables are also immoveable, for though land be immoveable, yet parts of it are moveable, and though houses are immoveable, parts of them are moveable, so far that they are physically capable of being detached and removed; but as they are not intended to be removed and are parts of a whole which is immoveable, they are therefore held to be immoveable. Thus things which are so fixed to immoveables as to become parts of them, and are not by their nature intended to follow the person, and are fixed to the immoveable thing not temporarily but *perpetui usus causa*, are held in law to be immoveable, though physically capable of being detached and moved.[b]

As for trees and vegetables, they are part of the land though they are not land, because they are produced out of the land, and cannot live if separated from it. *Fructus pendentes*, fruits hanging to the stem, are parts of the vegetable that produced them, and are therefore also *partes fundi*, parts of the land. But these things, as soon as they are detached, become moveable, on the principle *cessante ratione cessat effectus.*

Incorporeal things partake of the nature of the things which are their objects. Thus a right to land is immoveable, for though the right itself follows the person, yet it cannot be vindicated except where the land is situated.

Usucapion is defined as follows by Modestinus: *Usucapio est adjectio dominii per continuationem possessionis temporis lege definiti.*[c] Thus

[z] Cod. lib. vii. tit. xxxi. De Usucap. Transformanda, L. unic. Cod. lib. vii. tit. xxxiii. De Præscriptione Longi Temporis, L. ult. Hugonis Donelli Comment. De Jure Civili, lib. v. cap. iv. § 8.

[a] Pothier, Traité des Choses, part 2, § 1. Voet, Com. ad Pand. lib. i. tit. viii. De Rerum Divisione et Qualitate, num. 2, &c. [b] Voet ad Pand. ibid. n. 13.

[c] Pand. lib. xli. tit. iii. De Usurpat. et Usucap. L. 3. Fragment. Ulpian, tit. xix. § 3.

it appears that usucapion and prescription are modes of acquiring the right of dominion. But there is a species of prescription which in the English Law is called *limitation of actions.* This prescription operates not on the right itself but on the remedy, and entitles a debtor to plead that the demand of his creditor has been extinguished by lapse of a certain period of time.[d] That species of prescription when applied to *jura ad rem* is no more than the limitation of the duration of a right of action *ad rem*, and not a mode of acquiring dominion. Thus, if A. owe ten pounds to B. and B. permit his right of action to be extinguished by the effect of the Statute of Limitations, it cannot be correctly said that A. thereby acquires *dominium* over that sum, but rather that by the extinction of the right of B. to compel him to pay the money, A. avoids losing it.

But when this species of prescription is applied to *jura in re*, it is the same thing in effect as usucapion, with this difference, however, that the former has reference to the duration of the right of action of persons having right, while the latter has reference to the duration of the possession by which the *dominium* is acquired. Thus in the former the property is acquired by the possessor by the extinction of all adverse claims, so that he may have acquired it as against one claimant and not as against another; but in the latter, the possessor acquires the property by his own possession during a certain time, and therefore at the expiration of that time his right is established against all the world, except against a claimant who has interrupted his possession by an actual claim, or was unable from absence or incapacity to assert his claim.

Three things are required by the Roman Law for prescription, namely, 1, *Bona fides;* 2, possession for a period of time limited by the law; and 3, a just title. A purchaser from a person whom he believed to be the lawful proprietor of the thing, but who was not so, is a *bonâ fide* possessor, and the purchaser may acquire it by usucapion if he possess it for the requisite time. And Justinian enacted that moveables may be acquired by usucapion by possession during three years, and immoveables by *possessio longi temporis*, that is to say, for ten years if the parties be in the same province and for twenty years if they be not.[e] But the party must have a just and sufficient cause of possession or title.

[d] Pothier, Traité des Obligat. num. 677; and Alciatus defines it to be *Exceptionem quæ ex temporis lapsu substantiam capit, et actioni objicitur.*

[e] Instit. lib. ii. tit. vi. De Usucap. princip. Cod. lib. vii. tit. xxxiii. De Præscriptione Longi Temp. L. ult.

The first point to be considered is the just and sufficient title requisite for prescription.[f]

It must not be argued from this that a claimant of property has a right to call on the possessor to produce his title, for as Paulus says, *Ei incumbit probatio qui dicit, non qui negat*, and therefore *actori incumbit onus probandi.*[g] And Justinian says that it is far more advantageous to possess than to claim. The convenience of possession consists in this, that though the property be not his who possesses it, yet if the plaintiff cannot prove that it is his own, the possession remains where it was; for which reason where the rights of both parties are doubtful, it is the practice to decide against the plaintiff.[h] And thus the Emperor Antoninus says: *Possessori non incumbit necessitas probandi possessiones ad se pertinere, cum petitore in probatione cessante dominium apud eum* (*possessorem*) *remaneat:* and thus Venulejus says, *Adversus extraneos vitiosa possessio prodesse solet.*[i]

The meaning of the rule that a title is necessary for usucapion is, that if the link between the possessor and the person from whom he received the property be good, that is to say, if the former received it from the latter by a title capable of transferring dominion, usucapion will enable the possessor to keep the property even if it should be proved by a third party that the possessor derived the property from one who had no right or title to it, or who had no right to convey it to him.[k]

It follows that no man can prescribe who does not possess the thing by a just title, that is to say, a title capable of transferring the right of property. Such titles are as many as the transactions whereby the right of property passes from one man to another, but Trebonian and his colleagues have devoted a title of the Pandects to each of the most ordinary titles of acquisition and possession.

They are the following: The title *pro emptore; pro hærede; pro donato; pro derelicto; pro legato; pro dote;* and *pro soluto*. But these are all comprehended in the title *pro suo*, which includes all those modes or causes of possession which have not a special name of their own.[l]

[f] Cod. lib. iii. tit. xxxii. De Rei Vindicatione, L. 24.

[g] Pand. lib. xxii. tit. iii. De Probat. et Præsumpt. L. 2.

[h] Instit. lib. iv. tit. xv. De Interdictis, § 4.

[i] Cod. lib. iv. tit. xix. De Probation. L. 2. Pand. lib. xli. tit. ii. De Acquirenda vel Omittenda Possessione, L. ult.

[k] Instit. lib. i. tit. ix. Per quas Personas cuique Acquiritur Obligatio, § 6.

[l] Pand. lib. xli. tit. iv. et seq. Pand. lib. xli. tit. x. Pro Suo, L. 1, L. 2. Pothier, Traité de la Prescrip. part 1, chap. 3, § 7.

Another species of possession must be noticed; namely, possession *pro possessore*, which is that of a man who produces no title, but who, in the words of Ulpian, *Interrogatus cur possideat, responsurus sit, quia possideo.*[m] No possessor is bound to produce his title, and it follows therefrom, that every possessor is presumed to possess under a just title, until the contrary is proved: consequently, when a possessor has possessed during a great length of time, and he cannot be shown to possess under a defective title, his possession must be presumed to proceed from a just title.[n]

Such a possessor, *pro possessore*, may evidently prescribe. But one whose title is void—for instance, one who purchased from a lunatic or an infant, or whose title is tainted with *mala fides*, (for no man shall profit by his own wrong,) or one whose title was valid, indeed, but not capable of conveying the right of property, or *dominium*, (as, for instance, a lease or a loan,)—cannot prescribe by any period however long. This is the meaning of the maxim—*Melius est non habere titulum quam habere vitiosum.* As for those who possess lawfully, but by titles which have not the effect of transferring the right of property, the Emperor Alexander Severus says, *Non sibi sed dominio rei possident*, —their possession is the possession of the proprietor of the thing; and according to the rule of Salvius Julianus, *Causam possessionis nemo sibi mutare potest.* And no length of time will therefore enable them to prescribe.[o]

But no man can prescribe without *bona fides*, for no man may profit by his own wrong.[p] The principles of the law as to what constitutes *bonâ fide* possession, have already been sufficiently explained,[q] but it is necessary here to add an important exception to the law which enables *bonâ fide* possessors to prescribe.

Pomponius lays down the rule, *In jure erranti non procedit usucapio.*[r] Thus, as Pothier says, if your procurator sold your property without a special power to do so, to a man who believed a procurator to have as such a general power of alienation, that purchaser, though he purchased *bonâ fide*, cannot prescribe against you, for his *bona fides* proceeded from error in law.[s]

This is founded on a celebrated rule of Papinian, *Juris ignorantia non prodest adquirere volentibus: suum vero petentibus non nocit.*[t] The

[m] Pand. lib. v. tit. iii. De Hæred. Petit. L. 12.

[n] Pothier, Traité de la Possession, num. 10.

[o] Cod. lib. vii. tit. xxx. Communia de Usucap. L. 1. Pand. lib. xli. tit. v. Pro Hærede, L. 1.

[p] Pand. lib. l. tit. penult. L. 109.

[q] Vide supra, chap. xvi.

[r] Pand. lib. xli. tit. iii. De Usurp. et Usucap. L. 32, § 1. Pand. ibid. L. 31, pr.

[s] Pothier, Traité de la Préscrip. num. 39.

[t] Pand. lib. xxii. tit. vi. De Juris et Facti Ignor. L. 7, and L. 8.

law so far indulges men, that they are not deprived of their rights by the effect of their ignorance of law. Thus, if an heir give what he has inherited to a woman, believing that the law gives it to heirs female, the law will permit him to recover it from her. But the law will not allow men to benefit by their ignorance of its provisions which they ought to know, because by so doing it would deprive one man of his legal rights in consideration of the other party having been ignorant of the law.

The reason of this is, that it would be absurd to permit any man to profit by his ignorance of the law, which he ought to know, so as to place him in a more advantageous position than another who did not neglect to make himself acquainted with the rules to which every member of society is bound to conform his conduct.

But as to error in fact, the case is different, for though all men are bound to know the law, or to inquire what it commands or forbids, no man is bound to know every fact: besides, usucapion is founded on error in fact, since it is acquired by possession of a thing received from one who was not the proprietor, the alienee believing him to be the proprietor.

But the belief of the possessor that he has a title, when he has it not, will not of itself supply the place of a title.[u]

The next part of the Law of Usucapion is that touching the duration of the possession.

The lapse of time (says Justinian) *which benefited the deceased, may be continued for the benefit of the heir, though he knew the estate to be the property of another. But if the possession of the deceased had not a just commencement, the heir cannot prescribe, though he were ignorant of the vicious possession of the deceased.*[x]

Continued possession is requisite for usucapion.[y] But it need not be the possession of the same person during the whole period necessary for usucapion. The heir, however, (whether testamentary or *ab intestato,*) is one person with the deceased, and as Papinian lays it down: *Cum hæres in omne jus defuncti succedit, ignoratione suâ defuncti vitia non excludit.*[z] Therefore, though the heir inherited the property, believing it to have been possessed *pro suo* by the deceased, he cannot acquire it by usucapion if the deceased could not have done so.

The Emperor, however, decides that the heir may avail himself of the possession of the deceased, though he be aware that he inherited that which did not rightfully belong to the deceased. The reason is,

[u] Instit. lib. ii. tit. vi. § 6. [x] Ibid. § 7.

[y] Pand. lib. xli. tit. iii. De Usurp. et Usucap. L. 23, and L. 3.

[z] Pand. lib. xliv. tit. iii. De Divers. Temp. Præscript. L. 2.

that the Roman Law requires *bona fides* only at the commencement of the possession. Now as the possession of the heir is a continuation of the possession of the deceased, the commencement of the possession of the deceased is the commencement of that of the heir, so far that the heir possesses as if he were the same person as the deceased.[a]

But the Canon Law requires *bona fides* during the whole period of possession, so that if it come to the knowledge of the possessor that he possesses what belongs to another, as he at the same time contracts an obligation to restore it to the rightful owner, he from that time ceases to be capable of acquiring it by prescription, and his obligation descends upon his heir. Thus the Canon Law lays down the rule, *Possessor malæ fidei ullo tempore non præscribit*, and the obligation of restitution is perpetuated by the rule of Pope Boniface VIII. *Peccatum non dimittitur nisi restituatur ablatum.*[b]

Interruptions of the continuation of possession which stop prescription, are of two species, namely, natural or of fact, and civil or in law. The first is where the possessor ceases to hold the thing, as, for instance, if it be taken from him; and the second is where a claim against the possessor is brought before some court, and is contested or disputed by him.

The difference between the effects of these two species of interruption is as follows:—Natural interruption, or, in fact, has a general effect with respect to the claims of all men.[c] The reason of this is that thereby one of the essential requisites for usucapion, namely, possession, ceases in fact, therefore usucapion cannot take place at all, nor, consequently, against any one person more than another. But the effect of civil interruption, or interruption in law, by litiscontestation is not general but relative. So soon as a claim to the property is brought into court, the possessor is bound to relinquish it, if the claim be made good, and that obligation necessarily deprives him of the right of acquiring the property by usucapion as against that claimant. But such obligation towards that claimant cannot produce any legal effect with respect to other persons. Besides, *Lex Civilis vigilantibus scripta est*, and while the claimant must not be deprived of the benefit of his vigilance and activity, which enabled him to claim before usucapion was completed against him, there is no reason why his vigilance should benefit others who were not vigilant.

Justinian improved the law of civil interruption by enacting that it should take place by the *oblatio libelli*, that is to say, by the submission of the claim to the court; for the possessor might delay the litis-

[a] Pand. lib. xli. tit. i. De Acquir. Rerum Domin. L. 48, § 1.

[b] Sext. Decretal. tit. ultim. Reg. 2, Reg. 4.

[c] Pand. lib. xli. tit. iii. De Usurp. et Usucap. L. 5.

contestation by delaying to put in his exception or plea, and thereby retard the interruption.[d]

With respect to some persons, no interruption is necessary to prevent usucapion; namely, against those who are unable to assert their rights; for the rule of the law is this: *Contra non valentem agere nulla currit præscriptio.* Thus possession cannot affect by prescription the claims of infants, persons of unsound mind, and other persons under disabilities.

With respect to some things also, no possession, however uninterrupted, can produce usucapion, for where the law forbids usucapion, the good faith of the possessor is of no avail.[e]

It is true that two constitutions of the Emperors Honorius and Theodosius, and Anastasius enacted that no actions whatever should be brought after a silence of thirty, or, in some cases, of forty years; but those constitutions are construed to extend only to such things as are capaple of being acquired and possessed *pro suo* by law and by nature. This is called *præscriptio longissimi temporis.*[f] Justinian by his 119th Novell, extended the thirty years' prescription to cases where the property had been received from a *malâ fide* possessor, and possessed (though *bonâ fide*) without the knowledge of the rightful owner.

The principle of the continuation of possession for the purposes of prescription from one person to another, is not confined to cases of inheritance; for the Emperors Severus and Antoninus decided by their rescripts that the possession of a vendor is to be conjoined with that of a purchaser.[g] And this principle is applicable to all successors *singularis rei.* Thus, if a vendor possessed for ten years, and then sold the thing, the purchaser will, after ten years' possession, have held the property long enough to acquire it by the twenty years' prescription.[h] But if the vendor be not entitled to prescribe, the vice of his possession does not prevent the *bonâ fide* purchaser from prescribing. If, however, the purchaser avails himself of the possession of the vendor, it is expressly decided by Ulpian that he must be prejudiced by the vices of that possession.[i] This is in accordance with

[d] Cod. lib. vii. tit. xl. De Annali Exceptione Italici Contractus tollenda, L. penult. et ult.

[e] Pand. lib. xii. tit. iii. De Usurpationibus et Usucapionibus, L. 24. Instit. lib. ii. tit. vi. § 5. Hugon. Donelli Comment. Jur. Civil. lib. v. cap. vi. § 7, cap. xxxi. § 4.

[f] Cod. lib. vii. tit. xxxix. De Præcrip. XXX. vel XL. Annor. L. 45. Hugon. Donelli Comment. Jur. Civil. lib. v. tit. xxxi. § 7, &c.

[g] Instit. lib. ii. tit. vi. § 8.

the celebrated rule of Paulus: *Secundum naturam est commoda ejus rei eum sequi, quem sequuntur incommoda.*[k] The reverse of this rule is also good law. Thus, if the purchaser does not plead the possession of his alienor, he is not affected by it at all. As Vinnius says, *Neque nocet, neque prodest.*

CHAPTER XIX.

THE LAW OF THINGS.—ACQUISITIONS BY MUNICIPAL LAW.—DONATIONS.

Donation is the second of those which are classed by Trebonian among the modes of acquiring things by Civil or Municipal Law. Donation, *in genere*, is one of the most primitive and natural of all derivative modes of acquiring property, for the power of transferring it without consideration is inherent in the very nature of unlimited dominion. But Trebonian treats of the contract of donation in this part of the Institutes, because his intention is principally to describe two artificial species of donation, that is to say, *mortis causa*, and *propter nuptias.*

Donations are divided by Justinian into two classes :—*mortis causa*, and *non mortis causa* ;[l] but Julianus gives in the Pandects a superior classification.[m] He divides donations into simple or proper, and qualified or improper donations. A donation is a contract, whereby a person gratuitously dispossesses himself of something by transferring it to another to be his property, who accepts it.[n] The first is a contract or agreement, because it would otherwise be a mere offer analogous to a promise, which Ulpian defines to be *solius offerentis promissum*,[o] therefore it must be accepted by the donee. 2ndly, it must

[k] Pand. lib. l. tit. ult. De Reg. Jur. L. 10.

[l] Instit. lib. ii. tit. vii. princip. [m] Pand. lib. xxxix. tit. v. De Donat. L. 1.

[n] Argum. Pothier, Traité des Donations, artic. prélimin.

[o] Pand. lib. xxxix. tit. v. De Donat. L. 1. Voet ad Pand. Comment. lib. xxxix. tit. v. num. 2.

be gratuitous, because otherwise it would be a sale or exchange. A proper donation is that whereby a man gives as an act of mere munificence and liberality, intending the thing given to become immediately the property of the person accepting it; and not to revert to himself in any case, though the Roman Law allows donations to be revoked in five different cases of gross ingratitude, and (in the case of a gift by a freedman to his patron) on the birth of children, subsequent to the gift.[p]

An improper or qualified donation is where a man gives, intending the thing given to become the property of the donee accepting it, but to revert to himself if any event or act should or should not take place or be done.[q]

Of these improper donations one of the most remarkable is *Donatio mortis causa.*

A donation mortis causa (says Justinian) *is one that is made in contemplation of death, when a man gives anything that it may become the property of the donee in the event of the death of the donor, but with the intention that he may recover it if he lives, and also that he may be at liberty to revoke the gift at his pleasure, and that it may be void in the event of the donor outliving the donee. These donations are strictly analogous in law to legacies.*[r]

Indeed a donation *mortis causa* is where the donor desires rather to have the thing himself than that the donee should have it, but prefers that the donee should have it rather than the heir.[s] But though a donation of this kind is made in contemplation of death, if a man in perfect health and in no danger of losing his life deliver something to another with the intention that it should be a donation only in the event of his death, it is a valid donation *mortis causa.*[t]

The question whether a donation be or be not *mortis causa* is one of fact, that is to say, of intention, and the presumption is in favour of the affirmative when the donor gave the thing while danger was imminent, and in favour of the negative in the contrary case.

The antiquity of this contract is shown by a passage in the Odyssey, in which Telemachus makes a donation *mortis causa* to Piræus; and Vinnius cites another precedent from the Alcestes of Euripides.[u]

This species of donation, if accompanied with actual delivery, is *juris gentium*, as Blackstone observes; but it was subjected by the Roman

[p] Vinnii Comm. ad Instit. lib. ii. tit. vii. § 2.

[q] Pand. lib. xxxix. tit. v. De Donat. L. 1.

[r] Instit. lib. ii. tit. vii. § 1.

[s] Pand. lib. xxxix. tit. vi. De Mortis Causa Donat. L. 1. *Magis se vult habere quam eum cui donat, magisque eum cui donat quam hæredem suum.*

[t] Vinnii Comm. ad Instit. lib. ii. tit. vii. § 1.

[u] Odyss. xvii. v. 77, apud Justin. Instit. lib. ii. tit. vii. Eurip. Alcest. v. 1020.

Law to the same formalities of attestation as codicils, and is therefore artificial and *juris civilis* in the Roman Law.[x]

The donation not made *mortis causa*, but which is perfected as soon as the donor has expressed his will, either by writing or verbally, is called a simple donation or donation *inter vivos*. And by the Roman Law donations are good without delivery, and they produce an obligation to deliver the thing given.[y]

The difference between donations *inter vivos*, and *mortis causa*, is that the former are irrevocable, except in the instances above mentioned, and except in the case of donations *propter nuptias*, while the latter do not come into force until the death of the donor, previous to which they are revocable at his pleasure.[z] And donations *inter vivos* take effect immediately, whereas donations *mortis causa* do not until the death of the donor.

Until the law was altered by Justinian, delivery was requisite to complete a valid donation, but the Emperor enacted that actual donations, that is to say, where the donor says I give you (*verbis de præsenti*), and not I will give you (*verbis de futuro*), shall be enforced in the same manner as a sale.[a]

This is a remarkable instance of departure from the rule followed by the English Law, that no contract is capable of being enforced at law in which there is not, or there is not presumed to be, a consideration or mutual interest. That rule is invariably applied by the Roman Law only to those agreements which had not a specific name as contracts acknowledged by the law, as sale, or mandate, or partnership, or which were not invested with a certain formula, called stipulation, which was held to import deliberate intention. Thus though a sale cannot by its very nature exist without a price, which is the consideration on one side, and a thing sold, which is the consideration on the other, mandate is the undertaking of a gratuitous service, and there there is no consideration received by the gratuitous procurator or attorney.

It may be doubted, on grounds of morality as well as of legal policy, whether the sanction of the law should be confined to contracts in which there is a consideration or reciprocity. The argument of Blackstone that the rule of the English Law prevents the setting up of promises for which no good reason could be assigned, is rather assuming the question in dispute, since it assumes that the only good reason

[x] Blackst. Com. book ii. chap. xxxii. p. 513. Five witnesses are required. Cod. lib. viii. tit. lvii. L. 4.
[y] Instit. lib. ii. tit. vii. § 2.
[z] Pand. lib. xxxix. tit. vi. De Donat. Mortis Causa, L. 32.
[a] Cod. lib. viii. tit. liv. De Donat. L. 35.

for a promise is a consideration or reciprocal interest.[b] Indeed the English Common Law has itself acknowledged that the rule is not strongly founded on good reasons, by establishing that a consideration is to be presumed, and no proof to the contrary is to be received where the obligee has executed a deed, and also by allowing a mere nominal consideration to be as effectual in many instances as if it were full and sufficient.

In fact, whenever a man has bound himself deliberately and advisedly, so as to be subject to an obligation *in foro conscientiæ*, his obligation should be enforced on the general maxim of Ulpian, *Grave est fidem fallere*,[c] and he should not be permitted to plead against that maxim of natural law, that he had not an interest in making the engagement, or that he had received no benefit from the other party whom he injures by breaking faith towards him.

But on the other hand, the law should require proof of a sufficiently deliberate intention in the promisor, without which it cannot consistently with legal policy interfere. Agreeably with that policy, Justinian did not sanction promises to give, which are often very loose and inconsiderate; but enforced actual gifts by present words, which certainly import a degree of deliberation.

We now come to another species of qualified or improper donation, or donation which is revocable, namely, donation *ante nuptias*.

This contract is a gift by the bridegroom to the bride, subject to the tacit condition that it should be of no effect if, whether by act of the parties or otherwise, there be no marriage between the parties.[d] By a constitution of the Emperor Constantine, it is established that every donation before marriage by the bridegroom to the bride or the contrary should be subject to that tacit condition; but if either party break off the engagement, he or she cannot take advantage of the condition. If however the marriage be prevented by the death of the bridegroom after he had given the bride a kiss, she is entitled to retain half the gift *quasi osculi jure*.[e] There is also in the Civil Law the donation *propter nuptias* which is a gift made by the husband to the wife in augmentation of her *dos* or dower. But it must not exceed in amount the *dos* itself.[f]

These species of donations are a counterpart of the *dos* or marriage

[b] Blackst. Comm. book ii. chap. xxx. p. 445.

[c] Pand. lib. xiii. tit. v. De Constituta Pecunia, L. 1.

[d] Instit. lib. ii. tit. vii. § 3, et ibid. Comment. Vinnii.

[e] Cod. lib. v. tit. iii. De Donat. ante Nupt. L. 15, L. 16.

[f] Instit. lib. ii. tit. vii. § 3. Cod. lib. v. tit. iii. De Donat. ante Nupt. L. penult. Pand. lib. xxiv. tit. i. De Donat. inter Vir. et Ux. L. 1, et tot. tit.

portion. It follows from a constitution of Diocletian and Maximian, that *dos* or marriage portion is a gift by or in the name of the wife to the husband for the purpose of bearing the charges of marriage.[g] Ulpian says, *Dos sine matrimonio esse non potest*,[h] consequently a marriage portion is a species of donation *ante nuptias*, and these donations are *ad augendam dotem*, or as additions by the husband or future husband to the portion.

CHAPTER XX.

THE LAW OF THINGS.—POWERS OF, AND RESTRAINTS ON ALIENATION.

Restraint on Alienation by Owners.—Power of Alienation vested in Persons who are not Owners.—Instit. lib. ii. tit. viii. Quibus Alienare licet vel non licet, princip. § 1, 2.—Restrictions on the Alienation of the Dotal Estate.—Parapherna.—Alienation Defined.—The Canon Law as to Alienations of the Wife's Estate.—English Law.—Power of Alienating.—Property Pignorated.—Power of Persons under Guardianship. P. 125.

HAVING explained prescription and usucapion, and donations, which are modes of acquiring individual things by civil or municipal law, the next modes of acquisition expounded by Justinian are inheritances both testamentary and *ab intestato*. The latter are modes of acquiring things *per universitatem* by municipal law, for they vest in the heir not merely individual things but the whole estate of another. But the Emperor previously explains certain cases wherein a man who is the proprietor of a thing cannot alienate it because he cannot do so by law, and other cases in which one who is not the proprietor nevertheless has a legal power of alienation.

These apparent anomalies proceed either from the enactments of the law, or from the agreement of the parties. The first instance given by the Emperor is one of the former description.

In some cases the proprietor of a thing has not the power to alienate it; and in others he who is not the proprietor has that power. Thus the Lex Julia forbade the alienation of the dotal estate by the husband, without the will of the wife, though it is his as having been given to him for a marriage portion with his wife. But we, extending and

[g] Cod. lib. xxiii. tit. iii. De Jure Dot. L. 20.

[h] Pand. lib. xxiii. tit. iii. De Jure Dot. L. 3. See, on the subject of the Dos or Marriage portion, the very full Commentaries of Donellus, Comment. Jur. Civil. lib. xiv. cap. iv. et seq.; and Voet, Comm. ad Pand. lib. xxiii. tit. iii. et seq.

amending the provisions of the Julian Law, have enacted that all alienations and obligations of the dotal estate shall be unlawful even with the assent of the wife, in like manner as hypothecations are by the Julian Law, that the weakness of the female sex may not be made detrimental to their interests.[i]

Tryphoninus says, *Quamvis in bonis mariti dos sit, mulieris tamen est.*[k] This must be understood to mean that though the portion belongs to the estate, or is *in bonis* of the husband as having been given to him *ad onera matrimonii sustinenda*, yet his right over it is qualified by the beneficial interest of the wife. Thus we find that the interest of the wife is the object of the legislative restrictions laid upon the marital power over the dotal estate.

The *Lex Julia de Fundo Dotali*, which first imposed these restrictions, applied only to landed property, and indeed a prohibition to alienate moveables could not be enforced without great difficulty.[l]

But here a distinction must be drawn between dotal property, which was given to the husband to support the burthens of matrimony, and *parapherna*.[m] That term applies to things *extra dotem*, that is to say, things not given to the husband; and it is enacted by the Emperors Theodosius and Valentinian that he shall not, unless with the consent of the woman, interfere with them.[n] And Justinian made him liable and accountable, as an agent, for their administration.[o]

These do not come within the provisions of the *Lex Julia*, and they may be alienated by the wife alone, or by the husband, with her consent, but not without, because they are not his. Thus it appears that by the Civil Law the husband and wife are not considered to be one person as in our courts of Common Law, but as separate persons.

It is not consistent with the nature of this treatise to point out the changes made by Justinian in the *Lex Julia*. The result of those changes was to restrain the husband (even with his wife's consent) from alienating or hypothecating the dotal estate.[p] This was provided for the protection of the wife, as the Emperor expresses it: *Ne fragilitate naturæ suæ in repentinam deducatur inopiam.*

The Emperors Severus and Antoninus define alienation to be *omnis actus per quem dominium transfertur*. Now the Emperors say *dominium*, and not *dominium rei*, therefore alienation must in that law be taken to mean not merely the alienation of the thing, but that of any

[i] Instit. lib. ii. tit. viii. princip. [k] Pand. lib. xxiii. tit. iii. De Jure Dot. L. 75.

[l] Pand. lib. xxiii. tit. v. De Fundo Dotali. Voet ad Pand. Comment. ibid. num. 4.

[m] Voet, Comm. ad Pand. lib. xxiii. tit. ii. De Jure Dot. num. 2.

[n] Cod. lib. v. tit. xiv. De Pactis Convent. tam super Dote quam super Donatione propter Nuptias et Paraphernis, L. 8. [o] Cod. ibid. Lex. ult.

[p] Cod. lib. v. tit. xiii. De Rei Uxoriæ Actione, L. unic.

part of the dominion over it.[q] But this prohibition of alienation is relaxed in several cases where the alienation is for the benefit of the wife. When, however, the estate has been alienated illegally by the husband, the conveyance is void *ipso jure*, and the purchaser cannot prescribe against the wife while she remains under the authority of her husband, for *contra non valentem agere præscriptio non currit.*[r]

The Canon Law allows alienations by the husband to which the wife consents upon oath, and from that law the method of passing the estate of married women in the English Law may be derived. But it seems doubtful whether that modification did not make the law nugatory, since it is difficult for a woman to have it in her power to refuse her consent to the wishes of her husband if he be determined to obtain that consent. It is therefore best that the restrictions should be absolute, except where they are contrary to the interests of the woman whom it should be the object of the law to protect.

The English Common Law as absolutely forbade any act of the married woman to the prejudice of her interests as the Laws of Justinian; but that prohibition was evaded by the contrivance of a fine, together with the examination of the woman with regard to the freedom of her consent.[s]

The Emperor next gives an example of a power of alienation in a person who is not the proprietor of the thing.

On the other hand, the creditor has power to alienate the property pignorated, though it is not his. This power arises from the will of the proprietor, for he agreed that the creditor should have the power to sell the property pignorated, if the money due were not paid. But we have subjected the power of creditors over pignorated property to certain rules, that while creditors may not be impeded in the acquisition of that which is due to them, debtors may not unnecessarily lose their property.[t]

The power here described by Justinian is a power springing from contract, and regulated by law in a very judicious manner, but this subject will be more conveniently explained hereafter.

Another instance is next given by Justinian of a proprietor restrained from alienation, namely, that of persons under guardianship, who are disabled from alienating anything that is theirs without the authority of their guardians.[u] This is a restriction arising from the law alone, whereby a man is disabled from exercising his rights over his own property. But this subject has been already explained.

Acquisitions *per universitatem* are the next subject to be considered.

[q] Cod. lib. v. tit. xxiii. De Fundo Dotal. L. 1. Voet ad Pand. Comm. ad eund. tit. num. 2.

[r] Voet, Comm. ad Pand. ibid. num. 6.

[s] Co. Litt. 121 a. n. 1.

[t] Instit. lib. ii. tit. vii. § 1.

[u] Instit. ibid. § 2.

CHAPTER XXI.

THE LAW OF THINGS.

Of Testaments. — General Arrangement of the Remainder of the Institutes.— Division of the Testamentary Law into Three Parts.—Definition of an Inheritance.—Definitions of a Testament.—Persons incapable of making a Testament.—Execution of Testaments, Written and Nuncupative Testaments.— Solemn and not Solemn Testaments.—Registration of Wills.—Origin of Probate of Wills. P. 131.

The law of usucapion and donations having been explained, Justinian proceeds from the modes whereby the property in individual things is acquired, to that by which one man's estate passes *per universum* to another, namely, *inheritance;* the effect of which is that the whole estate of the deceased is transferred to his heir. Inheritance is of two kinds ; for it is acquired either by will, *ex testamento*, or without will, *ab intestato*.[x]

And first, of inheritance by will, or testamentary inheritance.

The Rubric of the tenth title of the 2nd Book of the Institutes is, *De Testamentis Ordinandis*, and the subject of testamentary law is developed at considerable length in the succeeding titles, occupying the remainder of the second book. The third book commences with inheritances *ab intestato*, and after that has been explained, the Emperor, leaving the subject of *jura in re*, or *dominium*, passes on to *jura ad rem*, which arise from obligations. With the law of obligations the second of the three divisions, namely, of *Things*, is concluded. Persons and Things having been considered, the Emperor then proceeds to the third division—of *Actions*.

From the tenth to the nineteenth titles inclusively, the text of the Imperial Institutes is almost entirely composed of historical deductions of the various changes in testamentary law from the earliest times to the reign of Justinian; of the obsolete law arising from the bondage of descendants under the paternal power, and the distinction between the Civil Law and the remedial jurisdiction of the Prætor; and of technical rules which have been superseded in almost all modern nations by positive enactments adapted to the changes which society has undergone. It will therefore be most convenient here to resort to the Pandects for an exposition of such parts of the Roman Testamentary Law as are now valuable, avoiding technical rules and mere

[x] Instit. lib. ii. tit. ix. § 6.

positive and obsolete law. But for the Law of Legacies, the Institutes will again be followed.

This portion of the Civil Law is divisible into three parts, as it regards, 1, the Testator; 2, the Testament; and 3, the Heir.

I. First, those persons are pointed out who are incapable of making a will, and the mode of executing a testament is described.[y]

II. Secondly, three titles are devoted to the law respecting the causes which may render a testament void or voidable, though duly executed, and those which make it void for irregularity, or from events subsequent to its execution; and to the exposition of the law relating to changes wrought upon the face of the testament or testamentary instrument.[z]

III. Thirdly, it is shown who may be made heir by testament, and how such heirs are made; and two titles follow regarding certain species of appointments of heirs, namely, substitutions, or the substitution of one heir in the event of the other not accepting the inheritance; and conditional appointment of heirs.[a]

An inheritance is thus defined by Gajus: *Hæreditas est successio in universum jus quod defunctus habuit.* And Ulpian says: *Hæreditas ejusdem potestatis jurisque est cujus fuit defunctus.*[b] The general principle of the law is that whoever binds himself binds his estate, and that men stipulate for the benefit of their heirs as well as for their own. The consequence is that the estate remains liable after the death of the proprietor, and, on the other hand, his heirs becoming the representatives of his person for his liabilities are also his representatives in his rights.

Grotius defines a testament to be a mode whereby a man alienates his property in the event of death, reserving to himself in the meanwhile as full a power over it as if he had not made any such disposal.[c]

That great jurist holds, with Pufendorf, that though the mode of exercising the testamentary power be variously regulated and restricted by the municipal law of different countries, yet the power of disposing of property in the event of death is *juris gentium*, and springs from natural law, being a part of the secondary law of nature, and included in the plenitude of the rights of property. But that power is limited by natural as well as by Civil Law. Thus no man may exercise it to the prejudice of his just creditors; for no man can transfer to another

[y] Pand. lib. xxviii. tit. i. Qui Testamenta facere possunt et quemadmodum Testamenta fiant.

[z] Pand. lib. xxviii. tit. ii. Ibid. tit. iii. Ibid. tit. iv.

[a] Pand. lib. xxviii. tit. v. Ibid. tit. vi. Ibid. tit. vii.

[b] Pand. lib. l. tit. penult. L. 24. Ibid. tit. ult. L. 59.

[c] Grot. liv. ii. chap. 16, § 14.

more right to a thing than he has himself. And, on principles of natural justice, no man can alienate his property in the event of his death, so as to leave destitute his children or others for whom he is bound to provide. The Civil Law of each country has also restricted the exercise of the testamentary power by positive enactments grounded on reasons of public good, as well as by laws declaratory of the natural law; and has moreover prescribed certain forms to be observed in the exercise of that power, with a view to prevent its freedom being destroyed by the influence of force, fear, or fraud.

These general principles having been established, it remains now to be examined, first, what persons may, or rather what persons may not make a testament, and secondly, how testaments are required to be executed.

A testament is thus defined by Modestinus: *Testamentum est voluntatis nostræ justa sententia, de eo quod quis post mortem suam fieri velit.*[d] The words *justa sententia* have the effect of excluding every expression of an intention which is either contrary to law, or not declared in a legal manner; for it follows, from a law of Gajus, that a void testament, like any other void title, is a nonentity in law.[e] Consequently the testament of a person incapable by law of making one, is not *justa sententia voluntatis*, and is void. And so a person who has not a rational and discriminating mind, is incapable of making a testament. Persons who by reason of a crime have been condemned to suffer civil death, or any penalty importing civil death, or who have legally forfeited their power of making a testament, must necessarily die intestate, unless they have made a valid testament before the commission of the offence;[f] and, indeed, in some cases the Criminal Law has a retroactive effect, avoiding any will previously executed by the offender.[g]

The Roman Law also disallows testaments executed by persons under real or presumed incapacity. It is necessary to point out who those persons are, in order to show who are capable of exercising the testamentary power, for the rule of the Civil Law is this: *Testamentum facere possunt omnes qui non inveniuntur prohibiti.*

Persons who have no power of discrimination, such as lunatics, idiots, and others who are deprived of the use of their reason, either from infirmity or voluntary causes, such as intoxication, are absolutely incapable of making a testament while subject to the influence of those affections, for an instrument executed under such circumstances,

[d] Pand. lib. xxviii. tit. i. Qui Testamenta facere possunt, L. 1.

[e] Pand. ibid. L. 4.

[f] Voet ad Pand. Comm. lib. xxviii. tit. i. num. 39.

[g] Voet ad Pand. Comm. ibid. num. 12.

is not *voluntatis justa sententia.* But it is for the person who asserts the testator to have been under incapacity, to prove that fact.[h]

Bodily infirmity does not produce any incapacity, for sanity of mind suffices.[i]

As for defect of age, though children at a very early age are incapable by nature to make a testament or to perform any other act requiring discretion; the precise duration of their incapacity is a matter of positive law; for the limit must be fixed somewhere to avoid perplexities arising from the great varieties in the more or less early development of men's intellect. The Roman Law limits the incapacity of children within the period below puberty.[k]

Ulpian expressly decides that the capacity to make a will commences in males at fourteen and in females at twelve years of age, and that the last year is to be considered as completed, so soon as the last day of that year has commenced.

Prodigals also are incapable of making a testament. Pomponius says: *Furiosi vel ejus cui bonis interdictum est nulla voluntas est.*[l] The law will not permit the acts of either to have any effect, for whether a man be unfit to manage his affairs by reason of insanity, or from any other cause, such as prodigality and extravagance, he has no will; for either he is naturally incapable of discrimination, or the law will not for his own good and that of others permit him to have any will of his own.

We have next to consider the mode in which the testator must declare his will, that is to say, with the formalities required by law, in order to render it valid after his death.[m]

Testaments by the Roman Law are of two kinds, *testamentum solemne*, and *testamentum minus solemne*, and again they may be either written, or nuncupative. And first of the *testamentum solemne.*

A written will of this kind must be signed by the testator or by some one in his name, according to a constitution of Theodosius and Valentinian, unless it be wholly written by himself.[n]

The subscription of the testator is required to be in the presence of witnesses, who must be *omni exceptione majores.* Thus a witness must not be a prodigal nor an infamous person, for they are unworthy of

[h] Voet, Comm. ad Pand. lib. xxviii. tit. i. Qui facere Testam. possunt, num. 35.

[i] Pand. lib. xxviii. tit. i. Qui Testam. facere poss. L. 2. Cod. eod. tit. L. 3.

[k] Pand. ibid. L. 5, and L. 19. Instit. lib. ii. tit. xii. Quibus non est Permiss. facere Testam. § 1. Co. Litt. 89 b, n. 6. Pand. lib. l. tit. penult. L. 134.

[l] Pand. lib. l. tit. ult. De Reg. Jur. L. 40.

[m] Instit. lib. ii. tit. x. De Testam. Ordinand. princip. Ulpian, Fragment. tit. 20.

[n] Cod. lib. vi. tit. xxiii. De Testam. L. 21.

belief; nor a woman nor a person below the age of puberty, for they are in general more easily imposed upon or influenced, than men of mature age; nor a legatee, nor the heir, for they have an interest in the validity of the instrument. Thus Paulus says, *Nullus idoneus testis in re sua intelligitur.*[o]

Also no person under the immediate power of another who has an interest in the will, is a legal witness to the instrument, for as Licinius Rufinus says, *Idonei non videntur testes quibus imperarii potest ut testes fiant.*[p] And the general rule obtains that all those persons whose testimony would not be trusted if they deposed to a fact in a court of justice, are *a fortiori* incapable of attesting the execution of a will.[q]

A nuncupative testament is a verbal declaration of the will of the testator made before seven sufficient witnesses. That number of witnesses is required in all testaments by the Roman Law.[r]

Testaments called *minus solemnia* may be either written, or nuncupative, and they are those which the law permits to be executed with fewer solemnities. Such are those executed during a pestilence, and where there are not the means of observing the formalities prescribed by law. Such also is the *testamentum militis,* which is valid though it consist of nothing more than a simple manifestation of the will of the soldier without any legal formality.[s]

Two constitutions of Arcadius and Honorius, and of Theodosius, show that the registration of testaments in the office of the *Magister Census*, or among the records of a court of justice, or of a Municipium, was in use among the Romans.[t]

The clergy attempted to obtain the privilege of registering wills, and they actually succeeded in doing so, but this usurpation is in strong terms denounced by the Emperor Justin, who after enacting that the registration of wills shall exclusively belong to the *Magister Census*, thus reproves the clergy:—"It is absurd to confuse duties by confounding different functions together, so that what is entrusted to

[o] Cod. lib. vi. tit. xxiii. De Testam. L. 9. Vinnii Comment. ad Inst. lib. ii. tit. x. De Testam. Ordinand. § 6. [p] Pand. lib. xxii. tit. iii. De Probat. L. 6.

[q] Voet, Comm. ad Pand. lib. xxviii. tit. i. Qui Testam. facere poss. num. 7.

[r] Pand. lib. xxviii. tit. i. Qui Test. facere poss. L. 21. Instit. lib. ii. tit. x. De Testam. Ordinand. § ult. The number of witnesses is derived from the antient form and fiction of Testaments, *per æs et libram.* See Heineccii Antiquit. lib. ii. tit. x. xi. § 7.

[s] Voet, Comm. ad Pand. lib. xxviii. tit. i. Qui Testam. facere poss. num. 12. Pand. lib. xxix. tit. i. De Militari Testam.

[t] Cod. lib. vi. tit. xxiii. De Testament. L. 17, L. 19.

one, another takes from him: and this is especially so with regard to the clergy, to whom it is opprobrious to endeavour to show themselves skilful in forensic matters." [u]

It appears from a remarkable law of the Emperor Leo, (which transferred the *insinuatio* or registration of wills, from the *Magister Census* to the *Quæstor* and certain other magistrates in Rome, and to the Præsides in the Provinces,) that the magistrate entrusted with that duty not only registered the instrument, but authenticated it under his seal upon the faith of the depositions of the subscribing witnesses.[x] From that proceeding the probate of wills in the English Ecclesiastical Courts is probably derived.

CHAPTER XXII.

THE LAW OF THINGS.—TESTAMENTS.

Of Testaments.—Causes rendering a Testament Void.—Disinheriting of Descendants.—*Quærela inofficiosi.*—*Legitim.*—*Injustum Testamentum.*—*Ruptum Testamentum.*—Revocation of Wills: by Birth of a Child; by a Subsequent Will.—Incompatible Wills.—*Irritum factum Testamentum.*—Appointment of an Heir.—What Persons are capable of being appointed.—Void Modes of Disposing.—Obscurity.—Distinction between Error of Law and of Fact.—Circumstantial Evidence.—Preconstituted Proofs—Substitutions.—Their Origin.—Time of Deliberation.—Inventory.—Substitutions, Vulgar, Pupillary, Quasi Pupillary, Fideicommissary.—Conditional Appointments.—Conditions Impossible, Foolish or Derisory, Casual, Potestative, and Mixed. P. 140.

Having explained in the preceding chapter the law regarding incapacity to make a testament, and the mode in which that instrument is required to be executed, it is now necessary to show the causes which render a testament void or voidable, *ab initio*, and those which cause its revocation, or annulling, though it be originally good and valid.

And first, a will is void by the Roman Law, unless it either disinherit for a cause admitted by the law, or institute heirs the children or other descendants under the paternal power of the testator, or his posthumous children, who, but for his death, would have been under his power. But the emancipated children have the *quærela inofficiosi*

[u] Cod. lib. vi. tit. xxiii. De Testam. L. 23. Cod. lib. i. tit. iii. De Episc. et Cleric. L. 41.

[x] Novel. Leonis, 44, near the end of the Corpus Juris.

if they be passed over in silence, or unjustly disinherited by the testator, and the law annuls the will by a fiction, supposing the testator not to have been of sane mind.[a] But if the testator bequeathed anything to the heir, the *quærela inofficiosi*, by the older Roman Law, was not admitted. The heir, however, had an action to obtain his *legitim*, that is to say, to make up, together with what was bequeathed to him, one-fourth of the share which he would have had if he had not been deprived of his full share.[b]

Justinian further restricted the power of disinheriting, by enacting that the heir should have the benefit of the *quærela inofficiosi*, even where the testator bequeathed to him his *legitim;* and after that alteration in the law, no heir could be disinherited, even in part, who was admitted by proximity of blood to the *quærela inofficiosi*, except for a sufficient reason.[c]

As for the Law of *Collatio Bonorum*, whereby heirs are bound to reckon as part of their share of the inheritance whatever they have received from the deceased during his lifetime, it will be more conveniently explained elsewhere.

We will next proceed to consider the substance of the title in the Pandects, *De Injusto, Rupto, Irrito facto Testamento.*[d]

Papinian defines an imperfect or irregular testament as follows:— *Testamentum non jure factum dicitur ubi solemnia juris deficiunt.* Such a testament is *testamentum injustum*, which denomination includes all those that are not *voluntatis justa sententia.*[e] It follows from this definition, that a testament obtained by force, fear, or fraud is in reality void from the beginning, because it is not *voluntatis justa sententia.* But as those vices or defects are extrinsic to the instrument, and require separate proof, they render the testament not void but voidable.[f]

It is however necessary to observe with regard to these vices in testaments, that no persuasions or assiduous attentions paid to the deceased for the purpose of obtaining his inheritance are sufficient grounds to avoid a testament made under that kind of influence, for it does not, by itself deprive him of the exercise of his free will and judgment.[g]

Various causes may revoke or annul a will, rendering it *ruptum testamentum*, though originally valid. The death of the testator alone

[a] Instit. lib. ii. tit. xviii. De Inofficioso Testamento.

[b] Instit. ibid. § 3. Vinnii Comment. ad Instit. ibid.

[c] Novel. 18. Novel. 115.

[d] Pand. lib. xxviii. tit. iii.

[e] Pand. lib. xxviii. tit. iii. De Injusto, Rupto, &c. Testam. L. 1.

[f] Voet, Comm. ad Pand. lib. xxix. tit. vi. Si Quis Aliquem testari prohibuit vel coegerit.

[g] Voet, Comm. ad Pand. ibid. num 3.

can render a will irrevocable, for, as Ulpian says, *Ambulatoria est voluntas testatoris usque ad vitæ exitum.*[h]

Thus the will may be revoked by the testator cancelling or destroying it. The birth of a child annuls a testament whereby that child's rights are expressly or tacitly set aside, or in other words, whereby the child is disinherited contrary to law.[i]

A will may also be revoked by a subsequent valid will.[k] By the Roman Law, as it prevailed in the time of Justinian, two wills could not coexist, and the last only could be valid as a will, though the first might be confirmed by it, so as to be a valid codicil. But by a codicil, an heir could not be appointed.[l] This rule rested on technical grounds and is not admitted in the modern Civil Law, which allows two wills to be valid together, and where they are incompatible, the latest in date has the preference. *Ea quæ postea geruntur prioribus derogant.*[m]

Whoever claims under one of several testaments has the onus cast upon him to prove that it is the latest; and where several testaments are incompatible with each other, and their priorities cannot be shown, they are of no effect so far as they are incompatible.[n]

Lastly, a testament is said in the Roman Law to be *irritum factum*, when the testator forfeits his estate for a crime, and where the heir refuses the inheritance, or the will is otherwise made ineffectual, though neither revoked nor otherwise invalidated. We will now return to revocation by the testator. The question whether a testament be revoked or no, is one of intention. That intention may be declared not only by express words of revocation contained in a subsequent will, but by acts. Thus if the testator cancel, or deface, or destroy the instrument, it is presumed that he did so, intending to revoke it, unless the contrary be proved.[o]

But a revocation, whether expressed or implied, is of no effect if it be grounded on error, that is to say, on the belief of something

[h] Pand. lib. xxxiv. tit. iv. De Adimendis vel Transferendis Legatis, L. 4.

[i] Pand. lib. xxviii. tit. iii. De Injust. Rupt. vel Irrito Facto Testamento, L. 1 et 3.

[k] Pand. ibid. L. 1 et 2. Instit. lib. ii. tit. xvii. Quibus Modis Testament. Infirmatur, § 7.

[l] Voet, Comm. ad Pand. ibid. num. 7.

[m] Voet, Comm. ad Pand. ibid. num. 8. In the modern Civil Law, the rule of the Pandects on this subject as to Milit. Wills and Codicils is extended to all wills. Pand. lib. xxix. tit. i. De Testam. Milit. L. 19. Ibid. tit. vii. De Jure Codicill. L. 8. Ibid. L. 6, § 2.

[n] Voet, Comm. ad Pand. lib. xxviii. tit. iii. De Injusto Rupto Irrito Facto Testamento, num. 9. Pand. lib. l. tit. ult. De Reg. Jur. L. 188. *Non jus deficit sed probatio,* as in Pand. lib. xxvi. tit. ii. De Testament. Tutela, L. 31.

[o] Voet, Comm. ad Pand. lib. xxviii. tit. iv. De his quæ in Testamentis delentur inducuntur, vel inscribuntur, num. 1.

that is not true,[p] or if it took place when the testator was under incapacity.

Testamentary law has now been considered with reference to the testator and to the testament. It must next be explained as it immediately regards the heir.

By the Roman Law an heir can be appointed by a testament only, and not by a codicil; but the appointment may be validly made by any words sufficiently denoting the intention of the testator.[q]

All persons, whether natural or artificial, that is to say bodies politic, are capable, unless the law make them incapable, of taking under testamentary dispositions. Persons are rendered incapable of being appointed heirs, either as a punishment for some delinquency, or from particular motives of legal policy,[r] as in the case of a guardian who is incapable of being made heir by his ward. And bodies politic cannot take under a will, unless they be lawfully incorporated by the Senate. But a bequest to the members of a body not lawfully incorporated is good.[s]

Certain modes of disposing are void as well as the appointment of certain persons to be heir. Thus, if the appointment be so obscure that it is incapable of being interpreted consistently with itself, it is void;[t] for a man who speaks ambiguously, does not say both propositions contained in the ambiguous words, but only that one which he means, and, therefore, whoever says what he does not mean, does not say what the words signify, because the intention is wanting, nor what he intends, because his words do not express it.[u] It follows that his words are of no effect; it also follows that if the intention be clear, the literal sense of the words, though not agreeable to that intention, do not subvert it.

An important consequence is to be drawn from these doctrines, namely, that every instrument and every act having effect as a manifestation of an intention, must be considered solely as evidence of that intention, and not as something substantive and separate from that

[p] Pand. lib. xxviii. tit. v. De Hæredibus Instituendis, L. ult.

[q] Voet, Comm. ad Pand. lib. xxviii. tit. v. De Hæredibus Instituendis, num. 1. Cod. lib. vi. tit. xxiii. De Testament. L. 15. Pand. lib. xxviii. tit. v. De Hæredibus Instituend. L. 1, § 5, 6.

[r] Voet, Comm. ad Pand. lib. xxviii. tit. v. De Hæredib. Instituend. num. 5, 8.

[s] Pand. lib. xxxiv. tit. v. De Rebus Dubiis, L. 20. . . . . *Non valebit nisi singulis legetur; hi autem, non quasi collegium sed quasi singuli homines admittuntur ad legatum.*

[t] Pand. lib. l. tit. ult. De Regulis Jur. L. 188.

[u] Pand. lib. xxxiv. tit. v. De Rebus Dubiis. *In ambiguo sermone non utrunque dicimus; sed id duntaxat, quod volumus; itaque qui aliud dicit quam vult, neque id dicit quod vox significat, quia non vult; neque id quod vult, quia id non loquitur.*

intention.[x] The lawful intention of the party must be carried into effect whenever it is clearly to be inferred from his act. Thus the Civil Law does not confine men to certain legal formulæ, in deeds and other instruments, so that none but certain words shall have effect though it is prudent to make use of those words which have a fixed and definite construction attached to them by the law. And the law requires particular acts to be done with due deliberation,[y] and therefore, in some cases, will not permit an intention to be manifested so as to have legal effect, otherwise than in a certain manner. And the law requires particular forms to be observed as security against fraud. Thus the Roman Law makes a form of question and answer called stipulation, necessary for the validity of some contracts. Thus, a testament, without the attestation of a certain number of witnesses, is void, because the law requires that number of witnesses as a security against fraud, and therefore refuses belief to a lesser number.

These restrictions, however, are justifiable only on the ground of the imperfection of all human power to judge of the intentions of men, and of the existence or nonexistence of alleged facts. Neratius truly observes in defining the difference between error in law and error in fact: *Jus finitum et potest esse et debet; facti interpretatio plerumque prudentissimos fallit.*[z] The meaning of this law is as follows. Law is definite or limited, and he who judges a question of law may have before him all the elements requisite for coming to a conclusion; consequently he can err only in drawing his inference from the premises, which are in themselves sufficient for a decision. But fact is not definite but indefinite. As nothing takes place without a sufficient cause, there is a chain of causes and effects whereby every fact or event is connected with those which precede it. It follows from this theory, that if it were possible in any particular case to become acquainted with all the causes by which any unknown fact was produced, that fact might be inferred or proved by induction with as much certainty as the degree of accuracy and power of reasoning of the judge would admit. Now this is so with regard to questions of law, for as the Roman Jurisconsult says, *jus finitum et potest esse et debet*; but to law he contradistinguishes fact which is invariable and finite only to Omniscience, and he therefore concludes *facti interpretatio plerumque prudentissimos fallit.*

He, however says *plerumque* and not *semper*, because where there is either such direct proof of a fact as excludes (as far as possible)

[x] Cod. lib. iv. tit. xix. De Probationibus, L. 12. Pand. lib. xxxi. De Legatis et Fideicommissis, Liber ii. L. 77, § 12.

[y] Pand. lib. l. tit. ult. De Reg. Jur. L. 76.

[z] Pand. lib. xxii. tit. vi. De Juris et Facti Ignorantia, L. 2.

the supposition of error or fraud in the instruments or other means whereby the fact is to be proved; or where the truth of the fact sought to be proved follows as an invariable inference from a number of distinct facts, each resting on sufficient and separate direct evidence, there is such certainty of the truth of that fact as warrants it being received as absolutely true.

But it is difficult to conceive a case of direct or circumstantial evidence, wherein some unknown fact may not exist, the want of knowledge of which may lead to an erroneous conclusion. It is this difficulty of deciding questions of fact (which indeed has led some philosophers to doubt everything) that justifies the establishment of what Bentham has denominated *preconstituted proofs*. They are those for which the law will receive no equivalent. But it is worth observing that even that species of evidence does not produce certainty. For instance, an instrument may be perfectly regular in all its forms, and yet it may have been extorted by fear, or obtained by fraud.

Preconstituted proofs may also frequently give rise to cases of hardship, and the harshness of the law in those instances is only justifiable on the ground, as Justinian expresses it, that *Quod communiter omnibus prodest, hoc privatæ utilitati præferendum.*[a] But in no branch of the law is there greater need of what Justinian designates as *Legibus amica simplicitas.*[b]

Two special modes of appointing heirs are next to be explained, that is to say, substitutions and conditions; and first of substitutions.

A substitution is a provision in a testament whereby more than one heir is appointed, and in which the heirs are to take not together, but one in default of the other.[c]

Substitutions are either *direct* or *fideicommissary*; and again *direct* substitutions are either *vulgar*, or *pupillary*, or *quasi pupillary*.

Substitutions drew their origin from the notion of the ancients that it was disgraceful to a citizen for his testament to remain unaccepted. That opinion was occasioned by the worship paid to the household gods, which became extinguished where the father of the family died without an heir.[d] To prevent this the ancients invented substitutions, whereby an heir was substituted to the instituted or appointed heir, to take in the event of the latter

[a] Cod. lib. vi. tit. l. De Caducis Tollendis, L. unic.

[b] Instit. lib. iii. tit. ii. De Legitima Agnatorum Success. § 3.

[c] Voet, Comm. ad Pand. lib. xxviii. tit. vi. De Vulgari et Pupillari Substitutione, princip.

[d] Heineccii Antiquit. lib. ii. tit. xv. xvi. Adoption in the Hindu Law, had its origin in a similar superstition.

declining the inheritance, and to the first substitute any number of others may be successively substituted.[e]

The reason of the frequent unwillingness of heirs to accept inheritances bequeathed to them was, that the heir becomes by the Roman Law, liable to all the heritable debts of the deceased. The Law, however, and the Prætor granted to heirs a space of time, called the time of deliberation, within which they might examine whether it would be expedient to accept or to refuse the inheritance. Justinian gave to them the benefit of inventory, that is to say, the power to provide an authentic inventory of the estate of the deceased, and thereby to discharge themselves from all liability to his debts beyond the value of the inheritance.[f]

Substitutions, however, still kept their ground, for an inheritance might give more trouble than advantage to the heir, though it subjected him only to a limited liability, and it was therefore the practice of testators to endeavour by that device to secure themselves from the final rejection of their wills.

Every substitution contains a condition. Thus the words *Si Titius hæres non erit, Mævius hæres esto,* are conditional in form. But a conditional substitution is one in which the substitute cannot avail himself of the refusal of the previous heir unless a certain condition be accomplished.[g]

Pupillary substitution is that whereby a father or other ancestor substituted an heir to succeed instead of or after his son or other descendant (being under his power) in the event of such son or other descendant dying during the life or after the death of the testator, before attaining puberty, and consequently without being capable of making a testament for himself.[h] Thus pupillary substitution implies two testaments in one,—that of the ancestor appointing an heir, and that of the same ancestor for his descendant appointing a substitute, or an heir to that heir. There are frequent allusions to this legal form in the antient writers. Thus Horace makes Tiresias advise Ulisses not to neglect to ingratiate himself with the rich man who has a sickly child:[i]

> . . . . Leniter in spem
> Arrepe officiosus ut et scribare secundus
> Hæres, et si quis casus puerum egerit Orco
> In vacuum venias.

---

[e] Pand. lib. xxviii. tit. vi. De Vulg. et Pupill. Substitut. L. 1.

[f] Instit. lib. ii. tit. xii. De Hæredum Qualitate, § 5. Cod. lib. vi. tit. xxx. De Jure Deliberandi, L. ult.

[g] Voet, Comm. ad Pand. lib. xxviii. tit. vi. De Vulgari et Pupill. Substitut. num. 3. Ibid. L. ult. § 1. This distinction was overlooked by Butler, Co. Litt. 191 a, n. 1.

[h] Heinecc. Antiquit. lib. ii. tit. xv. xvi. § 4.

[i] Horat. Sat. ii. v. ver. 45.

Quasi Pupillary, or *exemplar* substitution, was introduced by Justinian, and is that whereby the father or mother substitute an heir to take instead of or after, and as heir to their child, in the event of that child dying without having recovered from an infirmity causing an incapacity to make a will.[k] Direct substitutions are called *vulgar*, which are neither *pupillary* nor *quasi pupillary*.

There are also *fideicommissary*, which are contradistinguished from direct substitutions. A *fideicommissary* substitution is one whereby the heir is required by the testator to transfer the inheritance by virtue of a trust, to a substituted heir who is to succeed after the former.

Conditional institutions or appointments of an heir remain to be considered. Conditions may be added as well to testamentary dispositions of every description, as to acts *inter vivos*, such as contracts.[l] A conditional act may be defined to be one, the effect of which is suspended by a future and uncertain event, that is, an event which may or may not occur. It follows from this definition, that an impossible condition, and one, the event of which is certain, but its certainty is not known to the parties, and also one which is already accomplished or forfeited at the time of the act, are not strictly speaking conditions, because they do not suspend the effect of the act. But as they have the form, and in some cases even the uncertainty of conditions, at least so far as the knowledge of the parties is concerned, they are called conditions. But they have no actual suspensive effect, and therefore such conditions are called improper.

We have here only to consider testamentary conditions, asubject to which it will be necessary to revert for the purpose of explaining conditional legacies.

It is a general rule that impossible conditions, that is to say, those which cannot be accomplished at all, and those the accomplishment of which would involve a violation of positive law, or be *contra bonos mores*, are of no effect whatever to suspend the effect of testamentary dispositions.[m] *Impossibilis institutio (in testamentis) pro non scripto habetur.*[n] But it is otherwise in contracts.

Thus also conditions in wills, which are designated as *ineptæ et derisoriæ*, are not considered as legal conditions, and are passed over as if not written. Thus Marcian says—Papinian writes, that foolish dispositions of testators respecting their burial (as, for instance, that dresses, or any other unnecessary things be provided for their funeral)

[k] Voet, Comm. ad Pand. lib. xxviii. tit. vi. De Vulg. vel Pupill. Substit. num. 27.

[l] Voet, Comm. ad Pand. lib. xxviii. tit. vii. De Conditionibus Institutionum, num. 1.

[m] Pand. lib. xxviii. tit. vii. De Condition. Institut. L. 1, L. 14, L. 15. Pand. lib. xxx. De Legatis et Fideicommissis, Liber. 1, L. 112, § 3.

[n] Instit. lib. ii. tit. xiv. De Hæred. Instituendis, § 10.

are not valid.[o] And Scævola held a clause in a testament to be of no effect, whereby a woman desired to be buried with valuable ornaments.[p] And Ulpian expressly forbids the burial of valuables with the deceased person.[q] Modestinus, after deciding a foolish condition in a will to be void, very justly adds: But it is first to be considered whether a man who inserted such a condition was of sane mind.[r]

Conditions are either *potestative*, that is to say, such as the person who is to benefit by their accomplishment must himself perform, or the performance of which depend on him; or they are *casual*, that is, out of the power of that person; or else they partake of the nature of both potestative and casual conditions. The latter species are called *mixed* conditions.[s]

One general rule governs all species of conditions. It is this: Unless they be accomplished or the law dispense with their accomplishment during the life of the person designated by the testator, the testamentary disposition depending on the condition is void. The condition must be either fulfilled or dispensed with during the life of that person, because both inheritances and legacies are personal to the heir or legatee, *ob aliquam meritum*, and therefore the benefit of them cannot pass directly from the testator to the heir of such heir or legatee.

Upon the same principle of the personal nature of the benefit conferred by the testator, rests the rule of Papinian: *Dies incertus conditionem in testamento facit.*[t] The meaning of that celebrated rule is, that if the appointment or legacy itself be suspended for a term (and not merely its payment), as the term may expire either before or after the death of the heir or legatee, that term operates as a condition, because its expiration will not give effect to the legacy, unless it occur during the life of the person who is the object of the testator's bounty. Thus it produces that uncertainty which is the distinctive feature of a condition.[u]

Casual conditions must in all cases be fulfilled before the appointment or legacy can have effect, and the same rule applies to mixed conditions, so far as they partake of the nature of casual conditions; but it is otherwise with those which are called potestative conditions.

[o] Pand. lib. xxx. De Legatis et Fideicommissis, Liber. i. L. 113, § 5.

[p] Pand. lib. xxxiv. tit. ii. De Auro et Argento Legato, L. ult.

[q] Pand. lib. ii. tit. vii. De Religiosis et Sumptibus Funerum, 14, § 5.

[r] Pand. lib. xxviii. tit. vii. De Condition. Institutionum, L. 27.

[s] Voet, Comm. ad Pand. lib. xxviii. tit. vii. De Condit. Institutionum, num. 10.

[t] Pand. lib. xxxv. tit. i. De Conditionibus et Demonstrationibus, L. 75. Voet, Comm. ad Pand. lib. xxviii. tit. vii. num. 32.

[u] Pand. lib. xxxv. tit. i. De Conditionibus et Demonstrationibus, L. 1.

Nothing more is required of an heir or legatee under a potestative condition, than that he should do, or show himself willing to do, all that he can towards accomplishing it; and he is therefore discharged from the condition, if he be prevented from fulfilling it otherwise than by the act of the testator or his own.[x]

This doctrine arises from the liberal manner in which the will of the testator is construed by the Roman Law. This is reasonable and just, because the testator intended to benefit the heir or legatee, and it is impossible to look upon the accomplishment of the condition as a species of consideration, or *quid pro quo* in the nature of a bargain or contract, since the testator cannot be regarded in the light of a bargainer who acts with the sole or principal view of some advantage or emolument to himself. It may, therefore, very correctly be argued that if the performance of the condition be out of the power of the heir or legatee, the testator can hardly be presumed to intend to deprive of his bounty that person towards whom he must have been friendly or well-affected, upon the sole ground that he has been unsuccessful in his endeavours to accomplish the will of the deceased, or that, notwithstanding his good will to perform the condition, its performance is beyond his power.

This reasoning is particularly cogent in cases where the condition is slight, when compared to the benefit intended to be conferred by the testator: and it is also agreeable to the rule of Marcellus: *In re dubia benigniorem sententiam sequi non minus justius est quam tutius.*[y]

There are however cases where it is clear, that the testator had in view the strict accomplishment of the condition principally or solely. The intention of the testator is the rule to be observed, and therefore in such cases the heir or legatee cannot take unless he actually perform the condition.[z]

[x] Donelli Comment. Jur. Civil. lib. viii. cap. 34. But see Voet, Comm. ad Pand. lib. xxviii. tit. vii. De Condition. Institut. num. 19.

[y] Pand. lib. l. tit. ult. De Regul. Jur. L. 192, § 1.

[z] Pand. lib. xxxv. tit. i. De Conditionibus et Demonstrationibus, L. 84. Voet, Comm. ad Pand. lib. xxviii. tit. vii. num. 22.

CHAPTER XXIII.

THE LAW OF THINGS.—LEGACIES.

Of Legacies.—Instit. lib. ii. tit. xx. De Legatis, § 1—6, 9, 12, 16, 21—23, 29—31. —Definition of a Legacy.—Distinction between a Legacy and *Fideicommissum*, or a Trust.—Justinian's Law regarding both.—Bequest of Property of the Testator and of the Heir, and of a third party respectively, and of Mortgaged Property.—Legacy of Property of a third party, which becomes that of the Legatee after execution of the Testament.—Legacy of the Property of the Legatee to himself.—Cato's Rule.—Alienation of the Bequeathed Property by the Testator.—Destruction and Change of Condition of the Thing Bequeathed. —Legacies of Incorporeal Things.—Bequest of a Debt.—Bequest of a Specific Act.—Restraint on Alienation.—Right of Choice in Case of a general Legacy.—Bequest of an Option or Right of Choice.—Its Effect as to the Heir of the Legatee.—Distinction between a Legacy vested, but *solvendum in futuro*, and a Legacy not vested.—Effect of Erroneous Descriptions in Bequests.—Erroneous Reason or Motive of a Legacy. P. 148.

A LEGACY is not an acquisition *per universitatem*, and in that respect the subject of this chapter might be properly classed under the head of acquisitions of individual things. But as the Law of Legacies naturally arises out of that of testaments, it is placed by Justinian immediately after the titles of the Institutes containing the testamentary law; and with this chapter we return from the Pandects to the Institutes.

A legacy is defined by Justinian to be *a donation bequeathed by the deceased*, to be delivered *to the legatee by the heir*.[a]

The heir or the co-heirs, as the case may be, are by the Roman Law one person with the testator, and his representative in his whole estate. The heir therefore, or the co-heirs have imposed on them the obligation of delivering the legacy to the legatee. In the antient Roman Law a distinction was drawn between a legacy in direct terms giving the thing to the legatee, and a legacy in indirect words addressed to the heir, and making him a trustee to give the property to the legatee, which created a species of *fideicommissum* or trust. The former species of legacy arose from the Law of the Twelve Tables, and was subject to very technical and strict rules, while the latter was moulded by the equitable jurisdiction of the Prætor on a more rea-

[a] Instit. lib. ii. tit. xx. De Legatis, § 1. And see Pand. lib. xxx. Liber. ii. De Legatis, L. 36. Ibid. Liber i. De Legatis, L. 116.

sonable and liberal plan.[b] Justinian, without confounding legacies and trusts together, so far as they are expressions of two different intentions, subjected direct legacies, or legacies strictly so called, to the same equitable rules which governed *fideicommissa* or trusts, the chief of which consists in the liberal observance of the intention of the testator; and he at the same time gave to *fideicommissa* certain advantages as to legal enforcement (such, for instance, as a direct action for the thing itself, instead of an indirect one against the person of the heir) which previously belonged exclusively to direct legacies.[c] The title of the Institutes *De Legatis*, therefore, applies to both these kinds of testamentary dispositions, and the three books *De Legatis et Fideicommissis* which form the 30th, 31st and 32nd books of the Pandects treat promiscuously of direct legacies and testamentary trusts.

Justinian commences his exposition of the jurisprudence of legacies as follows, with a paragraph regarding things which are subjects of those dispositions.

Not only the property of the testator or of the heir, but that of a third party may *be bequeathed as a legacy, and the heir is in that case bound to purchase that property and deliver it to the legatee, or, if he be unable to do so, to pay an equivalent to him instead of the specific thing. But if the nature of the thing be such that it cannot possibly be given, because it is not in commercium, as for instance the Campus Martius, or a Basilica, no equivalent even is due to the legatee, for such a legacy is absolutely void.*

The position which we have laid down, that a bequest of the property of a third party is valid and effectual, must be understood as limited to the case in which the deceased was aware that the thing was the property of another, and does not apply to a case where he believed it to be his own. The reason of this distinction is, that probably if he had been aware that the thing belonged not to himself but to another, he would not have bequeathed it, and thus the Emperor Antoninus Pius decided by a rescript. And it is for him who claims, that is to say, the legatee, to prove that the testator was aware that the thing belonged to a third party, and not for the heir to prove him to have been ignorant of that fact. This is in conformity with the rule that the burthen of proof is laid on him who claims.[d]

All things corporeal and incorporeal, and acts as well as things strictly so called, may be the subject of legacies, except those which are incapable of being transferred at all, or of being transferred to the legatee. As to these the rule obtains, *Impossibilium nulla obligatio*

[b] Vinnii Comment. ad Instit. lib. ii. tit. xx. § 3.

[c] Instit. lib. ii. tit. xx. § 2, 3.

[d] Ibid. § 4.

est; and since the legacy produces no obligation upon the heir, it follows that he cannot be bound to give to the legatee any equivalent for the thing bequeathed.

The legacy of a thing belonging to the heir is evidently valid, since the heir has the power to give it to the legatee, and if he be unwilling to do so, he may decline to accept the inheritance. In like manner the heir has the power to purchase the property of a third party, and give it to the legatee unless that third party refuse to sell, in which case the bounty of the testator must not be defeated by such refusal, to the injury of the legatee and the emolument of the heir. The intentions of the testator must therefore be carried into effect so far as the circumstances will allow, by the legatee receiving the money which the testator virtually dedicated to the purchase of the thing bequeathed.

But if the testator made the bequest, believing the property to be his own, the law reasonably presumes that he would not have bequeathed it had he known it to belong to a third person.[e] And as it is the legatee who claims the legacy, he must show his title to it, and he therefore has the onus cast upon him of showing that the testator bequeathed it to him knowing it to belong to a third party. *Semper necessitas probandi incumbit illi qui agit.*[f] In a case of this nature it is most probable, *cæteris paribus,* that the testator believed the thing to be his own which he bequeathed; but by showing grounds for presuming the contrary, the legatee may cast the burthen of proof on the heir, for *Onus probandi transfertur in eum contra quem presumptio facit.*[g]

The Civil Law makes the following exception to the rule regarding an erroneous legacy of property to a third party:—

The Emperor Severus enacted that a bequest of the property of a third party should bind the heir to give either the thing itself or the price thereof, though the testator believed it to be his own, when the legatee is a person nearly related to the testator, such as his wife, or any other person to whom it must be presumed that he would have made the legacy, even had he known the property not to be his own.[h] Thus the law establishes a presumption destroying the ordinary presumption *Non legasset si scivisset alienam rem esse.*

The principles governing a legacy of the property of a third party are applicable also to a legacy of property subjected to a hypotheca-

[e] Pand. lib. xxxi. Liber ii. De Legatis, L. 67, § 8.

[f] And see Paulus, Pand. lib. xxii. tit. iii. De Probation. et Præsumption. L. 2. *Ei incumbit probatio qui dicit non qui negat.*

[g] Cujacii Recitat. Solemn. ad tit. Cod. De Probationibus, *paratit.* Cujac Op. tom. ix. col. 242. Pand. lib. xxii. tit. iii. De Probationibus et Præsumptionibus, L. 9.

[h] Cod. lib. vi. tit. xxxvii. De Legatis, L. 10.

tion or mortgage, which is, so far as the hypothecation extends, belonging to a third party,—namely, the mortgagee. In such cases the question to be decided is, whether the testator knew of the existence of the charge. If he did, the heir must redeem; if he did not, the heir is not bound to redeem, unless the legacy would be entirely illusory without such redemption, as where the property is charged up to its full value. In the latter case it is presumed that the testator would have intended the heir to redeem, had he known of the charge.[i]

When the property of a third party is bequeathed, it may so happen that it may become that of the legatee after the execution of the testament, and before or after[k] the death of the testator. If the legatee acquired the property by a *lucrative title*, such as a gift,—that is to say, without paying anything as consideration for it—the legacy is satisfied by anticipation; but if he acquired it by an *onerous title*, such as sale, for valuable consideration, he may recover from the heir what he gave for it, because, as Labeo says, *Videtur ei rem abesse cui pretium abest.*[l] The fundamental rule of law on which this decision is grounded, is that the debtor of a specific thing is set free from his obligation to deliver it, by its becoming the property of the creditor by a lucrative title, that is to say, without the creditor having given anything for it. But if the debtor received anything from the creditor as consideration for the thing, the latter may recover that consideration back.[m]

If a testator bequeath to a legatee property which already belongs to that legatee, the legacy is null and of no effect, because *Dominium non potest nisi ex una causa contingere.*[n] And such a legacy is void though the property has ceased to belong to the legatee at the time of the testator's death; for *Si ab initio non consistit legatum, ex post facto non convalescet.*[o] This is in accordance with the celebrated rule called Cato's rule, or the Catonian rule, which decides that what-

[i] Instit. lib. ii. tit. xx. § 5. Pand. lib. xxx. Liber i. De Legatis, L. 57.

[k] Vinnii Comm. ad Instit. lib. ii. tit. xx. § 6.

[l] Instit. ibid. § 6. Pand. lib. l. tit. penult. De Verbor. Signif. L. 14. See the converse in Pand. lib. l. tit. penult. De Signific. Verbor. L. 88.

[m] Pand. lib. xlvi. tit. iii. De Solutionibus, L. 61. *Quotiens id quod tibi debeam ad te pervenit, et nihil tibi abest, nec quod solutum est repeti possit, competit liberatio.* And see Pand. lib. xliv. tit. vii. De Obligationibus et Actionibus, L. 17. With regard to the proviso, *Nec quod solutum est repeti possit,* see Pand. lib. l. tit. penult. De Verbor. Signif. L. 71.

[n] Instit. ibid. § 9. Pand. lib. xli. tit. ii. De Acquir. vel Omit. Possess. L. 3, § 4.

[o] Instit. ibid. Pand, lib. xxx. Liber i. De Legatis, L. 41, § 2.

ever provision in a testament would be of no effect if the testator died at the time of executing the instrument, is void at whatever time he may die.[p] But this rule is not applicable to conditional provisions.

In the case of the alienation of property by the testator after he had executed a will bequeathing it as a legacy, the question to be decided is whether the testator intended such alienation to operate as a revocation of the legacy.[q] The general rule is, that a voluntary alienation raises a presumption of an intention to revoke; but an alienation of an opposite description, *ex necessitate rei familiaris*, or otherwise on compulsion, does not, and therefore leaves the heir liable to the legatee.[r]

A specific legacy is also revoked or extinguished by the destruction of the specific thing bequeathed, or its becoming such that it cannot be delivered to the legatee, provided such destruction or other ground of impossibility of delivery be not caused by the act of the heir.[s] This decision is governed by the general rule of the Civil Law that the debtor of a specific thing is freed from his obligation by that thing perishing. And a change in the thing whereby its delivery is rendered impossible, has the same legal effect as its perishing. But the debtor cannot defeat the creditor by his own act, and therefore if he by his own act render the specific performance of his own obligation impossible, he must pay an equivalent to the creditor. These principles apply to specific legacies, because the heir is the debtor of the legatee.[t]

Having thus explained some of the more interesting among the innumerable rules of the Civil Law respecting legacies of corporeal things, we will proceed to consider legacies of incorporeal things.

Not only corporeal but incorporeal things may be bequeathed: and what is owing to the deceased may be the subject of a legacy, so that the heir is bound to assign to the legatee his right of action, unless the testator demanded or received payment of the debt during his lifetime. In such case the legacy is extinguished. A legacy in the nature of the following examples would also be valid: I require my heir to repair the house of such a person, or to release, or to pay his debts.[u]

Ulpian says, *Et corpora legari omnia et jura possunt.*[x] And here we have three examples of legacies of the latter description.

With regard to the first (the bequest of a debt due to the testator),

[p] Pand. lib. xxxiv. tit. vii. De Regul. Caton. L. 1. [q] Instit. ibid. § 12.

[r] Pand. lib. xxxiv. tit. iv. De Adimendis Legatis, L. 18. And see Pand. lib. xxxii. Liber iii. De Legatis et Fideicommiss. L. 11, § 12. [s] Instit. ibid. § 16.

[t] Voet, Comm. ad Pand. tit. unic. De Legatis, num. 53.

[u] Instit. lib. ii. tit. xx. § 21.

[x] Pand. lib. xxx. Liber i. De Legatis et Fideicommiss. L. 41.

Justinian, by a constitution to be found in the Code, rendered unnecessary the assignment of the right of action by the heir to the legatee.[y] If the testator receive, or even demand[z] payment of the debt, it is presumed that the testator did so with an intention to revoke the legacy, but the legatee may show that there was not such intention, and thereby make a good title to the legacy.[a]

The other two examples given above show that the performance of a specific act as well as a specific thing, may be bequeathed by the Civil Law,[b] and a negative act may be the subject of a bequest. Thus an estate may be bequeathed with a prohibition to alienate it, provided a reason be assigned for such prohibition, and provided it be for the benefit of some specific person. And it is of no effect as against creditors of the legatee.[c] Having thus considered specific legacies, that is to say, legacies of specified things, we will proceed to the subject of general legacies, or bequests of things not specified, or things in *general.*

If either a slave or any other thing be bequeathed without specifying any particular individual slave or other thing, the legatee has the choice unless the testator expresses a contrary intention.[d]

The rule of the Roman Law in cases of this description is, that the choice is not arbitrary, for if it be vested in the legatee, he must not choose the best; and if it be vested in the heir, the latter must not choose the worst of the kind of thing, which is bequeathed. *Legato generaliter relicto observandum est ne optimus vel pessimus accipiatur.*[e]

The testator may expressly bequeath an option or a right of choice of one or more out of several things belonging to him, and by a law of Justinian this right passes to the heir of the legatee if he die without exercising it.[f]

Testamentary provisions are always held to be of a personal nature, and consequently if the person named by the testator do not survive him, the provision is *caducum* or lapsed, unless it be acquired by survivorship (*jure accrescendi*) between joint legatees.[g]

Upon the same principle, the heir of the person named by the testator cannot benefit by the accomplishment of a condition, nor by

[y] Cod. lib. vi. tit. xxxvii. De Legatis, L. 18.

[z] Pand. lib. xxx. Liber i. De Legat. et Fideicom. L. 72, § 2. Pand. lib. xxxiv. tit. iii. De Liberatione Legata, L. 21.

[a] Pand. lib. xxxiv. tit. iv. De Adimendis Legatis, L. penult.

[b] See Pand. lib. xxxii. Liber iii. De Legat. et Fideicom.

[c] Pand. lib. xxxi. Liber ii. De Legatis et Fideicom. L. 69, § 3. Pand. lib. xxx. Liber i. De Leg. et Fideicom. L. 114, § 15, § 14.

[d] Instit. lib. ii. tit. xx. § 22.

[e] Pand. lib. xxx. Liber i. De Legatis et Fideicom. L. 37.

[f] Instit. ibid. § 23.

[g] As to the *Jus accrescendi*, see Instit. lib. ii. tit. xx. § 8, and the Comm. of Vinnius thereon.

the expiration of a term limited in such a manner that the legacy may never become vested during the lifetime of the legatee.[h]

Thus a legacy to Titius, *when he reaches twenty-five years of age*, is not vested, for he may never reach that age ; but a legacy to Titius *to be paid* upon his reaching that age, suspends the payment only, and not the legacy, and is the same as if the testator had said, *payable in so many years ;* therefore the right to such a legacy is transmissible to the heirs of the legatee. In short, the general rule is that the legacy is not transmissible unless, to use the words of Pomponius, *Dies cessit vivo testatore.*[i] Pomponias says, *dies cessit*, which signifies not that the legacy is actually payable, which is expressed by the term, *dies venit, but that it is so vested in the legatee*, that it must at a future time become payable. *Certum est debitum iri.*

But the legatee cannot transmit to his heir a contingent interest, which the civilians call *spes debitum iri.*

An opinion prevailed that on these principles a legatee to whom an option or right of choice was bequeathed, could not transmit it to his heir, because it was held to be subject to the condition, *si legatarius optasset.* But Justinian very correctly settled the law contrary to that opinion, for in all cases where a condition may be implied upon the sole ground that the possession of the legacy cannot be obtained by a direct demand, it is only the payment and not the right that is suspended. *Dies non venit, verum dies cessit.* Thus Papinian says, *Conditiones extrinsecus non ex testamento venientes, id est quæ tacite inesse videntur, non faciunt legata conditionalia.*[k] Such legacies are not strictly conditional, for the apparent condition arises from the mode of the legacy, *extrinsecus non ex testamento*, and do not indicate any intention on the part of the testator to suspend the rights of the legatee so as to render them contingent.

With regard to the mode in which a bequest is expressed, the Civil Law holds it valid notwithstanding an error in the name or surname of the legatee, provided it appear who the testator meant to designate, because the purpose of names is to designate persons, and if the latter are known, their names are of no importance.[l] And the same principle obtains with regard to an error in the description or designation of a thing bequeathed : *Falsa demonstratio legatum non perimit.*[m] And so liberal is the construction of wills by the Roman Law, that the

[h] Pand. lib. xxxv. tit. i. De Conditionibus et Demonstrationibus, L. 1.

[i] Pand. ibid.

[k] Ibid. L. 99.

[l] Instit. lib. ii. tit. xx. § 29. Pand. lib. xxxiii. tit. iv. De Dote Prælegata, L. 1, § 8. *Quidquid demonstrandæ rei additur satis demonstratæ frustra est.*

[m] Instit. ibid. § 30. Hence the maxim, *Nil facit error nominis, si de corpore constat.*

erroneousness of a statement appended to a bequest, expressing the motive or reason inducing the testator to bestow the legacy, does not render the bequest void, unless it appear that without that motive or reason he would not have given it, as for instance, where the motive is expressed as a condition.[n]

Justinian devotes a separate title to the subject of the revocation and translation of legacies. It is entitled *De Ademptione et Translatione Legatorum.*[o] The first of these subjects has already been sufficiently explained, and questions arising on the second depend solely on the intentions of the testator, and present no general principle requiring explanation here, having regard to the plan of this treatise.

CHAPTER XXIV.

OF THE FALCIDIAN LAW.

Of the Falcidian Law.—Instit. lib. ii. tit. xxii. De Lege Falcidia.—Effect of the Lex Falcidia.—Mode of taking the Falcidian Fourth.—Payment of Debts.—Contribution of Legacies.—Distinction between Specific and General Legacies.—The Falcidian Fourth taken from both kinds of Legacies. P. 150.

Under the antient Roman Law founded on the Law of the Twelve Tables, the power of bequeathing legacies was unlimited. The Lex Furia and the Lex Voconia restricted this power. But those laws having been found ineffectual, the Lex Falcidia, a Plebiscitum deriving its name from Publius Falcidius a Tribune of the people in the time of Augustus, was enacted. That law restrained testators from bequeathing legacies amounting to above the value of three-fourths of the inheritance, and secured to the heir, or the co-heirs together, one-fourth of the estate.[a]

That fourth to which the heir or the co-heirs is or are entitled is taken from the estate in the following manner:—First, the debts and funeral expenses of the deceased, and any sums he may have left to manumit

[n] Instit. ibid. § 31. Pand. lib. xxxv. tit. i. De Condition. et Demonstrationibus, L. 17, § 2, 3. Ibid. L. 72, § 6. *Falsam causam legato non obesse verius est; quia ratio legandi legato non cohæret.* Pothier, Tr. des Testam. chap. 2, § 3.

[o] Instit. lib. ii. tit. xxi. Voet, Comm. ad Pand. lib. xxxiv. tit. iv. De Adimendis vel Transferendis Legatis, vel Fideicommissis.

[a] Instit. lib. ii. tit. xxii. princip.

slaves, must be deducted. Then the Falcidian fourth is taken out of the residue, and afterwards the remaining three-fourths of such residue is distributed *pro rata*, or proportionably among the legatees. The debts must be paid first, because the Civil Law holds that which the deceased owes not to be part of his property. *Bona intelligiuntur cujusque quæ deducto œre alieno supersunt.*[b] Thus, if the estate be insolvent, the legacies are not due.[c]

All the legacies do not contribute in the same manner, nor in every case, to the payment of the debts. Thus, specific legacies, that is to say, legacies of specific things, do not become subject to payment of the debts, unless the remainder of the estate be insufficient.[d] The reason of this is, that those specific things are separated from the estate by the testator, and become, by his death, the property of the respective legatees, who are therefore not bound to contribute to the payment of the debts, unless the creditors be unable to obtain full payment out of the corpus of the estate, which is primarily liable to the debts, according to the rule, *Æs alienum, universi patrimonii non singularum rerum onus est.*

The testator must, on the other hand, be presumed to have intended, where he gave no specific thing to a legatee, that the legatee should be paid out of the residue of the estate, after the separation of the things specifically bequeathed from the corpus of the inheritance. This intention implies a tacit condition that the general legacies shall be paid if and so far as the estate is sufficient to do so after the specific legacies have been paid. In this respect specific legacies and general legacies differ materially. But on the other hand, specific legacies are liable to be extinguished by the thing which is their object perishing, or otherwise becoming incapable of being given.

The Falcidian one-fourth, however, is deducted from the whole estate of the testator remaining, after payment of the debts, for the law expressly requires it to be one-fourth *omnium bonorum*, and those words apply to both species of legacies.[e]

As for the payment of funeral expenses, and the costs of freeing slaves, the first is held to be a debt of the deceased, and one, indeed, which ought to be paid, for reasons of public decency, before any other, and the second is a highly privileged legacy, because of the very peculiar and invariable favour with which the Civil Law looks upon the emancipation of slaves.

[b] Pand. lib. l. tit. penult. De Signif. Verbor. L. 39, § 1.

[c] Pand. lib. xlii. tit. viii. Quæ in Fraud. Creditorum facta sunt, ut restituantur, L. 23.

[d] Pothier, Des Testaments, chap. 4, § 5.

[e] Ibid.

CHAPTER XXV.

THE LAW OF THINGS.—FIDEICOMMISSARY INHERITANCES AND LEGACIES.

Fideicommissary Inheritances and Legacies.—Instit. lib. ii. tit. xxiii. De Fideicommissaris Hæreditatibus; tit. xxiv. De Singulis Rebus per Fideicommissum Relictis.—Definition of a Fideicommissum.—Difference between a Fideicommissum and a Substitution.—Fideicommissary Substitutions.—Origin and Legal Establishment of Fideicommissa.—The 159th Novell of Justinian not a Law restricting Fideicommissary Substitutions.—Restrictions adopted in Modern Times.—Registration.—The Trebellian and Pegasian Senatusconsulta.—Fideicommissa constituted by act *inter vivos*.—The Statute De Donis and Conditional Fees at Common Law.—Analogy of the English and the Roman Law.—The Extinction of Fideicommissa.—Use of a discretionary Power to break Fideicommissary Substitutions or Entails.—Protectors of Settlements under Stat. 3 & 4 Will. IV. cap. 74.—Sir E. Sugden's Remarks on their Powers.—Individual Things and Moveables subject to Fideicommissum by the Roman Law as well as Inheritances and Immoveables. P. 155.

All inheritances and legacies are either direct, or indirect, that is to say, *fideicommissary*, which species of disposition is very neatly defined by Vinnius as follows: *Fideicommissum est id omne de quo quis suprema defuncti voluntate rogatus est ut daret vel faceret.* A fideicommissum is constituted by *precative words*, that is to say, in the form of a request to the person to whom the property is first bequeathed or who is first appointed heir, to transmit it to some other person designated by the testator. Hence the difference appears between substitutions and fideicommissa, for in the former the substitute succeeds in default of the instituted heir, and each substitute after the first succeeds in default of the one who was named before him, whereas in the latter the fideicommissary takes, and then transmits the inheritance to the person designated to receive it. Thus the former is a direct and the latter an indirect inheritance.

But every fideicommissum is a species of substitution, though it differs from a substitution strictly so called inasmuch as it is an obligation or trust imposed on a person, binding him to give or to do something to or for another. And one person may be substituted to another by fideicommissum, so that the second should receive the property after its having been enjoyed even during life by the other.

In the same manner that one person may be requested to transmit the property to another, the second may be made a trustee for a third, and again the third for a fourth, and so on to any number of substitutes. And as alienation by any of the fideicommissaries is a breach of trust, this species of disposal of property produces something resembling what an entail was in the English Law, before any means were invented to break entails. But this analogy did not exist until a legal remedy was provided to enforce the obligations of the *fiduciarius* or *trustee.*

In former times (says Justinian) *all fideicommissa were ineffectual, because no one was compellable to execute the trust vested in him: for inheritances were transmitted to persons who could not validly be made heirs, by desiring others who were capable, to transfer the inheritance to them. These species of inheritances were called fideicommissa, because they were sanctioned by no bond of law, but only rested upon the honour and conscience of those to whom the request was addressed. The Emperor Augustus, however, influenced by a desire to favour persons placed in certain situations, or because a solemn adjuration was directed to him by testators, or indignant at the gross breach of faith of which some persons were guilty, ordered the Consuls to interpose their authority in these matters. And as this was both just and popular, there soon arose a permanent jurisdiction in matters of trust, and that jurisdiction became so great a favourite that a Prætor was appointed to decide upon matters of fideicommissum, who was called Prætor Fideicommissarius.*[a]

Fideicommissa were invented in Rome for the same general purpose for which uses were devised in England; that is to say, to evade the law. In Rome this evasion was very beneficial, because of the numerous and merely technical and unnecessary, and therefore unjust disqualifications of persons who were not permitted by the antient *Jus Civile* to be heirs.

This is an example of a curious fact to be found in the history of almost every system of legislation, namely, that the legislature does not keep pace with the innovations of time, nor with the growth and changes of the wants of the people, and that it would consequently be difficult to point out many instances of a bad or inconvenient or obsolete law that has not been evaded long before it was abrogated or amended. The ingenious contrivance of the action of ejectment in the English Law, is an instance of the evasion of the cumbersome forms of a complicated art, which under the specious pretence of providing a remedy for every possible wrong, threw great obstacles in the way of their redress, by rendering it a matter of difficulty in many cases to discover, not indeed the redress promised by the law, but the means provided for its attainment. Many other

[a] Instit. lib. ii. tit. xxiii. § 1.

instances could be given of reforms, or at least changes which have been effected indirectly by means of fictions and contrivances, because they could not be obtained from the legislature.

Justinian, in explaining the unprotected state of fiduciary rights, points out the difference between a legal or civil, and a mere natural or equitable right. *Ideo fideicommissa appellata sunt quia nullo vinculo juris, sed tantum pudore eorum qui rogabantur continebatur.* From the legal sanction given by the Emperor Augustus to fideicommissa, arose fideicommissary substitutions, which by restraining alienation made a very serious inroad upon the simplicity of the Roman Law. They consisted in the appointment of several persons, to take successively, so that none of them could alienate except the last.

It has been supposed that Justinian, by the 159th Novell, restricted fideicommissary substitutions to four degrees;[b] but that celebrated law was framed to provide for the case of a particular family, so that it cannot be interpreted to operate as a general law.

But in almost every country on the continent of Europe substitutions were limited by the policy of the modern civilians, who soon discovered the evils caused by entrusting so large a power to the hands of a private citizen as that of making his property inalienable in a particular line of succession established by himself, thereby rendering it less beneficial, not only to the public, but to his heirs themselves.

These restrictions of the power of alienating were not in every case effectual, and they are, with one exception, abolished by the French Code, on grounds of public policy.[c] The inconveniences of these substitutions were materially diminished in many parts of Europe, but especially in France, by the registration of instruments containing them. That precaution prevented secret substitutions, which might have been used for fraudulent purposes.

After the legal establishment of fideicommissa by Augustus, the Trebellian and Pegasian Senatusconsulta made important improvements in that branch of law.

The Trebellian Senatusconsultum, which derived its name from Trebellius Maximus, who was Consul together with Seneca in the time of Nero, enabled the Prætor to render directly liable to the charges on the estate the fideicommissarius, who had the benefit of the inheritance, and to exonerate the fiduciary heir.[d] That enactment was followed by

[b] Co. Litt. 191 a, note 1.

[c] French Code Civil, art. 896. By art. 1048, fathers and mothers may give property to one or more of their children, subject to the obligation of transmitting it to the children born or to be born of the settlers in the first degree only. And see Merlin, Repertoire, tom. xvi. p. 507.

[d] Instit. lib. ii. tit. xxiii. De Fid. Hæred. § 4.

the Pegasian Senatusconsultum, which extended the principles of the Falcidian Law to fideicommissa, thereby enabling the fiduciary heir to deduct for his own benefit one fourth part of the clear inheritance, before transmitting it according to the directions of the deceased.[e]

Justinian consolidated these laws together under the name of *Senatusconsultum Trebellianum*, whereby he provided for the apportionment of the charges on the estate between the fiduciary and the fideicommissary, and otherwise simplified and improved the law.

Fideicommissa may be constituted not only by testament and codicil, but by act *inter vivos*, which was most frequently by donation and dotal contracts. But when constituted by act *inter vivos*, they affect only the person of the fiduciary and not the property itself, unless the instrument containing them be registered.[f]

The mention of donations naturally suggests the subject of the English statute, *De Donis Conditionalibus*, and conditional fees at Common Law. Those estates were called conditional by reason of the condition expressed or implied in the donation, that if the donee died without heirs entitled to take it, the land should revert to the donor, and it was held at Common Law that the donee acquired full power over the property immediately on his having issue.[g] It is remarkable that precisely the same case and decision are to be found in the Roman Law of fideicommissary donations. The rule of the Civil Law in these cases is that *Qui sunt in conditione positi, non censentur in testamento vocati*, and that rule is applied as well to acts *inter vivos*, as to testaments, upon the ground given by Blackstone, namely, that the condition had a suspensive effect, and that its performance by birth of issue rendered the estate of the donee absolute.[h] The rule of the Civil Law has a more extensive effect than the similar principle of the Common Law, for by the former the performance of the condition extinguished the fideicommissum, but by the latter the heir succeeded under the qualifications of the conditional fee if the donee died without having taken advantage of the performance of the condition by alienating or otherwise disposed of the estate. But this peculiarity of the Common Law proceeded from the nature of feuds, which generally follow the rule of succession limited in their investiture, and it does not destroy the resemblance of the Common Law before the Statute de Donis to the Civil Law.

We have next to consider the extinction of fideicommissa.

[e] Instit. lib. ii. tit. xxiii. De Fid. Hæred. § 5.

[f] Voet, Comm. ad Pand. lib. xxxvi. tit. i. Ad Senatuscon. Trebell. num. 9.

[g] Blackst. Comm. book ii. chap. vii.

[h] Voet, Comm. ad Pand. lib. xxviii. tit. ii. De Liberis et Postliminis Hæredibus Instituendis, num. 9.

No fideicommissum is good against the creditors of him who creates it, nor even against his legatees, nor against the fisc or treasury.[i] Secondly, the restriction upon alienation does not prevent the dotation of daughters of the fideicommissary out of the estate. Thirdly, if all the persons having an interest in the fideicommissum consent to the alienation, the fideicommissum is avoided, and the alienation good.[k]

This important decision arises from the principle that the cause of a restraint on alienation must be clearly specified, and also the persons for whose benefit it is designed, otherwise it is *nudum præceptum*, and of no effect.[l] Thus the restraint is rendered personal: consequently it may be done away with by the persons for whose benefit it was designed.[m] Fourthly, it is presumed, unless the testator very clearly expressed a contrary intention, that the duration of the restraint is limited to four degrees, including the testator himself. Consequently, after four degrees, the fideicommissum is extinguished unless a contrary intention of the settler be clearly shown.[n] Fifthly, a fideicommissum may be extinguished by the dispensation of the sovereign upon good and sufficient grounds being shown, such as poverty or other necessities of the parties holding the property. There are indeed very high authorities among the modern civilians, who hold that in such cases a licence to alienate is unnecessary, and that the settler must be presumed not to have intended to place his family in difficulties, but to benefit them by binding them with a settlement, and that therefore when circumstances arise rendering the restraint on alienation prejudicial to their interests, he must be presumed to intend that restraint to cease.[o] This doctrine, applied as it was in Holland by a high court, would have the effect of placing property, subject to fideicommissary substitution, in a condition analogous to that of the immoveables of minors, which, by the Civil Law, cannot be alienated without a decree on good cause being shown for such alienation. Now assuming that restraints on alienation are in some cases beneficial, it may be argued that those restraints should not be broken (as in the old English Law by fine or recovery) at the discretion of the tenant in tail and at any time, but they should be relaxed only in those cases in which the restraint is prejudicial, instead of being

[i] Voet, Comm. ad Pand. lib. xxxvi. tit. i. Ad Senatuscon. Trebell. num. 62.

[k] Pand. lib. xxx. Liber i. De Legatis, L. 121, § 1. Cod. lib. vi. tit. xlii. De Fideicommiss. L. 11.

[l] Pand. lib. xxx. Liber i. De Legatis, L. 114, § 14. Pand. lib. xxxii. Liber iii. De Legatis, L. 93.

[m] See the rule in Pand. lib. iv. tit. iv. De Minoribus, L. 41.

[n] Voet, Comment. ad Pand. lib. xxxvi. tit. i. Ad Senatuscons. Trebellianum, num. 33.

[o] Voet, Comment. ad Pand. ibid. num. 70.

beneficial to the family for which it was imposed. The principle of vesting somewhere a discretionary power of permitting, or not, the alienation of property subject to a restriction of the power of alienation, has been adopted by the legislature in the stat. 3 & 4 Will. IV. ch. 74, which makes a protector of every settlement, without whose concurrence the estate cannot be alienated, nor the entail barred.

Sir Edward Sugden, however, shows that the power vested in the protector (which continues even after he has alienated the estate which he held under the settlement) is unwise, as being arbitrary and uncontrolled.[p] It may therefore deserve consideration whether the protector ought not to be required to act under the control of a court of equity, and whether he should not be subject to removal by such court in certain cases.

The Roman Law does not restrict fideicommissa to immoveable property, nor to entire inheritances. Individual things, such as land, silver, clothes, or money, may be bequeathed by way of fideicommissum, and either the heir or a legatee may be made a trustee to deliver them to the fideicommissary.[q]

Having thus given a sketch of the Law of Fideicommissa, we will proceed in the next chapter to the subject of codicils.

CHAPTER XXVI.

THE LAW OF THINGS.—CODICILS.

Of Codicils.—Instit. lib. ii. tit. xxv. De Codicillis.—Origin and History of Codicils.—Definition.—Execution of Codicils. P. 156.

Codicils were chiefly intended to mitigate the strictness of the antient Roman Law, which required, for the validity of a testament, the attestation of seven Roman citizens, *omni exceptione majores.* In its origin a codicil was no more than a letter addressed to the person to whom or (in the case of fideicommissa) through whom the testator desired to bequeath something. A legacy could be bequeathed, but an heir could not be appointed directly by codicil, though he might be made indirectly, that is to say, by way of fideicommissum. Thus

[p] Sugd. Vendor and Purch. vol. ii. p. 301.

[q] Instit. lib. ii. tit. xxiv. De Singulis Rebus per Fideicom. Relict. princip.

codicils were either substitutes for or supplementary additions to testaments.

The history of the rise of this species of disposition is as follows :—Lucius Lentulus dying in Africa, left codicils, confirmed by anticipation in a will of earlier date, and in those codicils requested the Emperor Augustus, by way of fideicommissum, to do something therein expressed. Augustus carried this will into effect, and the daughter of Lentulus paid legacies which she could not legally have been compelled to pay. Other persons executed similar fideicommissa. The Emperor then convoked an assembly of the learned (among whom was the celebrated Trebatius), and asked them whether the practice could be sanctioned consistently with the principles and policy of the law. And they advised him to declare that the practice in question was very useful and even necessary to the citizens, on account of the long journeys frequently undertaken at that time, that they might execute codicils where it would be impossible to make a testament. Afterwards, Labeo having executed codicils, no one entertained any doubt but those instruments were invested with the fullest legality.[a]

A codicil is a less solemn last will either of a testator or of an intestate. It is, therefore, either a substitute for or a supplement to a testament.[b] Thus, by the Roman Law, where there are codicils and a testament, the former in a manner derive their validity from the other, of which they are held to be a part, and the avoidance of the testament makes the codicils void.[c] But by the modern Dutch Civil Law, an heir may be made directly by codicil, and a codicil does not depend for its validity on the validity of the testament.[d]

Justinian lays it down that codicils require no solemnities of form or execution;[e] but this rule applies only to those which are confirmed by testament. And no codicil is valid that is not simultaneously attested by five witnesses, or by two witnesses and a notary. In the case of a nuncupative codicil, the presence of the same number of witnesses is required.[f]

These general rules must suffice for the purpose of this treatise, as the law of different countries varies respecting the mode of executing testaments and codicils. Codicils are unknown to the modern French Law.

[a] Instit. lib. ii. tit. xxv. De Codicillis, princip.

[b] Ibid. § 1. Voet ad Pand. lib. xxix. tit. vii. De Jure Codicillorum, num 1.

[c] Pand. ibid. L. 3, § ult.

[d] Voet, Comm. ad Pand. ibid. num. 5.

[e] Instit. ibid. § ult.

[f] Domat, L. Civil. liv. iv. tit. i. § 1, 2. Vinnii Comm. ad Instit. hoc tit. num. 3. Voet, Comm. ad Pand. lib. xxix. tit. vii. num. 1. Cod. lib. vi. tit. xxvi. L. ultim.

CHAPTER XXVII.

THE LAW OF THINGS.—INHERITANCE AB INTESTATO.

Inheritances *ab Intestato.*—Instit. lib. iii. tit. i. De Hæreditatibus quæ ab Intestato Deferuntur.—Definition of Intestacy and of Succession *ab Intestato.*—Origin and Foundation of the Right of Inheritance.—Its general Principles.—Roman Law of Inheritance.—The 118th Novell.—DESCENDANTS.—Right of Representation.—Succession *per Capita* and *per Stirpes.*—Posthumous Children.—Presumption of Legitimacy.—Period of Gestation.—ASCENDANTS.—Succession of Brothers and Sisters and their Descendants, with Ascendants. — COLLATERALS. — Right of Representation. — Husband and Wife. — Mode of reckoning Degrees of Kindred in the Civil Law.—*Agnati* and *Cognati.*—Affinity. —Kindred by the Canon Law.—*Collatio Bonorum.*—English Statute of Distributions. P. 166.

THE first species of acquisitions *per universitatem*, that is to say, Testamentary Inheritances, having been explained, the second, namely, successions by appointment, not of the deceased but of the law only, remain to be considered.

The portion of the Institutes relating to this subject is very intricate, and somewhat difficult, because it contains many details of obsolete law, and the modes whereby the equity of the Prætor mitigated the severity of the antient Roman jurisprudence, as well as the enactments which brought the rules of succession into a more reasonable and less artificial state. To Justinian is due the honour of having superseded this mass of legislation, and reduced this branch of the Civil Law to simple and consistent rules, which have been more or less imitated by every civilized nation in Europe.

Justinian's law of inheritance will, therefore, be the principal subject of this chapter, which is divided into four parts. In the first, intestacy is defined; the second contains the explanation of the rules of succession; the third relates to the rules of consanguinity and affinity; and the fourth gives a sketch of the law of *Collatio bonorum*, by which, to produce equality in the division of inheritances, those heirs who have received any part of the inheritance during the lifetime of the deceased, are required to reckon that part as a portion of their lawful share on the division of the inheritance.

And first, Justinian thus defines intestacy. *That man is intestate who either executed no will, or whose will is void; or whose will, though valid at its execution, was avoided subsequently, or is of no effect for want of an heir.*[a] It follows that inheritance or succession

[a] Instit. lib. iii. tit. i. princip.

ab intestato is that which arises by appointment of the law alone, that is to say, where there is no heir appointed by the deceased, or at least none validly or effectually so appointed. Secondly, the rules of succession *ab intestato*, or by force of the law alone, are to be considered.

We have already seen that the great civilian, Domat, classifies all law under two heads, namely, *obligations* by which civil society is kept together and its purposes are furthered for the welfare, both physical and mental, of mankind, and *successions*, whereby those obligations are perpetuated, and without which, therefore, civil society would last no more than during a single generation, and thus the shortness of human life would render it impossible that mankind should derive full benefit either from the institutions of the social order, or from the industry of individuals.[b]

It has already been shown that the institution of property is part of the secondary law of nature, because without it the social order which man is bound to cultivate could not be maintained; and because exclusive appropriation is necessary for the full enjoyment of most of those things which are designed for the use of man.

These doctrines lead to the conclusion that the law of succession, without which the institution of property could not be perpetuated, and without which every transaction would either remain incomplete or terminate by the death of one or more of the parties, must be part of the secondary natural law, whereby men are bound to all the consequences of those institutions, which are necessary or expedient for the welfare of mankind.

But the question is, in what manner are these principles to be carried into effect? The political and economical views of legislators, and perhaps still more, the struggles of different interests, and those hidden causes which produce events and institutions, and which under the name of chance often give to their offspring an appearance of prevision and wisdom which exercises the ingenuity and excites the admiration of succeeding ages, have applied the hereditary principle with a vast diversity of modifications. But the natural principles of the transmissibility of rights and obligations by descent lie within a small compass.

It is natural that men should be succeeded in their property by those who are so nearly connected with them in blood that to provide for and benefit such heirs is the duty and ought to be the wish of the deceased. In default of such near relations, a natural presumption may be followed, which is grounded on the probability that the

[b] Domat, Loix Civiles, Traité des Loix, chap. vii.

deceased is desirous rather to benefit those who are connected with him by affinity than any others; and this presumption is sufficient to justify a rule in itself useful and unobjectionable, and than which one more solidly founded on natural reason has not yet been discovered for the purpose for which it is intended.

Where no persons are found so connected with the deceased, or their connection is one which, from motives of legal policy or morality, is reprobated by the law, it is most advisable to avoid the contention and disorder arising from the vacancy of property by appointing an *ultimus hæres*, who cannot well be any other than some public authority, whose claim must, in a case of this nature, have greater weight than that of any private member of society.

One chief use of the testamentary power is to supply the want of a person designated by the law to take the place of the deceased: but that power is extended in all countries where it exists, so far as to supersede the appointment of the law. Thus the testamentary power is a compliment of, and a substitute for, the law of inheritance.

But the rights acquired by persons who have dealt with the deceased during his lifetime, must be superior to those of the heir, because *qui prior est tempore potior est jure:* and the transmissibility of property by descent would be deprived of much of its utility unless not only rights were transmitted, but the obligations also which are deductions from and diminutions of those rights.[c]

On these grounds, the Roman Law holds that the heir represents the person of the deceased, and the application of that rule to heirs *ab intestato,* and to heirs appointed by the deceased, is similar.

Having sketched out the general theory of successions by hereditary descent, we will proceed to the enactments of the 118th Novell of Justinian, which contains the Roman Law of inheritance.

That celebrated constitution is framed with the sole view to distribute the property among those whom the testator may be presumed to have wished to benefit.

On this principle the lines of succession are divided into three, which rank among themselves in the following order: 1st, Descendants; 2ndly, Ascendants; and 3rdly, Collaterals. And first of descendants.

Descendants are the children of the person from whom the descent is reckoned, and their descendants *in infinitum:* and they are preferred by Justinian to the two other lines. Descendants succeed without any distinction as to their proximity to the deceased. Thus grandchildren succeed, together with their uncles and aunts, children

[c] Pufendorf, Droit de la Nature et des Gens, liv. iv. chap. x. xi. Grotius, Droit de la Guerre et de la Paix, liv. ii. chap. vii.

of the deceased. This is by what is called the right of representation, which may be defined to be the succession of one or more persons to the right which another would have succeeded to if he had been living. It is thus explained by Grotius. As it is usual that a father and mother should take care of their children, the grandfather and grandmother are not held to be bound to maintain their grandchildren during the life of the parents. But when the father and mother, or one of them die, it is just that the grandfather and grandmother should provide for their grandchildren in the place and stead of their deceased son or daughter, and it is the same with regard to more distant ascendants. Hence comes the right by virtue of which a grandson succeeds in the place of the son, as Ulpian says. Modern jurists call this succession *per stirpes*, the right of representation.[d] This species of succession, by representation, is called succession *in stirpes*, because the number of the individuals is not considered, but they are all held to represent the one person in whose place and stead they take.

This is a consequence of the following rule of descent. The nearest descendants of the deceased exclude their own descendants, that is to say, those who are more distant in the same descending line from the deceased. The reason of this is that the more distant descendants succeed in process of time to those who are nearer in the same line, and the former are therefore not allowed to share the inheritance of the ancestor during the lifetime of his immediate descendants, their ancestors.

This being admitted, it would not be reasonable that the surviving sons, for instance, should share the inheritance equally with the children of a deceased son, otherwise the death of one of the immediate descendants of an intestate would prejudice the others, and the children of the surviving sons would be less favourably treated than the children of the deceased son; for the former would take on the death of their father no more than his share, as if they had taken *per stirpes*, while the latter would succeed *per capita* on an equal footing with the children of the deceased.

Thus the children of the intestate succeed to equal individual shares, or *per capita;* and their descendants, if such descendants survive the persons who stand between them and the deceased, and are thereby next to him at the time of his death, succeed by representation or *per stirpes*, to what their ancestor would have taken if he had been living. And they share that portion of the inheritance among them-

[d] Grot. Droit de la Guerre et de la Paix, liv. ii. chap. vii. § 6. Pand. lib. i. tit. vi. De His qui Sui vel Alieni Juris sunt, L. 7. Instit. lib. iii. tit. i. § 6.

selves equally or *per capita*, which they take as a line by right of representation.

If there are none but descendants in the same degree of proximity to the intestate, they all share alike or *per capita*.

The 118th Novell makes no distinction as to the nature of the property to be inherited, nor with reference to the sex or age of the persons to whom or through whom the inheritance falls.

As for posthumous children, the reasonable rule of Paulus is followed, *Qui nasci speratur, pro superstite est.*[e]

But no posthumous child is admitted to succeed, in favour of whom the presumption of legitimacy does not exist. Spurious children or bastards are those who cannot show a father, or who cannot show a lawful father.[f] Now wherever there is a marriage, the law presumes the children of the wife to be the children of the husband. *Pater is est quem justæ nuptiæ demonstrant, quidquid in contrarium vir et uxor dixerint.*[g] Nothing will destroy that presumption of legitimacy during the marriage, except evidence showing clearly the impossibility of the conclusion to which it leads. But when the marriage is at an end, the presumption continues no longer than the extreme period of gestation, reckoned from the latest time when the possibility existed on which the presumption of legitimacy is founded.

The modern Civil Law wisely fixes no invariable limit for the *justum tempus pariendi*. Paulus decides on the authority of Hippocrates, which was also followed by the Emperor Antoninus Pius, that seven months or 282 days are sufficient for the production of a perfect human animal,[h] and Ulpian lays it down on the other hand, that *Post decem menses natus, non admittitur ad legitimam hæreditatem.*[i] This rule, however, as it is only grounded on a presumption arising from what usually occurs, may be departed from by the discretionary power of the judge, having regard to the opinions of the learned, and the circumstances of the case.[k]

This equitable modification of the strict rule of Ulpian is grounded on the principle of a law of Justinian, which says in a case where

[e] Pand. lib. l. tit. penult. De Verbor. Signif. L. 231. Pand. lib. i. tit. v. De Statu Hominum, L. 7. See the same principle in Reeve *v.* Long, 3 Levinz, 408. Stat. 10 & 11 Will. III. cap. 16; and see Co. Litt. 55 b. n. 8.

[f] Pand. lib. i. tit. v. De Statu Homin. L. 23.

[g] Ibid. tit. vi. De His qui Sui vel Alieni Juris sunt, L. 6. Pand. lib. ii. tit. iv. De in jus Vocando, L. 5. Pand. lib. xxii. tit. iii. De Probat. L. 29.

[h] Pand. lib. i. tit. v. De Statu Homin. L. 12. Pand. lib. xxxviii. tit. xvi. De Suis et Legitim. Hered. L. 3, § ult.

[i] Ibid. § 11.

[k] Voet, Comm. ad Pand. lib. i. tit. vi. De His qui Sui vel Alieni Jur. sunt, num. 4. There is some inaccuracy on this subject in Co. Litt. p. 123 b, not. 2, which is however a very valuable note.

a woman above fifty years of age was alleged to have had a child: *Sancimus licet mirabilis hujusmodi partus inveniatur, et raro contingat; nihil tamen eorum quæ probabiliter a natura noscuntur esse producta respui.*[l] And thus the supreme court of Friesland admitted to the succession a child not born till 333 days from the husband's death, which period only wants three days of twelve lunar months.[m] And a Novell of Justinian seems to imply that a child born within the year (*circa terminum anni*) may be the issue of the deceased husband.[n]

It is important here to observe that, as a general principle, the law should be slow in deciding beforehand that anything is absolutely impossible so far as to receive no proof against common experience, except when it is necessary that a limit should be drawn somewhere, in which case the law ought to have regard to what may occur beyond what is frequent, though not to events of extreme rarity.[o]

The Roman Law provides minute precautions to prevent frauds by widows pretending to be with child; and from thence is probably derived the Common Law writ, *De ventre inspiciendo*.[p]

Next to the descending line, *ascendants*, that is to say, parents, and their parents who are comprised under the name of ancestors, are admitted to the succession as follows:—

Ascendants take whenever the deceased left no descendants, to the exclusion of all collaterals, except brothers and sisters of the whole blood and their descendants, who take by representation the share of their father or mother.[q]

The nearest ancestor excludes the others. Thus a father excludes a grandfather, and if the father be dead, the grandfather excludes the great grandfather.

No distinction is made between the paternal and maternal line, nor with reference to the derivation of the property; but the inheritance is divided into two equal parts, one of which is equally distributed among the paternal, and the other among the maternal ancestors in the same degree respectively.

If however the deceased left brothers or sisters of the whole blood, that is to say, by the same father and mother, they partake of the inheritance with the ancestor or ancestors in equal shares. Thus the

[l] Cod. lib. vi. tit. xlviii. De Legitim. Hered. L. 12.

[m] Co. Litt. ibid.

[n] Novella 39, cap. 2, § 1.

[o] *Prudentissimi juris auctores medietatem quandam secuti sunt, ut quod fieri non rarum admodum potest intueantur.* Pand. lib. v. tit. iv. Si Pars Heredit. petatur, L. 3. Paulus there says, *Sed et tergeminos senatores cinctos vidimus Horatios,* and he mentions several other, and still more extraordinary instances of the same nature.

[p] Pand. lib. xxv. tit. iv. De Inspiciendo Ventre.

[q] Novell. 127.

ancestors of each line respectively succeed *per capita* to the half which falls to such line, but if there be brothers and sisters they share with the ancestors *per capita*.

Justinian by his 127th Novell enlarges the privilege of collaterals by providing that the descendants of a deceased brother or sister shall succeed by representation to the share of their father or mother, together with the surviving brothers and sisters and the ascendants.

But when there are no brothers or sisters of the whole blood, or their descendants, then the collaterals are all excluded by the ascendants or ancestors.

We come now to the third and last order of heirs at law, namely, collaterals, who succeed to the whole inheritance where there are neither descendants nor ascendants. Collaterals are called to the succession after ascendants, because the latter are presumed to be nearer in affection to the deceased than the former, except brothers and sisters of the whole blood, who by reason of their great proximity are admitted together with the ascending lines.

Collateral heirs are all those who are lawfully descended from any person from whom the deceased was also descended, and they are admitted according to the proximity of their consanguinity to the deceased in the following order.

First, collaterals of the whole blood are preferred to collaterals of the half blood in the same line.

Secondly, those collaterals who are descended from a nearer ancestor of the deceased exclude those who spring from a more distant ancestor.

Thirdly, the nearest, in each line, to the common ancestor, that is to say, the ancestor from whom the line is traced, exclude those who are more remote, being separated from that common ancestor by a greater number of descents or generations.

By virtue of these rules, the first in the order of collateral succession are the brothers and sisters of the whole blood, that is, those who spring from the same father and mother as the deceased. If there be no brothers or sisters of the whole blood, those of the half-blood take. Brothers and sisters succeed *per capita* in equal shares: and the nearest descendants of deceased brothers and sisters succeed by representation and therefore *per stirpes*, or by lines, together with the surviving brothers and sisters, and take the share which such deceased brothers or sisters would have inherited if alive. That share is divided equally among the nearest descendants of the deceased brother or sister in the same degree.

It follows from the rule that descendants represent their deceased ancestor; that as the brothers and sisters of the whole blood exclude those of the half-blood, so it is with their descendants also.

Where there are no surviving brothers or sisters, their nearest descendants share equally or *per capita*. This is reasonable as they are all on the same footing,[r] and it is a more simple method of division than that *per stirpes*.

If there be no descendants from the nearest ancestors of the deceased, either by the whole or half-blood, then the descendants of the next ancestors, that is to say, of the parents of the father and of the mother, are called to the succession in the same order as those of the father and mother, but without distinction between the whole and the half-blood. This exception is probably intended for greater simplicity, to avoid difficulties which would arise in distinguishing between the whole and the half-blood where the ancestor is distant, and it is also reasonable, because the presumption of greater affection of the deceased for his relations by the whole than for those of the half-blood is considerably weakened or obliterated in proportion to the remoteness of the common ancestor.

The right of representation also does not extend beyond the descendants of brothers and sisters of the deceased.

The law of succession of collaterals more distant than the descendants of the parents, or one of the parents of the deceased, may be reduced to the following rules.

First, the descendants of the ancestors nearest to the deceased exclude the descendants of more distant ancestors.

Secondly, those among the descendants of each degree or generation of the ancestors of the deceased, who are separated by the smallest number of descents or generations from the common ancestor through whom they claim their consanguinity with the deceased, exclude those who are more remote from the common ancestors or ancestor.

Thirdly, the collaterals in the same degree of proximity to the common ancestors or ancestor share equally among them, *per capita*.

If there be neither descendants nor ascendants, nor collaterals, and the deceased left a husband or a wife, then he or she succeeds to the exclusion of the crown.[s]

This exposition of the rules of descent will render easy the third part of this chapter in which the mode of reckoning degrees of kindred in the Civil Law is now to be shown.[t]

[r] Vinnii Comm. ad Instit. lib. iii. tit. v. De Successione Cognatorum, § 5.

[s] Cod. lib. vi. tit. xviii. Unde Vir et Uxor, L. unic. Cod. lib. x. tit. x. De Bon Vacant. L. 1.

[t] Vinnii Comm. ad Instit. lib. iii. tit. vi. De Gradibus Cognationum, princip.

Kindred is divided into three lines or orders of consanguinity, namely, the ascending line, the descending line, and the transversal or collateral line. The first is composed of parents and other ancestors; the second of children, grandchildren and other descendants; and the third of persons descended from a common ancestor, such as brothers and sisters, uncles and aunts, and cousins. Thus consanguinity may be said to be of two kinds, namely, direct (including the ascending and descending lines) and collateral.

Every line of consanguinity is divided into degrees which, according to Paulus, are so called by comparison with steps, because one degree is below the other, and one springs from the other.[u] And every filiation or generation is a degree. To determine in what degree of kindred two persons stand towards each other by the Civil Law, it is only necessary to count the number of descents or filiations between those two persons. Thus, in the direct lines, the parent and child are to each other in the first degree, because there is but one descent or filiation between them. Thus in the collateral line, brothers are in the second degree to each other, because there are two filiations between them, and uncle and nephew are in the third degree, for *semper generata persona gradum adjicit.* So there is no first degree in the collateral line, because where there are two collaterals there must be two filiations or descents between them from the common ancestor.

The Roman Law distinguishes relations into *agnati*, and *cognati.* The former are relations though males and the latter through females.[x] But the words *cognati* and *cognatio* are sometimes used as a generic term to express kindred of both kinds.

As for affinity, it is the relationship which arises by marriage between a husband and the relations of his wife, or a wife and the relations of the husband. Those relations stand in the same degree to the husband as to the wife and *vice versa.*[y]

It has been shown in Chap. viii. that the Canon Law reckons the degrees of kindred among collaterals differently from the Civil Law, so as to make brothers related in the first degree, and uncles and nephews in the second, because the Canon Law reckons the degrees only on one side, and if the number on each is different, then on the side on which there are the greater number of degrees from the common ancestor.

Collatio bonorum remains to be explained, which is the subject of the fourth and last division of this chapter. This portion of the

[u] Pand lib. xxxviii. tit. x. De Gradibus et Adfinibus, L. 10, § 9, 10.

[x] Pand. ibid. § 2.

[y] Voet, Comm. ad Pand. lib. xxiii. tit. ii. De Ritu Nupt. num. 29.

Roman Law applies exclusively to successions in the direct descending line.[z]

It would be impossible to maintain fair equality in distributing an inheritance among co-heirs, without having regard to any portions thereof received by one or more of them in the lifetime of the deceased. Therefore the law of *Collatio Bonorum* (originally introduced by the equity of the Prætor) requires an heir claiming his share of the inheritance to collate or bring into account as part of that share, what he has already received from the deceased. The principle of the Civil Law is that no man shall enforce equity against another unless he on his part will observe and do equity.

Thus if a co-heir claims no share, he is not bound to collate. *Qui non vult hereditatem, non cogitur ad collationem.* And thus the very principle of *collatio bonorum* excludes from collation all those things which the heir acquired by an onerous title from the deceased, that is to say, by giving a valuable consideration for them.

Justinian by his 18th Novell, cap. vi., extends the law of collation to cases where a father appoints his children to be his co-heirs by testament, for it is presumed that he has an equal affection for them all.[a] But as *præsumptio veritati cedit,* if it appear that the testator did not intend that there should be collation it is excluded. And in the same manner collation may be excluded in successions *ab intestato* where an intention to do so is manifested by the deceased.[b]

From the Roman Law of *Collatio Bonorum* is said to be derived that part of the Statute of Distributions (22 & 23 Car. II. chap. 10, explained by 29 Car. II. chap. 3) where directions are given, that no child of the intestate (except his heir at law) on whom he settled in his lifetime any estate in lands or pecuniary portion equal to the distributive shares of the other children, shall have any part of the surplusage with their brothers and sisters; but if the estates so given to them by way of advancement be not quite equivalent to the other shares, the children so advanced shall now have so much as will make them equal. And the other provisions of the Statute of Distributions seem to have been derived from the 118th Novell of Justinian.

[z] Voet, Comm. lib. xxxvii. tit. vi. De Collatione Bonor. num. 1.

[a] Pand. lib. xxiii. tit. ii. De Ritu Nupt. L. 67. § 1.

[b] Voet ad Pand. lib. xxxvii. tit. vi. num. 27.

CHAPTER XXVIII.

THE LAW OF THINGS.

Of Obligations.—Instit. lib. iii. tit. xiv. De Obligationibus.—General Arrangement of the Subject.—*Dominium* or *Jura in Re*, and Obligations or *Jura ad Rem* or *in Personam*.—Derivation of Law and Obligations from Love of God and Love of Our Neighbour.—Obligations Generated; First, in Consequence of an Act of the Party; and secondly, by the Law alone.—Obligations Natural or Civil, and both Natural and Civil.—Classification of Obligations in the Roman Law: —*Ex Contractu, quasi ex Contractu, ex Delicto* and *quasi ex Delicto*.—Subdivision of Obligations *ex Contractu* into four Classes.—Definition of a Contract. —Division of Contracts into Nominate and Innominate. P. 172.

It has been shown that the second of the three general heads under which the Imperial Institutes are arranged, namely, 1. Persons; 2. Things; and 3. Actions, comprises not only those things which are under our dominion, and rights *in rem*, which are asserted by a legal demand of a specific thing as our property, but also *jura ad rem*, which are called obligations, or perhaps more strictly the beneficial interest in, or right of, requiring the fulfilment of obligations.

It has also been shown the whole law of *Things* may correctly be referred to two heads, *dominion* or property, and *obligations*, including under the former all rights *in re*, and under the latter all rights *ad rem*, which are also called *in personam*, because they are rights which have indeed for their object a thing, but which arise from an obligation of a person which causes or generates the right to the thing.

Domat argues that all law may be reduced to two heads, rights with their corresponding obligations and successions, and testaments whereby the former are transmitted from one generation to another. Domat built his theory of jurisprudence upon the text of the Gospel declaring that upon the love of God and the love of our neighbour hangs the whole law. From the love of God springs the obligatory force of the whole law of nature, which is sanctioned by the will of Heaven, promulgated by nature itself; and upon that principle the duty of obedience to the natural law is made independent of the hope of reward and the fear of punishment. From the duty of loving our neighbour spring all those obligations, the fulfilment of which is necessary for the welfare of mankind, and which we owe to our fellow men as a consequence of the primary or of the secondary natural law, including as part of the secondary natural law the duty of obedience to municipal law, without which obedience the social state either could not exist at all, or could not exist in tranquillity, or would not be capable of producing the greatest welfare of mankind, moral as well as physical.

Here all law is considered as included within two precepts, and therefore included under the head of obligations.

Looking at law under this aspect, it comprises all the actions of men who are capable of forming an idea of the nature of duty and obligation. Every human action must be in obedience to an obligation, or contrary to an obligation, or neither, that is to say, within the limits of lawful freedom. In this sense Ulpian says, *Jurisprudentia est divinarum et humanarum rerum notitia: justi et injusti scientia.*[a]

Every man possesses his own rights, limited by and subject to the rights of others, which he is bound not to violate, for there cannot be two conflicting rights;[b] and thus every right has a corresponding obligation. Those obligations are generated either in consequence of some act on the part of the person obliged, or without any such act. The former are obligations by consent, express or implied, that is to say, contracts and obligations of reparation and restitution; and the latter are obligations arising from the law alone, whether natural or municipal.

These general doctrines will facilitate the comprehension of the following definition of obligations which are enforced by Civil or Municipal Law.

Obligatio est juris vinculum quo necessitate adstringimur alicujus rei solvendi secundum nostræ civitatis jura.[c]

Pothier, in his celebrated treatise on obligations, observes that the term obligation has two significations. In its most extensive acceptation it includes imperfect obligations, the fulfilment of which consists in the exercise of virtues, such as charity or generosity. Obligation in this sense is synonymous with duty. But the term taken in its strict acceptation comprehends only those obligations which are called perfect or personal obligations, which give to the person towards whom we are bound by them a right to exact their fulfilment.[d]

The first division of obligations of this nature is with reference to the species of bond which they produce, that is to say, the authority by which we are bound to fulfil them. Under this aspect obligations are divisible into three classes; 1st, Natural and Civil Obligations; 2nd, Merely Civil Obligations; and 3rd, Merely Natural Obligations.[e]

[a] Pand. lib. i. tit. i. De Just. et Jur. L. 10, § 3.

[b] Pand. lib. xli. tit. ii. De Adquirenda et Omittenda Possessione L. 3, § 5.

[c] Instit. lib. iii. tit. xiv. De Obligat. princip.

[d] Pothier, Des Obligations, artic. prélim.

[e] Ibid. part 2, chap. 1, § 173.

A civil obligation is that above defined by Justinian as *vinculum juris*, and the Emperor adds *quo necessitate adstringimur*, because such obligations give a right to compel their fulfilment by recourse to courts of justice.

A natural obligation is defined by Papinian[f] to be *vinculum æquitatis*, and it is binding in conscience, so that he who neglects or refuses to fulfil is not only not virtuous, but also unjust. But the municipal law in many cases refuses to compel the performance of such natural obligations. The law however only allows a sort of impunity in such cases of injustice, and professes to compel the observance of good faith wherever it is possible to do so without inconvenience. Thus Ulpian says: *Quid tam congruum fidei humanæ quam ea quæ inter eos placuerunt servare.*[g]

Upon that principle Triphoninus decides that the repayment of money paid which was due in conscience, though not in law, cannot be required from the equitable creditor.[h]

Obligations are however most commonly both natural and civil; but they are sometimes civil only. For instance, if a man has had judgment against him unjustly in a court from whence there is no appeal, he does not really owe that which he is decreed to pay; but because the evil which would result from disobedience to final judgments is greater as affecting the commonwealth, than that which affects the individual to whom justice has not been done, he is bound for the good of society by law to abide by that judgment and obey it. Hence it appears that even in obedience to an unjust law (provided that obedience consist not in a wrong act, but in mere submission) there is a foundation of secondary natural law, for municipal law would be powerless and useless, and society would consequently not exist with tranquillity if every man were at liberty to resist and disobey so much of the law as he conceives to be contrary to his rights.

This doctrine must be understood as applicable to ordinary cases and to individuals considered as such, but not to large communities of men subjected to greater evils by cruel or unjust laws than would be caused by resistance to those laws. But the application to particular cases of this exception to the general principle of obedience is one of the most difficult and dangerous questions of public law.

Having now classified obligations with reference to the nature of their *vinculum* or binding power, we will proceed to their classification in the Imperial Institutes.

Obligations are divided into four classes. For they arise from

[f] Pand. lib. xlvi. tit. iii. De Solutionibus et Liberationibus, L. 95, § 4.

[g] Pand. lib. ii. tit. xiv. De Pactis, L. 1.

[h] Pand. lib. xii. tit. vi. De Condictione Indebiti, L. 64.

contract: from quasi contract: from delict: or from quasi delict. Those which arise from contract shall first be considered. They also are divisible into four species. Obligations arising from contract are produced by the possession of a thing, or by a verbal formula, or by writing, or by bare consent. Each species shall be separately considered.[i]

Here obligations are classified with reference to their efficient cause, and again subdivided with reference to the manner in which they are contracted. Trebonian and his colleagues were the authors of the classification of obligations under these four heads:—1. *Ex contractu*; 2. *Quasi ex contractu*; 3. *Ex delicto*; 4. *Quasi ex delicto*. The meaning of the last three of these terms alone requires explanation here.

A *quasi* contract is an obligation springing not from contract but from some act which is not culpable. Thus if a man receive a payment of what is not due to him, he is bound to repay it though he received it believing it to be due. Now this explanation shows that the term *quasi contract* is not correct, for the very word contract implies consent; whereas the obligations improperly called *quasi ex contractu* by Trebonian arise quite independently of any consent, express or implied.

The words *quasi ex contractu* once indeed occur in a law of Gajus in the Pandects,[k] but they are applied to the case of a guardian, and are made use of by way of illustration, and not as a general name for obligations arising neither from a contract, nor a culpable act. Though a guardian assumed his duties on compulsion by the law, yet, being so compelled, he might be held to have tacitly consented to do his duty. *Coactus voluit.* Gajus however thus gives the true cause of the mutual actions of persons against each other in those obligations which Trebonian calls *quasi* contracts. *Utilitatis causa*, he says, *receptum est eos invicem obligari.* It is in fact necessary that men should be held legally bound without their consent by the effect of the law either acting by itself, or operating on some act of their own.

The two remaining classes of obligations, *ex delicto*, and *quasi ex delicto*, are those which bind a person who has committed a crime, or who has done some injury arising from a fault such as carelessness.

We come now to the classification or subdivision of obligations of the first of these four classes,—those *ex contractu*. Here the equity of the Civil Law is mingled with a good deal of arbitrary and technical law, of which it is necessary to give a general idea.

[i] Instit. lib. iii. tit. xiv. § 2.
[k] Pand. lib. xliv. tit. vii. De Obligat. et Action. L. 5, § 1.

Obligations *ex contractu* arise, according to Justinian, in four ways, that is to say, *re contrahuntur, aut consensu, aut literis, aut verbis.* The first includes those obligations which cannot be generated otherwise than by possession of a thing. Such is the contract of deposit or loan. Such are all obligations to restitution. Obligations contracted *consensu* are those which, like sale or hire, are so generally in use and so definite, that the bare consent of the parties is by the Civil Law held sufficient to bind them to all the obligations belonging to those contracts. Obligations *quæ literis contrahuntur*, were made use of in only one case (which will be further explained hereafter), where a positive law gave effect to a written instrument. Those contracted *verbis*, by words, include a number of legal contracts not comprised in the three former classes, and they are called *verborum obligationes*, because they could not be entered into otherwise than by a formula of words consisting in question and answer. That formula is called in the Roman Law *stipulatio.* Having thus given a general explanation of Justinian's classification of obligations, we will commence with those of the first class, namely, obligations *ex contractu.*

A contract is a species of convention or agreement which the Romans called by the general names of *pactum* or *conventio.*[l] Thus Ulpian says, *Est pactio duorum pluriumve in unum placitum consensus.*[m] A contract is defined by Pothier to be "a convention or agreement by which the parties reciprocally promise, or one among them promises and engages towards the other or the others, to give him or them, or to do or not to do something."[n] Vinnius defines a contract somewhat differently, thus: *Contractus est conventio habens nomen speciale, aut eo deficiente civilem obligandi causam.*[o] This definition is taken from a law of Ulpian, where he lays it down that conventions *juris gentium,* that is to say, natural obligations by agreement are not all enforced by Civil Law.

Those which are so enforced, or in other words, which produce a right of action, are either sanctioned by the law under a particular name, such for instance as that of sale, loan, or deposit, or the more general denomination of *stipulatio*, or are founded on a cause or consideration: for instance, if A. give B. something in consideration of B. engaging to do something or to give something in return to A.[p]

The civilians have deduced therefrom the division of contracts into *nominati,* which are sanctioned by name, and *innominati,* which are

[l] Pothier, Des Obligations, part 1, chap. 1, num. 3.

[m] Pand. lib. ii. tit. xiv. De Pactis, L. 1, § 2, 3.

[n] Pothier, ubi Sup.

[o] Vinnii Comm. ad Instit. lib. iii. tit. xiv. § 2.

[p] Pand. lib. ii. tit. xiv. De Pactis, L. 7.

not so, but are enforced when there has been anything done on one side which binds the other party *vinculo juris*, to do something in return.[q]

These nameless contracts are divided into four classes.—1. *Do tibi ut des; 2. Facio ut Facias; 3. Facio ut des; and 4. Do ut facias.*[r]

In the next Chapter, the contracts which *re contrahuntur* will be explained.

CHAPTER XXIX.

THE LAW OF THINGS.—REAL CONTRACTS.

Contracts Produced by Delivery and Possession of a Thing.—Instit. lib. iii. tit. xv. Quibus Modis Re Contrahatur Obligatio.—Contract of *Mutuum.—Promutuum.* —*Solutio Indebiti* referred to.—Commodate or Loan.—Difference between Commodate and *Mutuum.*—The general Principle on which different Degrees of Diligence and Care are required in different Contracts.—*Vis Major* and Chance.—Effect of Delay or Default.—*Præcarium.—Actio Directa et Contraria.* —Deposit.—*Pignus* or Pledge.—Difference between *Pignus* and *Hypotheca* or Mortgage.—The Creditor's Power of selling the Pledge. P. 177.

Justinian, in the 14th chapter of the third book of his Institutes, explains four contracts which *re contrahuntur*, that is to say, which are produced by the possession of a thing. Contracts of this nature are properly four in number, namely, *Mutuum; Commodatum; Depositum; Pignus.* Except the first, they all come under the legal denomination of bailment in our English Law, because they are produced by a thing being bailed or delivered to a person who becomes bound in certain obligations respecting that thing, in consequence of its delivery for a certain purpose. And first, of the contract called *Mutuum.*

An obligation is contracted by the transfer of a thing, in the case of Mutuum. Mutuum is the loan of those things which are measured or estimated by number, weight and measure, and which we give in that manner with the intention that they may become absolutely the property of the person that accepts them from us. Such are oil, wine, corn, money, brass, or silver. And this species of loan is called Mutuum, because we give the thing with the intention that not the same identical substance, but another thing of the same nature and quality may be

[q] Grotius, Droit de la Guerre et de la Paix, liv. ii. chap. xii. § 3. And see Pand. lib. xix. tit. v. De Præscriptis Verbis.

[r] Pand. ibid. L. 5

given to us in return; and thus the property of the substance itself is transferred to the borrower.[a]

This is a contract of *do ut des*. It is defined by Pothier to be a contract, by which one of the contracting parties conveys the right of property in a certain number or quantity of some things or thing to be consumed by use, to the other party, who engages to repay him in the same kind.[b]

Here is an instance of the contracts which are called unilateral, because one party being bound by the act of the other, from which he has derived an advantage, the obligation is all on the side of him who received the benefit. Of the same nature is the obligation of restitution which arises whenever any one has received a payment, through error, of that which is not due to him. There the obligation arises from the erroneous receipt of the thing, and it may be enforced by action at law.[c] This is called by Pothier, after the example of Cujacius, ***Promutuum***, from its resemblance to *Mutuum*, which is also remarked by Gajus.[d]

But, in truth, this obligation does not arise from contract, because no consent of the party is required to give it existence, yet Trebonian classed the payment of what is not due, *solutio indebiti*, under the head of *Quasi Contractus*.

Commodate is where a thing is delivered to be used or is lent, without the lender receiving anything as a price for the use of the thing. If such a price be given, the contract becomes hire and letting of the thing.

Commodate is very different from Mutuum; for in Commodate, the thing lent is not delivered to become the property of the person to whom it is so delivered, which is the case in Mutuum; and therefore in commodate the borrower must restore to the lender the very identical thing lent. And in Mutuum the borrower remains bound to restitution, though the thing perish by a purely accidental or irresistible event.

But in commodate, the borrower is bound to use in the custody of the thing lent, exact and scrupulous care: nor is it sufficient if he bestowed on the thing lent the same degree of care as on his own property, if another person could have taken more attentive and diligent care of it. But he is not liable for the effects of irresistible force or of chance which he could not have foreseen, unless indeed that chance would not, but for his fault, have affected the thing lent. If you carry with you on a journey a thing lent to remain at your house, and

[a] Instit. lib. iii. tit. xv. princ.

[b] Pothier, Du Contr. de Pret. a Consomption, num. 1.

[c] Instit. ibid. § 1.

[d] Pand. lib. xliv. tit. vii. De Obligat. et Action. L. 5, § 3.

it is taken by robbers or lost in a storm, you are liable for the loss, and bound to make reparation.[e]

Whenever one man has possession of the property of, or what is due to another, and it is lost, or destroyed, or deteriorated, the question may arise which of the parties shall bear the loss.

Ulpian decides that in some contracts more, and in others less responsibility is cast on the party bound by them. Some contracts render men liable for *dolum* or fraud only, while in others a party is also liable for the effects of *culpa,* a fault on his part whereby the other party suffers damage.

Ulpian applies this distinction according to the following general rule.[f]

The party who derives no benefit from the contract is liable only for dole in dealing with the property of the other. But where the contract is beneficial to both parties, as in sale, or hire, or partnership, there both dole and fault (*dolus et culpa*) are included in the obligations and responsibility incident to the contract. In those contracts which are beneficial only to the party obliged by them, such as *commodatum,* he is not only liable for the effects of his dole and fault, but he is bound to be careful and diligent. *Talis diligentia præstanda est qualem quisque diligentissimus paterfamilias suis rebus adhibet.*[g]

The rules of law on this subject must however be understood to apply to those cases only where it is not otherwise agreed between the parties to the contract: *Legem enim contractus dedit.*[h]

But a stipulation in a contract *ne dolus præstetur* is null and void,[i] for it is contrary to good morals.

With regard to those irresistible events which Gajus denominates *vis major,* and generally those which cannot be resisted, the general rule of Ulpian is observed that no man is liable for their effects. And it is the same with fortuitous events which could not be foreseen.[k]

But this irresponsibility is limited by Ulpian to events *quæ sine culpa accidunt,* and the same exception is made by Gajus, who says, if I lend you plate to give a supper, and you carry it on a journey, in that case if it be lost by an irresistible event, you are responsible.[l]

[e] Instit. lib. iii. tit. xv. § 2. Pand. lib. xiii. tit. vi. Commodati, L. 18.

[f] Pand. lib. xiii. tit. vi. Commodati vel Contra. L. 5, § 2. Pand. lib. l. tit. ult. De Divers. Regul. Jur. L. 23. And see Coggs *v.* Bernard, 2 Lord Raym. 912; and Sir W. Jones, on the Law of Bailments, 4th edit. 1834.

[g] Pand. lib. xiii. tit. vi. Commodati, L. 18.

[h] Ibid. lib. l. tit. ult. De Divers. Reg. Jur. L. 23. Ibid. lib. ii. tit. xiv. De Pact. L. 7, § 15.

[i] Ibid. Ibid. lib. xiii. tit. vii. De Pignoratitia Actione, L. 27, § 3.

[k] Ibid. lib. xix. tit. ii. Locati Conducti, L. 25, § 6. Ibid. lib. xiii. tit. vi. Commodati, L. 18.

[l] Ibid. lib. xiii. tit. vi. Commodati, L. 18.

On the same principle are founded the decisions in the Pandects, that after a delay to deliver a thing which is due, the party guilty of delay is liable for even fortuitous and irresistible events.[m]

There is one species of commodate, called *precarium*, which is a loan of a specific thing during pleasure, whereas commodate, properly so called, is not revocable until the thing has been used for the time and purpose intended by the parties.[n]

The principles explained above are also applicable to the contract of deposit, which is thus described by Justinian.

If a thing be deposited with any one, he becomes bound by possession of the thing, and is under the obligation of restoring that thing, to which restitution he is compellable by direct action of deposit. His responsibility extends no further than to make him liable for the effects of his dole, and he is not responsible for a fault (*culpa*), *that is to say, indolence or negligence. He is therefore not liable if the thing deposited be stolen out of his custody in consequence of his want of diligent care: for he who delivered his property into the custody of a careless friend must bear the consequences of his own imprudence.*[o]

These rules spring from the gratuitous nature of the contract of deposit. But if the bailee in deposit be to receive a reward in consideration of his care and custody of the thing, the contract becomes one of *locatio conductio*, or hire, which is governed by different rules.

The *actio directa* here referred to by Justinian, is that which arises from the chief part of the contract, as contradistinguished from the *actio contraria*, which is the remedy to enforce obligations arising incidentally or subsequently. Thus the depositor has the *actio depositi directa* to recover the deposit: and the bailee in deposit has the *actio depositi contraria* to be indemnified by the depositor for all expenses incurred by him in the care and custody of the thing.[p] And here the contract of deposit differs from that of commodate, in which the borrower is entitled only to the repayment of extraordinary and unexpected expenses connected with the thing lent, and other charges incident to the ownership; while the small and ordinary expenses incident to the use of the thing fall on the borrower.[q] The reason of this diversity is that the deposit is a burthen, but the borrower derives an advantage from the loan. Two rules of the contract of deposit remain to be noticed.

[m] Pand. lib. xlv. tit. i. De Verborum Obligationibus, L. 23, 82, 91.

[n] Pand. lib. xliii. tit. xxvi. L. 1. Pand. lib. xiii. tit. vi. Commodati, L. 17, § 3.

[o] Instit. lib. iii. tit. xv. § 3.

[p] Vinnii Comm. ad Instit. ibid. Pand. lib. xvi. tit. iii. Depositi, L. 5.

[q] Pothier, Traité du Pret. a l'Usage, num. 81. Pand. lib. xiii. tit. vi. Commodati, L. 18, § 2.

As the thing is deposited solely for the convenience of the depositor, it follows that the bailee in deposit is bound to restore it on demand.[r] And upon the same principle, a person who has undertaken the custody and care of a deposit, cannot restore it of his own accord, until the time has expired during which he undertook that custody and care.[s]

Only one contract, which *re contrahitur*, remains to be considered. It is *pignus*, or pawn, which in the Scotch Law is called pledge.[t]

A creditor who accepts a pledge, is bound in a real contract by the acceptance of the thing; for he is bound to restore the identical thing. But as a pawn or pledge is given for the benefit of both parties (for the debtor, that he may obtain credit, and for the advantage of the creditor, that what is due to him may be the more secure); therefore the creditor is bound to be scrupulously diligent in the custody and care of the pledged property. If, notwithstanding that care, the thing be lost by accident, the creditor is not liable, and he may, nevertheless, sue the debtor for what is due to him.[u]

The Civil Law requires of the creditor *exactam diligentiam* in the custody of the pawn. He is bound to be as careful in that custody as the average of careful men usually are in their own affairs.[x]

Ulpian distinguishes pledge (*pignus*) from *hypotheca*, or mortgage, by defining that in the former the property is, and in the latter it is not delivered into the possession of the creditor. But in another place he says, that property may be subjected to the contract of pledge without delivery.[y] This contradiction, however, is only apparent; for in the latter case the contract without delivery would give the creditor a right of action to obtain possession of the pledged property, and the obligations properly belonging to the contract of pawn cannot be in existence until delivery.[z]

By delivery the following obligations are engendered.

The creditor is entitled to retain the pledge, and to sell it, and retain what is due to him out of the price, after the debtor is in delay of payment. But there must be a demand of payment, for Scævola says, *Nulla intelligitur mora ibi fieri ubi nulla petitio est.*[a]

This power of sale of the creditor is limited by a constitution of the Emperor Constantine, which declares illegal a contract that the pledge should be forfeited to the creditor, upon the debtor making default or delaying payment.[b]

[r] Pand. lib. xvi. tit. iii. Depositi, L. 1, § 45, 46. [s] Ibid. L. 5, § 2.

[t] Erskine, Instit. book iii. tit. i. § 33. [u] Instit. lib. iii. tit. xv. § 4.

[x] Pand. lib. xiii. tit. vii. De Pignoratitia Actione, L. 14.

[y] Pand. ibid. L. 9, § 2, and L. 1.

[z] Vinnii Comm. ad Instit. lib. iii. tit. xv. § 4.

[a] Pothier, Contract. de Nantissment, chap. 4, art. 2. Pand. lib. l. tit. penult. De Reg. Jur. L. 88. [b] Cod. lib. viii. tit. xxxv. De Pactis Pignorum. L. ultim.

This equitable provision is also to be found in the Liber Feudorum; and its principles are analogous to those of Statute 39 & 40 George III. ch. 99.[c]

But the constitution above referred to does not extend to a decision of Marcian, on the authority of Alexander Severus and Antoninus Pius, that a pledge may be forfeited for default or delay of payment, provided it be fairly valued, and forfeited only for the amount due to the creditor.[d] These principles arise from the very nature of the contract of pledge, which is no more than a security for the payment of the debt.

Thus the creditor is bound, so soon as the debt is fully paid or otherwise extinguished, to restore the pledge.[e]

If the creditor derived any advantage or profit, capable of being estimated, from the pledged property, he is bound to make a deduction to that amount from the debt.[f]

The debtor, on the other hand, is bound to indemnify the creditor for his expenses necessarily incurred for the preservation of the pledged property.[g] And if the debtor knowingly pawn what is not his, or if the creditor suffer any loss or damage by not having been warned by the debtor of some fact relating to the pledge, the debtor must indemnify him.[h]

CHAPTER XXX.

THE LAW OF THINGS.—OBLIGATIONS BY WORDS.

Of Obligations by Words.—Instit. lib. iii. tit. xvi. De Verborum Obligationibus, princip. § 1—3.—The Form of Stipulation.—Traces of it in the Coronation, Baptismal, and Marriage Ceremonies.—Principle on which Stipulation is Valid without Consideration.—Abolition of its Technicalities by the Emperor Leo.—Stipulations Absolute and Qualified.—Terms, Express and Implied, suspending the Performance of Contracts.—Terms limiting the Continuance of Contracts. P. 180.

THE second class of obligations, that is to say, obligations by words, are explained in this chapter.

It has been already shown that this species of obligations are those

[c] Lib. Feud. lib. i. tit. xxiii.

[d] Pand. lib. xx. tit. i. De Pignor. et Hypothec. L. 16, § 9.

[e] Pothier, Traité du Nantissement, chap. iv. art. 2, § 2. Pand. lib. xiii. tit. vii. Pignor. Actione, L. 9, § 3.

[f] Pothier, ibid.

[g] Pothier, ibid. § 3. Pand. ubi sup. L. 8.

[h] Ibid. L. 16, § 1.

contracted by virtue of the formula of question and answer, called *stipulatio*, which was requisite in the Roman Law, for the validity of contracts not designated by a proper name, and wherein nothing is executed on either side by way of consideration.

A good illustration of the use of this formula is to be found in the *Pseudolus* of Plautus. Pseudolus promises the young man, Calidorus, that he will either enable him to obtain Phœnicum, or pay a penalty of twenty *minæ;* but Calidorus distrusts him, and Pseudolus thus asseverates :[a]

> *Pseudol.* Roga me viginti minas :
> Ut me effecturum quod tibi promisi scias,
> Roga, obsecro Hercle. Gestio promittere.
> *Calidorus.* Dabisne argenti mi xx. minas ?
> *Pseudol.* Dabo ; molestus nunc jam ne sis mihi.

And in the same play, Simo, one of the two old men, and father to Calidorus, says to Ballio, who offers him a bet, in defiance of the machinations and "*doctum dolum*" of Pseudolus :[b]

> Nullum periculum 'st quod sciam stipularier.

It seems most probable that the form of interrogation and answer used in the Marriage and Baptismal services is derived from the Roman stipulation ; and that the interrogations addressed to the people in the Coronation service, which has been supposed to be a vestige of popular election, draws its origin from the same source.[c]

The rubric of this title of the Institutes includes all obligations to the constitution of which writing is not essential. And, indeed, where writing is requisite, it is only so as evidence of the lawful agreement which constitutes the intrinsic substance of the agreement. It follows, therefore, that those rules of stipulations, which are not special and technical, are applicable to all contracts, so far as they are not inconsistent with the peculiar legal principles and positive restrictions of each.[d]

The rules of obligations by words are, however, especially intended to govern those contracts which have no peculiar and specific name, as well as the special clauses and provisions which may be inserted in the regular or *nominate* contracts.

The contracts classed under the four heads, *Do ut des—Facio ut facias—Do ut facias*—and *Facio ut des*, produce a legal obligation

[a] Plaut. Pseudol. act. i. sc. 1, ver. 111, 116.

[b] Ibid. act iv. sc. 6, ver. 14; and See Terence, Andr. act. v. sc. 5, ver. 48.

[c] And see Heineccii Antiquitates, lib. iii. tit. xvi.—xx. as to the Antient History of *Stipulations*.

[d] Erskine, Instit. book iii. tit. ii.

and a right of action without the form of stipulation, provided something be done on one side by way of consideration to bind the other party. But according to the usages of the antients a stipulation required no consideration or reciprocity.

This was probably (as in the English Law with regard to deeds or instruments under seal) on account of the deliberate intention supposed to be implied by the formality of stipulation.[e] It appears then that contracts enforced by action in the Civil Law are either those sanctioned by name, or those in which there is a reciprocity of interests, with some act done by way of performance or part-performance on one side, whereby a civil obligation is engendered on the other.[f] And in this sense stipulation is in the class of nominate contracts, not requiring any consideration to make them valid. The technicalities and strict forms of stipulation are only matter of legal history, as they were abolished by a constitution of the Emperor Leo dated in the year 469.[g] The rules of this contract will therefore be considered here so far as they are grounded not on the subtilty of the Roman Law, but on natural equity.

And first, stipulations are either absolute, that is to say, unqualified, or qualified. Those of the latter species are qualified by a condition or a term. When a stipulation is unqualified, its execution becomes due immediately. But when it is qualified by a term, as, for instance, if the obligee promise to pay a sum of money at a future time, in that case, though the debt is due immediately, it is not payable until the term is expired, and the whole of the day specified for performance of the contract is past.[h]

Suspensive terms are of two species: 1st. Those which are expressly agreed on by the parties; and 2ndly, those implied by the nature of the obligation.[i] The latter are called *dilationes ex re.* Paulus says, *Interdum prior stipulatio ex re ipsa dilationem capit; veluti si fructus futuros aut domum edificari stipulatus est.*[k] And upon the same principle, in every contract the law allows the obligee a reasonable time within which to execute his obligation, and the length of that time must be judged of by the nature of the contract and the circumstances of the particular case. But where the obligation is absolute and unqualified, performance may be demanded immediately, and

[e] Grotius, Droit de la Guerre, liv. ii. chap. xi. § 4.

[f] Vinnii Comm. ad Instit. lib. iii. tit. xiv. princip. Voet, Comm. ad Pand. lib. xix. tit. v. princip.

[g] Voet, lib. xlv. tit. i. princip. Cod. lib. viii. tit. xxxviii. L. 10.

[h] Instit. lib. iii. tit. xvi. § 2.

[i] Pothier, Des Obligations, num. 228.

[k] Pand. lib. xlv. tit. i. Des Obligat. Verborum, L. 73. Instit. lib. iii. tit. xvi. § 5.

N 2

the debtor must perform his engagement as soon as it is possible to do so.[l]

A term suspends not the obligation but the performance only,[m] and a vested interest is in the creditor before the expiration of the term. The performance is *debitum in presenti, solvendum in futuro.* It follows that if the debtor pay before the expiration of the term, though by error, he cannot recover back what he paid; and that what is due during the term cannot be made a set-off; or, as the Civil and Scots Law calls it, a *compensation* to extinguish a debt due from the creditor to the debtor.[n]

The term is presumed, unless the contrary appears, to be intended for the benefit of the debtor or obligee, and therefore he may perform his engagement before the expiration of the term if he thinks fit.[o] A term may define the continuation of a contract, and not suspend its performance. Thus, if A. bind himself to pay ten pieces of gold so long as B. lives, the obligation is absolute as to its commencement, and takes effect immediately; but it ceases on the death of B.[p]

But where the duration of an obligation is limited by a term or a condition, the expiration or accomplishment of which is to extinguish it, the debtor may be obliged to pay after the expiration of the term, or the occurrence of the condition, if he was in delay of payment, after a demand made; because he may not profit by his own wrong.[q]

We come now to stipulations qualified by a condition. But this subject, involving the whole law of conditions, requires a separate chapter.

[l] Vinnii Comm. ad Instit. lib. iii. tit. xvi. § 2. Pand. lib. xlv. tit. i. De Verbor. Oblig. L. 118, § 1. And see L. 136; and Pand. lib. xlvi. tit. iii. De Solutionibus, L. 105. [m] Pand. lib. l. tit. penult. De Verborum Signif. L. 213.

[n] Pothier, Des Obligat. num. 230—232.

[o] Pand. lib. l. tit. ult. L. 17. Pand. lib. xlvi. tit. iii. De Solut. L. 70.

[p] Instit. ibid. § 3.

[q] Pothier, Des Obligat. num. 226. Pand. lib. xvii. tit. i. Mandati. L. 59, § 5. Pand. lib. l. tit. ult. De Regul. Jur. L. 134.

CHAPTER XXXI.

OF CONDITIONAL CONTRACTS.

Of Conditional Stipulations.—Instit. lib. iii. tit. xvi. De Verborum Obligationibus, § 4, 6, 7.—Definition of a Conditional Stipulation or Contract.—Distinction between a Condition and a Term.—Classification of Conditions.—Suspensive Conditions.—Resolutary Conditions.—Conditions Potestative, Casual, and Mixed.—Accomplishment of Conditions.—Impossible Conditions.—Several Conditions expressed in the Disjunctive or in the Conjunctive.—Distinction between the Effect of Conditions in Contracts and in Legacies.—Improper Conditions.—Distinction between Contracts to give and Contracts to perform.—Specific Performance.—Damages. P. 186.

Justinian thus defines conditional stipulations.[a]

A stipulation is conditional when the obligation is deferred until the event of an uncertain occurrence, so that the effect of the stipulation depends on that occurrence taking place or not. Such is a stipulation to give ten pieces of gold if Titius be elected consul. If a man bind himself by contract to pay a sum, provided the creditor does not go up to the capitol, it is the same as if he had bound himself to pay at the death of the creditor. A conditional contract produces a contingent right, or a hope that the debt may become due: and that hope is transmissible, on the death of the creditor, to his heir.

Voet defines a condition to be: *Casus adjectus actum suspendens propter incertum futurum eventum.* Vinnius describes a condition thus: *Conditio est adjectio qua id quod dari fierive volumus confertur in aliquem casum.*[b] This definition resembles that of Domat, quoted by Hargrave: "A condition is any paction or agreement which regulates what the parties have a mind should be done, if a case which they foresee should come to pass."[c]

It appears then that two features are essential to a condition: 1st, A delay suspending the obligation, and 2ndly, A delay depending on an uncertain event; that is to say, an event which may never come to pass, or which is uncertain from being unknown. Thus the uncertainty of the event distinguishes a condition from a term which only suspends the obligation so that the obligation is certain to take effect after the term has expired.

[a] Instit. lib. iii. tit. xvi. § 4.

[b] Voet, Comm. ad Pand. lib. xxviii. tit. vii. De Conditionibus Institutionum, princip. Vinnii Comm. ad Instit. lib. iii. tit. xvi. § 4.

[c] Co. Litt. 201 a.

The delay produced by virtue of a condition, may be a delay of the obligation itself, of the contract, or of some change in the obligation to which the parties have agreed by anticipation. Thus an obligation conditioned "if a ship arrive in a month," is suspended until the ship arrives: but in a contract to pay a monthly sum *until* the ship arrives, the obligation is not suspended, but the agreement that the money shall no longer be paid as soon as the ship arrives, is suspended or delayed until the arrival of the ship. As for the expression of Justinian in the paragraph given above, *Ex conditionali stipulatione tantum spes est debitum iri;* it applies only to those conditions which suspend the obligation of the contract.

Conditions are classified as follows by Pothier.[d] Conditions are either *suspensive* or *resolutory*. The former are those which suspend the obligation, and the latter are those which rescind that which has been agreed upon, in the event of a certain occurrence. Conditions suspensive resemble conditions precedent, and conditions resolutory resemble conditions subsequent in the English Law.[e]

Conditions are further divided by Pothier into three classes, that is to say, 1st, Potestative or optional, or those which it is in the power of the creditor to accomplish; 2ndly, Casual, the accomplishment of which depends upon chance, so far as the creditor is concerned; and 3rdly, Mixed conditions, the accomplishment of which depends on the union of the will of the creditor with that of a third party or with any event over which he has no control. Again, all these events upon which depends the coming into force of that which is subject to the condition, may be positive or negative. A positive condition depends on the accomplishment of a given event, and a negative condition depends on some event not occurring. Positive conditions are accomplished when the event which is the subject of the condition occurs.[f]

When a condition consists in doing or giving anything, it is requisite for the accomplishment of the condition, that the performance of that act be as the parties must most probably have intended. Thus as a general rule, the performance should be specific, but where the strictly specific performance is not essential, or of the essence of the contract, a performance, *per equipollens*, is sufficient in law.[g]

Upon the same principles depends the question whether the con-

[d] Pothier, Des Obligations, num. 199, &c. part 2, chap. 3, § 1, 2. And see the French Code Civil, art. 1168, &c.

[e] Co. Litt. Chap. of Estates upon Condition. passim.

[f] Pothier, Des Obligat. num. 206.

[g] Ibid. 207. And see Co. Litt. p. 237 a, n. 1, and Litt. § 552.

dition must be performed by the very person named in the contract, or may be performed by some other person.

But it is presumed that the parties intended their heirs to take their respective places with respect to the accomplishment of conditions.[h] But this rule does not extend to legacies.

When no period of time is defined, within which the condition is to be accomplished, it is held to have failed so soon as its accomplishment has become impossible, and this principle applies as well to negative as to positive conditions.[i]

There was a difference of opinion between the two schools of antient Jurisconsulti, whether the same rule is applicable to a condition in which the creditor has an actual interest.[k] For instance, if a man binds himself to pay 100 pieces of gold if he does not give the slave Pamphilus. Pothier decides according to the Sabinians and Papinian, that the debtor may in such a case be called upon by the creditor to perform his agreement, and that upon his failing to do so, the condition precedent must be held to be accomplished. Papinian says, *Fuisse voluntas probatur ut homo solvatur aut pecunia petatur.*[l] And this case differs from that of a condition, *si Capitolium ascendero*, for there the intention of the parties was that the party should not go up into the capitol, and therefore he cannot be called upon either to pay the penalty or to go up into the capitol.

It is a rule common to all conditions in obligations, that they are held to be accomplished when their accomplishment has been prevented by the debtor, who had an interest in their not being accomplished. *Quicumque sub conditione obligatus curavit ne conditio existeret, nihilominus obligatur.*[m] But it is otherwise where the debtor prevents the accomplishment of the condition by which he is discharged from the obligation, by doing something which he had both a right and an interest to do, and which not directly but only collaterally prevents the accomplishment of the condition, for *nullus videtur dolo facere qui suo jure utitur.*[n]

But if the creditor be prevented from accomplishing a potestative or mixed condition, by any cause not proceeding from an act of the debtor (as where an animal dies whose delivery is the condition under which the debtor is bound), the debtor has the benefit of the condition

[h] Instit. ubi supra. [i] Ibid.

[k] Pand. lib. xlv. tit. i. De Verbor. Obligat. L. 115, § 2.

[l] Pand. ibid. Pothier, Des Obligat. num. 211.

[m] Pand. lib. xlv. tit. i. De Verborum Obligationibus, L. 85, § 7. Pand. lib. l. tit. ult. De Regul. Jur. L. 39. Pand. lib. xxxv. tit. i. De Condition. et Demonstration. L. 81.

[n] Pand. lib. l tit. ult. L. 55. 151. Pothier, Des Obligat. num. 212.

not being accomplished, and he is freed from the obligation.[o] The reason is that contracts must be understood *uti sonant*, and against the creditor.[p] But it is otherwise as to testamentary dispositions, which are interpreted according to their fullest meaning, and therefore a legatee has the benefit of the accomplishment of the condition where it was prevented otherwise than by his default.[q]

Such are the chief rules touching the accomplishment of conditions: but it may be impossible from the very beginning. That impossibility may arise from the physical laws of nature, or from the moral laws of nature, or from the Municipal Law. In all these cases the condition is equally held to be impossible by the Civil Law. Papinian writes; *Quæ facta lædunt pietatem, existimationem, verecundiam nostram, et (ut generaliter dixerim) contra bonos mores fiunt, nec facere nos posse credendum est.*[r]

Such conditions, when they are *in faciendo*, render the contracts subject to them void and of no effect, as being illusory, or illegal. When they are *in non faciendo*, they do not render contracts void, if the impossibility be physical; but they may have that effect where the impossibility is moral or legal, because it is contrary to good faith and justice to stipulate for anything in consideration of abstaining from doing what is illegal or otherwise wrong.[s] And so in the English Law to omit to do something which is a duty is a void condition. And any obligation, to take effect on the occurrence of an impossible event, is void and can never exist.[t]

But it is otherwise in wills, in which impossible conditions are of no effect. *Impossibilis conditio pro non scripta habetur.*[u] And thus the disposition has effect as if there had been no condition.

These general rules will suffice with regard to the accomplishment of single conditions; but where several conditions are appended to one obligation or transaction, a distinction must be drawn[x] between the case where the conditions are connected by a disjunctive, such as *or*, and that where they are united by the conjunctive particle *and*. Where the words are in the disjunctive, the fulfilment of one condition is sufficient; but where they are in the conjunctive, the obligation

[o] Pothier, Des Obligat. num. 213. [p] Pand. lib. ii. tit. xiv. De Pact. L. 39.

[q] Pand. lib. xxx. tit. i. Liber i. De Legatis et Fideicommissis, L. 54, § 2. Pand. lib. xxxv. tit. i. De Condition. et Demonstr. L. 31.

[r] Pothier, Des Obligat. num. 204. Pand. lib. xxxv. tit. i. De Condit. Institutionum, L. 15. Pand. lib. l. tit. ult. De Reg. Jur. L. 185. Pand. lib. xxxv. tit. i. De Conditionibus et Demonstrationibus, L. 3.

[s] Pothier, ibid. num. 204. [t] Co. Litt. 206 b, n. 1; 237 a, n. 1; 219 a.

[u] Pand. lib. xxxv. tit. i. L. 3. Pand. lib. xxx. tit. i. Liber i. De Legatis et Fideicom. L. 104, § 1.

[x] Pand. lib. xlv. tit. i. De Verborum Obligat. L. 129.

depends on the fulfilment of both or all the conditions. And so it is in the English Law.[y]

An important distinction between the law of conditions in contracts, and in legacies, remains to be considered.

A condition suspends an obligation, so that *tantum spes est debitum iri;* but the benefit of that contingency descends to the heir of the party. *Eam spem in heredem transmittimus.*

The law is otherwise as to legacies. It follows, from the personal nature of legacies, that they do not descend to the heir of the legatee, unless they have become vested in the legatee, that is to say, due though not payable to him, in his lifetime. So a conditional legacy cannot be claimed by the heir of the legatee, if the condition was not accomplished in the lifetime of the legatee,—because a conditional legacy is not vested but contingent.[z] And so far is this principle carried in the Roman Law, that if a legacy be suspended by a term which may not expire during the life of the legatee, the legacy is not vested but contingent, and it therefore does not descend to the legatee's heir, if the legatee dies before the expiration of the term.[a]

There is a species of condition called *improper*, which does not produce a real but only an apparent suspensive effect, and which is uncertain only in this sense, that it is unknown. Such is the condition *if Titius has been consul*, or if Mævius *be now living*.[b] The difference between improper and proper conditions is, that in the former the event is or may be known to some men, but in the latter it can be known to no one, because it is future and uncertain, that is to say, it may happen, or it may never happen; or (in the case of potestative conditions) it depends on the will of one of the parties to the contract, which may also be unknown to all men.

The very nature of these improper conditions requires that both parties should be ignorant of the event, for if it be known to one party and not to the other, there is fraudulent concealment on the side of the former, who would thus profit by his own wrong.[c] This rule is of great importance in cases of insurance.

We come now to a very important passage of the Institutes, where Justinian distinguishes contracts *to give* from contracts *to perform.*

Not only things may be made the objects of contracts, but acts; as for instance, where a man stipulates that something shall be done or shall not be done. And in such contracts it is best to agree to a

[y] Co. Litt. § 364, p. 225 a.

[z] Pand. lib. xxxv. tit. i. De Condition. et Demonstrat. L. 1, 2.

[a] Pand. ibid.

[b] Instit. lib. iii. tit. xvi. § 6.

[c] Pothier, Des Oblig. num. 31. Pand. lib. iv. tit. iii. De Dolo Malo, L. 1, § 2. Pand. lib. ii. tit. xiv. De Pact. L. 7, § 9.

penalty in the event of non-performance, for the purpose of avoiding doubt and uncertainty in enforcing the contract.[d]

Pothier lays down the rule *Nemo potest precise cogi ad factum.* But this rule (which gave rise to an important difference of opinion between Vinnius and Heineccius) must be applied only to personal acts which it is impossible to compel the debtor to perform specifically, such as to paint a picture. In such cases, if the debtor be obstinate, there is no possibility of compelling him to specific performance.[e]

But to permit a man to discharge himself, as a matter of course, if he think fit, from the performance of his contract, by paying damages, would be to enable him to profit by his own wrong. It would also be contrary to the principle of the constitution of the Emperors Diocletian and Maximian, that the creditor cannot be obliged to receive payment otherwise than is agreed upon by the contract.[f] Pothier also holds that if an obligation *not to do* a certain thing be violated, the injured party may have things restored to their former state.[g] Heineccius argues with great force of reason, that the laws on which the maxim given above is founded are all negative on the question, for they only lay it down that the creditor may claim damages, but that no law has been produced showing that he is bound to be content with damages, foregoing specific performance. We may conclude that the Roman Law enforces specific performance of contracts wherever the nature of the case permits, but leaves the creditor his option between damages and specific performance.[h] And so it is in the English Law.

We have seen that Justinian recommends the insertion of a penalty in contracts, by way of liquidated damages, to be paid in case of non-performance. If no such provision be made, the damages must be estimated by the judge.

Damages of this nature are compensation for the loss suffered, or for the gain not received by reason of the non-performance or delay of performance or other violation of a contract.

The general rule on this subject is, that the creditor cannot demand compensation by way of damages for any loss except that which follows as a direct consequence of the violation of the contract, or which the debtor must have foreseen as the consequence of that violation.[i]

Instit. lib. iii. tit. xvi. § 7.

Vinnii Comm. ad Instit. lib. iii. tit. xvi. § 7. Heinecc. ibid. note.

Cod. lib. viii. tit. xlii. De Solutionibus et Liberation. L. 16.

Pothier, Des Obligat. num. 158. [h] Heinecc. ubi supr.

Pothier, Des Obligat. part 1, chap. 2, art. 3. Domat, Loix Civiles, liv. iii. tit. v.

CHAPTER XXXII.

OF JOINT CONTRACTS, OR OBLIGATIONS IN SOLIDUM.

Of Joint Contracts or Obligations *in Solidum*.—Instit. lib. iii. tit. xvii. De Duobus Reis Stipulandi vel Promittendi.—Description of Joint Contracts. Different Effects of the Particles *or* and *and*.—The 99th Novell of Justinian. Diversity between Joint Debtors and Sureties. Reference to the English Law. P. 188.

The 17th title of the 3rd book of the Institutes relates to contracts whereby several persons bind themselves jointly and severally to the performance of the whole obligation, as though each were the only person bound, with the express or implied stipulation that the performance of the obligation by one of them shall discharge all.

It also relates to contracts in which there are several obligors, or creditors, to each of whom separately the performance of the whole obligation is due, as though he were the sole creditor; but so that the performance to one of them is a sufficient discharge of the debtor with respect to all.[a]

Obligations of this kind are called in the Roman Law obligations *in solidum*. They are contracted as follows:—

The particle *or*, placed between the names of the obligees in a contract, constitutes an obligation *in solidum;* for the creditor then has a right to claim performance from any one of the debtors. But when the names of the debtors are connected by the word *and*, it is to be presumed that the parties intended that each should be separately liable for a portion of the obligation.[b]

The 99th Novell of Justinian made an important alteration in this part of the Roman Law. After that constitution it became established that, unless the intention of the parties to contract an obligation *in solidum* be expressed, each debtor is liable for an equal share of the performance. Even where that intention is expressed, the creditor cannot claim the entire performance of the obligation from one of the co debtors, unless the others are either absent or insolvent, or unless the debtor has renounced his privilege of sharing the liability with his co-debtors.[c] But this privilege and the 99th Novell are not received in Mercantile Law.

[a] Pothier, Des Obligat. num. 261 258.

[b] Vinnii Comm. ad Instit. lib. iii. tit. xvii. princip. Pand. lib. xxx. tit i Liber i. De Legatis, L. 8. Novell, 99. Vinnii Comm ibid.

It has been shown that in contracts *in solidum* each debtor is bound in the whole obligation, as if he were the sole debtor. And Papinian says, *Etsi maxime parem causam suscipiunt, nihilominus in cujusque persona propria singulorum consistit obligatio.*[d]

Thus Justinian lays it down that one joint debtor may be bound by an unqualified obligation, and another by an obligation qualified by a term or by a condition; nor will these qualifications exclude the creditor from availing himself of the unqualified nature of the obligation affecting the other joint debtor.[e] It is here important to notice the difference between joint debtors and sureties. Joint debtors are each bound towards the creditor as if they were sole debtors; for the creditor may sue whichever he pleases for the whole debt, and this rule is only modified by the privileges granted by Justinian to persons in that situation. But sureties are only bound collaterally, for the purpose of securing to the creditor an indemnity, in case of the default of the principal debtor. It follows that the obligation of sureties cannot extend beyond what is requisite for that purpose, otherwise the creditor would gain by the default of the principal debtor, since he would obtain from the surety what he would not be entitled to demand from the principal.

Joint obligations may arise from every species of contract.[f]

The joint debts, duties, obligations, and contracts and covenants which Littleton mentions as analogous to joint tenancy, in many respects resemble the contracts described in this part of Justinian's Institutes.[g]

[d] Vinnii Comm. ad Instit. lib. iii. tit. xvii. § 1, num. 1.

[e] Instit. lib. iii. tit. xvii. § 2.

[f] Pand. lib. xlv. tit. ii. De Duobus Reis Constituendis, L. 9.

[g] Litt. § 282.

CHAPTER XXXIII.

OF VOID CONTRACTS.

Of Void Contracts.—Instit. lib. iii. tit. xx. De Inutilibus Stipulationibus.—What Things may and what may not be the Object of Contracts.—Confirmation.—Promises regarding the Acts of Others.—In what Manner they may take effect.—Contracts Void for Want of Consent.—Effect of Error on Contracts.—Distinction between Efficacious and Concomitant or Collateral Error.—Error affecting a Motive or Inducement.—Incapacity of the Party.—Want of Privity of Interest.—Illegal Contracts. P. 196.

In the 30th title of the 3rd book of his Institutes the Emperor gives the chief rules of law showing what causes render contracts void. Some of those rules are purely technical, and proceed from the adherence of the Romans to the formula of stipulation, which they observed in most of the transactions of civil life, both public and private (including even the passing of laws) and with which all contracts might be clothed, though many needed it not.[a] But it is necessary here to pass over all those rules which are not grounded on reason and equity, or otherwise requisite to be explained as essential parts of the Roman Law.

The defects which render contracts void have reference to the thing which is the object of the obligation, or to the quality of the parties, or to the form or mode of contracting. Error, violence, dole, and lesion, are defects affecting the efficient cause of the contracts, and reducible under the heads above enumerated: but all these, except the first, do not, by the Roman Law, make the contract void, though they are reasons to avoid it *per exceptionem*, or upon plea pleaded. Justinian, therefore, expounds the three last-mentioned defects of contracts in the title of his Institutes devoted to the subject of exceptions or pleas.

The first subject here to be considered is what things may, and what may not be, the objects of contracts. *All things* (says Justinian) *which may be submitted to our dominion, may be the objects of contract, whether they be moveable or immoveable.*[b]

If a man stipulate for something which either is not or cannot be in existence, the stipulation is void and ineffectual.[c]

[a] Vinnii Comm. ad Instit. lib. iii. tit. xvi. princip. Heineccii Antiquitates Juris, lib. i. tit. ii. § 8.

[b] Instit. lib. iii. tit. xx. princip.

[c] Ibid. § 1. Pand. lib. l. tit. ult. L. 185.

This last paragraph is grounded on the maxim *impossibilium nulla obligatio*, from whence it also follows that a contract may be void because it is unintelligible, and that the debtor of a specific thing is set free from his obligation by the thing perishing without his *fault*.[d] And on the same principle of impossibility, a contract to give a thing appropriated to public use, or a thing consecrated, or a thing which is already the property of the stipulator, is void. And if anything which has been lawfully made the subject of a contract afterwards become incapable of being so, the contract is avoided, provided the charge in the nature of the thing took place otherwise than by the act of the debtor.[e] And Justinian expressly decides that a contract to deliver a certain man, in the event of his becoming a slave, is absolutely void, and never can have effect, because the law looks upon the subject-matter of the contract as naturally excluded from dominion.[f] The reason of this is, that what is absolutely void *ab initio* is incapable of confirmation *ex post facto*, according to the celebrated rule of Cato, *Quod initio vitiosum est non potest tractu temporis convalescere*.[g] A confirmation must take effect by supplying some defect in a title or right, which makes that title or right voidable or ineffectual in law. It cannot, therefore, operate upon what is void, and consequently never had any existence in law. And the English Law in this respect agrees with the Civil Law, for Lord Coke says: "A confirmation may make a voidable or defensible estate good, but it cannot work upon an estate that is void in law."[h] Hence is derived the common maxim, *Qui confirmat nihil dat*, which means that a confirmation does not create a new right, but only perfects an incomplete one.

Another consequence of the rule *impossibilium nulla obligatio est*, is that when the subject-matter of a contract, originally valid, becomes such, that under the same circumstances the contract could not have commenced, it is avoided. Thus Marcellus and Paulus give the rule: *Etiam quæ recte constiterunt resolvuntur cum in eum casum reciderunt a quo non potuissent consistere*.[i] So the debtor of a specific thing is discharged by the destruction of that thing. But when the debtor has by his own act caused the impossibility of performing his obligation, he is not discharged, for he is bound to indemnify the creditor.[k]

Pand. lib. l. tit. penult. L. 115. Vinnii Comm. ad Instit. hoc loc.

[e] Instit. ubi sup. § 2.

[f] Instit. lib. iii. tit. xx. § 2. *Quæ enim natura sui dominio nostro exempta sunt, in obligationem de luci nullo modo possunt.*

[g] Pand. lib. xxxiv. tit. vii. De Reg. Caton. Pand. lib. l. tit. ult. L. 29.

[h] Co. Litt. book iii. chap. ix. Of Confirm. § 515.

[i] Pand. lib. xlv. tit. i. De Verb. Oblig. L. 98. Ibid. L. penult. § ult.

[k] Instit. lib. iii. tit. xx. § 2.

We now come to those defects in contracts which regard, not the object of the contract only, but the parties, or their relation to that object.

If (says Justinian) *a man promise that another will do or give something, he is not bound. But if he promise that he will cause another to do or give something, he is bound by that agreement.*[l]

No man can either promise or stipulate touching matters affecting the rights of another,[m] and such a promise or stipulation is therefore void, as legally impossible to be executed. But there is no principle of law against a man promising to induce another to give or execute something, because he only promises his own act, and takes the risk of failure. If a man engage for another without his knowledge and consent, the contract is void. But the former may validly engage to pay something by way of penalty, in case of the latter not performing the contract.[n]

Pothier thus explains this rule of law: "When I promise that a third party shall do or give something for your benefit, without making myself liable in case of his not executing the contract, it is evident that I do not bind him, because no man can bind another without his consent; and that I do not bind myself, because it is assumed that I intended to bind not myself but another."

"But it is easily to be presumed that the person who promised that another would do or give something, did not promise *pure de alio,* but promised also *de se*, that is to say, he undertook upon his own peril, that the other should perform what he promised for him.

"In such cases the contract is valid, and renders the person who promised for the other liable in damages if the contract be not performed by the latter."[o]

The presumption that the contract was made not *pure de alio,* but *de alio et de se*, is supported by the rule that contracts are to be interpreted against the obligee, and Julianus says, *Quotiens ambigua oratio est, commodissimum est id accipi quo res de qua agitur magis valeat quam pereat.*[p]

Thus the rule of Ulpian, *inutiliter promittitur factum alienum,* applies only to contracts *pure de alio.*

The nature of a contract requires the concurrence of the intentions of the parties, for a contract or convention is defined by Ulpian to be

l Instit. lib. iii. tit. xx. § 3; and see § 20.

m Pand. lib. l. tit. ult. De Reg. Jur. L. 73, § 4, L. 74.

n Instit. ubi. sup. § 20.

o Pothier, Des Obligat. num. 56. Pand. lib. xlv. tit. i. De Verbor. Obligat. L. 81. *Qui alium sisti promittit, hoc promittit, id se acturum ut stet.* Ibid. L. 58, § 2.

p Pand. lib. xxxiv. tit. v. De Rebus Dubiis, L. 12, 21.

Duorum vel plurium in idem placitum consensus, and the same Jurisconsult says that to consent is *in unam sententiam decurrere*.[q] Thus Justinian decides that a stipulation is void if the stipulator puts the question, and the other person does not answer, or if one thing be stipulated for, and another promised, or if the stipulator puts the question unconditionally and the promise is made conditionally.[r]

The first of these cases is a mere nullity, and so is the converse, that is to say, a mere *pollicitatio* or offer not accepted. *Pollicitatio offerentis solius promissum est.* And *Invito beneficium non datur.*[s] And in the other cases there is no contract for want of consent.

But if a number of things be stipulated for and only the obligation to give some of them be taken, the contract is good as respecting those concerning which the parties agreed, because *in toto et pars continetur*, and though the parties did not agree as to all, they agreed as to a portion.[t]

On the same principle of want of consent, if the parties were in error and had in view different things as the subject matter of the contract, there is no obligation between them. Thus if Titius stipulate for the slave Stichus, and Sejus understand him to mean Pamphilus, there is no contract.[u]

This decision is founded on the rule *non consentiunt qui errant.*[x]

But error does not vitiate a contract or indeed any act in law, unless it bear on the very substance of the contract or other act. Thus it is a common rule in the Civil Law that *Nihil facit error nominis quum de corpore constat.*[y] The general rule on this subject is that error vitiates a contract where it falls either upon the thing itself, or upon the quality of the thing which the parties had principally in view, and which quality constitutes the substance of the thing.

This rule is governed by the distinction drawn by Pufendorf between *efficacious* error or ignorance, without which the act in question would not have been performed, and *concomitant* error or ignorance without the existence of which it would equally have been performed.[z]

[q] Pand. lib. ii. tit. xiv. De Pactis, L. 1, § 2, 3.

[r] Instit. lib. iii. tit. xx. § 5.

[s] Pand. lib. l. tit. xii. De Pollicit. L. 3. Ibid. tit. ult. L. 69.

[t] Pand. lib. xlv. tit. i. De Verbor. Oblig. L. 83, § 4, L. 1, § 4, et 3. Pand. lib. l. tit. ult. L. 113.

[u] Instit. ibid. § 22.

[x] Pand. lib. ii. tit. i. De Jurisdictione, L. 15. Pand. lib. l. tit. ult. De Regul. Jur. L. 116, § 2.

[y] Pand. lib. xviii. tit. i. De Contrahenda Emptione, L. 9, § 1. And see Pand. lib. xxx. tit. i. Liber i De Legatis, L. 4, as to nominal error in Legacies. Domat, Loix Civiles, lib. i. tit. xviii. Sect. 1, § 7, 8.

[z] Pufend. Devoir de l'Homme et du Citoyen. liv. i. chap. i. § 8, edit. Barbeyrac.

No error that is not *efficacious* can make void a contract; for unless the consent of the parties proceed from the error, it cannot vitiate their consent, to which it is only concomitant or collateral.

With respect to error touching the motive or reason which induced a man to enter into a contract (as for instance if he agree to buy something, erroneously believing that he requires it for a given purpose) Pothier holds with Barbeyrac that it does not vitiate the contract unless it be expressly agreed that the contract shall depend on the truth of the facts which cause the motive or reason.[a] On the same principle a legacy is good, though the motive which induced the testator to bequeath it was founded on error. *Ratio legandi legato non cohæret.*[b]

And herein a motive or inducement differs from a condition.

The want of consent also vitiates contracts entered into by persons incapable of giving consent. Such are persons insane and those within the *ætas infantiæ*, that is to say, below seven years; and the *ætas infantiæ proxima*, which is half the period between seven years of age and puberty.[c]

Persons insane cannot do any legal act. The Roman Law regards them as incapable of will, and as persons absent. *Furiosi nulla voluntas est. Furiosus absentis loco est.*[d]

A person below the age of puberty is legally capable of transacting business, provided the authority of his guardian be interposed where it is requisite, for instance, where the infant is to bind himself; for he may bind another person towards himself without his guardian. But this must be understood to apply only to those who have already some powers of comprehension, for infants (below seven years of age) and those who are of an age near to infancy (*infantiæ proxima*), are not materially different in law from persons insane. For their own advantage the law places those who are near to infancy on the same footing as those who are near puberty.[e]

But the subject of the capacity and incapacity of persons has already been explained in a former chapter.[f]

Another cause of nullity of contracts is the want of privity of interest between the stipulator and the person who is to be benefited by the contract.

It has already been laid down (says Justinian) *that no one can stipulate for the sole benefit of a third party. For civil contracts are designed*

[a] Pothier, Des Obligat. num. 20. Pufendorf, ubi sup.

[b] Pand. lib. xxxv. tit. i. De Condition. et Demonstration. L. 72, § 6.

[c] Vinnii Comm. ad Instit. lib. iii. tit. xx. § 9.

[d] Pand. lib. l. tit. ult. L. 40, L. 124, § 1.

[e] Instit. lib. iii. tit. xx. § 9, 10.

[f] Chap. x.

to enable men to obtain what they have an interest in obtaining, and the stipulator has no interest that something should be given to another person. But if it be desired to do this, a penalty must be added to the contract, to be due if the contract be not performed. When any one stipulates with a penal clause, it is not inquired what interest he has in the performance of the contract, but the penalty only is regarded.[g]

Pothier thus explains the law contained in this paragraph of the Institutes:—"When I stipulate something from you for the benefit of a third party, the convention between us on that stipulation is void, for you do not by that contract bind yourself civilly either towards that third party or towards me. It is evident that you contract no obligation towards the third party, because it is a principle of law that contracts can have effect only among the contracting parties; but you do not even contract any civil obligation towards me. That which I stipulated for the benefit of another, being a thing in which I have no interest capable of being estimated, no damages can be given to me against you if you break your engagement, and you may consequently break it with impunity. Now it is contrary to the very essence of a civil obligation that the debtor should be able to violate it with impunity; for a civil obligation is defined to be *juris vinculum quo necessitate adstringimur.* But these reasons cease where a penalty is stipulated for in the event of the contract not being performed.[h]

Grotius holds that a contract for the sole benefit of a third party, is valid in Natural though not in Civil Law; and this position is supported by the maxim of Papinian: *Beneficio adfici hominem interest hominis,* for there is a moral, though not a civil interest to support a contract of this nature.[i]

The reasons on which the rule *Alteri stipulari nemo potest* is grounded do not apply where the contract is not for the sole benefit of the third party, but the stipulator also has an interest in the performance of the contract. In such cases the contract is valid. Thus, if a man stipulate that something be given to his creditor, the stipulator may have an interest in the performance of the contract.[k]

Quod turpi ex causa promissum est non valet. Thus if a man promise to do anything illegal or immoral, the promise is void.[l] And upon the same principles, if anything be promised in consideration of

[g] Instit. lib. iii. tit. xx. § 19. *Alteri stipulari nemo potest.* Pand. lib. xlv. tit. i. De Verbor. Obligat. L. 38, § 17.

[h] Pothier, Des Obligat. num. 54.

[i] Grot Droit de la Guerre et de la Paix, liv. ii. chap. xi. § 18. And Pothier, ubi supra. Pand. lib. xviii. tit. vii De Servis Exportandis, L. 7. And see Pand. lib. xiii. tit. v. De Constituta Pecunia, L. 1.

[k] Instit. lib. iii. tit. xx. § 20.

[l] Instit. ibid. § 24. And see the distinction in Pand. lib. xlvi. tit. i. De Fidejussoribus, L. 70, § 5.

not doing an illegal act, that convention is void.[m] Such a contract is evidently *contra bonos mores.* These principles apply equally to all contracts involving anything illegal or contrary to the policy of the law. Thus Paulus decides that, *Inhonestum est vinculo pœnæ matrimonia obstringi*, and that therefore a contract for the payment of a sum of money by way of penalty or forfeit, if a marriage do not take place, is void.[n]

And Papinian says: *Jus publicum privatorum pactis mutari non potest.*[o]

If, however, anything has been actually given in performance of such a void contract, the law will not compel restitution, unless the party be innocent; for, as Paulus says, *Ubi dantis et accipientis turpitudo versatur, non posse repeti dicimus.*[p] But if the party seeking restitution of what he has given be not a wrong doer, the law will enforce restitution. *Quoties autem solius accipientis turpitudo versatur repeti potest.* The party claiming restitution must come into court with clean hands.

[m] Pand. lib. ii. tit. xiv. De Pactis, L. 7, § 3. *Si ob maleficium ne fiat promissum est, nulla est obligatio ex hac conventione.*

[n] Pand. ibid. L. 28, princip. *Contra Juris Civilis regulas, pacta conventa rata non habentur.* Pand. lib. xiv. tit. i. De Verborum Obligat. L. 134, princip.

[o] Pand. lib. ii. tit. xiv. De Pactis, L. 38.

[p] Pothier, Des Obligat. num. 43. Pand. lib. xii. tit. v. De Condictione ob Turpem Causam, L. 3. Pand. ibid. L. 4, § 2. At § 3, is this subtle decision:—*Sed quod meretrici datur repeti non potest, ut Labeo et Marcellus scribunt: sed nova ratione, non ea quod utriusque turpitudo versatur, sed solius dantis: illam enim turpiter facere quod sit meretrix; non turpiter accipere cum sit meretrix.* See on the subject of Contracts touching illicit things, Burlamaqui, Droit de la Nature et Des Gens, vol. iii. p. 37, &c.

CHAPTER XXXIV.

OF SURETIES, OR CAUTIONERS.

Of Sureties, or Cautioners.—Instit. lib. iii. tit. xxi. De Fidejussoribus.—Difference between Principal and Accessory Obligations.—Definitions of the Contract of Cautionary.—What Obligations may be secured thereby.—The *Beneficium Divisionis*.—The *Beneficium Ordinis*, or of Discussion.—Rules as to the Extent of the Obligation of Cautioners.—Their Remedy to obtain Repayment. P. 198.

All contracts or obligations are either principal or accessory. Principal obligations are those which the parties have chiefly in view, and which have a proper and distinct object of their own. Accessory obligations are those which the parties have not chiefly in view, and which have not a proper and distinct object exclusively their own, but are intended solely to insure the performance of some other obligation. The most important of these contracts is that of Sureties or Fidejussors. Fidejussio or Cautionary is a contract whereby a man binds himself towards a creditor, for a debtor, to pay to the former the whole or part of that which the latter owes to him in the event of the debtor not doing so himself.[a]

It is also defined by Erskine to be that obligation by which one becomes engaged for a debtor, who hath bound himself to pay a sum or do a deed, that he shall truly fulfil it.[b]

Every species of obligation, whether legal or only natural, may be secured by cautionary.[c]

As cautionary is an obligation accessory to that of the principal debtor, the execution of which it is its sole purpose to secure; the consequence is that unless there be a valid principal obligation, there can be no valid cautionary. This is agreeable to the rule *Cum principalis causa non consistit, ne ea quidem quæ sequuntur locum habent.*[d]

But though there must be a valid principal obligation, otherwise there can be no cautionary, the principal obligation need not be one which can be enforced by law, and so the obligation of the cautioner may be more strict than that of the principal. Thus Julianus says that the cautionary may be taken, *quotiens est aliqua obligatio natu-*

[a] Pothier, Des Obligat. num. 366. [b] Ersk. Institutes, book iii. tit. iii. § 61.

[c] Pand. lib. xlvi tit. i De Fidejussoribus, L. 1.

[d] Pand lib. l. tit. ult De Regul. Jur. L. 129, § 1. Pufendorf, Droit de la Nature et des Gens, liv. iii. chap. vi. § 11.

ralis vel civilis cui applicetur.[e] But a cautioner cannot validly engage to secure the performance of a contract, which though binding in conscience, is forbidden by the law.[f] Such a contract of fidejussion is contrary to the policy of the law, and therefore void.

Thus in order to decide whether a purely natural obligation be capable of being secured by cautionary, it is necessary to examine if that principal obligation be merely without a legal remedy to enforce it, or whether it be absolutely contrary to the policy or enactments of the law. In the former case the contract of cautionary or fidejussion is valid, and in the latter it is void.

The obligation of a fidejussor descends on his heir, as is the case with other contracts in the Roman Law.[g] The obligation of the fidejussor or cautioner may either precede or follow that of the principal debtor.[h] But as the sole object of this contract is to secure the performance of some other obligation, of which it is an accessory, the obligation of the cautioner must remain in suspense until that of the principal debtor is in existence, or is no longer suspended.[i]

Cautioners are allowed by the Roman Law, in cases where more than one are security for the same principal obligation, to divide their liability, and share it equally among themselves, for any one cautioner who is sued separately may (by virtue of a rescript of the Emperor Hadrian) require the creditor to sue him only for his share. But if any one of the co-cautioners be insolvent at the time of litiscontestation, the others are liable for his share. And if any one of them pay the whole, the others are set free, for it was his own neglect not to claim this privilege granted to joint cautioners by the Emperor Hadrian, which is called *beneficium divisionis.*[k]

Erskine observed that this *beneficium divisionis* was required in the Roman Law because cautioners were bound by the *verba solemnia* of stipulation, and were therefore in all cases liable for the whole debt; but that it is otherwise in the Scotch Law. "By our law (he says) all the co-cautioners are bound in the same writing, so that there is no room for this benefit: for where they become obliged conjointly and severally, the plain intention of the parties is that the obligation should not be divided; and where they are bound simply as cautioners, each co-cautioner is by the genuine nature of such obligation, without any privilege, liable only for his own proportion, while the other cautioners are solvent, except where the obligation itself is indivisible."[l]

[e] Pand. lib. xlvi. tit. i. De Fidejuss. L. 16, § 3, 4. Ersk. Instit. book iii. tit. iii. § 64.

[f] Cod. lib. iv. tit. xxix. Ad Senatusconsul. Villejanum. L. 14. Pand. lib. xvi. tit. i. Ad Senatusc. Vellej. L. 16, § 1. Pand. lib. xlvi. tit. i. De Fidejuss. L. 70, § 5

[g] Instit. lib. iii. tit. xxi De Fidejuss. § 2.

[h] Instit. ibid § 3.

[i] Pand. lib. xlvi tit. i. De Fidejuss L. 57.

[k] Ibid. ubi sup. § 4.

[l] Erskine, Instit. book iii tit. iii. § 63.

Justinian granted another equitable indulgence to cautioners, which in the Roman Law is called ***beneficium ordinis***, and in the Scotch Law *benefit of discussion*. By his 4th Novell he enacted that the principal creditor should be sued before the cautioner, unless the former was insolvent or absent; and that in case of the absence of the principal debtor, the cautioner should be allowed a respite within which to produce him. The effect of this law was practically to restrict the liability of the cautioner to what could not be obtained from the principal debtor.

This contract is further restricted by its legal nature.

Fidejussors cannot validly be bound (says Justinian) *so as to owe more than the principal debtor owes for whom they are bound: because their obligation is an accessory of the principal obligation. But they may be bound so as to owe less. Therefore, if the principal debtor owe ten pieces of gold, the cautioner may be bound for five pieces, but he cannot be bound for ten, if the principal debtor owe five.*[m]

Thus, if the principal debtor be bound absolutely, that is to say, in an unqualified obligation, the cautioner may be bound, subject to a condition or a suspensive term; but the converse of that case would be contrary to law, for *plus in accessione non potest esse quam in principali re.*[n]

If the law permitted the cautioner to owe more than the principal, the creditor would gain by the default or insolvency of the latter. This is contrary to the nature of the contract, which is intended not to give a gain to the creditor, but only to secure him against a loss. And if the law permitted the obligation of the cautioner to be otherwise more onerous than that of the principal, with regard either to certainty or to duration, the cautioner might remain liable after the obligation, the performance of which he was bound to secure, had ceased to exist. This is absurd, and repugnant to the nature of cautionary. Thus if the principal debtor be only bound to pay after the expiration of a term, the cautioner cannot be liable immediately. *Plus est enim statim aliquid dare, minus est post tempus dare.*[o]

It is on the principle of that rule that interest is due for delay of payment of debts.

Cautioners have an action against their principal debtor to recover whatever they have lawfully paid for him.[p] The Roman Law, however, does not permit a co-cautioner, who has paid more than his share, to sue his co-cautioners, unless he have received from the creditor before or at the time of the payment, an assignment of the creditor's right of action against them.[q]

[m] Instit. ubi sup. § 5.
[n] Instit. ibid.
[o] Instit. ibid.
[p] Instit. ibid. § 6.
[q] Vinnii Comm. ad Inst. lib. iii. tit. xxi. § 6.

CHAPTER XXXV.

THE LAW OF THINGS.—OF OBLIGATIONS BY WRITING.

Of Obligations by Writing.—Instit. lib. iii. tit. xxii De Literarum Obligationibus.—Explanation of *Literarum Obligationes*. *Presumptio Veritatis*—*Presumptio Solemnitatis*.—Rule that Extrinsic Solemnities are not presumed.—Distinction between them and Intrinsic Solemnities. P. 200.

If a man admit by a written instrument having borrowed what in fact never was paid or delivered to him, the Roman Law allows him to protect himself from the suit of the supposed creditor by the plea called *Exceptio non numeratæ pecuniæ*. But Justinian provided[a] that that plea should not be admitted after two years from the date of the instrument.

Obligations contracted in that manner are called by Justinian, *Literarum obligationes*, which in the Institutes, but not in the Pandects, are set down as the third species of obligations *ex contractu*.[b]

Before the expiration of two years from the date of the instrument of admission, the creditor must prove that the money was in fact lent to the debtor, if the latter plead that he did not receive it. The reason of this is that the debtor is not required to prove a negative. Besides it is to be presumed that if it had been paid, the creditor would be able to give evidence of the fact.[c]

But after two years are elapsed without the debtor taking any proceedings, the law presumes that the loan was carried into effect, and then the debtor is not heard to the contrary. But by the modern usage of most countries, the supposed debtor is allowed (though the presumption of law is against him) to prove after the two years have expired, that he did not in fact receive the loan. The presumption casts the *onus probandi* on the debtor, which, before the expiration of the two years, was upon the creditor.[d]

It is necessary to observe, that these *literarum obligationes* were only in cases of the admission of a loan, and the law on this subject is founded on peculiar reasons.

[a] Cod. lib. iv. tit. iv. De non Numerata Pecunia, L. 14.

[b] Cujacii Notæ ad Instit. lib. iii. tit. xxi. Cujac. Op. tom. i. col. 180, edit. Venet. Mutin.

[c] Vinnii Comm. ad Instit. ibid. num. 4. Cod. lib. iv. tit. xix. De Probation. L. 23.

[d] Vinn. ibid num 10.

In other cases the contents of an instrument legally constituted in its external form are presumed to be true as against the parties by whom it is executed, until that presumption is rebutted by contrary evidence.[e] This is what is called *presumptio veritatis.* This principle arises from the nature of presumptions, which are defined to be *conjecturæ ex signo verisimili;* for it is highly probable that a man himself knows, or has ascertained the truth of what he states in a solemn instrument.

On analogous principles, where an instrument is legal upon the face of it, it is presumed that all forms were duly observed in its execution,[f] until the contrary is proved. *Videri omnia solemniter esse acta.* This is called *presumptio solemnitatis.*

The party who produces an instrument admitted or proved to be genuine, has the advantage over the other who, though it be upon the face of it legal, alleges that some legal forms were omitted in its execution. The latter must therefore prove his allegation, and if he fail in the proof, the presumption prevails.[g]

But *Extrinsica solemnitas non præsumitur.* The meaning of this rule is, that where something is legally required which does not regard the execution and perfection of the instrument taken by itself,—that extrinsic requisite is not presumed, but must be proved. Thus Gajus decides, that whoever purchases from a person below puberty (*pupillus*) must prove *tutore auctore, lege non prohibente se emisse.*[h]

The rule therefore is, that intrinsic solemnities are presumed, and extrinsic solemnities are not;[i] that is to say, they are not presumed from the apparent legality of the act, though they may be presumed from other circumstances, such, for instance, as long and undisturbed possession; for they may be (in general) proved by circumstantial as well as by direct evidence.

The title of the Institutes, *De Literarum Obligationibus*, is of little practical use. And this species of obligations has no foundation in Natural Law.[k]

[e] Instit. lib. iii. tit. xx. De Inutil. Stipul. § 12, beginning with the words *Item verborum.*

[f] Pand. lib. xlv. tit. i. De Verbor. Obligat. L. 30. Instit. lib. iii. tit. xxii. § ultim.

[g] Voet, Comm. ad Pand. lib. xxii. tit. iii. De Probat. num. 15.

[h] Pand. lib. vi. tit. ii. De Publiciana in Rem Actione, L. 13, § ultim.

[i] Menochius, De Præsumptionibus, lib. iii. Præsumptio 132; et vide lib. ii. Præsumpt. 23, num. 2, 3.

[k] Pufendorf, Droit de la Nature et des Gens, liv. v. chap. ii. § 6, note 5.

CHAPTER XXXVI.

THE LAW OF THINGS.—OF OBLIGATIONS BY CONSENT.

Of the Contract of Buying and Selling and of Exchange.—Instit. lib. iii. tit. xxiii. De Obligationibus ex Consensu.—Explanation of the Nature of this Class of Contracts. Instit. lib. iii. tit. xxiv. De Emptione et Venditione.—Nature of Contracts *ex Consensu*.—The Contract of Sale defined. When it is Complete. —Effect of Error. Representations and Statements by the Vendor.—Sale of a Future Thing.—Sale of a Chance.—Legal Principles as to the Price.—Difference and Resemblance between Sale and Exchange.—Rules of the Civil Law, as to the Risk and Profit of the Thing after Sale and before Delivery.—Rules of Natural Law.—Conditions in Sales.—Conditions Precedent and Subsequent. —*Pactum de Retrovadendo.—Addictio in Diem.—Lex Commissoria.*—Sale of Things not *in Commercio*.—Sale of the Property of a Third Party.—Sale of the Same Thing to several Purchasers.—Rules of the Roman Law.—Principles of Natural Law. P. 211.

THE fourth class of obligations, *ex contractu*, consists of those which are called obligations *ex consensu*. Contracts of this class are so called in the Roman Law, not because other contracts are made without the consent of the parties, but because these are the only contracts which create an obligation from the moment that the parties have declared their consent by proper outward signs, and without its being necessary that anything should be delivered or that anything else should be done beyond that consent.[a] *Sufficit eos qui negotium gerunt consentire.* These contracts are all *named contracts*, (*contractus nominati,*) in the strictest sense of the term, and not merely as contradistinguished from those which are not valid in the Roman Law unless there be a valuable consideration to support them, in which latter sense even a stipulation by question and answer is a named contract.

These contracts by consent are *nominati*, because their frequent use is such that their name suffices to express all their consequences and incidents.

But all these distinctions are unknown to natural law as well as the technical consequences drawn from them by the Civil Law. And indeed the distinction between named and anonymous contracts is not to be found, at least in so many words, in the Corpus Juris.[b] Contracts, *ex consensu*, are four in number, namely, *Buying and Selling, Letting and Hiring, Societies or Partnerships, and Mandates.*[c]

[a] Pufendorf, Droit de la Nature, L. 5, chap. 2, § 6. Instit. lib. iii. tit. xxiii.

[b] Grotius, Droit de la Guerre et de la Paix, liv. ii. chap. xii. § 3, et n. 3.

[c] Instit. ubi sup.

And first, of the contract of sale, which is perhaps the most important of all.

Pothier defines that contract as follows. The contract of sale is a contract in which one of the parties who is the vendor binds himself towards the other, who is the purchasor, to give him to possess as proprietor a thing in return for a sum of money, which the purchaser, on his part, engages to give to the vendor.[d]

The same learned civilian writes that sale is a synellagmatic contract as contradistinguished from an unilateral contract, and that it is also a commutative contract, that is to say, one in which it is the intention of each of the parties to receive an equivalent for what he gives. Three things are essential to every contract of sale. 1st, A thing which is the object of the contract; 2nd, A price agreed upon; and 3rd, The consent of the contracting parties.[e]

The contract of sale (says Justinian) *is complete as soon as the price is agreed upon, though nothing has been paid, and no arrha or earnest has been given, for the earnest is only the evidence of a sale having been contracted.*[f]

This is the general rule, but sales which are required by law or agreement to be contracted by a written instrument, are not perfected and complete until that instrument has been executed. And so it is where the sale is required to be contracted by a notarial instrument. There all the formalities required for that kind of instrument must be completed before the sale is valid. The purchaser refusing to perform the contract, forfeits the earnest if he has given any.[g] And the vendor so refusing forfeits double the amount of the earnest. It is to be presumed however (where there is room for doubt) that the written instrument is intended only to be evidence of the contract, and not to be an essential part of it.[h]

Ulpian lays down this rule: *Sive in ipsa emptione dissentiant, sive in pretio, sive in quo alio, emptio imperfecta est.*[i] But the want of assent as to the thing sold must be respecting something essential, otherwise it does not invalidate the contract. Thus an error *in corpore*, as, if the purchaser meant to buy the horse A, and the vendor intended to sell the horse B, renders the sale void. But it is otherwise if the error was only as to the name, for, *Nihil facit error nominis si de corpore constat.*[k]

If, however, there be an error *in substantia*, though the parties

[d] Pothier du Contr. de Vente, art. prelim. [e] Ibid. 2 3.
[f] Instit. lib. iii. tit. xxiv. princip. [g] Instit. ibid. § 1.
[h] Grotius, Droit de la Guerre et de la Paix, liv. ii. chap. xvi. § 30.
[i] Pand lib. xviii tit 1. De Contrahenda Emptione, L. 9. [k] Ibid. § 1.

agree as to the specific thing, the sale is void. Thus, if a man sold lead for silver, or copper for gold, the rule of Ulpian is applied, *Quotiens in materia erratur nulla est venditio.*[l] It is otherwise where the consent fails only as to the quality of the thing, as for instance its goodness or badness. Paulus says, *Si* (res) *deterius fuit quam emptor existimaret, tunc emptio valet.*[m] But this rule applies only where the purchaser was able to perceive the quality of the thing, for if the vendor took advantage of the inability of the purchaser to do so, the sale is void.[n]

The purchaser may, however, (where the contract is not void) obtain an abatement of price by the action *quanti minoris,* or *exempto,* in consideration of the vendor having induced the purchaser to buy the thing for a higher price than it was worth, by false representations respecting its qualities; though the vendor is not liable for mere praises of his merchandise, *quæ commendandi causa in venditionibus dicuntur.*[o]

Where the purchaser has an opportunity of seeing whether the praises bestowed by the vendor upon his property are well founded, he must judge for himself.[p] But if the vendor do not confine himself to general praises, nor to assertions the truth of which the purchaser may ascertain, but make statements respecting the property, for the truth of which the purchaser naturally and properly relies upon the knowledge of the vendor and is thereby induced to give a higher price than he would otherwise have done, the purchaser has an action against him to abate the price.

Though the thing sold must be certain, that is to say specified, as well as the price (otherwise there can be no consent to it), the sale of a future thing, that is to say, a thing not in existence at the time of the contract, is valid. Thus the sale of the future profits of an estate, or the future offspring of an animal, is valid.[q] And even a mere hope or chance, as the future draft of a net, may be validly sold.[r] But there is an important distinction between the sale of a future thing and the sale of a chance or hope. In the first species of case, the law holds the

[l] Pand. lib. xviii. tit. i. De Contrahenda Emptione, L. 9, et vide L. 41.

[m] Pand. ibid. L. 10.

[n] Pand. ibid. L. 11. And see Pand. lib. xxi. tit. i. De Ædilitio Edicto et Redhibitione et Quanti Minoris.

[o] Pand. lib. xix. tit. i. De Actione Empti. et Vendititi, L. 13, § 4. Pand. lib. xviii. tit. i. De Contr. Emptione, L. 43. Sugden, Vendors and Purchasers, vol. i. p. 3.

[p] Pand. lib. xviii. tit. i. De Contrah. Empt. L. 43, § 1. *Pollicitationes venditorem non obligant si ita in promptu res est ut eam emptor non ignoraverit.* Pand. lib. iv. tit. vi. Ex Quibus Causis Majores xxv. Annis in Integrum restituuntur. L. 16.

[q] Pand. lib. xviii. tit. i. De Contrahenda Emptione, L. 8. [r] Ibid. L. 8, § 1.

contract to be conditional, and to be of no effect, unless the thing which is its object comes into existence. So if I sell the future young of a particular animal, and the animal has none, the contract is of no effect, and the price is not to be paid. But in the second species of case, a chance is sold, and not a specific though future thing. Thus when the cast of a net is sold, the contract partakes of chance: therefore, if no fish are caught, the purchaser must nevertheless pay the price. In every case the question is one of intention,—whether the parties intended to buy and sell a future thing, or a mere chance.[s]

We come now to the principles of the Civil Law respecting the price. In the first place the price must be certain and definite, or (which is the same in principle) data must be settled whereby it may be rendered certain and definite, for otherwise there cannot be a consent of the parties to the price, without which the contract is void. Thus it may be agreed that the price shall be a given sum, or that it shall be settled by a third party, or generally by arbitration.[t] And if the third party do not settle the price, or if the arbitration be ineffectual, the contract is void. And the same principle governs the contract of letting and hiring.[u]

Ulpian says, *Sine pretio nulla venditio est.*[v] And the price must have three requisites. 1st. It must be a true and not a fictitious price, though it be inadequate. 2ndly. It must be certain and definite, or capable of being defined. And 3rdly. It must consist of money.[x] If the price be illusory, the transaction is a gift and not a sale; if the price be not certain, or capable of being rendered so, which is the same in principle, (for *certum est quod certum reddi potest,*) there is no consent of the parties to the price, and therefore no sale: and if what is given, or to be given, on one side be not money, the transaction is an exchange and not a sale.

The rule of the Civil Law is, that *Pretium in numerata pecunia consistere debit.* There was some difference of opinion on this matter among the antient Jurisconsulti, but that of Nerva and Poculus was confirmed by several Emperors.[y] They held, with Paulus and Ulpian, that the difference between sale and exchange (*permutatio*) is that in the former there is a distinction between the vendor and the purchaser, as there is between the thing sold and the price, which consists of money: but in the latter there is no such distinction, because it consists in the mutual transfer of things one in consideration of the

[s] Voet, Comm. ad Pand. lib. xviii. tit. i. num. 13.

[t] Pothier, Traite du Contr. de Vente. num. 26.

[u] Instit lib. iii. tit. xxiv. § 1

[v] Pand. lib. xviii. tit. i. De Contrahenda Empt. L. 2, § 1.

[x] Pothier, Contr. de Vente, num. 18—21.

[y] Instit. ubi sup. § 2.

other. *In permutatione discerni non potest uter venditor vel uter emptor sit.*[z]

All the rules respecting the contract of sale are however applicable to that of exchange, except those which arise from the difference between the obligations of vendor and purchaser, for *permutatio vicem emptionis obtinet.*[a] And Paulus shows that the contract of buying and selling derives its origin from exchange.[b]

According to these principles, Pothier decides that if besides the payment of a price in money, the purchaser engages to give or to perform something as a complement of the price, the contract is nevertheless a sale and not an exchange, because there is *merx* and *pretium*. And so Pomponius holds.[c]

We have now to consider a very important paragraph of the Institutes. It is as follows: —

When the contract of buying and selling is contracted, (and this as we have observed is effected so soon as the price is agreed upon, when the contract is not by written instrument) the thing sold is at the risk of the purchaser, though it has not yet been delivered to him. Therefore if after sale a slave die or receive any hurt, or if a building or any part of it be consumed by fire, or if lands sold, or any portion of them be washed away by a torrent, or injured by an inundation or a storm, the loss in all these cases must be borne by the purchaser, who is obliged to pay the price agreed upon though he never had possession of the thing. Whatever may happen to the thing sold without the dole or fault of the vendor, the vendor is not liable. But if, on the other hand, after the sale any accession be made to the land by alluvion or otherwise, this increase is to the sole profit of the purchaser, for Commodum ejus esse debet cujus periculum est. But if a slave who is sold, either run away or be stolen before delivery, and neither fraud nor negligence can be imputed to the vendor, the question arises

[z] Pand. lib. xix. tit. iv. De Rerum Permutatione, L. 1. Pand. lib. xviii. tit. i. De Contrah. Empt. L. 1.

[a] Cod. lib. xix. tit. iv. De Rerum Permut. L. 2.

[b] Pothier, Contr. de Vente, num 30. Pand. lib. xix. tit. i. De Actione Empti. et Venditi. L. 6, § 1.

[c] This is a very curious passage, as a specimen of antient political economy. Origo emendi vendendique a permutationibus cæpit. Olim enim non erat nummus: neque aliud *merx*, aliud *pretium* vocabatur: sed unusquisque secundum necessitatem temporum, ac rerum, utilibus inutilia permutabat, quando plerunque evenit ut quod alteri superest alteri desit. Sed quia non semper nec facile concurrabat, ut cum tu haberes quod ego desiderarem, invicem haberem quod tu accipere velles, electa materia est cujus publica et perpetua æstimatio, difficultatibus permutationum æqualitate quantitatis subveniret: ea que) materia forma publica percussa, usum dominiumque non tam ex substantia præbet, quam ex quantitate: nec ultra *merx* utrumque, sed alterum *pretium* vocatur. Pand. lib. xviii. tit. i. De Contrah. Empt. L. 1.

whether the vendor undertook the safe custody of the slave until delivery. If he did, then the risk of such casual occurrences falls upon him, but if not, the loss falls on the purchaser. And so it is with regard to other animals and things. But (as against third parties) *the vendor is held to be owner of the property until delivery, and therefore whenever any such loss occurs, he must transfer to the purchaser his rights of action, whether real or personal, if required. And so it is with regard to actions for theft and damage.*[c]

The principles contained in this paragraph are founded on the rule that the debtor of a specific thing is set free from his obligation by that thing perishing without its loss being imputable to him.[d] As soon as the contract of sale is perfected, the vendor becomes debtor of the thing sold, and the purchaser becomes debtor of the price, and therefore as the thing sold is the subject-matter of the obligation of the vendor, that obligation must perish with the thing unless its loss be legally imputable to the vendor.

And this doctrine is not contrary to the rule *Res perit domino suo*,[e] though Justinian lays it down that until delivery the vendor continues to be proprietor of the thing sold; for this is as between him and third parties who are not affected by the contract;[f] according to the general rule of the Roman Law, that property is transferred, not by contract, but by delivery.[g] But as between the parties to the contract, the thing sold is the property of the purchaser before delivery, for he has an action to obtain delivery, and *Is qui actionem habet ad rem recuperandam, ipsam rem habere videtur.*[h]

It follows from the legal principles governing this subject, that though the destruction of the thing sold sets free the vendor, the purchaser remains liable to pay the price, for if it were otherwise, he could not be said to bear the loss.

On the other hand, the purchaser is entitled to the benefit of any improvement or increase of, or profit from the thing sold, arising before delivery, for *Secundum naturam est commoda cujusque rei eum sequi quem sequuntur incommoda;* and *Ubi periculum, ibi et lucrum collocatur.*[i]

[c] Instit. ibid. § 3.

[d] Pothier, Des Obligat. num. 657. Poth. Contr. de Vente, part 4. Pand. lib. xlv. tit. i. De Verbor. Oblig. L. 37.

[e] Cod. lib. iv. tit. xxiv. De Pignoratitia Actione, L. 9.

[f] Grotius, Droit de la Guerre et de la Paix, liv. ii. chap. xii. § 15, n. 6.

[g] Cod. lib. ii. tit. iii. De Pactis, L. 20. Cod. lib. ix. tit. xxxiv. De Crimine Stellionatus, L. 2.

[h] Pand. lib. l. tit. ult. L. 15; tit. penult. L. 143. Pand. lib. xli. tit. i. De Acquirendo Rerum Dominio, L. 52.

[i] Pand. lib. l. tit. ult. L. 10. Cod. lib. vi. tit. ii. De Furtis, L. ult. § 3.

If the vendor caused the impossibility of delivering the thing, or its deterioration, by any act, positive or negative, contrary to his obligations towards the purchaser, the former must compensate the latter for his loss. Paulus says, *Factum suum cuique, non adversario nocere debet*[j], and the purchaser should not suffer for the act of the vendor. And Ulpian rules that *Qui dolo desierit possidere pro possidente damnatur, quia pro possessione dolus est;*[k] which means that he who by dole ceases to possess is liable as though he still possessed, for he becomes liable by reason of his dole, as he before was by reason of his possession. From this principle it follows, that if the vendor wrongfully lost possession of the thing sold, he remains liable towards the purchaser.

But Paulus says, *Nemo damnum fecit nisi qui id fecit quod facere jus non habet.*[l] It follows, therefore, that the vendor is liable towards the purchaser for no acts or omissions affecting the thing sold, but such as he had not a right to do or to omit. This subject requires consideration. The responsibility of the vendor is governed by this celebrated rule, taken from a law of Ulpian. *In contractibus in quibus utriusque contrahentis utilitas versatur, levis culpa, non etiam levissima præstatur.*[m] Therefore that degree of care and diligence is required of the vendor which is usually bestowed on their own property by reasonable and careful men. *Media diligentia, id est talis qualem vulgo bonus et frugi paterfamilias suis rebus adhibet.*[n]

But if the purchaser delay to take possession of the property sold to him, the vendor is then relieved from all liability except for dole.[o] And therein is included gross fault or negligence, for Ulpian says, *Lata culpa dolo comparatur;* and Paulus says, *Magna culpa dolus est.*[p]

The responsibility of the vendor may, however, be varied by the agreement of the parties, provided that agreement be not contrary to law; as, for instance, an agreement that there should be no liability for dole or fraud.[q]

It is necessary to observe that the general rule, that after sale and before delivery the risk of the thing sold is upon the purchaser, applies only where the contract is a sale of a specific thing, as, for instance, a

[j] Pand. lib. l. tit. ult. L. 155.

[k] Pand. ibid. L. 131, 157, § 1.

[l] Pand. ibid. L. 151.

[m] Pand. lib. xiii. tit. vi. Commodati, L. 5, § 2. Pand. lib. xviii. tit. i. De Contrah. Empt. L. 35, § 4. Pand. lib. l. tit. ult. L. 23.

[n] Vinnii Comm. ad Instit. lib. iii. tit. xxiv. § 3, num. 10.

[o] Pand. lib. xviii. tit. vi. De Periculo et Commodo Rei Venditæ, L. 17.

[p] Pand. lib. ii. tit. vi. Si Mensor Falsum Modum dixerit, L. 1, § 1; lib. l. tit. penult. L. 226.

[q] Pand. lib. l. tit. ult. L. 23.

particular horse; and where the sale is not of a specific thing, but of a thing *in genera*, as, for instance, *a horse*, and not the horse A or B; there, after the vendor has chosen what horse he will deliver, the horse remains at his risk until delivery, unless the purchaser accepted the horse.[r]

It is evident that if the vendor sold *a horse* without specifying any individual horse, and afterwards procured or chose a horse for the purpose of its being delivered, and the horse died before acceptation, he is not discharged from his obligation by that event; for he cannot plead the impossibility of performing his part of the contract, since though he cannot deliver *that horse*, he can deliver *a horse*, which was what he engaged to do.[s] In such cases the vendor is not the debtor of a specific thing, but of a thing *in genere*,—and he is therefore not discharged by the thing perishing.

Such are the chief rules of the Roman Law on this celebrated head of law, *De Periculo et Commodo Rei Venditæ*. But Pufendorf holds them not to be entirely in accordance with Natural Law. He is of opinion that, by natural equity, the loss ought in two cases to fall on the vendor after the conclusion of the contract, namely, wherever either he is in delay to deliver the thing sold, or the thing has not been delivered because it is at a distance from the place where the bargain was struck. In the former case he is liable by the Roman Law, as well as on obvious principles of justice. In the latter the vendor is bound to put the purchaser in possession; and though the vendor is discharged by the impossibility of doing so arising without his default, yet the purchaser ought to be discharged from liability to pay the price, because he has not received the equivalent due to him, and thus the contract is void and of no effect on both sides.

But if the thing perish after the purchaser is in delay to take possession of it, he must pay the price, for the vendor is not to suffer a loss by the default of the purchaser.[t] These principles seem to be very equitable, and they would probably be observed in a question of this kind arising between nations, in preference to those of the Roman Law.

The contract of sale, like other contracts, may be subject to a condition. Thus a horse may be sold with this condition,—provided the purchaser be satisfied with it after a certain time.[u] There the contract is in suspense. One effect of that suspense is, that the thing sold

[r] Pand. lib. v. tit. penult. De Verborum Obligat. L. 23.

[s] See the same principle in the distinction between *mutuum* and *commodatum*, Instit. lib. iii. tit. xv. § 2.

[t] Pufendorf, Droit de la Nature et des Gens, liv. v. chap. v. § 3.

[u] Instit. lib. iii. tit. xxv. § 4.

remains the property of the vendor, and is at his risk until the condition is accomplished.[x] It is indeed evident that the thing sold cannot be at the peril of the purchaser while the contract is suspended by the condition; for, as Ulpian neatly expresses it: *Quod pendet non est pro eo quasi sit*,[y] and therefore there is no sale and no transfer of property until the condition is accomplished.

A sale may also be subject to a condition subsequent, that is to say, to be good until a given event. And thus an unlimited power may be vested in the purchaser to return the thing sold, and recover the price.[z]

Of the same nature is the *pactum de retrovadendo*, or *jus retractus conventionalis*, which consists of an agreement that the vendor, or the vendor and his heirs, shall be at liberty for ever, or within a certain time, to re-purchase the thing sold.[a]

The most remarkable species of conditions subsequent in sales by the Roman Law are *addictio in diem*, whereby the sale is annulled if a more favourable offer be made to the vendor within a given time; and *lex commissoria*, which is an agreement that if the price be not paid within a certain time, the sale shall be void.[b]

The rules of law respecting conditions, which has been explained elsewhere,[c] are applicable as well to sales as to other contracts.

If a man knowingly purchase something not *in commercio*, as for instance a thing sacred or public, the contract is void and of no effect. But if he purchase it, being deceived as to its nature by the vendor, he has an action against the vendor, to obtain damages for the deceit practised upon him.[d]

Paulus says, *Quas (res) natura vel gentium jus, vel mores civitatis commercio exuerunt, earum nulla venditio est.*[e] The reason is that no man can convey to another a right which he has no power over, that is to say, which he has not himself. *Nemo plus juris ad alium transferre potest quam ipse habet.*[f] But the vendor cannot exonerate himself from the contract by pleading an impossibility of which he was aware from the beginning, for no man shall profit by his own wrong.[g]

[x] Pand. lib. xviii. tit. vi. De Periculo et Commodo Rei Venditæ, L. 8.

[y] Pand. lib. l. tit ult. L. 109, § 1.

[z] Pand. lib. xxi. tit. i. De Ædilitio Edicto. L. 31, § 22.

[a] Cod. lib. iv. tit. liv. De Pactis inter Emptor. et Venditor. L. 2.

[b] Pand. lib. xviii. tit. ii. De in Diem Addict. L. 1. Pand. lib. xviii. tit. iii. De Lege Commissoria, L. 1; ibid. L. 3.

[c] Chap. xxxi.

[d] Instit. lib. iii. tit. xxv. § 5.

[e] Pand. lib. xviii. tit. i. De Contrahenda Vendit. L. 34, § 1. Instit. lib. iii. tit. xx.

[f] Pand. lib. l. tit. ult. L. 54.

[g] Ibid. L. 134. Pand. lib. xvii. tit. ii. Pro Socio, L. 63, § 7, Non est æquum dolum suum quemquam relevare.

He is therefore liable to compensate the purchaser in an action for damages.

But though no man can convey to another a right which he has not himself,—a thing may be validly sold which belongs to a third party and not to the vendor. That species of sale is valid though it does not transfer the property of the thing sold to the purchaser. It is a contract binding the vendor to obtain the thing sold from the owner, and deliver it to the purchaser, or to compensate him in damages for breach of the contract.[h] And if the vendor delivered the property erroneously sold, believing it on probable grounds to be his own, and the purchaser be evicted, he is liable to the purchaser, but not if there be no eviction, for the sale is *primâ facie* good, and the vendor gave the purchaser as good a title as he could.

The same thing may be purchased by different persons either from the same or different vendors.

Neratius decides that in such cases whichever purchased from the real owner shall have the preference; but that if each purchaser purchased from the same vendor, or if they all purchased from vendors whose titles were bad, there whoever first obtained possession, must be preferred, provided he be a *bonâ fide* purchaser, that is to say, provided he had reason to believe his vendor's title to be valid.[i]

So long as there has been no delivery, priority of time prevails, and *qui prior est tempore potior est jure*;[k] for no man can convey a title which he has already divested himself of,[l] and therefore the first conveyance prevails.

But where one purchaser has obtained possession with a *bonâ fide* title, he is preferred to a purchaser prior in date, for *in pari causa possessor potior est*; and, moreover, he is not to be deprived of the fruits of his care and vigilance in obtaining possession. *Jus Civile vigilantibus scriptum est.*[m]

The rule of the Roman Law, that property is transferred by delivery rather than by contract (except as between the parties) is founded on sound views of legal policy. The principles of natural law, however, are somewhat different, for they prefer priority of title to priority of possession,—because the effect of the first sale (provided it be such as

[h] Pand. lib. xviii. tit. i. De Contrahend. Empt. L. 28. Voet, Comm. ad Pand. lib. xviii. tit. i. num. 14.

[i] Pand. lib. xix. tit. i. De Actionibus Empt. et Venditi. L. 31, § 2.

[k] Pand. lib. xx. tit. iv. Qui Potiores in Pignore, L. 14. Sext. Decretal, tit. ult. Regula 54.

[l] Pand. lib. l. tit. ult. L. 54.

[m] Ibid. L. 129. Pand. lib. xlii. tit. viii. Quæ in Fraud. Creditor. L. 24. See Co. Litt. 290 b, note 1, § 15.

to convey the *dominium* of the thing sold) is to divest the right of the vendor and transfer it to the purchaser. The vendor cannot therefore afterwards dispose of that right, for *Nemo dat quod non habet.* Such is the doctrine of Grotius, which seems the most conformable to reason, though his commentator, Barbeyrac, maintains that when one of the several subsequent purchasers has obtained possession, accompanied with *bona fides*, the thing is, as it were, lost to the others, though prior in date, and that they must therefore be content with their action for damages against the vendor.[n]

CHAPTER XXXVII.

LOCATION OR HIRE, AND EMPHYTEUSIS.

Location, or Hire, and Emphyteusis.—Instit. lib. iii. tit. xxv. De Locatione Conductione.—Analogy of Location to Sale.—Legal Nature of the Possession of a Lessee.—*Locatio Rei*, and *Locatio Operis* defined.—Rules as to the Hire.—A Species of Exchange resembling Location.—Emphyteusis defined and compared to Feudal Tenures.—A Species of Sale resembling Location.—The Obligations of the Conductor or Lessee.—What Care and Diligence are required of him.—*Imperitia culpæ adnumeratur.*—Rules of the Civil Law respecting Damage by Fire. P. 216.

The contract of location or hire is the second of the contracts *ex consensu*, as they are placed in the Institutes, and it is governed by almost the same rules as the contract of sale.[a] Location is a contract where a hire is stipulated for the use of things or the service of persons.[b] It may be considered not improperly as a species of sale, wherein the subject sold is the use or service, and the hire is the price. On these principles is founded the decision of Ulpian, that a lessee *does not possess*; which must be understood to mean that he does not possess as proprietor, and that therefore his possession is the possession of the lessor.[c]

The possession of the lessee is what Cujacius denominates natural possession, and *rei detentio*, as contradistinguished from civil possession or *animo domini detentio*, and he lays it down that *qui incumbunt rei alienæ, non possident, sed alii possident per eos.*[d]

[n] Grot. Droit de la Guerre et de la Paix, liv. ii. chap. xii. § 15, num. 4, and note 6.

[a] Instit. lib. iii. tit. xxv. princip. [b] Erskine, Instit. book iii. tit. iii. § 14.

[c] Pand. lib. vi. tit. i. De Rei Vindicatione, L. 9.

[d] Cujacii Comm. ad Legem 9, Pand. lib. vi. tit. i. De Rei Vindicatione. Cujac. Op. tom. vii. col. 249. edit. Venet. Mutin.

With regard to the mode of constituting the contract, Justinian says: *As vending and purchasing is contracted directly the price is settled, so letting and hiring is contracted so soon as the hire is settled and agreed upon. And the lessor has the action locati, and the lessee the action conducti.*[e]

Location is of two species, namely, *locatio rei,* and *locatio operis.*

Locatio rei is a contract whereby one of the parties obliges himself to give to the other the use and enjoyment of a certain thing for a period of time agreed upon between them, and in consideration of a price which the latter binds himself to pay in return.[f]

Locatio operis is a contract whereby one of the parties gives a certain work or service to be done by the other, who binds himself towards the former to do that work in consideration of a price which he who gives the work or service to be done binds himself to pay to him who undertakes to do it.[g] And in the French code it is defined to be a contract by which one of the parties engages to do something for the other in consideration of a price or hire agreed upon between them.[h]

The party who lets his work or service, or the use of his property to hire, is the *locator* or lessor, and the other is the *conductor* or lessee.

The amount of the hire may, like that of the price in a sale, be agreed to be referred to a third party, or generally to be defined by arbitration. But if the hire be left to be matter of future arrangement between the parties, the Roman Law considers the contract as not strictly location, but the anonymous contract of *facio ut des,* or *do ut des,* as the case may be, and the party entitled to the hire may recover what is fairly due to him by an action, *præscriptis verbis,* or *on the case.*[i] The reason of this is, that the action *locati* is inapplicable, because the amount of the hire is left to be determined by future agreement of the parties, or by a court of law. But this is a purely technical point of the Roman Law, though there may be cases where no court could settle the amount of the hire, and the contract would consequently be void for uncertainty, without some subsequent agreement of the parties.

As the mutual transfer of things, the one in consideration of the other, is not sale, if one of them do not consist of money, but exchange; so a similar mutual transfer of the use of things is not location but a peculiar contract.[k] It is a species of exchange, because there is no distinction therein between the lessor and the lessee, which distinction

[e] Instit lib. iii tit. xxv. princip. Grotius, Droit de la Guerre et de la Paix, liv. ii. chap xii. § 18.

[f] Pothier, Contr. de Louage, num. 1.

[g] Ibid. num. 392.

[h] Code Civil. art 1710.

[i] Instit. ubi sup. § 1.

[k] Ibid. § 2.

is essential to the contract of location. It is a contract of *do ut des*, and an exchange of labour or service is *facio ut facias*.

It follows that there can be no proper contract of *locatio rei*, unless the hire consist of money, or at least of something valued in money, as is the case with a corn rent. But that rule does not apply, except technically, and under the rule of the Roman Law distinguishing anonymous from named contracts, to *locatio operis*. This is evident, for in a contract to give a thing, though not money, nor valued in money, in consideration of a work or service, the distinction exists between the lessor and the lessee.[l] It is, therefore, location.

There is in the Roman Law a contract called *Emphyteusis*, which bears so much analogy to sale and to location, that it was disputed among the antients which of those two denominations it should bear. The Emperor Zeno, however, determined that it is a contract by itself, and of a distinct nature.

Emphyteusis consists of alienation of immoveable property, subject to a perpetual payment in the nature of rent, called the *canon*, to the landlord.[m] This contract may be subject to a variety of agreements or pactions, but if there be no special provisos to the contrary therein, the total destruction of the thing falls on the landlord, who thereby loses his rent, and the partial destruction or injury to it falls on the tenant.[n]

Erskine observes that *Emphyteusis* greatly resembles *feu holdings* in the Scotch Law.[o] Cujacius writes that it is a species of usufruct, because the grantor retains the proprietorship, or, as the English Law expresses it, *the legal estate*; and he deduces the origin of fiefs from those qualified beneficial ownerships in the Roman Law. Hargrave disputes this position,[p] because the *Emphyteuticarii* were merely occupiers of land under contracts of hiring; but it would seem that that sort of occupation may easily have led to the introduction of feudal occupation of land, as both have the grand characteristic of the separation of the *dominium utile* from the *dominium directum*.[q] And Cujacius fully recognises the difference between *emphyteusis* and fiefs, for he defines the latter thus: *Jus prædio alieno in perpetuum utendi fruendi, quod pro beneficio dominus dat ea lege, ut qui accipit, sibi fidem et militiæ munus aliudve servitium exhibeat.*[r]

An *emphyteusis* is properly perpetual, but it may be granted for a

[l] Voet. Comm. ad Pand. lib. xix. tit. ii. num. 8. Pand. lib. xix. tit. ii. Locati Conducti, L. 19, § 3. [m] Instit. lib. iii. tit. xxv. § 3. [n] Ibid.

[o] Ersk. Instit. lib. ii. tit. iv. § 6. Cujac. in Lib. Feudor. lib. 1. princip. et tit. v. Opera, tom. ii. col. 1066 and 1094, edit. Venet. Mutin.

[p] Co. Litt. 64 a, note 1; 191 a, note. [q] Co. Litt. 1.

[r] Cujac. Com. ad Lib. Feudor. princip. Oper. tom. ii. col 1067

long term of years, or for any other long period, subject to the payment of the *canon*, and the obligation of improving which belongs to this contract, that is to say, of cultivating the estate.[s]

Justinian gives another instance of a contract partaking of the nature of location and of sale. It is this: If Titius agrees with an artisan to pay him a sum of money for rings to be made by the latter out of his own materials, the transaction is, according to Cassius, a sale of the materials and hire of the labour or workmanship. Justinian, however, decides that it is a sale only. But if Titius himself furnished the workman with the materials, it is only a hire of the workmanship.[t]

The reason of this decision of Justinian is, that the transaction in question is the sale of a future thing to be produced by the workman, in which the workmanship is paid for as well as the materials. But the fact that the workmanship is paid for, does not in itself make the contract *locatio operis*, for in a sale the form or workmanship of the thing is considered, as well as the materials, in estimating the value, and whether the thing be purchased before it is made or afterwards, the nature of the contract is the same.[u] The obligations of the lessee or *conductor* are next to be considered. They are thus generally described by the Emperor.

The lessee (or conductor) is bound to do all things according to the tenour of the lease or contract of hire, and, if anything be omitted therein, he is, nevertheless, bound to it by equity. He who gave or promised hire for anything, is bound to such care in the custody thereof as a diligent father of a family bestows on his property. And if, notwithstanding that care, the thing be lost, he is no longer bound to the obligation of restitution.[x]

It appears by this text, that in location, as in other contracts, the agreement between the parties gives the law to the transaction.[y] And the consequences of the contract flow from the equity of the law, though not expressly agreed upon. *Si quid in lege prætermissum fuerit, id ex bono et æquo præstare oportet.*

The lessee becomes, after the expiration of the term of the hire, debtor of the thing hired to the lessor. The former, being the debtor of a specific thing, is therefore set free from his obligation by that thing perishing without his fault.

As this is a contract for the benefit of both parties, it includes

[s] Voet. Comm. ad Pand. lib. vi. tit. iii. num. 3. Donelli, Comm. Jur. Civ. lib. ix. cap. xiii. § 3, 19, &c.

[t] Instit. lib. iii. tit. xxv. § 4.

[u] Pand. lib. xviii. tit. i. De Contrahend. Emptione, L. 20.

[x] Instit. lib. iii. tit. xxv. § 4.

[y] Pand. lib. l. tit. ult. De Reg. Jur. L. 23. Cod. lib. iv. tit. lxv. De Locato et Conducto, L. 16. Instit. lib. iii. tit. xxv. § 5. Pand. lib. l. tit. ult. L. 90.

responsibility for fault as well as for dole.[z] The lessee is liable for *levis culpa*, but not for *levissima culpa*, a degree of liability which attaches to a party deriving the sole benefit from the contract, as, for instance, a borrower.[a]

Where a gem is given to be set or graven, and it breaks in the hands of the workman, if it broke *vitio materiæ*, he is not liable; but if it was spoilt by his want of skill (*imperitia facientis*), he is responsible to his employer.[b]

All cases where a man undertakes to do something with materials belonging to another in consideration of a hire, are governed by the celebrated rule of Celsus, Ulpian, and Paulus, that, *Imperitia culpæ adnumeratur*. The reason of this rule is that no man ought to undertake to do anything which may cause damage or injury to another, unless he possesses the skill necessary to guard against that danger.[c]

On the other hand, if the lessee be injured by some defect in the thing let, the lessor is liable. Thus if vessels be let, and there be a flaw in them whereby wine escapes and is lost, the lessor is liable for the damage, and he shall not be excused on the plea of ignorance. And where pastures are let, and the cattle are killed or injured by poisonous herbs growing there, the lessor is liable in damages if he knew of the defect of the pasture, and if not, he may not claim any rent, that is to say, in both cases the contract is at an end.[d] The Civil Law has a special rule touching fire. Paulus says: *Plerumque incendia fiunt culpa inhabitatum:* and Alfenus Varus says: *Incendium sine culpa fieri non potest.*[e] It follows from these texts, that the presumption of the law is against the person in whose premises the fire commenced. But Varus concludes that if he took those precautions which careful men usually take, he is not responsible for damage done by the fire communicating to neighbouring houses.

The last paragraph of this title of the Institutes applies to location, the general presumption arising in all contracts that men enter into contracts for their heirs as well as themselves.[f]

[z] Pand. lib. xiii. tit. vi. Commodati, L. 5, § 2. Pand. lib. l. tit. ult. L. 23.

[a] Vinnius, Comm. ad Instit. lib. iii. tit. xxv. § 5.

[b] Pand. lib. xix. tit. ii. Locati Conducti, L. 13, § 5.

[c] Pand. lib. i. tit. xviii. De Officio Præsidis, L. 6, § 7. Pand. lib. xix. tit. ii. Locati Conducti, L. 9, § 5. Pand. lib. l. tit. ult. L. 132.

[d] Pand. lib. xix. tit. ii. Locati Conducti, L. xix. § 1. Pand. lib. xix. tit. i. De Actione Empti. et Vend. L. 6, § 4.

[e] Pand. lib. i. tit. xv. De Officio Præfect. Vigilum, L. 3, § 1 Pand. lib. xviii. tit. vi. De Periculo et Commodo Rei Vendit. L. 11.

[f] Pothier, Des Obligat. num. 673.

If the lessee die within the time of the letting, his heir succeeds to his rights.[g] And so it is with lessors. But the presumption ceases where the performance of the contract is matter of skill, or otherwise personal to the party deceased, as in the case of a contract of hire to paint a picture.[h]

CHAPTER XXXVIII.

OF SOCIETY, COPARTNERY OR PARTNERSHIP.

Of Society, Copartnery or Partnership.—Instit. lib. iii. tit. xxvi. De Societate.—Definitions of the Contract of Society.—Its Four Essential Features.—Distinction between Partnership and Community of Property. Partnerships: 1. Universal, or 2. Particular. Partnerships of Things or of the Use of Things.—Partnerships in Professions or Arts.—Commercial Partnerships of Three Kinds: 1. Partnerships with a Collective Name; 2. Partnerships *en Commendite*, or Sleeping Partnerships; 3. Anonymous Societies or Joint-stock Companies.—Rules as to the Proportions of Gain and Loss, and the Liability of Partners.—Corporate Bodies.—Analogy and Difference between them and Anonymous Societies.—Dissolution of Partnership.—Effect of Withdrawal and of Death of a Partner.—Extent of the Duty of a Partner, and his Liability for Dole and Fault. P. 224.

THE third *consensual* contract, that is to say, society or partnership, is the subject of this chapter.

This contract is defined by Pothier to be a contract whereby two or more persons either place, or bind themselves to place something in common, for the purpose of lawfully making a common profit, for which they agree to be mutually accountable to each other.[a] It is perfected by consent without more, and it is synellagmatic or bilateral and commutative, which means that each party intends to receive an equivalent for what he gives.[b] Erskine more briefly defines this contract to be that by which several partners agree concerning the communication of loss or gain arising from the subject of the contract.[c] There are four features essential to society or co-partnership.

1st. Each partner must either bring, or engage to bring, something to the common stock, whether it be money or other property, or something else, as labour, industry, or skill.[d]

[g] Instit. lib. iii. tit. xxv. § 6.

[h] Pothier, Des Obligat. num. 674, 675.

[a] Pothier, Traité de la Societé, art. prélimin. And see Pufendorf, Droit de la Nature et des Gens, liv. v. chap. viii.

[b] Ibid. num. 5 7.

[c] Ersk. Instit. lib. iii. tit. iii. § 18.

[d] Pothier, Traité de la Societé, num. 8. Cod. lib. iv. tit xxxvii. Pro Socio, L. 1.

2ndly. The contract of society must be entered into with a view to the common interest of the partnership, that is to say, in order to *commune negotium genere*, otherwise it is the contract called *mandate* [e]

3rdly. The parties should have in view a profit or gain in which each of them may hope to have a share in consideration of what he has brought to the common stock, otherwise the contract would be *societas leonina*, unjust and void. *Iniquum enim genus societatis est ex qua quis damnum, non etiam lucrum spectet.*[f]

4thly. It is necessary for the validity of a contract of society that its subject-matter or object be lawful, and that the profit in view be honest and fair. *Nec enim ulla societas maleficiorum. Nec societas nec mandatum flagitiosæ rei ullos vires habet.*[g]

These rules show that it is the voluntary association of persons for a given purpose that distinguishes partnership from community of property, or joint ownership. Thus Papinian calls partnership *voluntarium consortium.* So where property devolves upon several persons together they are joint owners, but not partners, for there is no agreement between them to be partners.[h]

Partnerships are either universal or particular.

There are in the Civil Law two species of universal society or partnership, namely, *Societas universorum bonorum*, and *Societas universorum quæ ex quæstu veniunt.*

Partnership *universorum bonorum* is that wherein the parties agree to place in common all their property, present and future.[i] It is never presumed that this species of partnership has been contracted. The intention of the parties to do so must therefore be express, or otherwise clearly indicated.[k]

Ulpian and Paulus define partnership *universorum quæ ex quæstu veniunt*, to be that in which the parties place to the common account or profit all that they acquire by any species of industry or commercial transaction, but not what they derive from liberality, as a legacy or donation; and this kind of society is presumed to have been contracted when the parties entered into the contract of society generally without specifying the precise kind of society.[l]

Thus also the partnership is not liable to the debts of the individual

[e] Pothier, Traité de la Societé, num. 11. Pand. lib. xvii. tit. ii. Pro Socio, L. 52, princip.

[f] Pothier, ibid. num. 12. Pand. lib. xvii. tit. ii. Pro Socio, L. 29, § 2.

[g] Pothier, ibid. num. 14.

[h] Pand. lib. xvii. tit. ii. Pro Soc. L. 52, § 8. Ibid. L. 31.

[i] Pothier, ibid. num. 29.

[k] Pand. lib. xvii. tit. ii. Pro Socio, L. 7. Ibid. L. 52, § 8.

[l] Ibid. L. 7, L. 8, L. 52, § 8, L. 9, L. 11. Pothier, ubi sup. num. 51.

partners contracted before the partnership was entered into, for such debts are personal to the partner who incurred them.[m] And the partnership is not liable even to debts contracted during its existence, unless they be contracted in the partnership affairs.[n] Such are the chief rules of the two kinds of universal or general partnership.

Particular or special partnerships are of three kinds, namely, 1st. Those contracted to have in common certain things for the purpose of sharing their fruits or produce; 2ndly, Those wherein the object of the copartners is to pursue in common some profession or art; and 3rdly, Commercial societies or companies.[o]

Ulpian writes, *Societates contrahuntur unius rei*.[p] In this, as well as the other species of partnerships, either the things themselves included in the contract are placed in common, or only the use of those things. Upon this distinction is grounded the following celebrated decision of Celsus.[q] Two men possessed, one three, and the other one horse, and they agreed to sell the four together as a *quadriga*, and to share the price, the owner of the three horses taking three-fourths, and the proprietor of the one horse one-fourth of the produce. Before the sale, the single horse, which belonged to one of the partners, died, and he claimed nevertheless to have a share in the profits arising from the sale of the other three. But Celsus held the claim to be bad, because it was the use of the horses for the purpose of sale, and not the animals themselves, that was made common property and brought into partnership. *Non enim habendæ sed vendendæ quadrigæ coitam societatem*. But the Jurisconsult held that if the intention of the parties had been to make the *quadriga* common or partnership property, the partnership would not be determined by the share perishing which one partner thus brought into a common stock.[r]

This decision agrees with the rule *Res perit domino suo*, for in the first case the horses remained the sole property of their original owners; therefore each must bear the loss of his horse: but in the latter case, the horses would have been all and each, jointly and severally, the property of the partnership or the common property of the partners, therefore the loss must fall upon the society. In that case, therefore, the party who brought the one horse into partnership must bear one-fourth of the loss, and the other partner the remaining three-fourths.

We come now to partnerships in arts or professions. In them the

[m] Pothier, Traité de la Societé, num. 52.

[n] Ibid. n. 53. Pand. lib. xvii. tit. ii. Pro Soc. L. 12.

[o] Pothier, ibid. chap. ii. § 2.

[p] Pand. ubi sup. L. 5. Pothier, ubi sup. num. 34.

[q] Pand. ibid. L. 58.

[r] Ibid. *Si id actum dicatur ut quadriga fieret, eaque communicaretur, tuque in ea tres partes haberes, ego quartam; non dubie adhuc socii sumus.*

partners are to bring to the common account all gains arising from the exercise of the profession, art, or trade, in the pursuit of which they have associated themselves together for common profit.[s]

Commercial partnerships, which are the third class of particular or special partnerships, are divided by commercial law into three species.[t] First, *Partnership with a collective name or firm.* This is where several traders agree to trade in common in the name of the parties to the contract. In these all the partnership affairs are transacted in the name of the partnership, as for instance, A. B. and C., or A. B. and Company. But the partnership is entitled only to what the partners acquire in the name of the firm. Thus it is decided by the Emperors Diocletian and Maximian that a partner who purchased something in his own name with the partnership moneys acquired it for himself, though he was accountable to the society for the money.[u] As the society was not bound by the sale, it cannot profit thereby, according to the rule that contracts have effect only between the parties. If however the purchase made by the partner be within the purposes of the society, his copartners may compel him to share the profits with them, for he was guilty of a breach of contract towards them by appropriating to himself a profit which it was the object of that contract to obtain in common.[x]

The second species of commercial partnership is called *Commendite.* It is where one party trades in his own name and another furnishes the stock or money. There the sleeping partner shares the profits with the acting partner, but bears the losses and liabilities only up to the amount of the value which he puts into the common stock, or so far as he has agreed to be liable. The reason of this limited liability is, that the sleeping partner does not give his name to the partnership and takes no share in the business, and therefore no one can have dealt with the partnership with a view to his liability and credit; consequently he is not personally liable towards third parties; and he is liable towards his copartners only up to the amount of his contribution, or so far as he by his contract with them made himself liable.[y]

The third species are anonymous societies, or joint-stock societies, or companies. These are where two or more persons agree to participate in a certain business which is to be done in the name of one of them,[z] or under a collective name, designating the object of the association.[a] The partners in anonymous societies are not liable directly to third parties,[b] because those third parties do not look to the credit of the

[s] Pothier, Traité de la Societé, num. 55. [t] Ibid. num. 56.
[u] Cod. lib. iii. tit. xxxviii. Communia utriusque Judicii, L. 4.
[x] Pothier, ubi sup. num. 60. [y] Ibid. [z] Ibid. num. 61.
[a] Code de Commerce, art. 29—31. [b] Pothier, ubi sup. num. 63.

partners individually, who in this respect resemble sleeping partners. But they are bound to the extent of their interest in the enterprise (though beyond what they have contributed) to indemnify the acting partner or other agent of the society for what debts he has incurred in the partnership affairs.

The particular cases in which this obligation attaches must be determined by the rules of the Civil Law, regarding the contracts of society and *mandatum* or agency.

As for companies, incorporated or otherwise, authorized by law, they have certain privileges, accompanied by regulations for the prevention of fraud; but they are not within the scope of this chapter, as they depend more on public law than on contract.

Justinian gives this general rule as to the proportions of gain and loss to be enjoyed and borne by partners. If no express agreement has been made between the partners concerning their shares of profit and loss, the loss must be equally borne, and the profit equally divided.[c]

This rule is grounded on a presumption of law that the parties so intended; but where they did not contribute to the common stock in equal shares, the presumption ceases, and they share the loss and profit in proportion to their several contributions of capital, skill, or industry.[d]

If, however, there be any special agreement between the partners as to their shares of profit and loss, it must be observed. Thus three persons may validly agree that two shares of profit and loss shall belong to one partner, and that the other shall have the remaining third.[e] And a contract is valid in which a partner has secured to him two thirds of the profit, with liability to only one third of the loss, for the co-operation of some persons may be so valuable that it may be fair for them to be admitted into partnership on very favourable terms.[f] And of this the parties to the contract are to judge. *Legem contractus dedit.* So one partner may contribute money while the other only contributes his services; and a partner may (as it was held by Servius Sulpicius) be entitled to share the profit without liability to any part of the loss:[g] though it cannot be lawfully agreed that a partner shall be liable to loss and have no share in the profits, for this is *societas leonina*, which is unjust.[h]

With regard to the mode of determining the profit and loss, it is to be understood that if profit has been obtained in one business, and a

[c] Instit. lib. iii. tit. xxvi. § 1.

[d] Voet, Comm. ad Pand. lib. xvii. tit. ii. num. 8. Pand. ibid. L. 80, L. 6. L. 29.

[e] Instit. ubi sup.

[f] Instit. ibid. § 2. Pand. lib. xvii. tit. ii. Pro Socio, L. 29.

[g] Ibid.

[h] Pand. lib. xvii. tit. ii. Pro Socio, L. 29, § 2

loss suffered in another, the surplus of gain over loss is to be considered as the gain.[i] *Neque lucrum intelligitur nisi omni deducto damno; neque damnum nisi omni lucro deducto.*[k]

If in any contract of society, the proportions of gain only, or of loss only, be specified and settled, the same proportions are to be preserved with regard to loss or to gain, as the case may be.[l] This rule is grounded on an equitable presumption of the intention of the parties.

It is important here to note that, as a general rule, the restrictions and limitations of the liability of partners, by virtue of the contract of partnership entered into between them, do not affect the rights of third parties, creditors of the partnership, unless the latter dealt with the partnership on that footing. Thus it has been shown that it is peculiar to sleeping partners (because credit is not given to them as partners by third parties) that they are liable to third parties only up to the amount of their share in the concern.

This is the great distinction between a corporate body or an aggregate of persons to act as a body politic, and a partnership or society.

In the former, the individuals are perfectly distinct as such from the body which they compose, and those who deal with that body deal with it considered as a person, and not with the individual members. Thus Ulpian says: *Si quid universitati debetur, singulis non debetur; nec quod debet universitas singuli debent.*[m]

But copartnerships have not the legal character of bodies politic or persons in law; therefore, the individuals composing them (who hold out their credit as partners) are bound in their individual capacity by the partnership contracts with third parties.

With regard to anonymous societies or companies[n] they bear a modified analogy to corporate bodies, in this respect: Those who deal with them do not deal with the individuals; but this is because they do not look to the credit of the partners, who are a species of sleeping partners, but to the credit of the society. These societies, on the other hand, differ from corporate bodies in this, among other things: The partners are liable to the agents of the society in their individual capacity, which is not so with the members of corporations, for *quod universitas debet, singuli non debent.* Thus it appears that as regards third parties, anonymous societies are in the nature of bodies corporate.

[i] Instit. ubi sup.

[k] Pand. lib. xvii. tit. ii. Pro Socio, L. 30.

[l] Instit. ubi sup. § 3.

[m] Pand. lib. iii. tit. iv. Quod Cujuscunque Universitatis Nomine, L. 7, § 1.

[n] Pothier, Traité du Contr. de Societe, num. 63.

And so in the French Law they cannot be established without Public authorization.[o]

It now remains to be explained in what manner partnerships are dissolved.

No partnership can be indissoluble. *Nulla societatis in æternum coitio est.*[p] And the general rule is that partnership exists only so long as the parties continue in the intention of remaining partners. Thus, if one of them renounce the partnership, the society is dissolved. If, however, a partner renounced with fraudulent intent that he might have the sole benefit of an expected gain, as, for instance, where an universal partner (*totorum bonorum*) renounced in order to obtain the sole benefit of an inheritance, he may be compelled to share that profit with the other partners. It is otherwise if, after renouncing, the partner receive some profit which he had not in view at the time of his renunciation; for the whole is his own. But those from whom a partner has separated himself by renunciation, are entitled to the exclusive benefit of whatever they acquire after such renunciation.[q] These rules are grounded on abundant equity. Though partnership lasts only so long as each and all the partners are willing to remain associated together,[r] no man can renounce fraudulently, or so as to injure the rights of his copartners, otherwise he would profit by his own wrong; and *Nemo potest mutare consilium in alterius injuriam.*[s] Thus a partner who withdraws to secure a profit for himself alone, which by the terms of the contract he ought to share with his copartners, is guilty of fraud, and he remains bound to them, though they are no longer bound to him.[t] And so a partner cannot lawfully renounce at a time when his so doing would injure his copartners. An unseasonable renunciation (*intempestiva renunciatio*) does not set him free from his obligations, but renders him liable for the consequences.[u] Without this rule, no partnership would be safe, and it is essential to the fidelity and honesty which are necessary in this contract.

The effect of the retirement of one of the partners is (as we have seen) to dissolve the society with regard to all. *Cum aliquis renunciaverit societati, solvitur societas.*[x] And so it is in case of the death of a partner; for it may be that he was the person with a view to whom principally the society was formed, or without whom its business

[o] Code de Commerce, art. 37.

[p] Pand. lib. xvii. tit. ii. Pro Socio, L. 70.

[q] Instit. ubi sup. § 4.

[r] Cod. lib. iv. tit. xxxvii. Pro Socio, L. 5.

[s] Pand. lib. xvii. tit. ii. Pro Socio, L. 63, § 7. Ibid. lib. l. tit. ult. L. 75.

[t] Pand. lib. xvii. tit. ii. Pro Socio, L. 65, § 3.

[u] Ibid. L. 17, tit. ii. Pro Socio. L. 17, § 2, L. 65, § 5. Pufendorf, Droit de la Nat. liv. v. chap. viii. § 4.

[x] Instit. ubi sup. § 4.

cannot be beneficially carried on.[y] Men enter into this contract having regard to the persons with whom they associate themselves,[z] and any change of persons renders the partnership no longer the same, therefore the partnership is extinguished by the death or renunciation of one partner.

It follows, from the personal nature of this contract, that the heir of a deceased partner does not become a partner as such heir, without a special agreement to that effect. He, however, succeeds to the rights and obligations of the deceased partner, so far as they are not personal to him, and arise from community of property. Thus the heir succeeds only to the share of right and liability which the deceased had at the time of his death, as well as to the necessary consequences of those rights and liabilities; but not to the future rights and liabilities of the society.[a]

Another consequence of the rule that the contract of society is *voluntarium consortium*, is that no new partner can be made a member of the society without the consent of all the partners. *Socii mei socius meus socius non est.*[b]

A partnership is also determined by the conclusion of the business for which it was contracted.[c] This is evident, for *legem contractus dedit;* and on the same principle if a partnership be contracted for a time, it expires by the lapse of that time.[d]

The confiscation of all the property of one of the partners dissolves the partnership, for as the fisc succeeds to his property, he is held to be civilly dead.[e]

Also if a partner, being pressed by his debts, make a surrender of his goods (*cessio bonorum*), and they are sold to pay his debts, the partnership is dissolved. And in this case, if the partners (including the bankrupt) still consent to remain associated together in partnership, it is the commencement of a new society.[f] But this is not so in the case of confiscation, so far as the partner suffering that penalty is concerned, for he is civilly dead, and civil death has the same legal effect as natural death.

The question remains to be considered, whether a partner, as such, is liable to the society for dole only, as is the case with one who suffers property to be deposited with him, or for fault also, that is to say, for negligence or indolence.

[y] Pand. lib. xvii. tit. ii. Pro Socio, L. 65, § 5.

[z] Instit. ubi sup. § 5. The rule is *Qui societatem contrahit, certam personam sibi elegit.* Pand. ubi sup. L. 52, § 8.

[a] Pothier, Traité du Contr. de Societé, num. 144.

[b] Pand. ubi sup. L. 19, L. 20.

[c] Instit. ubi sup. § 6.

[d] Pand. ubi sup. L. 63, § 6.

[e] Instit. ubi sup. § 7.

[f] Ibid. § 8.

It is established law that he is liable, not only for dole, but for fault.[g] And as society is one of the contracts mutually beneficial to the parties, it follows that a partner is liable for fault, that is to say, *levis culpa*, though not for *levissima culpa:* so that it suffices if he use that degree of care and diligence which careful men of business usually apply to their own affairs.[h]

In that sense is to be understood the rule laid down by Justinian, that it suffices if a partner act with the same care and diligence in the partnership business which he uses in his own, and that whoever chooses a partner wanting in diligence must blame himself. For Justinian says: *Culpa autem non ad exactissimam diligentiam dirigenda est*, thereby implying that *exacta diligentia* is required.[i]

CHAPTER XXXIX.

OF MANDATE, OR PROCURATION.

Of Mandate or Procuration.—Instit. lib. iii. tit. xxvii. De Mandato.—Definition of Mandate.—The *Actio Mandati, Directa* and *Contraria*.—Three Things essential to this Contract.—The Five Modes or Kinds of Mandate.—Express and Tacit Mandate.—Ratification equivalent to Mandate.—Mandates General and Special.—Principles of Grotius as to Ambassadors.—Secret Powers and Instructions.—Powers Judicial and Extra-judicial.—Mandate for the sole Benefit of the Mandator.—Mandate for the Benefit of both Parties.—Mandate *Aliena Gratia*.—Mandate *Mandantis et Aliena Gratia*.—Mandate for the sole Benefit of the Procurator.—Liability of an Adviser for Advice given.—Responsibility of Advisers of the Crown.—Illegal Mandates.—The Execution of a Mandate.—The Four Modes in which Mandate terminates.—Care and Diligence required of the Mandatary or Procurator.—*Honorarium*. P. 232.

One of the contracts perfected by consent alone remains to be explained, namely, Mandate.

Mandate is a contract whereby one of the parties entrusts the other with the transaction of one or more affairs, to manage them in his place and at his risk; while the other engages to perform the trust

[g] Instit. ubi sup. § 9.

[h] Vinnii Comment. ad Instit. lib. iii. tit. xxvi. § 9. Pand. lib. xiii. tit. vi. Commodati, L. 5, § 2. Pand. lib. l. tit. ult. L. 23.

[i] Instit. ubi sup. Pand. lib xvii. tit. ii. Pro Socio, L. 72, 52, § 2. Pufendorf, Droit de la Nature et des Gens, liv. v. chap. viii. § 4.

gratuitously, and to be accountable to the former for the performance.[a]

The party who entrusts the other with the business is called the *mandator*, and he who undertakes it is called the *mandatarius* or procurator.

This contract is gratuitous, and in most instances has for its object the sole interest of the mandator; and it is synallagmatic or binding on both sides. But it is called by Pothier, *imperfectly* synallagmatic, for the primary obligation is on one side only, on the side of the procurator who has undertaken the trust. This is enforced by the *actio mandati directa.* But by the procurator performing the trust, the constituent becomes bound *ex post facto* to indemnify him if he has been put to any expense, or has contracted any obligation in the execution of the mandate. This obligation, which does not arise unless the execution of the trust has given it birth, is enforced by the *actio mandati contraria.*[b]

This contract is peculiarly important, because ambassadors and other public ministers are mandataries or procurators.[c] Pothier enumerates three things essential to the contract of mandate, namely; 1st. There must be an affair or transaction which is its subject-matter or object; 2ndly. The mandator and the procurator must have the intention to contract reciprocal obligations, the procurator to be accountable and responsible towards his constituent touching his trust, and the mandator to indemnify the procurator; and 3rdly. The mandate must be gratuitous.

Such are the general principles of this contract. The Emperor thus classifies the different kinds of mandate with reference to their purpose or object.

The contract of mandate is entered into in five modes. It may be given solely for the benefit of the mandator; or partly for his benefit and partly for that of the mandatary; or solely for the service of some third person; or partly for the profit of the mandator, and partly for the service of a third person; or for the benefit of the mandator and partly for the use of a third person. But if a mandate be given solely for the sake of the mandatary, the mandate is useless, and no obligation or right of action can arise therefrom.[d]

This contract may also be divided with reference to the mode in which it is entered into. Thus a mandate may be expressed, or tacit.[e]

[a] Pothier, Contr. de Mandat. art. prélimin. Burlamaqui, Principes du Droit de la Nature, tom. iii. p. 248, part iv. chap. xii. [b] Ibid. § 2, chap. i.

[c] Vattel, Droit des Gens, liv. iv. chap. v. § 56. Bynkershoek, De Foro Legatorum, cap. 7. [d] Instit. lib. iii. tit. xxvii. princip.

[e] Pand. lib. xvii. tit. i. Mandati, L. 18, L. 6, § 2. Pand. lib. l. tit. ult. L. 60.

And where business has been done by a person *negotium gerens*, that is to say, for another without his knowledge, if the latter ratify what has been done, he is bound by the contract of mandate. Ulpian says, *Si quis ratum habuerit quod gestum est: obstringitur actione mandati.*[f] And Ulpian gives the rule that ratification has the same effect as mandate, *Rati habitio mandato comparatur.*[g]

The doctrine of Grotius respecting the ratification of treaties is in accordance with this part of the Civil Law.[h]

Mandates may be either general, comprehending all the mandator's affairs, or special, that is to say, confined to certain specified matters or a single business. It must however be observed that the general nature of the mandate or procuration, whether with or without the clause *cum liberâ administratione*, gives the procurator no power beyond that of administration, which, according to the rule of Baldus, does not include the power of alienation.[i] And so Modestinus decides that a *procurator omnium bonorum* cannot alienate anything belonging to his constituent without a special power or mandate for that purpose, excepting fruits of the property and such other things as must perish, and thus subject the constituent or mandator to a loss if they be not alienated.[k]

But the *procurator omnium bonorum* may mortgage or pledge the property of his constituent where the power of doing so is incident to the management of the affairs or estate.[l]

This decision rests on the general principle of Grotius applied by him to the acts of ambassadors and ministers of state and other public officers, that "whoever gives a commission or power, gives at the same time, so far as depends on himself, the moral powers necessary for its execution."[m]

Thus in another part of his great work Grotius writes: "Persons are bound not only by their own act, but by the act of others, where it appears that they have appointed another to be the instrument, by means of which, they intend to bind themselves." "This may be either by a special commission or power for a certain affair, or by a general commission or power for a certain species of affairs."

"When the procurator or commissioner acts under a general power,

[f] Pand. lib. l. tit. ult. L. 60.

[g] Pand. lib. xlvi. tit. iii. De Solutionibus, L. 12, § 4. Pand. lib. iii. tit. v. De Negotiis Gestis, L. 6, § 9.

[h] Grot. Droit de la Guerre et de la Paix, liv. iii. chap. xxii. § 3, num. 2.

[i] Vinnii Comm. ad Instit. lib. ii. tit. i. De Rerum Divisione, § 42.

[k] Pand lib. iii tit. iii. De Procuratoribus, L. 63.

[l] Pand. lib. xiii. tit. vii. De Pignoratitiâ Actione, L. 12.

[m] Grot. Droit de la Guerre et de la Paix, liv. iii. chap. xxii. § 2, num. 2. Pand. lib. i. tit. xxi. De Officio Ejus, &c. L. 5. Pand. lib. ii. tit. i. De Jurisdictione, L. 2.

it may happen that the constituent may be bound by the act of the agent, though that act was contrary to the will of the constituent, which will however was known to the procurator only." "The reason of this is that there are two distinct wills or intentions in the transaction on the part of the constituent: one by which he engages to ratify and hold good all that the constituent may do in the matter committed to him; and the other, whereby he stipulates with the agent that the latter will not exceed his secret instructions."[n]

The argument of Grotius that the secret contract between the constituent and the agent cannot affect third parties is in accordance with the maxim of Paulus: *Animadvertendum est ne conventio aliâ re facta aut cum aliâ personâ, in aliâ re aliâve personâ noceat.*[o] Grotius holds that on these principles must be decided the case of an ambassador, who by virtue of his credentials has promised anything in the name of his sovereign, which is beyond his secret instructions.

That illustrious writer thus sums up these doctrines: "If the agent exceeded his secret instructions, his constituent is nevertheless bound, provided the agent did not exceed the limits of the power incident to the nature of his employment."[p]

Grotius cites in support of this legal theory several passages from the Pandects, in which it is laid down by Ulpian that a trader is bound by the act of his agent or factor so far as regards the affairs which the agent is appointed to manage; and that if the disavowal of the agent and the revocation of his power be not known to all men, the constituent is bound by the obligations contracted in his name by the agent towards persons ignorant of the revocation.[q]

The leading principle in this head of law is the rule of the Canon Law: *Qui facit per alium, est perinde ac si faciat per se ipsum.*[r] The mandator may, however, reserve to himself the power of ratifying or disavowing the acts of his mandatary.[s] The third division and classification of mandates has reference to the nature of its subject-matter or objects. Mandates or procurations may be *judicial*, that is to say, relating to judicial proceedings; or *extrajudicial*, that is, regarding other things. Having sketched out these various divisions, we will return to the classification adopted in Justinian's Institutes. And first, of mandates, for the benefit of the mandator or constituent.

[n] Grot. Droit de la Guerre et de la Paix, liv. ii. chap. ii. § 12.

[o] Pand. lib. ii. tit. xiv. L. 27, § 4.

[p] Grot. Droit de la Guerre et de la Paix, liv. iii. chap. xxii. § 4. Pufendorf, Droit de la Nature et des Gens, liv. iii. chap. ix. § 2.

[q] Pand. lib. xiv. tit. iii. De Institoriâ Actione, L. 5, § 11, L. 12, § 2, 4.

[r] Sext. Decretal. tit. ultim. Regul. 72.

[s] Burlamaqui, Principes du Droit de la Nature et des Gens, tom. iii. p. 65, part iv. chap. iv.

A mandate is for the sole benefit of the mandator ; if, for instance, some one request you to transact his business, or to buy him an estate, or to become surety for him.[t]

A mandate is for the benefit of the mandator, and also of the procurator or mandatary ; as, for instance, where a man requests another to lend money at interest to a third, which money is to be used in the affairs of the mandator : or if a debtor request his creditor to accept as debtor in his stead a third person.[u]

Mandate *alienâ gratiâ* is as follows: *The mandate is for the benefit of a third party only; where, for instance, a man requests another to transact the business of a third, or to buy an estate for him.*[x]

This passage seems at first sight at variance with the rule that no man can legally stipulate for the sole benefit of a third party. But it is not so, for though the mandator has no interest in the mandatary undertaking the mandate, yet so soon as the mandatary has entered on the discharge of that trust the mandator has an interest, because he is liable towards the third party for the administration of the mandate.[y] But the right of action does not accrue to the mandator until such interest arises. *Mandati actio tunc competit cum interesse cœpit ejus qui mandavit.*[z]

The next species are *Mandatum mandantis et alienâ gratiâ*, and *Mandatarii et aliena.*

The mandate is for the benefit of the mandator and of a third party, where (for instance) a person requests another to transact the joint affairs of the mandator, and of a third party, or to be surety for him and a third party.[a]

The mandate is for the benefit of the mandatary and of a third party, where (for instance) you are requested to lend money at interest to Titius ; for if the mandate were to lend it without interest, the mandate would be for the sole benefit of Titius.[b]

The last kind of mandate is *Mandatarii tantum gratia.*

The mandate is for the benefit of the mandatary or procurator alone, if (for instance) it recommend you to invest your money in land rather than at interest, or the contrary. This is not properly mandate, but advice, and it therefore produces no obligation (whether it be followed or no), for no one is liable for the effects of advice given, though it be not

[t] Instit. lib. iii. tit. xxvii. § 1.

[u] Ibid. § 2. One passage is omitted which relates to the Law of Sureties before the Novell. 4.

[x] Ibid. § 3.

[y] Pand. lib. iii. tit. v. De Negotiis Gestis, L. 28.

[z] Pand. lib. xvii. tit. i. Mandati, L. 8, § 6.

[a] Instit. ubi sup. § 4.

[b] Ibid. § 5.

such as is expedient to be acted upon, for every man is at liberty to consider for himself whether advice given to him be good or no. Therefore if you had money lying unprofitably in your house, and some one advised and exhorted you to lend it out at interest, or to buy something with it, he is not thereby liable to an action of mandate, though you invested your money unprofitably, or lost it in consequence of following his advice.[c]

This passage is governed by the rule of Ulpian, *Consilii non fraudulenti nulla obligatio est: cæterum si dolus et calliditas intercessit, de dolo competit actio.*[d] And the reason of this rule is well given by Justinian. It is because the man who receives the advice may judge for himself whether it be expedient or no.[e] But it is otherwise with fraudulent advice; for where an adviser uses fraud or deceit to induce the person whom he professes to counsel, to follow his suggestions, he, as far as in him lies, deprives that person of the full benefit of his own judgment whether the advice had best be followed or rejected. The adviser is therefore responsible.

And those who advise the commission of a crime, or even who encourage in any way a person who is disposed to commit a crime, are liable to punishment.[f]

With regard to those who are bound by their public employments to give advice to princes and governors, they may be liable for the consequences of advice given without fraud or deceit. The reason of this is that they have a positive duty of advising and counselling, cast upon them by virtue of their offices, which they have voluntarily undertaken,[g] and indeed in some instances no measure can be adopted without such advice.

Thus the advisers of the crown are responsible for the policy and wisdom as well as for the legality of the measures of government, because they are bound to use all their endeavours in the service of the crown; and on the other hand deserve punishment, if they undertake so important a duty without possessing the ability requisite for its discharge. *Nec videtur iniquum si infirmitas culpæ adnumeretur; cum affectare quisque non debeat in quo intelligit, vel intelligere debet infirmitatem suam alii periculosam futuram.*[h]

A mandate contrary to law or to good morals is void, not only on the principles applicable to all other contracts, but because no man can authorize another to do in his name what he cannot do himself,

[c] Instit. ubi sup. § 6.

[d] Pand. lib. l. tit. ultim. L. 47.

[e] Instit. ubi sup.

[f] Grotius, Droit de la Guerre et de la Paix, liv. ii. chap. xxi. § 1.

[g] Domat, Droit Public, liv. i. tit. ii. § 2.

[h] Pand. lib. ix. tit. ii. Ad Legem Aquiliam, L. 8.

because it is essentially illegal or wrong.[i] *Quod quis suo nomine exercere prohibetur; id nec per subjectam personam agere debet.*[k]

He who executes a mandate must not exceed the limits of that mandate. For instance, if any one empowered you by mandate to purchase an estate for him for the price of 100 *pieces of gold, you should not exceed that price, otherwise you will not have an action of mandate against him for repayment of the money; and Cassius and Sabinus carried this doctrine so far as to be of opinion that you could not recover even the amount which you were authorized by the mandate to spend. But the Pegasians were justly of opinion that in this case you would be entitled to recover the amount which you were empowered to give. This opinion is the most equitable. But if you purchase the estate for your mandator for a less sum than he specified in the mandate, you have an action against him; for he who directs that an estate may be purchased for him for* 100 *pieces, must be understood to have directed that if possible it may be purchased for a less sum.*[l]

The leading rule respecting the power of the procurator to depart from the strict letter of the mandate is to be found in a law of Paulus; *Melior causa mandantis fieri potest, deterior vero nunquam.*[m]

The termination of mandate is next to be considered. That contract is extinguished in four modes. They are, two proceeding from the mandator, namely, revocation and the death of the mandator; and two proceeding from the procurator, that is to say, his death and his renunciation. And first of the extinction of the mandate by revocation.

A lawfully contracted mandate is dissolved if it be revoked by the mandator before anything has been executed by the procurator.[n]

As mandate is for the benefit, or at least is accepted at the request of the mandator, he may therefore revoke it whenever he pleases, so far as the procurator is concerned. *Extinctum est mandatum finitâ voluntate.*[o]

But Paulus decides that if before the revocation become known to the procurator he had already executed the mandate, he has a right to be indemnified. It is otherwise if he knew of the revocation.[p] *Also, if before any part of the mandate has been executed, either of the*

[i] Instit. ubi sup. § 7. Pand. lib. l. tit. ult. L. 54.

[k] Pand. lib. l. tit. viii. De Administratione Rerum ad Civitates Pertinentes, L. 2, § 1.

[l] Instit. ubi sup. § 8. Diligenter fines mandati custodiendi sunt: nam qui excessit, aliud quid facere videtur. Pand. lib. xvii. tit. i. Mandati, L. 5.

[m] Pand. ibid. L. 3. Pand lib. l. tit. ult. L. 113.

[n] Instit. ibid. § 9. And in the Canon Law, see Lancelot, Instit. lib. i. tit. vi. § 13.

[o] Pand. lib. xvii. tit. i. Mandati, L. 12, penult.

[p] Ibid. L. 15 Pand. lib. xlvi. tit. iii. De Solutionibus, L. 12, § 2.

parties die, the mandate is dissolved. But it has been established as law, that the procurator may have an action to be indemnified, if he executed the mandate while in ignorance of the death of the mandator, provided his ignorance was justifiable and probable. If the law were otherwise, the procurator would suffer for his justifiable ignorance of the fact of the death of the mandator. Upon similar principles it was decided that if the debtors of Titius paid their debts to his slave who was his steward, not knowing that the slave had been emancipated, they are freed from their debts by the payment, though, according to strict law, the payment was not valid, since they paid to one who was not the person to whom they should have paid.[q]

The law here laid down by Justinian, that the death of the mandator extinguishes the mandate, rests on the rule, *Extinctum est mandatum finitâ voluntate*, and on the peculiarly personal nature of the obligation of the mandatary or procurator.[r] The reason why, on the other hand, the mandate is dissolved by the death of the procurator, is that he was the person trusted, and the trust does not pass to his heir.[s]

According to strict principle, the mandate ceases from the very moment of the death of the mandator; but *Bonæ fidei non congruit de apicibus juris disputare*, and, for the sake of convenience, it is established that the procuration is affected by the death of the mandator only from the time that it is known to the procurator.[t]

And, on the same equitable principles, is decided the case of a payment to a reputed agent by a person who did not know that the agency had been revoked.[u]

Any man is at liberty not to accept or undertake a mandate; but if he accept it, he must execute the mandate, or give notice with all speed to the mandator of his renunciation, in order that the mandator may either do himself what is the object of the mandate, or find another mandatary. For unless the procurator resign or renounce the mandate so that the mandator suffer no injury thereby, he is liable in an action of mandate, unless he have a sufficient justification to plead for not having given timely notice of his renunciation, or he had a good and sufficient cause of renouncing at a time when his renunciation was injurious to the mandator's interests.[x]

If the procurator be either unable to execute the mandate, or unable to give notice of his inability or renunciation, he is not liable for those omissions. *Impossibilium nulla obligatio est.* And the Roman Law allows the procurator to renounce, though to the injury of the mandator,

[q] Instit. ubi sup. § 10. [r] Voet, Comm. ad Pand. lib. xvii. tit. i. num 15.

[s] Pand. lib. xvii. tit. i. Mandati, L. 57. [t] Ibid. L. 29, § 4.

[u] Pand. lib. xlvi. tit. iii. De Solutionibus, L. 12, § 2, L. 18, L. 34, § 3.

[x] Instit. lib iii. tit xxvii § 11. Mandatum non suscipere cuilibet liberum est: susceptum autem consummandum est. Pand lib xvii. tit i. Mandati, L. 22, § ult

if by the insolvency of the latter he become incapable of indemnifying his procurator, or if capital enmity arise between the parties.[y]

As for the degree of care and diligence which the law requires of a mandatary, Pothier and Vinnius agree that although the contract is gratuitous, yet the procurator is responsible not only for dole and gross fault, but for slight fault (*levem culpam*) also: and they justify this exception to the general legal principle regarding the degrees of responsibility imposed by various contracts, by the argument that the procurator engages himself to more than a person with whom property is deposited for safe custody, because he undertakes, not mere custody, but the transaction of some business, which is a greater undertaking. *Spondet diligentiam et industriam gerendo negotio parem.*[z]

The contract of mandate may be qualified by a term, or suspended by a condition.[a]

Mandate, unless it be gratuitous, becomes another contract. For if a hire or reward be agreed upon, it becomes hiring and letting (locatio conductio). And we may lay down the general rule, that in those cases where the office or duty being undertaken gratuitously is deposit or mandate, it becomes hiring and letting if it be for hire. Therefore, if a man give clothes to be cleaned by a fuller gratuitously,[b] *the contract is mandate.*[c]

But if there be a remuneration given or promised by way of *honorarium*, the contract is still mandate.[d] Such a remuneration differs from a hire, inasmuch as it is not an equivalent for the estimated value of the services, and it is merely collateral to the services rendered.[e]

Thus it is with the salaries of ambassadors and ministers of state, and other great officers, who all stand in the relation of mandataries or procurators towards the sovereign power. And the same principle is applicable to the revenues which are provided for the sustenance of the clergy.[f]

With this chapter the subject of obligations *ex contractu* comes to a close.

[y] Vinnii Comm. ad Instit. lib. iii. tit. xxvii. § 11, num. 3.

[z] Pothier, Du Mandat. chap. 2, art. 2. Vinnii Comm. ad Instit. ubi sup. num. 2. Pand. lib. l. tit. ult. L. 23. Cod. lib. iv. tit. xxxv. Mandati, L. 13.

[a] Instit. ubi sup. § 12.

[b] Pand. lib. xix. tit. v. De Præscript. Verbis, L. 22.

[c] Instit. ubi sup. § 13. Pand. lib. xvii. tit. i. Mandati, L. 1, § 4.

[d] Pand. ibid. L. 6.

[e] Pothier, Du Mandat. n. 23. Voet, ad Pand. lib. xvii. tit. i. num. 2. Vinnii Comm. ad Instit. lib. iii. tit. xxvii. § 13.

[f] Devoti, Instit. Canon. lib. iv. tit. ix. De Simoniâ, § 6.

CHAPTER XL.

OF OBLIGATIONS ARISING NEITHER FROM CONTRACT, NOR FROM A WRONG.

Of Obligations arising neither from Contract, nor from a Wrong.—Instit. lib. iii. tit. xxviii. De Obligationibus quæ Quasi ex Contractu nascuntur.—Incorrectness of the term Obligation *Quasi ex Contractu.*—The true Source and Nature of these Obligations explained.—The Will of Man and the Law are the two Causes of Obligations.—The Fiction of every Man being a Consenting Party to the Law.—The Fiction of an Original Contract.—Danger of Fictions in Public Law.—Classification of Obligations without Consent. P. 237.

Next to obligations *ex contractu*, Justinian places that class which he calls obligations arising *quasi ex contractu*, because they spring neither from a contract, nor from a wrong.[a]

This subject has already been touched upon,[b] but it requires full explanation here. Justinian does not define a *quasi contract*, but shows what it is not, inferring that as it springs neither from contract, nor from a wrong, therefore it must be called an obligation *quasi ex contractu.*

This obscurity or rather incompleteness in the Institutes has caused much research among the modern civilians as to the nature of a *quasi contract.*

Some allege the tacit consent of the party bound, as the foundation of this species of obligation. But tacit consent is consent. Therefore the obligation would, under this hypothesis, be *ex consensu*, that is to say, *ex contractu.*

Other writers hold a *quasi contract* to be a presumed or feigned contract, from whence an obligation arises.[c] Thus Heineccius defines a *quasi contract* to be a lawful action whereby a man is bound, even without his knowledge, by reason of his consent, which is presumed, or feigned by equity. Thus he argues that when any one receives by mistake a payment which is not due to him, the law presumes or feigns that he consents to make restitution, because it is not just that he should acquire a gain by injuring another, and therefore commands him to restore what he has received.

But the argument implied in this definition is unsound. It is as

[a] Instit. lib. iii. tit. xxviii. princip.

[b] Chap. xxviii.

[c] Heineccii Element. lib. iii. tit. xxviii.

follows:—The consent of the party is implied or presumed by the law, because every man must be presumed to consent to do what justice requires that he should do. Now as the consent of the party is presumed because he is bound by equity to consent, it is evident that his obligation arises from equity; and the superaddition of a presumed consent on his part for the purpose of producing another source of obligation is superfluous. And the consent of a man to do what he is already bound to do by equity must always be superfluous so far as the obligation is concerned, because whether he consent or no, he is equally bound to obey justice.

It follows that a *quasi contract* is not a tacit contract; and that the obligation derived *quasi ex contractu* by Justinian springs not from a presumed or feigned contract, but from the law independently of any consent, real or implied, of the party.

The real grounds and nature of this class of obligations are as follow.[d] Every lawful act of man from which one person derives an emolument to the detriment of another and contrary to his rights, binds the former by an obligation to restore the gain which he has received.

This important principle springs from the very nature of the rights of property, which are not extinguished by the loss of the possession of that which is their object, according to the rule of Pomponius: *Id quod nostrum est, sine nostro facto ad alium transferri non potest.*[e] It follows from this rule that if anything be transferred from one man to another, without an intention of the proprietor to part with his property; he who receives it is bound to make restitution. But on the same principles, if the *bonâ fide* possessor incurred any expense for the preservation or improvement of the property, the owner who claims it is bound on his side to indemnify him, otherwise the owner would make a gain to the injury of another, contrary to equity.

The conclusion is that what Trebonian calls an obligation arising from *quasi contract*, is an obligation springing from the law of property which does not admit of any gain being retained contrary to the two rules of equity:—*Id quod nostrum est, sine facto nostro ad alium transferri non potest:* and *Æquum est neminem cum alterius detrimento locupletari.*

Trebonian probably adopted this denomination of *quasi contractus*, attracted by a species of symmetry in the names which he affixed to the four classes of causes of obligations. Thus he argues that as certain obligations arise neither from contract nor from a wrong, they

[d] Toullier, Droit Civil, liv. III. tit. iv. § 20.
[e] Ibid. § 18, 19. Pand. lib. l. tit. ult. L 11

seem to spring *quasi ex contractu;* and as he divided the sources of obligations *ex maleficio* into *delicta* and *quasi delicta*, he separated the other sources into two classes, and called them *contractus* and *quasi contractus.*

From this classification may be deduced the conclusion that there are but two causes whereby obligations are generated, namely, the will of man and the law.[f]

The freedom and the intelligent nature of man enable him to bind himself by his own consent to others: and his obligations contracted in that manner spring not from the Municipal Law, but from his consent, because the law would not bind him by those obligations, if he had not consented to bind himself, and because if the Municipal Law did not bind him by enforcing the performance of his obligations, those obligations would still exist. They are, therefore, correctly denominated obligations *ex consensu*, because the Civil or Municipal Law does not produce them, but only enforces them, and the natural law *grave est fidem fallere* is the remote, while the consent or convention is the immediate cause of the obligation.

But obligations not produced by consent and the free will of man, can proceed from no other source than the law, the commands of which are obligatory on all its subjects. *Legis virtus hæc est, imperare, vetare, permittere, punire.*[g]

It may, perhaps, be argued that Municipal Law is founded on general consent, which is binding on every member of the community as if he had expressly consented. But this doctrine, which can hardly be applied to any community, except a pure republic, wherein every citizen has a legislative power by himself or his representatives, is liable to great and numerous difficulties in its practical application: and the obligation of obedience to Municipal Law is far more safely rested on that natural law which obliges man to seek by the cultivation and furtherance of the social state, the welfare and improvement of the human race, than on any such fiction of universal consent.

Thus every man is bound to obey the Municipal Law of his country, because if it were not obeyed, no social constitution could exist: and on this principle are grounded the duties of the citizen deduced from the social nature of man, and from the obligations imposed on him as a consequence of that nature by the will of the Creator.

Blackstone derives the duties of the subject from an implied original contract; but the doctrine explained above shows that that contract (the existence of which, as Barbeyrac observes, never has been proved)

[f] Toullier, Droit Civil, liv. iii. tit. iv. § 3, &c

[g] Pand. lib. i. tit. iii. De Legibus, L. 7

is unnecessary, since the obligations of the subject to the sovereign power rest on the same ground as the institution of property, of the social state, and of civil government, which all belong to the secondary law of nature.[h]

Besides, no subject may by the English Law renounce his allegiance without the consent of the sovereign; consequently, his remaining a member of the nation cannot be said to imply any acquiescence in the supposed social compact; for a will or intention implies a contrary power or freedom of choice. *Ejus est non nolle qui potest velle.*[i]

It is indeed dangerous to introduce fictions into public law. The fiction of the social compact may be used to support even a grinding tyranny. It will be, perhaps, argued that this fiction is raised on grounds of reason, and the welfare of mankind, which are the roots of natural law, and inapplicable to the rule of the tyrant: but it must then be admitted that the theory of government is based not on the fiction but on those grounds, and consequently that the fiction is unnecessary, and calculated to mislead men from the true fundamental principles of public law.

Obligations arising from the law without consent or agreement are of two classes. 1st. Those which spring from the law alone without any act of the person upon whom the obligation is imposed. 2ndly. Those which arise from the law upon the occasion of an act of the person obliged, or of an act of the person to whom he becomes bound, or of a fortuitous occurrence.

The obligations whereby every man is bound to pay taxes, and to perform certain public duties, such as serving on juries, are instances of obligations proceeding from the law alone.

Obligations of the first class arise mediately as those of the second spring immediately from the law, for every obligation must proceed from the law, either natural or municipal.

Obligations arising mediately from the law are brought into existence by the law on the occasion of some act. Thus the obligation of a thief to restore stolen goods arises from the law of property, to which law he renders himself amenable by violating it.

The act of the person to be bound, thus precedes the obligation, and is a condition precedent to the existence of the obligation, but the obligation springs from the law on the occasion of the act.[k]

That act may be lawful, or unlawful. Of the first nature are those obligations which Trebonian derives *quasi ex contractu*, and of the second are those which he deduces *ex delicto* and *quasi ex delicto*.

[h] Blackst. Comm. book iii. chap. ix.

[i] Pand. lib. l. tit. ult. De Reg. Jur. L. 3.

[k] Toullier, Droit Civil, liv. iii. tit. iv. § 8.

The former are founded on the doctrines already explained; and the latter arise from the principle of natural law that *every one must repair whatever damage or detriment he has caused to another by his fault or wrongful act.*[1] But on this more shall be said hereafter.[m]

The latter (obligations arising from the law on the occasion of a lawful act) may obtain on the occasion either of an act of the person bound thereby, as when a man through error receives what is not due to him; or of the act of the other party, as where one incurs expense for another by which the latter profits. In that case he who receives the benefit is bound in equity to indemnify the other who relied on his sense of justice that he would not refuse to do so. A multitude of various circumstances, which are called fortuitous, because they do not proceed from the will of the parties, may also impose obligations on persons without their consent.

These doctrines may be thus summed up. Every obligation owes its origin either to a convention or agreement, or to the law without any convention or agreement. Those which arise from the law are of two species:—1st. Those which spring from the authority of the law only; and 2ndly, Obligations which arise from the law on the occasion of an act of the person bound thereby, or of the person to whom the other is bound by the effect of that act, or of a fortuitous event.[n] They are said by Trebonian to arise *quasi ex contractu.*

In the ensuing chapter the five obligations called *Quasi Contracts* will be successively explained.

[1] Pothier, Des Obligat. num. 123. And see the French Code, art. 1382. Grotius, Droit de la Guerre et de la Paix, liv. ii. chap. xvii.

[m] See chap. xliii. xliv.

[n] Toullier, Droit Civ. liv. iii. tit. iv. § 9.

CHAPTER XLI.

OF THE FIVE OBLIGATIONS CALLED OBLIGATIONS QUASI EX CONTRACTU.

Of the Five Obligations called Obligations *Quasi ex Contractu.*—Instit. lib. iii. tit. xxviii. De Obligationibus quæ Quasi ex Contractu nascuntur.—*Negotiorum Gestio.*—*Actio Directa* et *Actio Contraria.*—Extent of the Responsibility of the *Negotiorum Gestor.*—Guardianship.—Extent of the Responsibility of Guardians and Curators.—*Actio Tutelæ, Directa et Contraria.* Joint Ownership.—The Obligations of Joint Proprietors.—The Right of Division. The Right of Veto of Joint Owners.—The Actions *Communi Dividundo* and *Familiæ Erciscundæ.*—Community of Profits. Damage done by a Joint Owner to the Common Property.—Extent of Responsibility of Joint Owners.—Obligation of an Heir towards Legatees and Creditors. *Condictio Indebiti,* or Restitution of Payments made through Error.—Distinction between Ignorance of Fact and of Law.—*Condictio Indebiti* obtains in both Kinds of Error.—*Condictio Causâ Datâ, Causâ non Secutâ. Condictio sine Causâ.*—Cases where an erroneous Payment cannot be recovered.—Exception where the Debt is forbidden by Law. —Case of Parties *in Pari Delicto.* P. 246.

The first of the five species of obligations which form the subject of this chapter is *negotiorum gestio.* It is thus described by Justinian.

When any one has transacted business of an absent man (negotia absentis gesserit) there arise mutual rights of action between them, which are called actions negotiorum gestorum. The person who has received the service has the actio directa, and the other, or negotiorum gestor, has the actio contraria.

These actions spring from no contract, for they obtain where any one spontaneously undertook business, or the management of the property of another, without any mandate or authorization; therefore this kind of obligation is binding even upon those who are ignorant of the favour or service done to them. This law was received by reason of its utility, that the business of those who are absent without having been able to commit their interests to any one might not be neglected: for no one would take this care upon himself unless he had an action to recover what he had expended. But as the negotiorum gestor who has managed the business properly has a right to be indemnified by the principal, so the latter is in his turn bound towards and accountable to the owner for his administration. In such a case he is liable and responsible, so far that he is bound to bestow the utmost care and diligence on the task which he has undertaken; and it is not sufficient for him to be as careful as in his own affairs, if any one else might have conducted the business with greater diligence and advantage.[a]

The general principle on which the engagement of *negotiorum gestio* is founded is the rule that no man shall derive advantage by causing detriment to another.[b]

By virtue of this rule, if any one benefit another with the knowledge of the latter and his express consent whether previous or *ex post facto*,[c] the person deriving the benefit is a mandator and must indemnify him who confers it for any loss or injury caused by the service rendered. And the same principle is applicable to a case where the party received the benefit in his absence and without his knowledge of the fact.

Even supposing that the party derives no advantage from the administration of his affairs by the other, notwithstanding the utmost care and diligence of the *negotiorum gestor*, he is equally bound to indemnify the latter; for if it were otherwise, a principal would have the full benefit of the services of the *negotiorum gestor*, without being exposed to the uncertainty and the chances of adverse circumstances incident to human affairs. Thus the *negotiorum gestor* would be exposed to all the risk, and the owner would have all the benefit, contrary to justice.[d]

The extent of the responsibility of the *negotiorum gestor* is equal to that of persons who derive the entire benefit from any transaction,[e] because no man ought rashly to undertake the affairs of another without his consent, and he therefore does it at his peril. *Culpa est immiscere se rei ad se non pertinenti.*[f] But, on the other hand, it is most important for absent persons that some one should take charge of their interests.[g] It follows, then, that a *negotiorum gestor* is legally justifiable for his interference only where there is need of that interference, and where he managed the business as well as, under the circumstances, it could be managed.

Such is the general rule. Thus, if the *negotiorum gestor* exposed the interests of the owner to an unwarrantable risk, by undertaking something new in which he had never dealt before, the responsibility of the *negotiorum gestor* extends so far as to make him liable even for the consequences of fortuitous events.[h]

But where a man from friendship or charity undertakes an urgent

[a] Instit. lib. iii. tit. xxviii. § 1. Pand. lib. l. tit. ult. L. 60.

[b] Toullier, Droit Civil, liv. iii. tit. iv. § 23.

[c] Pand. lib. xvii. tit. ii. Pro Socio, L. 55.

[d] Instit. lib. iii. tit. xxviii. § 1. Pand. lib. xiii. tit. vi. Commodati, L. 5, § 2.

[f] Pand. lib. l. tit. ult. L. 36.

[g] Pand. lib. iii. tit. v. De Negotiis Gestis. L. 1.

[h] Pand. ibid. L. 11. And see the English Law as to *Executor de son tort*, 2 Stephen, Comm. p. 244.

affair requiring immediate execution, his responsibility is more limited. In such cases the *negotiorum gestor* is liable only for gross faults, that is to say, for dole and *lata culpa*.[i]

The reason of this exception to the general rule is, that the *negotiorum gestor* undertakes the affair upon an emergency, and without the possibility of calculating his own degree of capacity, or the chances that a more careful and fit person might be found to manage it. The law therefore considers his good intentions, and applies liberally the principle of Gajus, *Iniquum est damnosum cuique esse officium suum*.[k]

We will now proceed from the obligations arising from a voluntary to those occasioned by a compulsory administration, namely, guardianship. They are founded on the same grounds of equity as those of a *negotiorum gestor*, but the responsibility of the guardian is less extensive.

Guardians also who are subject to an action of tutelage, cannot be said to be bound by contract, for there is no agreement between guardian and ward. And as they are not engaged ex maleficio, it appears that they are bound by quasi contract. And both guardian and ward have mutual remedies by action against each other. For not only the ward has a direct action against his guardian; but the guardian, if he has expended his own money in the affairs of his ward, or has been bound for him, or has mortgaged his own property to creditors, is entitled to the action tutelæ contraria.[l]

The extent of the responsibility of guardians and curators is settled by a constitution[m] of the Emperors Diocletian and Maximian, which declares them liable for whatever the ward lost, and whatever advantage he did not obtain in consequence of the dole, *lata culpa* and *levis culpa*, of such guardian or curator. The same rule is laid down in a law of Papinian,[n] and it is grounded on the equitable principle that those should be fully protected by the law who are unable to protect themselves. It follows that the guardian or curator is bound to use that diligence and care in the performance of his duties which are employed by the average of careful men in the transaction of their own affairs.[o]

[i] Pand. lib. iii. tit. v. De Negotiis Gestis, L. 3, § 9. Erskine, Instit. book iii. tit. iii. § 33.

[k] Pand. lib. xxix. tit. iii. Testamenta Quem ad Modum aperiantur, L. 7.

[l] Instit. lib. iii. tit. xxviii. § 2. Pothier, Traité des Obligations, part 1, chap. 1, § 1. And see Donelli Comment. lib. xv. cap. xviii. &c.

[m] Cod. lib. v. tit. li. Arbitrium Tutelæ, L. 7.

[n] Pand. lib. xxvii. tit. iii. De Tutelis et Rationibus Distrahendis, L. 18.

[o] Pand. lib. xxvi. tit. vii. De Administratione et Periculo Tutorum, L. 33. A tutoribus et curatoribus pupillorum eadem diligentia exigenda est circa administrationem rerum pupillarium quam paterfamilias rebus suis ex bonâ fide præbere debet.

But the responsibility does not extend to a very slight degree of fault (*culpa lævissima*), nor consequently does the obligation of guardians and curators require the diligence of *diligentissimus paterfamilias*, because the office and duties are not assumed voluntarily, but undertaken in obedience to the law.

The guardian or curator has on his side a right of action to be indemnified by his ward for any outlay or loss occasioned by the performance of his duties.[p] All these rules apply equally to guardians and to curators.[q]

The next paragraph relates to the obligations of joint owners.

Also when anything is the common property of several persons, without any partnership between them with respect to that thing; as, for instance, if a thing be jointly bequeathed, or given to them all, they are reciprocally bound towards each other in the action communi dividundo, *to restore whatever one of them has received alone, beyond his share of the profits arising therefrom, or to repay whatever necessary expences one of them has incurred touching the common property.*[r]

The same law prevails in the action Familiæ erciscundæ, *for the division and distribution of an inheritance among co-heirs.*[s]

Justinian here gives instances of obligations arising on the occasion of an act of a third party, which, so far as regards the parties engaged thereby, is a casual event. These engagements must not be confounded with those the sole and immediate cause of which is the law, and which are called by Lord Stair *obediential* obligations, such as the duty of parents to aliment their children.[t]

The distinction between the obligations of co-proprietors and those of partners has been already explained;[u] but as the contract of society is where some thing or things are placed in common for the purpose of deriving from them a common advantage or profit, it follows that every partnership includes a community of property; consequently, so soon as the partnership has ceased, the partnership effects may be divided by the proceeding called *communi dividundo*.[x]

The first and principal obligation of co-proprietors is to submit to a division at the will of any one of them. *Nemo invitus compellitur ad communionem.*[y] This rule is grounded on the same reasons of legal

[p] Pand. lib. xxvii. tit. iv. De Contraria et Utili Actione Tutelæ, L. 1, 6. Cod. lib. v. tit. lviii. De Contrario Judicio Tutelæ.

[q] Vinnii Comm. ad Instit. lib. iii. tit. xxviii. § 2, in fine.

[r] Instit. lib. iii. tit. xxviii. § 3.

[s] Ibid, § 4.

[t] Erskine, Instit. book iii. tit. i. § 9. Pothier, Des Obligat. part i. chap. i. § 3.

[u] Chap. xxxviii.

[x] Pand. lib. x. tit. iii. Comm. Dividundo, L. 2.

[y] Pand. lib. xii. tit. vi. xxvi. § 4. Cod. lib. iii. tit. xxxvii. Communi Dividundo, L. 5.

policy as that which obliges partners to submit to a dissolution of partnership.

Every co-proprietor has a right of veto (*jus prohibendi*) to forbid anything being done to the common property without his consent. *In re pari potiorem causam prohibentis esse constat.*[z]

The mode of dividing common property in general by the proceeding called *communi dividundo*, and of distributing common inheritances among co-heirs, by the *judicium familiæ erciscundæ* will be more properly considered in commenting on the part of the Institutes, entituled *De Officio Judicis.*[a]

It follows, from a law of Ulpian, that co-proprietors are accountable towards each other for any benefit derived from the common property by one or more of them exclusive of the rest, and for damage done by one or more of them to the property, and that if one or more co-proprietors bear any expence for the benefit of all, the others must indemnify them.[b]

The property being common, the profits accruing therefrom must be common also; consequently, every co-proprietor is bound to share with his fellows.

As for damage done by a joint-owner to the common property, he is bound to indemnify the others on the general principle, *Factum suum cuique noceat.* But his responsibility in this respect only extends so far as to render him liable for the consequences of the want of so much care and diligence in the common business as he bestows on his own separate interests. *Talem diligentiam præstare debet qualem in suis rebus.* The reason of this limitation of responsibility is (so far as regards co-heirs) the involuntary nature of that connexion, and in other cases that each co-proprietor has a common interest in the property.[c]

It is, however, necessary to remember the rule *Lata culpa dolus est,* by virtue of which a joint-proprietor may be liable towards his fellows for a fault which, from gross habitual negligence, he would have committed in his own separate affairs. For an act which, in a man's own affairs, may be only gross negligence or absurdity, becomes dishonest when the interests of another are at stake.

The next species of obligation which Justinian explains is that of heirs towards the legatees and creditors of the deceased. But the legal nature of those obligations has already been sufficiently considered.[d]

[z] Pand. lib. xii. tit. vi. xxvi. L. 28. [a] Chap. lii.

[b] Pand. lib. x. tit. iii. Communi Dividundo, L. 3.

[c] Pand. lib. x. tit. ii. Familiæ Erciscundæ, L. 25, § 16. Vinnii Comm. ad Instit. lib. iii. tit. xxviii. § 3. [d] Instit. lib. iii. tit. xxviii. § 5.

The rights of legatees spring from the same source as those of the heir, that is to say, the will of the deceased; and those of the creditors are in principle the same after, as before, the death of their debtor, because he could not give to the heir more of right than he himself had.

Only one of the *quasi* contracts explained in the Institutes remains to be considered. It is *condictio indebiti*, or the right to obtain the repayment of that which, not being due, was paid through error.

Also he to whom any one paid through error what was not due to him, is bound quasi ex contractu, and his obligation resembles that of a person who receives a loan. He is therefore bound to restore what he received.[e]

The leading principle on this subject is the law of Pomponius, *Æquum est neminem cum alterius detrimento fieri locupletiorem.*[f] Now where a man receives that which is not due to him, and which the proprietor had not the real intention of transferring to him,[g] since his intention was founded on error and is therefore void, he cannot retain that thing consistently with the fundamental rule, *Id quod nostrum est sine nostro facto ad alium transferri non potest*, nor without acquiring a gain to the detriment of another. He is therefore bound to make restitution.

But it is essential to this obligation that the thing should have been paid through error. *Cujus per errorem dati repetitio est, ejus consulto dati donatio est.*[h]

As for the nature of the error, it is evident that there is no difference on principle in this respect between error in fact and error in law, for the equitable principles on which *condictio indebiti* is founded, are equally applicable to both.[i]

It has been indeed argued that no man ought to be ignorant of law, and that consequently no man can be permitted to plead ignorance of law. Paulus says, *Juris ignorantia cuique nocet, facti vero ignorantia non nocet.*[k] But that general rule must be limited by two celebrated laws of Papinian, where he determines that ignorance of law shall prejudice no one so far as to make him lose that which is his, though no man may plead ignorance of law for the purpose of placing himself in a position more advantageous than he would have been in had he known the law. *Juris ignorantia non prodest adquirere volentibus,*

Instit. lib. III. tit. XXVIII. § 6.

Pand. lib. XII. tit. VI. De Condictione Indebiti, L. 14.

Non videtur qui errat consentire. Pand. lib. l. tit ult L 116

[h] Pand. lib l. tit ult. L. 53. [i] Vinnii Comm. ad Instit lib III tit. XXVIII. § 6

[k] Pand. lib. XXII. tit. VI. De Juris et Facti Ignorantia, L. 9.

suum vero petentibus non nocet.[l] In other words, no one can exempt himself from the operation of the law by pleading ignorance of its provisions, but no man shall be wronged by reason of his ignorance of law.

It follows from the text just cited, that where one person has, and another has not, a right to the thing in dispute, the error of the former, though it be error of law, cannot prejudice him to the advantage of the latter, who would otherwise derive an emolument from the injury done to another. And Florentius Clemens says, *Iniquissimum videtur ignorantiam alterius alii profuturam.*[m]

We may conclude therefore that *condictio indebiti* obtains as well where the payment was made through ignorance of law as when it was caused by error of fact.[n] And so Erskine holds the law of Scotland to be, but some late cases have been decided on the contrary principle.[o]

On the principles of *condictio indebiti,* introduced by equity to restore property belonging to one man, and in the possession of another but without cause,[p] is grounded the right to claim restitution of whatever was given for a cause that has afterwards failed, and to be set free from an obligation which has been shown to be without cause. These rights are enforced by the proceedings called, *condictio causa data causa non secuta*, and *condictio sine causâ.*[q]

This subject may be aptly concluded with the following law of Papinian: *Ex his omnibus causis quæ jure non valuerunt, vel non habuerunt effectum, secuta per errorem solutione, condictioni locum erit.*[r]

Those cases remain to be explained where a payment cannot be recovered though made in error, and not due to the person to whom it was made.

It has been already shown that there are obligations arising from natural law and duty, which the Municipal Law declines for reasons of policy or necessity to enforce. But as the Municipal Law does not and, indeed, cannot nullify those obligations,[s] therefore that which a

[l] Pand. lib. xxii. tit. vi. De Juris et Facti Ignorantiâ, L. 7, 8.

[m] Ibid. L. 5.

[n] Vinnius, Domat and Toullier so hold. Voet and Heineccius are of a contrary opinion.

[o] Erskine, Instit. book iii. tit. iii. § 54, note.

[p] Pand. lib. xii. tit. vi. De Condictione Indebiti, L. 66.

[q] Pand. lib. xii. tit. vii. De Condictione sine Causâ, L. 1, 4, &c.

[r] Pand. lib. xii. tit. vi. De Condictione Indebiti, L. 54.

[s] Instit. lib. i. tit. ii. § 11. Pand. lib. iv. tit. v. De Capiti Minutis, L. 8. Civilis ratio naturalia jura corrumpere non potest.

man ought to pay, though he could not be compelled by law to do so is held not to be *indebitum.* The law denies the remedy, but not the right. Consequently, where a man pays that which he ought to pay, believing himself erroneously to be bound by the Municipal Law to do so, he cannot recover it. *Debiti vel indebiti ratio in condictione naturaliter intelligenda est.*[t]

These principles extend even to cases where that which was paid was due only by reason of an imperfect obligation or mere duty. Thus, where a mother believing herself liable by law to give a marriage portion to her daughter, gave it; Papinian held that she could not recover the portion. *Sublata falsâ opinione, relinquitur pietatis causâ;* and the law will not assist her to undo so commendable an action.[u]

As *condictio indebiti* springs from equity, it can only be excluded by an equitable plea. Such a plea arises where a person does through error that which he ought to have done if he had not been in error. There are cases, however, wherein, though there is a natural obligation, yet that which has been paid may not be recovered, because the obligation and the payment are totally forbidden by the Municipal Law.

This is decided by Marcian, who holds that where an exception or plea is allowed for the advantage and favour of the defendant, to exclude a demand, he may recover what he has paid through error; but that where the exception is granted *in odio* of the plaintiff, that is to say, because his demand is forbidden, it is otherwise, and what has been paid cannot be recovered.[x]

The reason of this is, that where the law introduces an exception in favour of some persons, such, for instance, as women and minors, because they are liable to be imposed upon, and for their protection, the same reasons are sufficient to give them restitution of whatever they have paid contrary to the privilege which the law grants to them, though it must be remembered that even those persons are liable *in quantum lucrati sunt*, because the law intends only to protect them against loss, and not to enable them to obtain gain.

But where the law gives the exception or plea, not in favour of one party, but *in odio* of the other, there that which was paid cannot be recovered, for the very payment was a violation of the law as well as the obligation; consequently, though the receiver or payee may be punished, and what he received taken from him, that he may

[t] Pand. lib. XII. tit. VII. De Condictione Indebiti, L. 64.

[u] Pand. ibid. L. 32, according to the reading of Cujacius.

[x] Pand. lib. XII. tit. VII. De Condictione Indebiti, L. 40.

not profit by his own wrong, yet the other party cannot complain if he suffers the loss of that which he gave, in consequence of a transaction into which he should not have entered. *Quod quis ex culpâ suâ damnum sentit, non videtur damnum sentire.*[y]

Upon this principle is founded the rule: *Ubi et dantis et accipientis turpitudo versatur, non posse repeti dicimus.*[z]

CHAPTER XLII.

OF THE EXTINCTION OF OBLIGATIONS.

Of the Extinction of Obligations.—Instit. lib. iii. tit. 30, Quibus Modis Obligatio Tollitur.—Of Payments.—Meaning of the word *Solutio* in the Civil Law.—Part Payments. Time of Payment.—Place of Payment. Payment must transfer the Thing Paid.—To whom and by whom it may be made. Effect of Payment by a Third Party. Imputation or Application of Payments.—*Acceptilation* or Release.—Tacit or Presumed Release, and Express Release.—Real Releases and Personal Discharges.—Novation.—Transfer of Hypothecs on Novations.—Principles as to subsequent Creditors.—*Delegation.*—Dissolution of Contracts by Consent.—*Compensation* or *Set-off.*—*Confusion.* P. 260.

HAVING propounded the Law of Obligations arising from contract and from quasi contract, Justinian proceeds to the extinction or dissolution of obligations. This subject might, perhaps, have been more properly placed after the two remaining species of obligations, namely, obligations *ex delicto* and *quasi ex delicto*: but Trebonian probably adopted this arrangement, because obligations arising on the occasion of a wrong are seldom extinguished otherwise than by the payment of damages, while the species of obligations hitherto considered are frequently extinguished by the peculiar modes of payment, which are the subject of this title, *Quibus Modis Obligatio tollitur.*

They are numerous. Several among the modes whereby obligations are dissolved have already been considered. Justinian defers the explanation of those which extinguish obligations by exception, that is to say, by a plea pleaded in answer to an action, and confines himself in this title to the four principal modes whereby they are dissolved *ipso jure.*

[y] Pand. lib. l. tit. ult. L. 203.

[z] Pand. lib. xii. tit. v. De Condictione ob Turpem Causam, L. 3. And see above, at the end of chap. xxxiii.

Obligations are dissolved by actual payment, or by other modes which have the same effect as payment. And first of actual payment.

Obligations are extinguished by the payment of that which is due; or if any one, with the consent of the creditor, give (by way of payment) something instead of that which should have been paid. And it is the same whether the debtor himself pay or some other person for him; for he is set free from the obligation by the payment made by another, whether with or without his consent, and even against his will. And if the debtor pay, those who were sureties for him are set free. It is the same on the other hand if the surety pay, for he is set free, and the obligation of the debtor to the creditor is dissolved.[a]

The word *solutio* used by Justinian in this paragraph has in the Civil Law a very extensive meaning, embracing every species of satisfaction and dissolution of an obligation. And Ulpian says, *Solvere eum dicimus qui facit quod facere promisit.*[b] It is in this sense of the word *solutio* that an obligation is defined to be *Vinculum juris quo necessitate adstringimur alicujus rei solvendæ.*[c] Thus the term *solutio* signifies in its strictest acceptation the specific performance of what is due. *Solutio est naturalis præstatio ejus quod debetur.*[d] Thus Pothier says—"Real payment is the specific accomplishment of what the debtor bound himself to perform or give. When the obligation is *to do* something, the real payment proper to that obligation consists in the performance of what the debtor is bound to do. When the obligation is *to give* something, the real payment proper to that obligation is the giving and transferring the dominion or property of that thing."[e]

It follows from these definitions, and from the text of the Institutes, *Tollitur obligatio . . . . si quis consentiente creditore aliud pro alio solverit,* that the creditor cannot be compelled to receive any payment not specifically that to which the debtor is bound by the obligation.[f] The payment must correspond with all the modes or essential features of the obligation, for a man cannot be said to perform his obligation towards another, *suum ei tribuere*, unless he perform it as it was agreed upon; and the debtor can change nothing in his

[a] Instit. lib. ii. tit. xxx. princip. Tollitur autem omnis obligatio solutione ejus quod debetur . . . . nec interest quis solvat.

[b] Voet, Comm. ad Pand. lib. xlvi. tit. iii. De Solutionibus, num. 1. Pand. lib. l. tit. penult. L. 176.

[c] Instit. lib. iii. tit. xiv. princip.

[d] Voet, ubi sup.

[e] Pothier, Des Obligations, part 3, chap. 1, num. 494.

[f] Instit. lib. iii. tit. xxx. princip. Pand. lib. xii. tit. i. De Rebus Creditis, L. 2, § 1. Pand. lib. xlvi. tit. iii. De Solutionibus, L. 98, § 6.

obligation to the prejudice of the rights of the creditor, for as Papinian says, *Nemo potest mutare consilium suum in alterius injuriam.*[g]

But on the other hand, as *bonæ fidei non congruit de apicibus juris disputare,*[h] the creditor cannot insist on a specific form of payment, unless he have an interest therein; that is to say, unless he would suffer some injury, loss, or inconvenience, if that form were not adhered to.[i]

Whether the subject-matter of the obligation, that is to say, the debt, be divisible or indivisible, the creditor cannot be compelled to receive a part payment of what is due to him.[k] Thus Modestinus decides, that where the contract does not give the debtor the power of paying the debt by instalments, he cannot by tendering and depositing as part payment a part of the sum due. stop the accumulation of interest, even with regard to the amount tendered and deposited.[l]

These rules may be summed up in the words of Pomponius, *Prout quidquid contractum est, ita et solvi debet.*[m] And as one thing cannot be paid instead of another, so on the same principle part of a thing due cannot be paid instead of the whole.

But the rule that one thing cannot be paid instead of another must not be extended to those cases where specific performance has become impossible without the obligation being extinguished by that impossibility. In such cases the debtor is freed from the obligation by payment of damages.[n]

As for the time of payment, a term is presumed to have been agreed upon for the benefit of the debtor. Ulpian says, *In stipulationibus, promissoris gratiâ tempus adjicitur,* and on that rule he decides that a term of payment of a legacy must be held to have been limited by the testator for the convenience and benefit of the heir.[o]

On this principle Celsus decides that though the creditor cannot require the debtor to pay until the term has elapsed, the debtor may compel the creditor to receive payment before its expiration.[p]

But the circumstances of the case may destroy this presumption, by showing that the term was intended for the benefit of both parties. And this is presumed in Mercantile Law where a term of payment is

[g] Pand. lib. l. tit. ult. L. 75. [h] Pand. lib. xvii. tit. i. Mandati, L. 29, § 4.

[i] Pand. lib. xlvi. tit. iii. De Solutionibus, L. 99.

[k] Pothier, Des Obligations, num. 534.

[l] Pand. lib. xxii. tit. i. De Usuris et Fructibus, L. 41, § 1.

[m] Pand. lib. xlvi. tit. iii. De Solutionibus, L. 80.

[n] Vinnii Comm. ad Instit. lib. iii. tit. xxx. princip. num. 3.

[o] Pand. lib. l. tit. ult. L. 17.

[p] Pand. lib. xlvi. tit. iii. De Solutionibus, L. 70.

limited in a bill of exchange, because the punctuality of payments at specified times may be very important to persons engaged in trade.[q]

With respect to the place of payment, it is presumed to have been specified for the benefit of both parties.[r] But if no place of payment be specified, it is presumed that the parties intend that payment should be made in the place where the obligation was contracted, unless the nature of the obligation, or the circumstances of the case, show them to have had in view any other locality. And the debtor is not bound to seek the creditor for the purpose of paying him, unless he agreed to do so.[s] Hence the common rule of Bartholus the Glossator: *Nulla mora ubi nulla petitio.*

Though when the place of payment is specified, the debtor is bound to pay in that place, yet he may make the payment elsewhere, provided he tender to the creditor at the same time compensation for the change of place. But if the creditor accept the payment without such compensation, he cannot afterwards claim it.[t]

Unless whatever is paid or given in payment to the creditor be transferred so as to be made his property, the obligation is not dissolved, for Paulus says, *Non videntur data quæ eo tempore quo dantur, accipientis non fiunt.*[u] And on this principle he decides that a debtor is not freed by the payment of a thing which by reason of the defectiveness of his title is subsequently taken from the creditor; but that if the title of the creditor to the property, though bad from a defect in that of the debtor at the time when the creditor received it, become good afterwards, the obligation is then dissolved.[x]

Upon these principles, if a creditor receive in payment, through error, that which was already his own property, the payment is void, for *Quod meum est amplius meum esse non potest.*[y]

And as a payment is void unless the property of the thing paid be transferred to the creditor, and a part payment made without the consent of the creditor is void,—it follows that if part of that which was paid be taken from the creditor, because the property over the whole was not transferred to him by the debtor, the payment is entirely avoided.[z]

[q] Pothier, Des Obligations, num. 233.

[r] Instit. lib. iv. tit. vi. § 33. Voet, Comm. ad Pand. lib. xiii. tit. iv. De eo quod in Certo Loco, num. 5, 7.

[s] Voet, Comm. ad Pand. lib. lxvi. tit. iii. num. 12.

[t] Voet, Comm. ad Pand. lib. xlvi. tit. iii. num. 7.

[u] Pand. lib. l. tit. ult. L. 167.

[x] Pand. lib. xlvi. tit. iii. De Solutionibus, L. 20, 60.

[y] Pothier, Des Obligations, part 3, num. 541.

[z] Pand. lib. xlvi. tit. iii. De Solutionibus, L. 46.

Payment must be made either to the creditor himself or to some one authorized by him, or having power to receive it.[a] And if the creditor ratify a payment made to a person unauthorized to receive it, the payment becomes valid.[b]

But we have seen that Justinian decides that a payment is good and valid though it be not made by, nor with the consent of the debtor.[c]

When the condition of the debtor is improved by the debt being paid by another, this decision may be grounded on the reason given by Gajus, that the Civil Law allows—*Etiam ignorantis invitique meliorem conditionem facere.*[d] But this reason is inapplicable to payments made without the knowledge of the debtor, in cases where the payment is not beneficial to the debtor, but only substitutes one creditor for another. In such cases, however, the debtor has no right to object to that being done by another person which he ought to have done himself. And the law favours the payment of debts, and therefore considers the advantage to the creditor of receiving what is due, rather than the possible inconvenience which may result to the debtor by the change of creditors.

The creditor is bound to accept payment from a third person as he is from the debtor. And the tender of payment by a third party is as effectual as if made by the debtor.[e]

But this doctrine is not applicable to obligations *faciendi*; for in almost every case of that description it is an essential part of the contract that it should be performed by the person specified, and therefore the creditor cannot be required to accept performance by any other.[f]

The effect of payment by a third party with respect to that party is this: If it be made against the will of the debtor, the third party has no remedy to recover the amount from him.[g] But if the third party paid with the knowledge or express consent of the debtor, he has the action *mandati* to recover the amount, for he acted as the procurator of the debtor. *Qui non prohibit pro se intervenire, mandare creditur.*[h] And it is the same when the debtor approves or ratifies a payment made for him to his creditor without his knowledge. *Ratihabitio mandato comparatur.*[i]

[a] Pothier, Des Obligations, part 3, num. 501. Pand. lib. l. tit. ult. L. 180. Pothier, Des Obligations, part 3, chap. i. § 2, 3.

[b] Pand. lib. xlvi. tit. iii. De Solutionibus, L. 49.

[c] Instit. lib. iii. tit. xxx. princip. Cod. lib. viii. tit. xliii. De Solutionibus, L. 17.

[d] Pand. lib. xlvi. tit. iii. De Solutionibus, L. 53.

[e] Cod. lib. viii. tit. xliii. De Solutionibus, L. 9, 17.

[f] Pand. lib. xlvi. tit. iii. De Solutionibus, L. 31.

[g] Pand. lib. xvii. tit. i. Mandati, L. 40. Cod. lib. ii. tit. xix. De Negotiis Gestis, L. 24.

[h] Pand. lib. l. tit. ult. L. 60.

[i] Pand. ibid. Pand. lib. xlvi. tit. iii. De Solutionibus, L. 12, § 4.

If the third party paid the debt without the knowledge of the debtor, he has the action *negotiorum gestorum* against the debtor to recover what he paid.[k]

Where a debtor owes several distinct debts to the same creditor, the creditor is bound to receive payment of each of them separately; and questions may therefore arise as to the application, or, in the language of the Civil Law, the *imputation* of such payments. For the decision of such cases, the following rules are laid down by the Emperor Antoninus Pius and by Ulpian.[l]

The debtor may, at the time of payment, *impute* it to whichever of the separate debts he desires to pay in preference to the others. The reason of this rule is, that the priority of a debt over others (which is the only ground on which a compulsory priority of payment can be supported) is not a sufficient reason to render the payment of one debt before that of another obligatory on the debtor, since they are all equally due, and the creditor may therefore demand payment of any one, or of all the debts. Now if the debtor had not that privilege of choice, the creditor would have the power to prevent his extinguishing any debt subsequent in date to a debt which the debtor might not be able to pay at the time. Thus, supposing a man to owe a debt of £1000, and another debt, subsequent in date, of £100, there the debtor, if he had not the power of choosing which debt he would pay first, would be subject to a hardship. For, though able to pay the small debt, he would be precluded from doing so because he had not previously paid the larger debt. And this would be unjust, because the creditor, by giving credit to a man already his debtor, may fairly be argued to have placed the second debt on the same footing as the first, the payment of which he might have required before giving the fresh credit. Another principle on which all these rules are founded, is, that these indulgences granted to the debtor, without prejudice to the right of the creditor to enforce the payment of all the debts, greatly contribute to facilitate the liberation of debtors, which is beneficial to the parties and also to the community.

If the debtor do not impute the payment, the creditor may do so, but he must observe this most just rule of Ulpian: *In id constituat solutum, in quod ipse si deberet esset soluturus. Æquissimum enim visum est creditorem ita agere rem debitoris ut suam ageret.*[m]

[k] Pand. lib. xvii. tit. i. Mandati, L. 6, § 2.

[l] Cod. lib. viii. tit. xliii. De Solutionibus, L. 1. Pand. lib. xlv. tit. iii. L. 1. And see on this subject the French Code Civil, art. 1253, &c. And for the English Law) Harrison's Digest. (1844 , col. 2331.

[m] Pand. lib. xlvi. tit. iii. De Solutionibus, L. 1. He is not so restricted by the English Law. Campbell *v.* Hodgson, Gow. 74. Hall *v.* Wood, 14 East, 243 n.

The case in which no imputation of the payment is made by either debtor or creditor remains to be explained. It is governed by the same rules which the creditor is bound to observe in applying a payment according to the general principle of Ulpian just given above.

Ulpian says *Quotiens indistincte quid solvitur, in graviorem causam videri solutum; si vero nulla prægravat, in antiquiorem.*[n]

Thus the most onerous debt—that is to say, the debt which bears hardest on the debtor—has the preference, and the priority of date is resorted to only *cæteris paribus*.

By virtue of this rule the payment is imputed rather on what the debtor owes in his own name, than upon what he owes as surety for another, and rather on what he owes under a penalty or forfeiture than on a simple debt.[o] And Ulpian decides that the payment must be imputed on a debt actually due rather than on one not actually due or which is disputed [p]

On the same principles a payment should be imputed on a debt the nonpayment of which imports legal infamy, rather than on any other: and if the payment accepted by the creditor be greater than the amount of the debt upon which it is imputed, the surplus is imputed on the debt on which the payment would have been imputed if the other had not had the preference.[q]

A payment is imputed rather on a debt which bears interest and one secured on mortgage or by *fidejussion* than on one of an opposite description.[r] But in the Scotch law this rule is improved, by applying indefinite payments, in preference to those debts which are least secured, provided some debt be not thereby left unsatisfied, the nonpayment of which would expose the debtor to a rigorous forfeiture.[s]

If principal and interest be due, the payment must be imputed first on the interest, and the surplus (if there be any) must be applied to the payment of the principal so far as it will go.[t] The reason of this rule is that the principal and interest being, as it were, one debt, since they are due by virtue of one obligation, it is just towards the creditor that he should be paid first the interest for the delay in the payment of which he is entitled to no compensation, and then the principal which, if it be not paid, produces interest. But the creditor cannot be compelled to receive payment of the interest without the

[n] Pand. lib. xlvi. tit. iii. De Solutionibus, L. 1, 3. Cod. ibid. L. 1.
[o] Pand. ibid. L. 4. [p] Pand. ibid. L. 1, 103.
[q] Pand. ibid. L. 97.
[r] Pothier, Des Obligations, num. 567. Corollaire, 3.
[s] Erskine, Instit. book iii. tit. iv. § ii.
[t] Cod. lib. viii. tit. xlii. De Solutionibus, L. 1.

principal, because both together are one debt, under one obligation.[u] If however there be a fair doubt whether the interest be due or no, the creditor may be compelled, at the discretion of the judge, to receive what is acknowledged to be due without prejudice to his ulterior claims.[x]

We will now proceed to the next paragraph of the Institutes, which relates to *acceptilatio* or release.

Also obligations are extinguished by acceptilation, which is a feigned payment.[y]

The peculiar form of question and answer by which releases were effected in the old Civil Law arises from the technical formula of question and answer, called ***stipulation***. It was consequently applicable only to obligations contracted in that particular mode, until it was ingeniously extended to every other species of obligation by that profound technical lawyer, Aquilius Gallus.[z] But the technical part of the law of acceptilation is little more than a mere object of curiosity to modern civilians, and the extinction of obligations by release must therefore be here considered unencumbered by those ingenious legal niceties which are arbitrary and obsolete.

A release may be tacit or express. Paulus decides that if the creditor returned to the debtor the instrument containing the obligation, he must be presumed to have released him from the debt; and it is decided by Modestinus that the same presumption arises where the instrument has been erased.[a] But there may be other ways of accounting for those facts on which the presumption rests, showing that the creditor did not intend to release the debt, and therefore he may give proofs to rebut the presumption.[b]

A release may be presumed from other circumstances.

Thus it is decided by Labeo and Paulus that when one party to a bilateral contract releases the other, the former is presumed to be discharged on his side, and so the release is presumed (unless the contrary appear) to have been mutual.[c]

Upon the same principle of looking above all to the intention of the parties, Pothier holds on the authority of a law of Paulus, that the omission of any mention of a debt in the acquittance or release of

[u] Cod. lib. viii. tit. xliii. De Solutionibus, L. 1. Pand. lib. xlvi. tit. iii. De Solutionibus, L. 97, 1.

[x] Pand. lib. xii. tit. i. De Rebus Creditis, L. 21. Pand. lib. v. tit. iv. Si Pars Hereditatis Petatur, L. 8.

[y] Instit. lib. iii. tit. xxx. § 1.

[z] Instit. ibid. § 1, 2.

[a] Pand. lib. ii. tit. xiv. De Pactis, L. 2. Pand. lib. xxii. tit. iii. De Probationibus, L. 24.

[b] Cod. lib. viii. tit. xliii. De Solutionibus, L. 14, 15.

[c] Pand. lib. xlvi. tit. iv. De Acceptilationibus, L. 23. Pand. lib. xviii. tit. v. De Rescindendâ Venditione, L. 5.

another debt does not raise any presumption of the release of the former. Error is presumed in that case rather than an intention to release the debt, for there is no sufficient probability to raise the presumption, and *Nemo donare facile presumitur.*[d] Thus Modestinus decides that the restitution to the debtor by the creditor of the property which was given as security for the repayment of the debt, raises no presumption of a release of the debt, because that restitution was probably made with the intention only to give up the security.[e]

We will now proceed from tacit or presumed, to express releases.

They are of two species, namely, real or actual releases, and personal discharges.[f] A real or actual release is when the creditor declares that he holds the debt as satisfied, or where he gives a receipt or acknowledgment of having received the amount, though he did not in fact receive it: and this species of release is equivalent to payment in law, since the form of acceptilation has become obsolete; for while that form was in use, a receipt had no effect except as evidence of payment.[g]

A personal release or discharge is that whereby the creditor only discharges the debtor from the obligation. Such a release extinguishes the debt only where the debtor to whom it is granted is the sole debtor, for *magis eximit personam debitoris ab obligatione quam extinguit obligationem*; whereas a real release has the direct effect of extinguishing the debt itself.[h] It follows that a release by way of personal discharge does not set free a co-debtor of the debtor to whom it is granted, but it is otherwise with a real release.

We come now to the extinction of a debt by *novation.* This is the substitution of a new debt to the former debt, which is thereby extinguished.[i]

Also obligations are extinguished by novation; as, for instance, if you stipulate from Titius what Sejus owes you. For by the intervention of a new person, a new obligation arises, and the former obligation is extinguished and merged in the second; so far even that the former is extinguished, though the latter be not valid. As, for example, supposing that you stipulate from a ward without the authority of the guardian that which Titius owes you. In such a case the creditor loses his debt, for the former obligation is discharged, and the latter obligation is void. But if the second obligation be contracted by the same

[d] Pand. lib. xliv. tit. vii. De Obligationibus et Actionibus, L. 29. Pothier, Des Obligations, num. 613. [e] Pand. lib. ii. tit. xiv. De Pactis, L. 3.

[f] Pothier, Des Obligations, num. 616.

[g] Pand. lib. xlvi. tit. iv. De Acceptilationibus, L. 19.

[h] Pothier, Des Obligations, num. 617.

[i] Code Civil of France, liv. iii. § 2, art 1271.

person who was bound by the former, there is no novation, unless that second obligation be different from the former one; as, for instance, if a term, or a condition, or a surety be added or be omitted. But the position, that the addition of a condition in the latter obligation causes novation, must be understood thus: If the condition to which the second obligation is subject be accomplished, the novation takes effect, and if it be not, the former obligation continues to exist.

The antients held that there was novation where the second obligation was entered into with that intention; and frequent doubts and difficulties arose from that indefinite state of the law, depending on presumption. We have, therefore, enacted by our constitution that there shall in no case be novation, unless with the express intention of the parties, and that wherever that intention is not expressed, the former obligations shall remain in force, together with the latter.[k]

This paragraph deserves attentive consideration.

Novation is the substitution of a new debt to the old one, and the former obligation is extinguished by the new one contracted in its place, whether the latter be civil or merely natural.[l] Now the decision of Justinian, that a stipulation from a ward without the authority of the guardian, may, though not valid, extinguish a prior legal obligation, is grounded upon this doctrine, that novation may be, by the substitution of a natural to a civil or legal obligation. But if the second contract be not merely void by municipal law but by natural law also, the former obligation is not extinguished thereby.

On the same principle is founded the decision of Justinian, that where the second obligation is conditional (meaning, where it is suspended by a condition) there is no novation, unless and until the condition is accomplished,[m] for until the condition is accomplished the obligation has no effect. Cujacius says, *Conditio est dies vel eventus incertus ex quo suspenditur obligatio ut possit esse vel non esse:* therefore, while the condition is pending, the obligation does not exist. *Quod pendet non est pro eo quasi sit.*[n] The intention of the parties, moreover, is to substitute one obligation for another, and therefore the intention of producing one obligation is inseparable from that of extinguishing the other. It follows then that they cannot be held to have intended to extinguish the first unless the second exist and take effect either legally or naturally.

[k] Instit. lib. iii. tit. xxx. § 3. Cod. lib.viii. tit. xlii. De Novationibus et Delegationibus, L. ult. Code Civil of France, art. 1273.

[l] Pand. lib. xlvi. tit. ii. De Novationibus et Delegationibus, L. 1.

[m] Instit. lib. iii. tit. xxx. § 3.

[n] Pand. lib. l. tit. ult. L. 169, § 1. Pand. lib. xlvi. tit. ii. De Novationibus L. 8, § 1.

We have seen that novation may be by the creditor substituting a new debtor to the former one, or by the substitution of a new obligation of the same debtor to the former obligation. It may also be by substituting a new creditor in the place and at the desire or with the consent of the former creditor: and there is a peculiar species of novation called delegation, which is when the debtor, to discharge himself from the debt, gives to his creditor another debtor, who binds himself towards the creditor, or binds himself towards a third party at the desire of the creditor.[o]

It is clear that the decision of Justinian, in the paragraph given above, that there is no novation unless the second obligation be different from the first, is not applicable to the case of novation accomplished by a change in the person of the debtor. That decision is grounded on the same reason as the doctrine that a legacy by a debtor to a creditor, of that which is already due to him, is of no effect, where there is not more in the legacy than in the debt.[p]

But it follows from these principles that where the change in the date of the obligation (which change is incident to novation as well as the change in the identity of the obligation itself) is material, the novation is validly effected, though the subsequent obligation be similar to the preceding one in every respect, except as to the date.

The principal effect of novation is to extinguish the former obligation, whereby it also extinguishes all the obligations accessory to it, such as hypothecs, pledges, and fidejussions.[q] The accessory obligation of the fidejussor follows the principal obligation.[r] And the fidejussor cannot be made surety to the new obligation, unless he consent to enter into a new fidejussion.

But Papinian decides that the creditor may, in accomplishing the novation, transfer to the new debt his right of hypothec, by which the former debt was secured, and retain the priority of that hypothec for an amount equal to that of the first debt.[s]

The reason of this important determination is as follows:—

The preference of hypothecary creditors one to the other, by reason of the priorities of their respective securities, is grounded on the rule *Qui prior est tempore potior est jure.* Now the reason of that rule is, that the debtor who has hypothecated his property has thereby diminished his right over it, and therefore cannot convey to any one

[o] Voet, Comm. ad Pand. lib. xlvi. tit. ii. num. 11.

[p] Pothier, Des Obligations, part 3, chap. 2, § 4.

[q] Pothier, Des Obligations, num. 599. Pand. lib. xlvi. tit. ii. De Novationibus et Delegationibus, L. 18.

[r] Pand. lib. l. tit. ult. L. 128, § 1.

[s] Pand. lib. xx. tit. iv. Qui potiores in Pignore, L. 3, princip. Ibid. L. 12, § 5.

any right over the property, except subject to such diminution. *Nemo plus juris ad alium transferre potest quam ipse habet.*[t]

It follows, from this doctrine, that the transfer of a security from a former debt to a new debt substituted for it is no violation of the rule *Prior potior est.* It is the transfer of a right vested in the creditor, and which he may so transfer with the concurrence of the debtor, preserving its priority; for, by so doing, he in no respect violates the rights of the subsequent creditors, who thereby lose no advantage that they before possessed.

But it is implied by this reasoning, that the prior hypothec cannot be transferred to the subsequent debt by novation, so as to make it a security for a greater amount than that of the former debt which is extinguished by novation.[u]

It must be observed here, that the transfer of the hypothec from one debt to another, cannot be made without the consent of the person to whom the hypothecated property belongs. That consent may be included in the novation in the cases considered above. But if the novation be made by substituting one debtor for another, though the novation itself may be validly effected without the participation of the original debtor, yet the transfer of the hypothec on which the first debt is secured, to the debt contracted in its stead by the second debtor, requires the consent of the first debtor.[v]

But though a subsequent hypothecary creditor may, by paying off a prior one, take his security with its priority, a stranger cannot do so, nor a creditor who has not a hypothec on the property, unless with the concurrence of the debtor or the prior creditor.[x]

We will now briefly consider the species of novation called *delegation.*[y]

Delegation is when a debtor, to acquit himself towards his creditor, gives to him a third person, who binds himself instead of the former debtor, either to the creditor or to a third person. Ulpian says: *Delegare est vice sua alium reum dare creditori vel cui jusserit.*[z]

Delegation includes a novation, for the transaction has the effect of extinguishing the debt of the delegator, and binding the delegate in his place: and when the delegate is a debtor of the delegator, there is

[t] Pand. lib. l. tit. ult. L. 54.

[u] Pand. lib. xx. tit. iv. Qui Potiores in Pignore, L. 12, § 5. Voet, Comm. ad Pand. lib. xx. tit. iv. num. 32.

[v] Pand. lib. xlvi. tit. ii. De Novationibus et Delegationibus, L. 30.

[x] Voet, Comm. ad Pand. lib. xx. tit. xxxiv.

[y] Pothier, Des Obligations, num. 600.

[z] Pand. lib. xlvi. tit. ii. De Novationibus et Delegationibus, L. 11.

also a further novation by the substitution of the debtor of the delegator in the place of the delegator himself.

It follows from the definition, that delegation requires the concurrence of three persons,—namely, 1st, the delegator; 2ndly, the delegate or person substituted for the delegator; and, 3rdly, the creditor who accepts the delegate instead of the delegator. It follows also that there may be a fourth party to the transaction, namely, the person to whom the delegate binds himself at the desire of the creditor. The consent of such three or four parties, as the case may be, is requisite for the validity of the delegation; each of them either discharges himself by contract, or binds himself, or else accepts a right.

As the delegation includes the extinction of the former debt, and the entire discharge of the former debtor (the delegator), it follows that the insolvency of the delegate after the delegation does not render the former debtor liable: and if the insolvency of the delegate at the time of the delegation was known to the creditor, it does not render the former debtor (the delegator) liable to indemnify him.[a]

The next paragraph of the Institutes relates to the dissolution of contracts by the mutual consent of the parties.

Also all obligations contracted by consent are dissolved by a contrary will. For if Titius and Sejus agreed, the former to sell and the latter to buy the Tusculan estate, and before the payment of the price, or the delivery of the estate, they agree to break off the sale, they are reciprocally set free.[b]

The technical form of *stipulation* having been rejected by the modern civilians, the law contained in this paragraph is applicable to all contracts (as well as to those contracted *consensu*) in which nothing has been executed on either side. If anything has been executed, mere consent will not dissolve the contract; for there must be a release, or something by way of restitution or indemnification on account of that which has been performed.[c] But to such cases also the rule of Justinian applies—*Obligationes quæ consensu contrahuntur contraria voluntate dissolvuntur*,—so far as anything remains to be done on either side. The general maxim of Ulpian on which this paragraph of the Institutes is founded, is important in public as well as in private law. *Nihil tam naturale est quam eo genere quidque dissolvere quo colligatum est.*[d]

[a] Pothier, Des Obligations, num. 504. [b] Instit. lib. iii. tit. xxx. § 4.

[c] Cod. lib. iv. tit. xlv. Quando liceat ab Emptione discedere, L. 1, 2.

Pand. lib. l. tit. ult. L. 35.

The corresponding rule in the opposite species of case, namely, that in which all the parties do not consent to dissolve the contract, is thus laid down by Diocletian and Maximian: *Sicut initio libera potestas unicuique est habendi vel non habendi contractus, ita renunciare semel constitutæ obligationi adversario non consentiente nemo potest.*[e]

But when an already entirely executed contract is reversed by consent of the parties, the transaction is not a dissolution, but a new contract, having a contrary effect to the former.[f]

There are peculiar reasons (which have been already shown) why the contracts of mandate and society are not subject to the rule that one party cannot dissolve a contract without the consent of the others. But they also are subject to the rule, *Nemo potest mutare consilium suum in alterius detrimentum.*[g]

The explanation of the last title of the third book of Justinian's Institutes is now concluded. A few words must be added respecting a very important mode whereby obligations are extinguished, namely, *compensation*, which in the English law is called a *set off*.

Compensation is the extinction of debts, of which two persons are reciprocally debtors towards each other by means of the obligations whereby they are reciprocally creditors towards each other. Modestinus says, *Compensatio est debiti et crediti inter se contributio.*[h] Thus if Titius owe Sempronius £100 and Sempronius owe Titius £50, it would follow that the balance, that is to say only £50 is owing to Sempronius. This is according to the common rule of the Civil Law, *Dolo facit qui petit quod redditurus est.*[i] Two persons cannot be reciprocally bound at the same time by identical obligations having the same object, or indefinite objects of an identical nature, such as the payment of a certain value. Such obligations and the rights which correspond with them, are incompatible in the person of each party, and therefore extinguish each other.

It follows from these principles that there is no compensation unless the mutual obligations be identical, consequently the debtor of a specific thing, such as a horse or an ox, is not discharged from his obligation in consequence of his having a right to receive a specific

[e] Cod. lib. iv. tit. x. De Obligationibus et Actionibus, L. 5. Cod. lib. xviii. tit. v. De Rescindenda Venditione, L. 3. [f] Pand. lib. ii. tit. xiv. De Pactis, L. 58.

[g] Pand. lib. l. tit. ult. L. 66.

[h] Pothier, Des Obligations, num. 623. Pand. lib. xvi. tit. ii. De Compensationibus, L. 1. And see Julii Pauli Receptæ Sententiæ (one of the additions at the end of the Corpus Juris, lib. ii. tit. v. §. 3.

[i] See this rule in the Canon Law, Sext. Decretal. tit. ult. De Regulis Juris, Reg. 59.

thing of the same kind from his creditor,[k] because the mutual obligations have different objects. Those objects are indeed similar, but they are not identical. The rule cited above, *Dolo facit qui petit quod redditurus est*, is not applicable to this species of case.

Another consequence of the same principles is, that unless the two reciprocal debts be both due and payable, and liquid, that is to say certain or definite, there is no compensation.[l]

Also they must be due to the creditors in the same characters, otherwise there are in law three persons and not two. So a debtor from whom Gajus claims money in the character of a guardian, cannot plead compensation, because Gajus owes him money in his private capacity.[m]

Ulpian decides that a natural debt and a civil debt may produce compensation and extinguish the legal obligation or the legal right. *Etiam quod natura debitur venit in compensationem.*[n] The reason of this is, that it would be contrary to equity to compel a man to pay to another that which the latter ought in equity to return, and should not have demanded. The effect of compensation is to extinguish, *ipso jure*, the reciprocal obligations from the moment that they coexist, so as to admit compensation.[o] Compensation therefore stops the accumulation of interest.[p]

The immediate effect, *ipso jure*, of compensation distinguishes it from a *set off* in the English Law, which takes effect only by being pleaded as an answer to the plaintiff's demand, and the Law of Scotland in this respect resembles that of England.[q]

Confusion, which is another mode whereby obligations are extinguished, is grounded on principles similar to those of compensation. Confusion is where the obligation of debtor and the right of creditor concur by one becoming the heir and accepting the inheritance of the other.[r] *Nemo potest sibi debere*, and therefore this concurrence of right and obligation in one person extinguishes both.

The next chapter will treat of obligations *ex delicto*, a subject with which Justinian commences the fourth book of his Institutes.

[k] The word creditor is used here on the authority of Pand. lib. l. tit. ultim. L. 10—12.

[l] Pand. lib. xvi. tit. ii. De Compensationibus, L. 7. Cod. lib. iv. tit. xxxi. De Compens. L. ultim. § 1.

[m] Pand. ibid. L. 23. The Law 18 of the same title is in accordance with these principles.

[n] Pand. lib. xvi. tit. ii. De Compens. L. 6.

[o] Cod. lib. iv. tit. xxxi. De Compensationibus, L. 14, princip.

[p] Pand. lib. xvi. tit. ii. De Compensationibus, L. 11, 12.

[q] Blackst. Comm. book iii. p. 304. Erskine, Instit. book iii. tit. iv. § 12.

[r] Voet, Comm. ad Pand. lib. xlvi. tit. iii. num. 18.

CHAPTER XLIII.

THE LAW OF THINGS. OBLIGATIONS ARISING EX MALEFICIO.—THEFT.

Obligations arising *ex Maleficio.* — Theft.—Instit. lib. iv. tit. i. De Obligationibus quæ ex Delicto nascuntur. Nature of Obligations *ex Delicto* and *quasi ex Delicto.* General Principle from which they spring. Distinction between *Damnum* and *Injuria,* and Definition of a Wrong. Rule deduced from the Definition of Liberty by Florentinus.—Wrongs offending Natural Law, and Wrongs offending Municipal Law. — A Delict or Malefice defined by Boehmerus.— Distinction between *Delictum* and *quasi Delictum.*—Examination of the Distinction between Public and Private Wrongs, and Criminal and Civil Law.— Definition of Theft explained in Detail, and the Civil Law of Theft compared with the Law of England. P. 270.

In the fourth book of the Institutes, Justinian, having given the elements of obligations springing from contract and from *quasi contract,* proceeds to those which arise from *delicta* or wrongs, and from *quasi delicta,* which are actions *maleficio proximi.*

It has already been shown that all obligations proceed from the law mediately, or immediately; that every obligation is by consent, or without consent, and that the latter sort of obligations arise either from the law directly, as is the case with those called by Lord Stair obediential; or from the law upon the occasion of an act or event.

Obligations arising upon the occasion of an act are divided into two classes, for the act may be either lawful or unlawful. Obligations arising upon the occasion of a lawful act are those called obligations *quasi ex contractu:* and those which arise on the occasion of an unlawful act are obligations *ex delicto,* and *quasi ex delicto.*

All obligations *ex maleficio,* or from wrong, are of the same species in this respect,—that they all equally spring from the law on the occasion of an act such as a theft, or injury to property, or rapine.[a]

The general principle from which all obligations *ex delicto* and *quasi ex delicto* spring, is, that *every act of any man which causes damage to another obliges him by whose fault that damage was caused to make reparation.*[b]

That principle is a corollary of the precepts of natural law, *Alterum non lædere, suum cuique tribuere.*[c]

[a] Instit. lib. xiv. tit. i. princip.

[b] Grotius, Droit de la Guerre et de la Paix, liv. ii. chap. xvii. § 1, § 3. Code Civil Français, art. 1382. Pand. lib. i. tit. i. De Just. et Jur. L. 10. § 1.

But not every act of one man which causes damage to another gives rise to an obligation to make reparation, for that obligation attaches to him *by whose fault the damage was caused.* It is therefore necessary to inquire what legally constitutes *fault.*

Ulpian defines an injury or wrong to be, *Quod non jure factum est, hoc est contra jus:*[d] and as the obligation to make reparation for the damage arises from the fault, and not from the intention to do injury, he adds, *Injuriam hic damnum accipimus culpa datum etiam ab eo qui nocere noluit.* This negligence or imprudence renders a man responsible for the consequences because the natural precept *Alterum non lædere* includes the obligation of taking care not to do anything nor to omit any act so as to prejudice the rights of others; and the obligation to indemnify the person thus injured follows as a natural consequence of the responsibility.

It follows from the definition of a wrong, *quod non jure factum est,* that if an act be not against right (*contra jus*) no one that suffers inconvenience or loss thereby can demand compensation. Thus Gajus says, *Nullus videtur dolo facere qui suo jure utitur.*[e]

But every man is bound to make such use of his rights as not to cause detriment to others.[f] It must however not be concluded that wherever the exercise of a right by one man is contrary to the interests of another, the right ceases to exist, for as Paulus writes, *Nemo damnum facit, nisi qui id fecit quod facere jus non habuit.*[g] Therefore when a man does that which he has a right to do, he is not bound to indemnify another whose interests are injured thereby, provided he used his rights in such a manner as to affect others as little as possible. Upon this principle Celsus decides that a person having a right of passage over the land of another, is not justified in passing over the cultivated parts, when he might, by using his right in a different manner, cause less or no inconvenience to the proprietor.[h] And no man ought to choose a mode which is prejudicial to others of doing what he has a right to do, when he can derive full benefit from his rights without injuring any one.

But every man has a right to derive the fullest benefit from that which is his, and as every one's interest cannot always be in harmony with that of others, it would be impossible to carry into effect by legal

[d] Pand. lib. IX. tit. II. Ad Legem Aquiliam, L. 5, § 1, 2.

[e] Pand. lib. L. tit. ult. L. 55. Matthæus de Criminibus, Comm. tit. iii. cap. i.

[f] Pand. lib. XXXIX. tit. III. De Aqua et Aquæ Pluviæ Arcendæ, L. 1, § 2. *Prodesse sibi unusquisque dum alii non nocet non prohibetur.*

[g] Pand. lib. L. tit. ult. L. 151.

[h] Pand. lib. VIII. tit. i. De Servitutibus, L. 9, and see the celebrated Law, Pand. lib VI tit. I. De Rei Vindicatione, L. 38.

means in the fullest manner the precept *Love your neighbour as yourself* (on which Domat founded his legal doctrines) without converting the law into a system of philanthropy and self-abnegation, which could not be enforced by means of courts of justice.

On the principle, *Nemo damnum facit nisi qui id facit quod facere jus non habet*, a man who by digging in his own ground caused a spring in the ground of his neighbour to dry up is not liable to indemnify the latter.[i]

And thus every man has a right to do whatever is necessary for the cultivation of his land, though it be injurious to the land of a neighbour; but he must not wantonly and unnecessarily do anything in the cultivation of his land which is mischievous to others,[k] for the general rule is this:—*Sic debere quem meliorem agrum suum facere, ne vicini deteriorem faciat.*[l]

Upon the same principles, in Public Law, no nation is bound to prefer the interests of another nation to its own.[m]

Such is the manner in which the Roman Law construes the rule of Paulus: *Nemo damnum facit nisi qui id facit quod facere jus non habet.* But it remains to be shown what general rule determines the actions which men have, and those which they have not a right to do.

That rule is to be found in the celebrated definition of liberty by Florentinus: *Libertas est naturalis facultas, ejus quod cuique facere libet, nisi si quid vi aut jure prohibetur.*[n] Now as no action is a wrong which in its object and mode is such as the person doing it has a right to do; and as, on the other hand, a man is legally at liberty to do whatever is not contrary to law—*quod jure non prohibetur*, it follows that no act is a *delict*, or *maleficium*, or wrong, that is not forbidden by law.

But there are actions forbidden by Natural Law and not by Municipal Law, and the contrary. Paulus says: *Non omne quod licet honestum est.*[o]

Every wrong must be a violation of law. When that law is Natural Law, the wrong is naturally a delict; and where it is a Municipal or Voluntary Law, the wrong is a civil wrong or delict. *Probra quædam natura turpia sunt, quædam civiliter et quasi more civitatis.*[p]

In many cases, as the Municipal Law is for the most part declaratory

[i] Pand. lib. l. tit. ult. L. 151. Pand. lib. xxxix. tit. iii. De Aqua et Aquæ Pluviæ Arcendæ, L. 1, § 12. [k] Pand. ibid. § 3—5. [l] Pand. ibid. § 4.

[m] Vattel, Droit des Gens, liv. ii. chap. i. § 16, 17.

[n] Pand. lib. i. tit. v. De Statu Hominum, L. 4.

[o] Pand. lib. l. tit. ult. L. 144 197. And see Barbeyrac, Traité de la Permission des Loix. [p] Pand. lib l tit penult De Signif. Verbor. L. 42.

of the Natural Law, an offence against the latter is also an offence against the former; but as a variety of arbitrary or voluntary laws are requisite for the welfare, and even the existence of the community, it is difficult to conceive an offence against Municipal Law (provided it be not unjust) which would not also be a violation of the secondary Natural Law whereby men are bound to obey the laws of the community to which they belong or in which they live.

But the Municipal Law declines to give a remedy for, and even to punish certain wrongs, on the same grounds that it refuses to enforce certain rights.

The imperfection of human means, and the moral imperfections of human nature are such, that it would be impossible that Municipal Law should provide a remedy for every violation of natural right, and to enforce the whole Law of Nature: and it is to avoid greater inconvenience, that the law in many cases leaves the enforcement of natural right, and the reparation of wrongs, to morality, conscience, and religion.

Such is the general nature of a wrong, *delict*, or *maleficium*. It is well defined as follows by Boehmerus: *Delicta sunt spontaneæ actiones vel omissiones legibus contrariæ.*[q] They are spontaneous, that is to say, voluntary or free actions, because no man is liable for violating the law when he had it not in his power to obey the law. Upon the same principles, those who are incapable of discrimination, and who, wherefore, if they either obey or violate the law, do so by accident, and consequently cannot obey the law in the correct sense of the term, are incapable of committing a delict or wrong.[r]

An omission, as well as a positive act, may be a delict; for where a man, by not doing what he ought to do, causes detriment to others, it is the same in principle as if he had caused that detriment unlawfully by a positive act. Thus if a man had it in his power to prevent a wrong, and did not, he is liable, provided he was bound to prevent it; for otherwise, his omission would not be an unlawful act.[s] Thus those who have under their power persons incapable of discrimination, are responsible for the damage done by such persons, if they might have prevented the injury and did not. So also persons are responsible for damage done through their fault by animals belonging to them, and even for damage by inanimate things which they were bound to prevent.[t]

[q] Boehmer. Elem. Jur. sect. i. § 29. And see Matthæus De Criminibus, Comment. prologomena, cap. 1.

[r] Pothier, Des Obligations, num. 178.

[s] Pand. lib. xlix. tit. xxvi. De Re Militari, L. 3, § 22, L. 6, § 8.

[t] Pothier, Des Obligations, num. 118. Code Civil. Franç. art. 1385. Pand. lib. 1 tit. ult L 109.

Delicta, taking the word in its widest sense, are divided into two classes,—namely, *vera delicta*, or *delicta* strictly so called: and *quasi delicta*.[u] A delict is an act whereby a person with dole or malice, that is to say, with an intent to injure, causes damage or injury to another.[x]

A *quasi delict* is an act whereby a person, without malice, but by fault or imprudence not legally excusable, causes injury to another.

Delicts are either public or private, according as they are regarded as injuring the community, or individuals in their private capacity.[y]

A *quasi delict* may also be either public or private. Negligence in the affairs of the community may be a high crime, which in a private matter would only be ground for an action for damages.

The boundary between public and private wrongs cannot be marked out by any clear and invariable rule, for every wrong to an individual is a wrong to the community to which he belongs or in which he lives, and which is established (among other things) for the protection of the rights of individuals. There are, indeed, offences directly affecting the commonwealth, and others which, by reason of their pernicious nature, are injuries as well to society as to the individual persons directly affected by them. But it is difficult to say that a petty theft is more pernicious to society than the wrongful detaining of an estate or a debt from the lawful owner or creditor.

Blackstone holds that private wrongs or civil injuries are an infringement or privation of the civil rights which belong to individuals, considered merely as such.[z] But theft comes within this description. Blackstone accordingly enumerates, as public wrongs, a number of instances, all consisting either of an offence against the state, or against the public peace, or including a violation of a right of the community. And the great commentator thus indicates the true reason why some wrongs are visited with punishment as offences against the community, while in others the law only awards reparation to the party injured. "The law has a double view, namely, not only to redress the party injured, but also to secure to the public the benefit of society, by preventing or punishing every breach of those laws which the sovereign power has established for the tranquillity and government of the whole."

From this definition of Municipal Law and government may be deduced, that where the wrong is sufficiently redressed, and the wrong-

[u] Boehmer. Elementa Jur. Crimin. sect. i. § 29.

[x] Pothier, Des Obligations, num. 116.

Vinnii Comment. ad Instit. lib. iv. tit. i. paratit.

Blackst. Comm. book iv. chap. i. § 1.

doer sufficiently discouraged by the reparation which he is compelled to make to the injured person, the wrong may be treated as private; but where the nature of the wrong is such that reparation is impossible, or must be inadequate, and where the enforcement of the obligation of reparation is ineffectual for the purpose of discouragement,—in such cases society is bound, for the protection of its members, to threaten and inflict punishment, as well as in those cases in which the grave nature, or the object of the crime, render it public by reason of its being an injury direct or indirect to the community.

It follows that the distinction between Civil and Criminal Law is matter of public policy, which may vary according to circumstances and the requirements of society.

Thus, for instance, a refusal to pay rent legally due is a civil wrong, and sufficiently repaired by civil remedies; but if there were a general refusal to pay rent throughout a country, the number of private wrongs might become so serious in its effect that it might be the duty of the legislature to stop the progress of the evil by adding a public prosecution and penalty to the inadequate remedies of the Civil Law; and yet each of the refractory tenants might be actuated by no design against the community.

Thus, again, the offence of calumniating a private individual cannot, strictly speaking, be an offence against society or a public wrong, unless it have a tendency to produce a breach of the peace, which in many instances may not be so; but a mere compensation to the party injured may be entirely, or in a great degree ineffectual either for indemnifying the party or discouraging offenders; for rich men will run the risk of being made to pay damages, and poor men know that they cannot be forced to do so. It follows, then, that society is bound (because the protection of individuals is its first duty) to punish calumny as a public crime, besides allowing the person injured to sue for damages, as compensation for the detriment suffered therefrom.

On the same principles, theft would be very inadequately discouraged by the mere civil remedy of restitution, since the thief would have nothing to lose and everything to gain by his crime; and he could evade even the obligation of restitution, by secreting or destroying the stolen goods, if he could not, by reason of poverty, be made to pay an equivalent; and for this reason, stealing even a thing of trifling value is a public crime in all civilized countries, while the refusal to pay a debt, though of great amount, is merely visited with a civil action.[a]

For the same reasons, because civil remedies are an insufficient

[a] Bowyer, Comment. on the Constit. Law of England, chap. xv. p. 232-3, 2nd edition.

protection against that species of fraud, the Insolvent Law visits with punishment persons who incur debts without having the means of meeting their engagements.

Private wrongs only are here to be treated of, that is to say, wrongs considered as injuries to the rights of individuals, and with reference to the redress provided by the Civil Law, without regard to the punishment which, in some instances, the Criminal Law inflicts on the wrong-doers.

Of these private wrongs, from which obligations *ex maleficio* spring, four are enumerated by Justinian and Gajus, and to some one or other of them all others may be reduced and referred. They are, *furtum*, *damnum*, *rapina*, and *injuria*.[b] The first,—theft, is thus defined by Justinian and Paulus:

Theft is the fraudulent taking of either a thing or its use or possession, for the purpose of gain: which is contrary to the Law of Nature.[c]

Furtum est contrectatio rei fraudulosa lucri faciendi gratia, vel ipsius rei, vel etiam usus ejus possessionisve: quod lege naturali prohibitum est admittere.[d]

Each part of these definitions must now be separately explained. And, in the first place, theft is evidently contrary to Natural Law, because it is a violation of the law of property, which is part of the secondary Natural Law; and Ulpian accordingly includes theft among the offences which are naturally disgraceful or sinful.[e]

Secondly, theft consists in taking, *contrectatio*. To constitute theft the locality of the thing must be changed. *Furtum sine contrectatione fieri non potest, nec animo furtum admittitur.*[f] *Cogitationis pœnam nemo patitur.*[g] Therefore the intention to deprive the owner of his property must be shown by an overt act; and that intention does not appear from mere manual apprehension of the thing, without taking it from the person who has a right to it, or from the place where it was.

And whether a man take a thing from the owner, or cause the owner by fraudulent representations to give it to him, it is the same

[b] Pand. lib. xliv. tit. vii. De Obligationibus et Actionibus, L. 4. Voet, Comm. ad Pand. lib. xlvii. tit. i. De Privatis Delictis, num. 3. [c] Instit. lib. iv. tit. i. § 1.

[d] Pand. lib. xlvii. tit. ii. De Furtis, L. 1, § 3. And see Matthæus De Criminibus, Comment. tit. i. cap. 1, De Furtis.

[e] Pand. lib. i. tit. i. De Justitia et Jure, L. 5, lib. l. tit. penult. De Signific. Verbor. L. 42.

[f] Pand. lib. xli. tit. ii. De Adquirenda et Omittenda Possessione, L. 3, § 18. Lib. x. tit. iv. Ad Exhibendum, L. 15.

[g] Pand. lib. xlviii. tit. ix. De Pœnis, L. 18.

in principle. The thing is in both cases taken without the consent of the owner, for *Non videtur qui errat consentire.* Thus he commits theft who knowingly receives money which is not due, or which he has no right to receive.[h] In these cases the false pretence used is only the means whereby the laws of property are violated, and therefore the Civil Law holds the wrong thereby committed to be theft, and not a distinct offence as in the English Law.

The Civil Law also holds that to detain and keep a thing from the owner is theft, because it is the same in principle as taking it from him, and so to hide anything from the owner is theft if it be done with intent to take it, that is to say to steal it.[i]

It follows from these doctrines that immoveables cannot be the subject of theft.[k] The reason of this is that a person wrongfully taking possession of immoveables without asserting a title and keeping possession by force against the owner is guilty of breach of the peace, and the party injured has his remedy by the interdict *unde vi.*[l] And immoveables are incapable of *contrectatio*, which implies a moving or withdrawal from the pursuit of the owner.[m]

But all portions and accessories of immoveables which are capable of *contrectation* and withdrawal from the pursuit and knowledge of the owner, such as trees, fruit, stones and earth, may be subjects of theft, because the principles applicable to the immoveables, of which they are parts or accessories, do not apply to them.[n] This distinction is unknown to the English Law, which is therefore encumbered with arbitrary rules as to what things may and what may not be the subjects of theft.[o]

With respect to the value of the thing, it need be but barely capable of estimation to render the thing the subject of theft.[p] By this simple principle the Civil Law avoids the numerous and complicated rules and distinctions whereby the English Law attempts to settle what things are of such value as to be the subjects of theft.

[h] Pand. lib. xiii. tit. i. De Condictione Furtiva, L. 18. Cod. lib. vi. tit. ii. De Furtis, L. 19. Voet, Comm. ad Pand. lib. xlvii. tit. ii. De Furtis, num. 6.

[i] Instit. lib. iv. tit. i. § 6. Cod. lib. vi. tit. ii. De Furtis, L. 6. Voet, Comm. ad Pand. ubi sup. Pand. lib xlvii. tit. ii. De Furtis, L. 1. § 2.

[k] Pand. lib. xlvii. tit. ii. De Furtis, L. 25.

[l] Pand. lib. xliii. tit. xvi. Vi et Vi Armata, L. 3, § 8.

[m] Erskine, Instit. book iv. tit. iv. § 58.

[n] Pand. lib. xlvii. tit. ii. De Furtis, L. 25, L. 57.

First Report on the Criminal Law, 1834. Digest of the Law of Theft, § 1.

Boehmer. Elem. Jur. Crim. cap. De Furtis, § 166. Carmignani Elem. Jur. Crim. lib iii. De Furt. § 990.

We come now to the second part of the definition. *Furtum est contrectatio rei fraudulosa.*

The taking must be fraudulent, for if it be forcible the offence is not theft but robbery—the offence *Vi bonorum raptorum*, and if it be not wrongful, it is no wrong. The *animus furandi* is essential to the offence of theft. *Maleficia voluntas et propositum delinquentis distinguit.*[q]

This point is further explained by the last words of the definition, namely, *lucri faciendi gratia. Furtum est contrectatio rei fraudulosa lucri faciendi gratia.*

The object of theft must be to acquire the thing stolen, or to derive some advantage from it to the injury of another. Thus if the defendant merely took possession of the thing to destroy it, the offence is not theft, but a worse offence.[r]

But where a man takes that which is not his, and gives it away, he is guilty of theft, because the power of disposing of the property is a sort of lucre. *Species lucri est ex alieno largiri.*[s] And thus he has the *animus furandi.* The last eight words only of the definition of theft remain for consideration. *Furtum est contrectatio rei fraudulosa lucri faciendi gratia, vel ipsius rei vel etiam usus ejus possessionisve.*

The wrongful making use of or deriving of profit from the property of another is by the Civil Law theft, though the thing itself be not taken. It is a theft of the use and profit, and so the violation of a mere right of possession by taking the thing, is a theft of the possession.[t] But here again the *animus furandi* is essential to constitute the offence; so that if the use or profit be derived under a probable and *bonâ fide* belief that the owner permitted or would permit such use or profit there is no theft, though the person using the property must indemnify the owner for any loss or injury caused by its unauthorized use.[u]

There is no theft if the owner of the property be willing that it be taken. *Nemo videtur fraudare eos qui sciunt et consentiunt.*[x] But if the owner permitted it to be taken only for the purpose of catching the thief, the offence of theft is complete, for the owner had no intention of giving his property away, but merely of detecting the

[q] Pand. lib. xlvii. tit. ii. De Furtis, L. 53. Cremani De Jure Crimin. vol. ii. p. 376.

[r] Voet, Comm. ad Pand. lib. xlvii. tit. ii. De Furtis, num. 8. Pand. lib. xlvii. tit. ii. L 53, L. 39.

[s] Pand. lib. xlvii. tit. ii. De Furtis, L. 54.

[t] Instit. lib. iv. tit. l. § 6. Voet, Comm. ad Pand. lib. xlvii. tit. ii. De Furtis, num. 5.

[u] Instit. ubi supra, § 7. Pand. ubi supra, L. 46, § 7.

[x] Pand. ubi supra, L. 46, § 8. Pand. lib. l. tit. ult. L. 145.

thief.[y] Therefore the rule *Volenti non fit injuria* does not apply to that case.

The Roman Law concerning the *maleficium* of theft, from whence springs the obligation of restitution of the stolen property with damages, has now been sufficiently explained.

CHAPTER XLIV.

OBLIGATIONS EX MALEFICIO.—OF RAPINE.—DAMAGE TO PROPERTY.—INJURY TO PERSONS.—OBLIGATIONS QUASI EX DELICTO.

Of Rapine.—Damage to Property.—Injury to Persons.—Instit. lib. iv. tit. ii. De Vi Bonorum Raptorum.—*Rapine* Defined.—Where the Use of Force is, and where it is not Justifiable.—Instit. lib. iv. tit. iii. De Lege Aquilia.—*Damnum* defined.—What Damage is Wrongful.—Where a Lawful Thing is done in a Wrongful Manner.—Damage arising from Neglect of Duty and Incapacity.—Institut. lib. iv. tit. iv. De Injuriis.—*Injuria* defined.—Classification of *Injuria*. Verbal Injuries.—Uttered or by Writing.—Where the Truth of the Imputation may be proved in Justification.—Action by a Husband or Father for Injury to his Wife or Children.—Instit. lib. iv. tit. v. De Obligationibus quæ quasi ex Delicto nascuntur.—*Quasi Delict* defined.—A Judge making a Cause his own.—Damage done by Things dropping from a House.—Liability of the Owners and Keepers of Ships, Inns, Taverns, and Stables, for the Acts of their Servants.—Observation of Grotius as to the Liability of Partowners of Ships. P. 277.

At the beginning of the fourth book of the Imperial Institutes, four species of private wrongs or *maleficia* are enumerated, namely, *furtum*, *rapina*, *damnum*, and *injuria*. The first of these has been explained. Rapine is a wrong of the same nature as theft, but committed by other means, that is to say not by stealth or fraud, but by force.

This offence is however no longer a distinct head in modern criminal law, which distinguishes two kinds of theft, namely, simple and qualified. Rapine or theft, accompanied with force, is an aggravated species of qualified theft, which is called qualified because it comprehends a violation not only of the law of property, but of some other law.

All injuries by violence are punished as public wrongs by the criminal law as well as redressed by the Civil Law.[a] And indeed

[y] Instit. ubi supra, § 8. Cod. lib. vi. tit. ii. De Furtis, L. 20.

[a] Pand. lib. xlviii. tit. vii. Ad Leg. Juliam de Vi Privata; lib. xlviii. tit. vi. Ad Leg. Juliam de Vi Publica.

the public wrong of violence is so much considered by the law, that it is punished though the private detriment suffered be very slight. And on the general principle that no violence is to be permitted, no man is allowed to obtain by violence even that which is his, or to which he is legally entitled.[b] The rule of the Roman Law is, that what may be done by an appeal to the law must not be effected by individuals taking the law into their own hands.[c] But where the power of the law cannot be resorted to it is otherwise, for in such cases men are left to the maintenance of their own rights.[d] Upon these principles rest the limitations of the right of self-defence in civil society.[e]

We come now to the wrongs comprehended under the word *damnum*, which are treated of in the title of the Institutes on the Aquilian Law.[f]

Damnum or damage means in the Roman Law, when taken into strict acceptation, the detriment which arises from the wrongful destruction of, or injury to, property, for which remedies are provided by the Aquilian Law.[g]

The act must in the first place be wrongful. Thus, to kill an animal wrongfully is to kill without having any right to do so. Consequently Justinian decides that a man who kills a robber (a slave) is not liable provided he could not in any other way avoid the danger.[h]

When damage is caused by inexcusable negligence, it is *injuria*, for it is *quod non jure factum est*, and within the remedies of the Aquilian Law.[i] That law thus embraces damage done by *quasi delict* or unintentional though inexcusable wrong, as well as by *delict* or intentional and malicious wrong. And as persons incapable of dole must *a fortiori* be incapable of fault, they are not liable to the Aquilian Law. So no one is liable for casual events beyond his power.[k]

As no act is an injury or wrong that is not done against right, it follows that where a man has a right to do the damage, it is no wrong. Thus damage done in lawful self defence is no wrong.[l] But it is not lawful to do anything in self-defence beyond what is necessary for

[b] Pand. lib. iv. tit. ii. Quod Metus Causa, L. 13. Gravina, Histor. cap. xci.

[c] Pand. lib. l. tit. ult. L. 176.

[d] Pand. lib. xlii. tit. viii. Quæ in Fraudem Creditorum, L. 10, § 1. Instit. lib. iv. tit. ii. De Vi Bonorum Raptorum, § 1.

[e] Pufendorf, Droit de la Nat. et des Gens, liv. ii. chap. v. § 4.

[f] Instit. lib. iv. tit. iii. De Lege Aquilia. [g] Instit. ibid. princip.

[h] Instit. ibid. § 2. Pand. lib. ix. tit. ii. Ad Leg. Aquiliam, L. 5, § 1.

[i] Pand. ibid. L. 5, § 1, L. 44. *In Lege Aquilia et Lævissima Culpa venit.*

[k] Pand. ibid. L. 7, § 3, L. 52, § 2.

[l] Pand. ibid. L. 4, 45, § 4. Pand. lib. i. tit. i. De Justitia et Jure, L. 3.

that purpose. On the principle of the right of self-preservation rests the decision that a man may destroy the house of his neighbour which is on fire, for the purpose of preventing the fire from extending to his own.[m] But it is otherwise where the house destroyed for the purpose of arresting the fire was not already on fire: and to that case the principles of the Rhodian Law are applied by several civilians of great authority. The Rhodian Law provides that when goods are thrown into the sea for the purpose of relieving a ship, the loss shall be borne by all those who have goods on board and by the owner of the ship.[n] This law is grounded on the equitable rule that no man shall gain or derive advantage by the injury of another. Now the same principle is applicable wherever one man's property is destroyed to prevent the communication of fire to that of another. But Voet is of a different opinion.

The law requires that a man should not do even what he has a right to do in a manner which he ought not to adopt. On this subject Justinian teaches as follows:—

If a man by throwing a javelin for his diversion or exercise happen to kill a slave who is passing, a distinction must be drawn. If the slave be killed by a soldier while he is exercising in a place appointed for that purpose, the soldier is not in fault: but if any other person did it, that person is legally guilty of a fault (culpa). And so it is if a soldier exercise himself by throwing darts in a place not set apart for that purpose.[o]

Also if a man lopping off branches from a tree killed your slave who was going by, he is guilty of a fault if this was done near a public road or way, and he did not call out that passers by might avoid the fall of the branch: but if he gave warning and the passer by did not take care of himself, the lopper is not liable. He is equally free from fault if he was at work away from a road or in the middle of a field, though he did not give warning, for no stranger had a right to go there.[p]

These two paragraphs rest on the principle that when a man does that which he has a right to do, in such a manner that no mischief can reasonably be apprehended therefrom, whatever mischief does in fact arise is fortuitous, so far as he is concerned, and therefore he is not liable. But even in the performance of a duty, care must be taken not to cause mischief by exceeding the limits of that duty. Thus a teacher is liable for any mischief which he has done to a

[m] Voet, Comm. ad Pand. lib. ix. tit. ii. num. 28.

[n] See the writers cited by Voet, Comm. ad Pand. lib. xiv. tit. ii. Ad Legem Rhodiam, num. 18. Pand. lib. xiv. tit. ii. L. 2, De Lege Rhodia.

[o] Instit. lib. iv. tit. iii. § 4.

[p] Instit. ibid. § 5.

scholar by undue severity, for *Levis dumtaxat castigatio concessa est docenti*, and *præceptoris nimia sævitia culpæ adnumeratur.*[q] The same principles are applicable to the conduct of magistrates and public officers, who must abstain from *nimia sævitia.*

The Emperor next proceeds to the subject of damage produced by neglect of duty and incapacity. And first of neglect of duty.

Also if a physician caused the death of your slave by giving up the cure after performing an operation on him, he is legally guilty of a fault.[r]

Also unskilfulness is held to be a fault; as for instance if a physician killed your slave by unskilfully operating upon him, or by administering to him the wrong medicine.[s]

Also if a mule driver be unable, through unskilfulness, to restrain the mules, and they kill your slave, the driver is liable. And even if he could not manage them for want of strength, when another could have done so, he is responsible for the damage as being guilty of fault. The same law holds good in the case of a rider who, through want of skill or strength, is unable to restrain his horse.[t]

Justinian here lays down the rule, *Imperitia culpæ adnumeratur.*[u] No man has a right, unless he be skilful, to profess himself able, and undertake to do that which, if it be not done with competent skill, may probably cause injury to others.[x] Thus, a physician is not indeed liable for the natural result of a disease, but whatever consequences follow from his want of skill, are legally imputed to him.[y]

And the same principles apply to cases of damage done through incapacity other than want of skill (as insufficiency of strength or power) by a person voluntarily undertaking what he is unable to perform, with the knowledge that he may probably cause such damage. But the degree of blame attaching to a person guilty of such imprudence, is a question of fact, and depends on the circumstances of the case.

The Aquilian Law gives (with certain distinctions, which it is not necessary here to particularize) a remedy by action for every species of malicious or culpable damage, consisting in the injury or destruction of property.

[q] Voet, Comm. ad Pand. lib. ix. tit. ii. num. 15. Pand. ibid. L. 5, § 3, L. 6.

[r] Instit. ubi sup. § 6. [s] Ibid. § 7. [t] Ibid. § 8.

[u] Pand. lib. l. tit. ult. L. 132.

[x] Voet, Comm. ad Pand. lib. ix. tit. ii. num. 23. Pand. lib. ix. tit. ii. Ad Leg. Aquil. L. 8.

[y] Pand. lib. i. tit. xviii. De Officio Præsidis, L. 6, § 7. Pufendorf, Droit de la Nat. et des Gens, L. 3, chap. 1, § 7. Pand. lib. xix. tit. ii. Locati Conducti, L. 9, § 5, L. 13, § 5. Stephen, Comment. on the Law of England, vol. iii. p. 472.

We come now to the subject of injuries to persons, which are all included under the general denomination of the four species of delict enumerated by Justinian,—namely, *injuria*. *Injuria*, or an injury in the technical sense of the term, is a delict committed in contempt or outrage of any one, whereby his body, his dignity, or his reputation, is maliciously injured.[z]

Labeo divides *injuria* into two classes, with reference to the means used by the wrong-doer,—namely, *words* and *acts*. Thus, for instance, if a man be calumniated or abused, he is injured by words; and if he be beaten, he is injured by acts. And Ulpian goes on with Labeo to classify *injuria* with reference to their objects, dividing them into three species, namely, *in corpus, ad dignitatem*, and *ad infamiam*.[a] An injury is against the body or person, as where a man is struck, laid hands on, or otherwise assaulted, though without being actually struck or laid hands on. It is against the dignity, when anything is done implying contempt or gross disrespect. It is *ad infamiam*, when done for the purpose of injuring the reputation of any one.[b]

Those of the first class can only be committed *by act:* but the two last may be committed as well *by words* as *by act* (*aut re aut verbis*), and an injury which consists only in an indignity, or *injuria ad dignitatem*, may also be detrimental to the reputation, and so be *ad infamiam*, or against the reputation also.

Verbal injuries are either by words uttered, or by writing. By these two means every species of injury, except the first (*in corpus*), may be committed; whereas *real* injuries, or injuries by act, may be of any of the three classes.

A verbal injury may be either by insulting or outrageous words, which is *ad dignitatem*, or by an imputation, which is *ad infamiam*. A malicious intent is essential to constitute a verbal injury. Thus the law excuses injurious expressions uttered without malicious intent, that is to say, without an intent to injure.[c] And so it is with what is uttered in the heat of anger, provided it be retracted afterwards.[d]

A person who injures or endeavours to injure the reputation of another by a malicious imputation, is liable, whether he be the inventor, the writer, the utterer, or the publisher of the libel, and whatever be its form.[e]

[z] Voet, Comm. ad Pand. lib. xlvii. tit. x. De Injuriis, num. 1.

[a] Pand. lib. xlvii. tit. x. De Injuriis et Famosis Libellis, L. 1, § 1, 2.

[b] Instit. lib. iv. tit. iv. De Injuriis, § 1. Pand. lib. xlvii. tit. x. De Injuriis, L. 15, § 1, L. 5, § 1. Voet, Comm. ad Pand. dict. tit. num. 7.

[c] Cod. lib. ix. tit. xxxv. De Injuriis, L. 5.

[d] Pand. lib. l. tit. ult. L. 48.

[e] Pand. lib. xlvii. tit. x. De Injuriis, L. 5, § 9. Cod. lib. ix. tit. xxxvi. De Famosis Libellis, L. unic.

As for the truth or untruth of the imputations, it is irrelevant, unless it be for the public good that the truth should be made known, in which case the defendant may justify himself by proving the truth of the allegations complained of.[f] On the principle (which has been adopted into the English Law by Stat. 6 & 7 Vict., ch. 96) that the publication of a fact, the knowledge of which is beneficial to the community, is not a wrong,—imputations against any one which have the effect of discovering a wrong-doer are decided by Paulus to be justifiable.[g] But in the Code, the application of this principle is in some degree modified as regards written libels: for the Emperors Valentinian and Valens enact that the author of a libel (*libellum famosum*) imputing an offence against the law to any one, shall bring an accusation against the person libelled, and shall be justified and escape punishment only if the accusation turn out true, in which case he shall be rewarded for bringing the offender to justice.[h]

The Civil Law holds that one person may have an action for an injury to another who is identified in interest with him. Thus a man may suffer an injury, not merely in his own person, but in that of his children or of his wife.[i]

The Civil Law allows the person complaining of *injuria* to proceed, either civilly for damages, proportioned to the injury and the circumstances of the case (a method originally introduced by the equity of the Prætor), or criminally, for a punishment to be inflicted on the offender by the office of the judge; and not only the principal wrongdoers are liable to these remedies, but also whoever instigated, advised, or in any way procured it to be perpetrated.[k]

The Law contained in the title of the Institutes, *De Injuriis*, has now been sufficiently explained, having regard to the plan and objects of this treatise. We will therefore proceed to the next title, the Rubric of which is, De Obligationibus quæ quasi ex Delicto nascuntur.

It will be remembered that a *quasi delict* is an act whereby a wrong is done without dole or malice, but by inexcusable imprudence or other default. The foundation of obligations springing *quasi ex delicto* has been shown in the first part of this chapter, and several instances of *quasi delict* have already been explained. It is therefore only necessary to add a brief notice of the particular cases here given by Justinian.

A Judge who, by a gross error, decided a cause wrongfully, was held by the old Civil Law to make the cause his own—*litem suam*

[f] Voet, Comm. ad Pand. lib. xlvii. tit. x. De Injuriis, num. 9.
[g] Pand. lib. xlvii. tit. x. De Injuriis, L. 18, 70, 33.
[h] Cod. lib. ix. tit. xxxvi. De Famosis Libellis, L. unic.
[i] Instit. lib. iv. tit. iv. § 2.
[k] Instit. ibid. § 10, 7, 11.

facere—which signifies that he made himself liable for the result, *quasi ex delicto.* But this part of the Civil Law of Justinian has in modern times become obsolete, and the remedy of appeal only can be resorted to in such cases.[l]

If anything be thrown or dropped from any chamber, and injure any one by its fall, the occupier of the room is liable *quasi ex maleficio.* Thus whoever has anything placed or suspended where by its fall it may do mischief, is liable for such mischief if it occur.[m]

The Civil Law holds the inhabitant or occupier liable for such damage done, even without his knowledge, by his family or servants, because he ought to be careful, lest the negligence of those over whom he has or ought to have a control produce mischief. *Habitator suam suorumque culpam præstare debet.*[n] But it must be observed that he is liable only because, by care and attention, he might have prevented the mischief; or upon the general principle that redress must be given to the party injured, and that in many cases it would bedifficult or impossible to obtain reparation from the person actually and directly guilty of the imprudence or negligence.

The owner or keeper is liable *quasi ex delicto* to be sued on account of every damage or theft committed in his ship, tavern, inn or stable, if he be guilty of no *maleficium,* but the offence be by any of those whose services he uses there. The reason given by Justinian is, that he is not in such cases liable *ex maleficio,* nor *ex contractu,* and yet he is guilty of a fault, because he uses the services of evil-disposed persons. Therefore he is bound *quasi ex maleficio.*[o]

Persons in those employments or trades are liable as such to two species of obligation, one *ex contractu,* and the other *quasi ex delicto.*

They are liable *ex contractu* (tacit or express) for the safe custody of the property which they profess and offer to receive and take care of, and to restore or deliver safely.[p]

They are also liable *quasi ex delicto* for damage done by their servants, because they are bound to keep a watchful eye on such persons. *Culpæ reus est qui malorum hominum opera utitur.*[q] And the law considers this severity necessary to prevent innkeepers, and carriers, and others in like employments from connecting themselves with thieves. It is moreover to be considered that they voluntarily embrace that mode of subsistence, though after they have done so

[l] Instit. lib. iv. tit. v. princip. et Vinnii Comment. ibid. [m] Ibid. § 1.

[n] Pand. lib. ix. tit. iii. De his quæ effuderint vel dejecerint, L. 6.

[o] Instit. ibid. § 3, and see 8 Coke's Reports, 32, Caly's case. Pand. lib. xliv. tit. vii. De Obligationibus et Actionibus, L. 5, § 6.

[p] Pand. lib. iv. tit. ix. Nautæ Caupones Stabularii ut Recepta restituant, L. 3.

[q] Pand. lib. xliv. tit. vii. L. 5, § 6.

they cannot without a sufficient cause refuse their services to those who require lodging and entertainment.[r]

In some cases however the law may operate harshly. And Grotius observes that the rule of the Roman Law making each of several part owners of a ship liable for the act of the master is not in accordance with equity, which requires that they should be liable only to the extent of their respective shares.[s]

Here ends the second part of the Institutes which treats of Things. The third and last part, which regards Actions, now remains to be explained.

CHAPTER XLV.

OF ACTIONS.

Of Actions.—Instit. lib. iv. tit. vi. De Actionibus, princip.—Actions are Necessary, and *Juris Gentium*.—Their General Nature.—Formulæ or *Actiones Legis*.—Their Abolition.—Use of the Names of Actions.—Their Use dispensed with by the Canon Law, and the Modern Civil Law.—An Action defined by Justinian.—Form of the First Stage of Actions.—The *Libellum*, Libel or Bill.—What it must contain.—Amendments.—Plurality of Actions in one Libel. The Libel in Criminal Causes.—Proceedings *ex Officio* or by Inquisition. P. 283.

With this chapter commences the last of the three parts into which Justinian divided his Institutes with reference to the objects of law, namely, that which relates to actions: and it is properly the last, for all law is administered to persons, respecting things, and by means of actions and judgments.[a]

Thus actions are considered in this portion of the Institutes, not as a right possessed, or property in action, which Ulpian mentions as a thing *in bonis*;[b] but as the means whereby the precept *suum cuique tribuere* is enforced and the law is applied to individual cases, or whereby we obtain that to which we have a legal right, from those who would not act justly towards us unless they were compelled to do so by the public power, or who require to be told by an authority which must be obeyed what they owe to others.

[r] Voet, Comm. ad Pand. lib. iv. tit. ix. num. 3, 4.

[s] Grot. Droit de la Guerre, liv. ii. chap. xi. § 13.

[a] Omne jus redditur personis, de rebus, per actiones et judicia. Wesenbecii, Comm. in Pand. lib. i. tit. v. § 1.

Pand. lib. l. tit. penult. De Verbor. Signif. L. 49.

The necessity of actions in the widest sense of the word, as legal remedies whereby right is enforced and wrongs are vindicated or redressed, the impossibility of maintaining in existence any human society without such remedies, and the very object of society itself, which is not only the promotion of the general welfare of man, but specially the enforcement of right and the redressing of wrongs; these considerations show that actions and judgments rest upon the same foundations of secondary or derived natural law, as all the other institutions which are necessary for the existence of man in that state in which it is his duty to live.

All government and every scheme of society or commonwealth would be illusory if men were allowed to be the arbiters and vindicators of their own rights. And it may be said with reason that human society could better exist without any laws than without judges or arbiters; and that it would be better that there should be no law than that every citizen should be invested with an irresponsible power of interpreting and applying the law; for the rule would give rise to more pretences for subverting right than that mode of administering the law would afford instances of its just application.

It may be concluded therefore that as actions and judgments are necessary for the existence of human society, and also because it is repugnant to natural reason that any man should be judge in his own cause,[c] they are *juris gentium*, and part of the natural law which binds man as a member of society.

From these reasons springs the doctrine of Antoninus Pius, Callistratus, and Paulus,[d] that no man is permitted to take the law into his own hands, and to do himself that which the civil magistrate is instituted by the public law to do, when the civil power is able and ready to maintain his rights.

From the same principles springs the maxim *Res judicata pro veritate habetur*, and thus the Prætor is said to do right (*jus dicere*) even where he decides erroneously,[e] for a judgment must be obeyed until it is reversed or set aside by a superior authority.

Such are the general foundation and nature of actions considered as the means whereby men obtain that to which they have a legal right when it is not voluntarily given to them; and thus legal obligations are enforced. But the word actions also signifies, in its more confined sense, the formulæ given by the Civil Law for proceeding

[c] Cod. lib. III. tit. v. Ne Quis in Sua Causa, L. unic. and see Hobart's Reports, 87.

[d] Pand. lib. IV. tit. II. Quod Metus Causa, L. 13. Pand. lib. l. tit. ult. L. 176.

[e] Pand. lib. I. tit. i. De Justitia et Jure, L. 11.

before the magistrate,[f] which were called *actiones legis*, and which resembled the Original Writs in the English Law. These formulæ however were abolished by the Emperor Constantine, and the Emperors Theodosius and Valentinian enact that no form of action shall be excepted to, provided it be adapted to and competent for the matter in hand.[g]

But the abolition of the formulæ did not get rid of the distinctive names of the several actions.[h] The insertion of the name of the action, as for instance *Pro socio* or *Mandati*, in the *libellum* or petition whereby the suit is brought into court, was still required by the Civil Law. But the Canon Law, which the modern civilians have adopted in this particular, further improved the law of judicial proceedings by dispensing with that formality where the narrative in the libel is sufficiently explicit without the nature of the action being specified by name.[i]

The names of the actions in the antient law are therefore important only for the purpose of scientific classification, and for understanding the more antient authorities.

An action in the general sense of the term is defined by Justinian to be *the right of demanding before a court of justice that which is due to the demandant or plaintiff.*[k] It is the means, of which the definition of a legal obligation contains the end. *Obligatio est juris vinculum quo necessitate adstringimur alicujus rei solvendæ secundum nostræ civitatis jura.*[l]

It has been shown that actions are *juris gentium:* but they derive their form from the Municipal Law. A general description of that form, so far as regards the first stage of actions, that is to say, the propounding of the plaintiff's suit, will now be given.

To propound an action, *edere actionem*, is to make known the exact nature of the claim or demand which the party proposes to pursue; and Ulpian holds such a declaration to be necessary on grounds of equity,[m] that the defendant may be enabled to judge whether he should give way, or contest the suit, and in case he should choose the latter alternative, he may come *instructus ad agendum*,

[f] Pand. lib. i. tit. ii. De Origine Juris, L. 2, § 6. Blackst. Comm. book iii. chap. viii. commencement.

[g] Cod. lib. ii. tit. lviii. De Formulis et Impetrationibus Actionum Sublatis, L 1, 2.

[h] Voet ad Pand. lib. ii. tit. xiii. De Edendo, num. 8.

[i] Ibid. Lancelotti, Institut. Jur. Canon, lib. iii. tit. vii.

[k] Instit. lib. iv. tit. vi. princip. Pand. lib. xliv. tit. vii. De Obligationibus et Actionibus. Actio est jus quod sibi debetur in judicio persequendi.

[l] Instit. lib. iii. tit. xiv. De Obligat. princip.

[m] Pand. lib. ii. tit xiii. De Edendo, L 1

and sufficiently informed of the nature of the demand made upon him.

In matters of small import the plaintiff may *actionem edere*, by merely stating the cause of action in the presence of his adversary before the judge; and this is the practice in summary proceedings; but in all other cases a *libellum*, *libel* or *bill*, is necessary.[n]

The libel is a written statement of the cause and demand, and consists of a narration and a conclusion; thus presenting the form of a syllogism without the major premise. The major premise is the law on which the demand is grounded, and it is omitted, because it is within the judicial knowledge of the court. The narration showing the cause of action is therefore the first part of the substance of the libel, and the conclusion, that is to say the demand or prayer for relief, is the second and last.[o]

The libel must be specific, and clear, and reasonable in all its parts; otherwise it may be excepted to for obscurity or absurdity: but if the defendant do not except, ambiguities are to be interpreted in favour of the plaintiff, because the defendant might by excepting have compelled him to be more specific. *Potuit cogere eum intentionem apertius conscribere.*[p]

Obscure parts of the libel should also be construed in the mode most concordant with the remainder: they should be interpreted so as to take effect: *Ut res magis valeat quam pereat*; and the judge may, even after the suit is contested, call on the *actor* or plaintiff for an explanation of his meaning and intention, without which the court could not give judgment with that certainty which the law requires.[q]

To avoid obscurity it is requisite that the libel should specify as clearly as the nature of the case will permit, who sues, and against whom; what is demanded, and from whom, and before what judge, and what is the cause of action.[r]

Not only the name of the parties must be expressed, but also the character in which they are to stand before the judge, as, for instance, in that of a guardian, or in their own names, or as an heir, or as a procurator.

That which is demanded ought to be clearly specified in the libel. Thus that instrument should show what it is in identity, quality, and quantity, so far as the nature of the case will permit. Thus general

[n] Voet, Comm. ad Pand. lib. ii. tit. xiii. De Edendo, num. 1.

[o] Ibid. num. 2.

[p] Ibid. num. 3. Pand. lib. v. tit. i. De Judiciis, L. 66. Pand. lib. l. tit. ult. L. 172.

[q] Voet, ubi sup. Pand. lib. v. tit. i. De Judiciis, L. 59, § 2.

[r] Voet, ubi sup. num. 4.

words may be used in the petition of an inheritance, and quantity or value only may be stated in a suit for a pecuniary debt.[s]

The name of the judge and of the court should be inserted in the libel, that the defendant may know whether he may object to either by declinatory exception.[t]

It is of great importance that the cause of action (*causa petendi*) be clearly set forth; and that cause is either general (which is also called *proxima*) or special, which is sometimes called remote.

The general cause of action in actions *in personam*, is an obligation; for all such actions are founded on an obligation of one person to another; and in actions *in rem*, it is dominion or the right by virtue of which the thing which is, or is alleged to be the object of the action, is totally or partly the property of the plaintiff.

In actions *in personam*, the *causa petendi* is the contract or other transaction, *in specie*, upon which the demand is founded; and it must be clearly and specifically set forth in the libel, because if an obligation *in genere* be set forth, the defendant cannot see the nature of the demand; for the same thing, as well as the same quantity or value, may be due to the same person by virtue of more than one obligation.[u]

But in actions *in rem*, the general cause of action is sufficient, because a thing cannot be the property of any one by several titles. Thus it is sufficient for the plaintiff to demand a particular estate, or a particular horse as his, without stating the special cause of petition, that is to say, how it is his.[x]

It must be observed that the specific allegation of the exact nature of the *jus in re*, or general cause of petition, is essential to the completeness of the libel; and as the special cause (the title of the plaintiff) must be single, the defendant may, in most cases, discover it by the examination of his own title, upon which it must ultimately or immediately turn.

If the rules of law respecting the libel be not correctly followed, the party is permitted at any period of the proceedings before judgment, to amend his libel, on payment of whatever costs the defendant has been put to by the error.[y]

The Civil Law does not allow more than one action to be inserted in one libel, except where the plaintiff (*actor*) is doubtful as to the nature of the action which he ought to use; and where the possession is claimed at the same time as the property or dominium, two libels are

[s] Voet, ubi sup. num. 5.

[t] Novell 52, cap. 3.

[u] Pand. lib. xliv. tit. ii. De Exceptione Rei Judicatæ, L. 14, § 3.

[x] Pand. ibid. L. 14, § 2.

[y] Voet, ubi sup. num. 9.

requisite. But the modern civilians follow the Canon Law, which permits several actions to be brought in the same libel, to obtain separate things from the same person. In such cases the libel is dealt with as several separate libels, namely, so many as it contains actions, each action being separately considered.

These conjoined actions must, however, not be repugnant to each other, nor have the same object or purpose; nor be against different debtors for separate debts; for in these cases the plurality of actions would produce confusion.

In criminal proceedings the libel must be equally certain and clearly expressed. It must specify the name of the accuser, the exact nature of the crime charged, and the year and the month in which it is alleged to have been committed.[z]

But in some offences, such as forgery, the locality in which the offence was committed cannot without too much difficulty be discovered, and in those cases the place need not be specified.[a]

As for the time of the commission of the offence, the year and month are generally sufficient; but the accused person may call upon the accuser to specify the day, with a view to proving an *alibi*. It must, however, be observed that all these rules tend to give the accused the fullest advantage of whatever means he may possess of showing his innocence, by rendering the accusation as definite and explicit as possible, that it may be more easily grappled with, and for such purpose that the accused may be as fully acquainted as possible with the charges against him. But the only really essential part of the accusation, and that on which the judge has to decide, is the crime charged in the libel. It follows that if the crime be sufficiently proved, the other circumstances become immaterial so far as regards the guilt or innocence of the accused, and it is of no consequence whether they be proved or not. If it were otherwise, the rules which are intended for the protection of innocence would be made to shelter guilt.

Such are the analogies between a libel in civil and in criminal proceedings. But in other respects those proceedings differ greatly.[b]

A striking diversity between criminal and civil proceedings is that the former may not only be commenced by libel like the latter, but by inquisition, which is an inquiry commenced *ex officio* by the judge,

[z] Voet, Comm. ad Pand. lib. ii. tit. xiii. De Edendo, num. 15. Reiffenstuel, Jus Canon. Univers. lib. v. tit. i. § 1.

[a] Voet, ibid. num. 2.

[b] Boehmerus, Element. Jur. Crim. sect. i. chap. iv. § 76. Lancelot, Institut. Jur. Canon, lib. iv. tit. i. Voet, Comm. ad Pand. lib. xlviii. tit. ii. De Accusationibus, num. 2.

ob legitimas causas, that is to say, upon a denunciation worthy of attention, or on strong grounds of suspicion or public report.[c]

By the modern practice of the Roman Law accusations are usually proceeded upon with a previous inquisition; and so it is in the Canon Law,[d] and this practice has been adopted into the English Law by Stat 3 & 4 Vict. ch. 76, commonly called the "Church Discipline Act."[e]

These are the chief rules of law respecting the mode of propounding the plaintiff's demands in a civil action, and of commencing a criminal proceeding.

CHAPTER XLVI.

OF ACTIONS.

Of Actions.—Instit. lib. iv. tit. vi. De Actionibus, § 1, 2, 6.—Actions divided into two Classes, namely, Actions *in Rem* (*Vindicationes*) and Actions *in Personam* *Condictiones*).—Explanation of the Nature of both Classes.—Real Actions.—Actions concerning Servitudes.—Their Division into Confessory and Negatory.—Why all Real Actions for Corporeal Things are Confessory or Affirmative.—The Paulian Action to revoke Alienations made in Fraud of Creditors. P. 289.

The chief classification of actions is that which divides them into actions *in rem*, and actions *in personam*. The former spring from *jus in re* or *dominium*, and are used where the plaintiff asserts a right of ownership: and the latter arise from *jus ad rem*, and are used where the plaintiff alleges the defendant to be bound towards him by an obligation *ex contractu*, or *quasi ex contractu*, or *ex delicto*, or *quasi ex delicto*.[a]

Every action rests on an asserted right to something, and on the obligation *suum cuique tribuendi*. But the rights and obligations which are enforced by action are of two distinct species.

It has been already shown that the Law of Things is divisible into two parts, namely, *dominion* or ownership, and obligations. Dominion is the right which we have to that which is ours, *jus quo res nostra est:*

[c] Voet, ibid. num. 17. Boehmerus, ibid. sect. i. cap. v. § 86. Lancelot, Instit. Jur. Canon. lib. iv. tit. i. § 4. Reiffenstuel, Jus Canon. Univers. L. 5, tit. i. § 3.

[d] Cremani, De Jure Criminali, lib. iii. cap. vi. § 4. Van Espen, Jus Eccles. pars iii. tit. viii. cap. i. num. 19.

[e] Bowyer, Comment. on the Constit. Law of England, p. 269, &c.

[a] Instit lib iv tit vi. § 1; lib. iii. tit. xiv § 2. Story, Conflict of Laws, § 530.

and an obligation is a bond of law whereby a man is bound to the performance of something.[b] Here the term obligation is taken in its strict sense, as contradistinguished from that general obligation arising from dominion, which binds every man who possesses that which is not his, to restore it to its owner.

Where this is the case, the natural duty *suum cuique tribuendi*, imposes the obligation of restitution on the possessor: and thus the right of dominion in one person produces an obligation in another, as indeed every right must have a corresponding obligation, active or passive, resting on a precept or prohibition. But it is evident that when a man claims a thing by virtue of a right of dominion, he claims it because it is his, and not because it is in the hands of a particular person; and that the possessor is bound to give it to the owner, because it is the property of the latter. It is not the property of the owner because the possessor is bound to deliver it to him, but the possessor is bound to deliver it to him because it is his.

Now the right by which a man demands a thing because it is his, is called *jus in re;* and it is vindicated and enforced by action *in rem*, which is called by the Civil Law *vindicatio*, whereby the general obligation arising from dominion is enforced.[c]

We come now to actions *in personam* which are called *condictiones*. Where a man is bound by any obligation not arising directly from the right of dominion in some one else, that obligation is indeed comprehended within the precept *suum cuique tribuere*, but the right in the one person springs from the obligation in the other, and not the obligation from the right.

Thus if Titius promise to give anything to Sempronius, he is bound to do so because *grave est fidem fallere*, and if the contract whereby he is bound be legally valid, Sempronius has a legal right to that thing. But he has that right because Titius is bound to give it to him, and Titius is not bound to give it to him because it is his, nor because he has a right to it, but because Titius has bound himself towards Sempronius. Thus the obligation of Titius does not spring from any anterior right of Sempronius, but the right of Sempronius springs from the obligation of Titius.

All this must, however, be understood without forgetting that every obligation springs mediately or immediately from the law. Now the right whereby a man demands anything not because it is his, but because it is due to him by virtue of an obligation, is called *jus ad rem;* or the right to obtain a thing. And here, the term a thing

[b] Voet, Comm. ad Pand. lib. vi. tit. i. De Rei Vindicatione, num 1.

[c] Instit. lib. iv. tit. vi. § 15.

must be taken to include an act as well as a thing in the stricter sense, for *jus ad rem* has for its object obligations *faciendi,* as well as obligations *dandi.*

Jura ad rem are enforced by actions *in personam.* They are so called because their object is to compel a person to do that which he is bound to do by virtue of an obligation arising from the act of that person or of some one whom he represents, or from the law, and not merely from the possession of something which the plaintiff has a right to as his property.

Thus Ulpian says, that an action *in re* (*vindicatio*) is that whereby we demand what is ours from the possession of another; and it is always brought against him who possesses the property. And an action *in personam* (*condictio*) is that by which we proceed against him who is bound to us by an obligation to do or to give something, and it is always competent against that person or his representative.[d]

One of the most striking diversities between actions *in personam* and actions *in rem,* is that the former follow the person liable, and the latter follow the thing which is their object, without reference to the person of its possessor. Thus we have seen that an action *in personam* is brought against the person bound by the obligation, and an action *in rem* is against the person who possesses the thing demanded.[e]

But a person having a right of action *in personam* may alienate it to another by *cession,* that is to say assignment, whereby the former gives to the latter a mandate to be used for his own benefit, thus constituting him *procurator in rem suam.*[f] This does not render the action less personal to the debtor or defendant.

And notwithstanding the real nature of actions *in rem,* if the possessor lose the possession by dole, that is to say *malâ fide,* or to defraud the claimant, he remains liable though he has ceased to possess. He is liable by reason of his dole, as he was liable by reason of his possession. *Pro possessione dolus est.*[g] But if he lost possession *bonâ fide,* that is to say without dole, even after litiscontestation, he is no longer liable to the action.[h]

On the same principles on which possessors are liable for dole, they

[d] Pand. lib. xliv. tit. vii. De Obligationibus et Actionibus, L. 25. The term *mixed actions* is not correct as a third division. Vinnii Comm. ad Instit. lib. iv. tit. vi. § 2. Voet, Comm. ad Pand. lib. v. tit. iii. De Hereditatis Petitione, num. 1, 13.

[e] Pand. lib. xliv. tit. vii. De Obligationibus et Actionibus. L. 25.

[f] Pand. lib. ii. tit. xiv. De Pactis, L. 11. Cod. lib. xiv. tit. xxxix. De Hereditate vel Actione Vendita, L. 5, 8. Voet, Comm. ad Pand. lib. iii. tit. iii. De Procuratoribus, num. 8.

[g] Pand. lib. vi. tit. i. De Rei Vindicatione, L. 22. [h] Pand. ibid. L. 27, § 1.

are also liable for fault (*culpa*) whereby the thing sued for is placed beyond the reach of the plaintiff after they had become aware of the suit.[i]

And the general rule is that the possessor of a thing demanded in a real action is a debtor of a specific thing by reason of his possession of that thing, and therefore subject to the rules which apply to other debtors of a specific thing.

Not only the full *jus in re* or full dominion, but every other *jus in re*, such as servitudes, may be maintained by action *in rem*.[k] And thus it is an action *in rem* where an action is brought for a right of use, or usufruct, or of walking, riding, or driving over or drawing water on the property of another. And of the same nature are actions for rights of servitude over urban tenements, as where a man asserts by action his right of raising his building.[l]

Actions for incorporeal real rights or *jura in re* such as those above mentioned have this peculiarity, that they may be of two kinds, *confessory* or *affirmative, and negatory*, whereas real actions for corporeal things can only be *confessory* or *affirmative*. A confessory action is one by which a servitude is asserted and claimed, and a negatory action is one whereby its existence is denied by the owner of the property alleged to be subject to the servitude.

Both these actions are *in rem;* the first because it consists of an assertion and claim of part of the dominion over the thing alleged to be subject to the servitude; and the second because it consists of an assertion of the dominion over the thing undiminished and not dismembered by the existence of the servitude.

But all actions for corporeal things are confessory or affirmative,[m] for the following reasons.

The general rule of law is this: *De suo, non de alieno jure quemque agere oportet.*[n] An *actor* or plaintiff must assert and proceed upon his own right and not on that of another. Now if a person in possession of a corporeal thing brought an action against another, whereby he denied the right of the latter to that thing, he would not thereby assert his own right (*jus suum*); for the successful denial of the right of another does not necessarily imply the assertion or establishment of the right of him who denies, since the thing in litigation may belong to neither party. But where the proprietor of a thing denies a right of servitude over it, he asserts thereby the freedom of his property and

[i] Voet, Comm. ad Pand. lib. vi. tit. i. De Rei Vindicatione, num. 33. Pand. ibid. L. 36, § 1.

[k] Gaji Instit. lib. iv. tit. De Actionibus, § 3, and ibid. Comment. G. Heffter.

[l] Instit. lib. iv. tit. vi. § 2, et ibid. Comment. Vinnii. [m] Ibid.

[n] Pand. lib. vii. tit. vi. Si Ususfructus petatur, L. 5.

the integrity of his right of dominion with respect to the person whom he sues. Therefore, *de suo, non de alieno jure agit.*[o] Thus a negatory action contains an assertion; and the right of servitude in the defendant being disproved, the right becomes established as part of the dominion or ownership of the proprietor, the residue of which was not in dispute.

And a negatory action would be unnecessary to the possessor of a corporeal thing, because his possession is sufficient,[p] and cannot be subverted unless another proves a superior title; but possession of an incorporeal thing, such as servitude, is not necessarily evident to the senses, since a man may have a right of this kind without exercising it, and therefore one person may conceive himself to hold his property subject to no servitude, while another claims a servitude over it, without asserting his claim so as to enable the owner of the property to dispute it. For this reason it is necessary that proprietors should have a remedy by action, for the purpose of obtaining a judicial declaration of the freedom of their property.

On the same grounds a confessory action may be brought for a servitude though the plaintiff be in possession,—that is to say in *quasi* possession of it. As a servitude is a right of deriving benefit from that which is not ours, the enjoyment of that benefit may be defeated without our knowledge, and the possession thereby subverted.[q]

It may be concluded that no one has an action for a corporeal thing who is in possession; but that incorporeal things may be claimed as the property of the claimant though he be in (quasi) possession.

After defining these actions which are given by the Civil Law, Justinian passes to those which spring from the Prætorian Law, being granted by the equity of the Prætor, for the purpose of furthering the remedies, supplying the omissions, and correcting the defects of the Civil Law. But enough has already been said respecting the Prætorian jurisdiction.[r] And, agreeably to the plan of this treatise, they will here be examined without reference to their origin, and (omitting what is purely technical and arbitrary) only so far as they are founded on principles of equity and reason.

The first of the Prætorian actions to be here explained is the Paulian action, by which fraudulent alienations are revoked at the suit of creditors.

If after the estate of a debtor has been delivered by course of law to

[o] Pand. lib. viii. tit. v. Si Servitus vindicetur, L. 4, § 7.

[p] Pand. lib. l. tit. ult. L. 128, princip.

[q] Vinnii Comm. ad Instit. lib. iv. tit. vi. § 2.

[r] Chap. i. vii.

his creditors, he transferred any of his property to any one in fraud of his creditors, they may obtain the decree of the supreme magistrate to rescind the transfer and claim the property as never having passed from their debtor.[s]

This (setting aside the fiction of the Prætor) is an action *ad rem,* that is to say, *in personam,* for it is grounded on a wrongful act of the debtor. Thus it is not competent unless the creditors be defrauded in fact by the alienation, because otherwise there is no wrong, and the Paulian action is grounded on the rule that no man shall profit by his own wrong.[t]

A distinction must be drawn between alienations without valuable consideration, by which the alienee acquires *titulo lucrativo,* that is to say, without giving anything in return, as by donation ; and alienations for valuable consideration, whereby the property is acquired *titulo oneroso,* that is to say in consideration of the payment of an equivalent, as, for instance, by sale.

If the alienation be of the former description, it is set aside by the Paulian action, provided either party were guilty or cognizant of fraud. And first, unless the alienation be fraudulent on the part of the alienee, it cannot be avoided whether it be lucrative or onerous. But the alienation is held to be fraudulent, not only when it was made with intent to defraud the creditor, but when the debtor knew, or ought to have known, that by diminishing his estate he rendered it, or that it was,[u] insufficient to pay his creditors, that is to say, insolvent;—and thus the fraudulent intent of the debtor, in point of fact, is not necessary to give the creditors the benefit of this remedy.[x] And the law holds every man to know that which he ought to know,—*Ne melioris conditionis sint stulti quam periti.*[y]

If there be no fraudulent intention, and the effect of the alienation be to defraud, it is *dolum ex re,* or fraud in fact, though not *dolum ex proposito,* or fraud by intention. *Res ipsa in se dolum habet.*[z]

If the alienee *titulo lucrativo* retain the property to the prejudice of the creditors, he profits by the wrongful act of the debtor. The creditors ask only what is due to them, while the alienee seeks a gain ;

[s] Instit. lib. iv. tit. vi. § 6. The technical part of this section is omitted, which by fiction changes the character of the action.

[t] Pand. lib. xlii. tit. viii. Quæ in Fraudem Creditorum, L. 15.

[u] Pand. lib. l. tit. penult. De Signif. Verbor. L. 114.

[x] Voet, Comm. ad Pand. lib. xlii. tit. viii. num. 14. Pand. lib. xlii. tit. viii. Quæ in Fraudem Creditorum, L. 10.

[y] Pand. lib. xliii. tit. xxiv. Quod Vi aut Clam. L. 4.

[z] Pand. lib. l. tit. ult. L. 36.

and Ulpian says, *In re obscura melius est favere repetitioni quam adventitio lucro.*[a] The alienee seeks a gain, while the creditors seek to avoid a loss, and they are therefore to be preferred.[b]

If the alienee was cognizant of the fraud, he must not only refund what he actually gained, but also indemnify the creditors from whatever loss they suffered by the alienation.[c]

If the alienation be *titulo oneroso*, that is to say, for valuable consideration, the alienee is not liable to a revocation, unless he be cognizant of the fraud.[d] The reason is that, *In pari causa possessor potior est.*[e] And this is law, though the alienee be below puberty (*pupillus*) and therefore not legally capable of being held liable for fraud; for he ought not to make a gain to the prejudice of the creditors by reason of his own incapacity.[f]

The words of the edict of the Prætor include all transactions, whatever be their nature, in fraud of creditors.[g] But the edict does not include omissions on the part of the debtor to acquire anything; for it applies to those who diminish their estate, and not to those who omit to augment it. The reason of this is that the creditors have a right in equity to payment out of what the debtor possessed; but not out of uncertain advantages which they could not have had in view in dealing with and giving credit to him.[h]

And a creditor who receives what is legally due to him before the estate of the debtor has been vested in the creditors or the *curator bonorum*, is not bound to refund, though the payment make the debtor insolvent. The reason of this is that the creditor who obtained payment ought not to be deprived of the fruits of his vigilance, or at any rate he has the legal advantage over the others which the law gives to a possessor. *Jus civile vigilantibus scriptum est. In pari causa possessor potior est.*[i] But after the estate of the debtor has passed to the creditors, or to the *curator bonorum*, the debtor has no power to pay one creditor in preference to another.[k]

[a] Pand. lib. l. tit. ult. L. 41, § 1.

[b] Pand. lib. xi. tit. vii. De Religiosis, L. 14, § 1.

[c] Voet, Comm. ad Pand. lib. xlii. tit. viii. num. 5.

[d] Ibid. num. 8. Pand. eodem titulo, L. 9. [e] Pand. lib. l. tit. ult. L. 128.

[f] Pand. lib. xlii. tit. viii. Quæ in Fraudem Creditorum, L. 6, § 10; L. 10, § 5.

[g] Pand. ibid. L. 1.

[h] Pand. ibid. L. 6. Voet ad Pand. lib. xlii. tit. viii. num. 16, 17. Pand. lib. l tit. ult. L. 134.

Pand. lib. xlii. tit. viii. Quæ in Fraudem Creditorum, L. 25, L. 6, § 7. Pand. lib. l. tit. ult. L. 128.

[k] The law of England on this subject somewhat differs from the Civil Law, though founded on the same reasons. See 2 Stephen, Comment. p. 207, Stat. 2 & 3 Vict. cap. 29.

CHAPTER XLVII.

OF ACTIONS.

Of Actions.—Instit. lib. iv. tit. vi. De Actionibus, § vii.—Servian and *Quasi* Servian Actions respecting Pawns and Hypothecs.—Difference between *Pignus* and *Hypotheca*.—What the Creditor must Prove in these Actions.—The Rule *Res transit cum Onere*.—The Law as to Moveables.—General and Special Hypothecs. —*Pactum Antichresios*.—*Pactum Commissorium*.—The Creditor's Power of Sale.—Dissolution of the *Vinculum Pignoris*.—The Rule *Qui Prior est Tempore Potior est Jure*.—The Action *De Constituta Pecunia*. P. 295.

Justinian passes from the subject of fraudulent alienations and their revocation at the suit of creditors, to the Servian and *quasi* Servian actions, whereby the Prætor Servius Sulpicius (the celebrated contemporary of Cicero)[a] completed the legal security of creditors by supplying the omissions of the Civil Law respecting pledges and hypothecs. And these Prætorian remedies provided by Sulpicius are first defined by the Emperor to be the action by which men enforce their right of pledge over the property of their tenant to secure the rent; and that whereby creditors pursue rights of pledge or of hypothec.

There is no difference between *pignus* or pledge, and hypothec, so far as regards the hypothecary action; for whenever the debtor and creditor agree that anything shall be pledged as security for the debt, the action has the same name. But in other respects there is a diversity between pledge and hypothec. The denomination *pignus* properly designates a thing delivered into the possession of the creditor, and more particularly if it be moveable. But property bound by a mere contract without delivery, is called hypothec.[b]

Such is the substance of Justinian's description of the Servian and *quasi* Servian action.[c]

The hypothecary action is evidently *in rem*, whether it be Servian or *quasi* Servian; for it is *ad rem persequendam;* and the right of the creditor over property pledged to him is *jus in re*, being a dismem-

[a] Heineccii Antiquitates, lib. iv. tit. vi. § 29. Pand. lib. i. tit. ii. De Origine Juris, L. 2, § 43. Gravina De Ortu et Progressu Jur. Civ. § 64.

[b] Instit. lib. iv. tit. vi. § 7.

[c] The *quasi* Servian action is Prætorian. See Vinnius, Comm. ad Instit. lib. iv. tit. vi. § 7, num. 6.

berment or separate portion of the *jus dominii* vested in the owner and debtor.[d]

Upon the principle that the hypothecary action is *in rem*, Marcianus decides that no change in the thing, or in the possession of the thing hypothecated, has any effect on the rights of the creditor; but that in every case he who does not possess it is not liable unless he fraudulently ceased to possess it; and that he who does possess it must either pay the debt, or surrender the property. *Aut pecuniam solvat aut rem restituat.*[e]

The creditor has two points to prove in the hypothecary action; first, that he has a right of pledge over the property, and secondly, that it is in the possession of the person against whom the action is brought.

And if it be in the possession not of the debtor, but of a third party, the plaintiff must prove that it was part of the estate of the debtor at the time of the contract, provided it be a special hypothec of certain property, or that it was so at or subsequent to that time, if it be a general hypothec extending over all the debtor's property present and future.[f]

It is, however, not necessary for the creditor to prove the actual dominion of his debtor upon whose title his hypothec depends. It is sufficient if the property was *in bonis* of the debtor, that is to say, possessed by him *pro suo*, and *bonâ fide* by a title in itself capable of transferring dominion.[g]

The reason of this is that the title of the debtor is held good by the law against all except any one claiming by a title paramount to his. Thus if he lose possession of it before he has held possession during a length of time sufficient to give him the *dominium* by usucapion, the Prætor will nevertheless give him relief by the Publician action to recover the property as though he had acquired the *dominium*.[h] The Publician action is founded on the reason that though the title of the possessor be imperfect from the imperfection of the title of the person from whom he derived it, yet his own immediate title is sufficient in itself to justify his possession *pro suo*, since it is *justa causa transferendi dominium*, and therefore he may acquire that dominion by continued possession and usucapion.

[d] Pand. lib. xx. tit. i. De Pignoribus et Hypothecis, L. 17, 16, § 2, 3. Voet, Comm. ad Pand. lib. v. tit. ii. De Inofficioso Testamento, num. 2.

[e] Pand. lib. xx. tit. i. De Pignoribus et Hypothecis, L. 16, § 2, 3.

[f] Voet ad Pand. lib. xx. tit. i. De Pignoribus et Hypothecis, num. 4. Pand. ibid. L. 15, § 1.

[g] Pand. ibid. L. 18. Instit. lib. iv. tit. vi. § 4, et ibid. Vinnii Comment.

[h] Instit. lib. iv. tit. vi. § 4.

It follows that as a possession of this nature is capable of being subverted only by some one who has the dominion, it must be protected by the law except against that person having the superior title. And as the title of the debtor is thus maintained by the Publician action, that title must equally be held good for the security of his creditors.

It follows from these doctrines that a thing is incapable of being pignorated which cannot be possessed *pro suo*, or which cannot be conveyed.[i]

The hypothecary right follows the property subject to it. *Res transit cum onere* whether the alienee acquired it by lucrative title (as gift) or by onerous title (as by sale); but the modern civilians have restricted the operation of this rule to immoveables by introducing the principle *Mobilia non habent sequelam*, a principle grounded on the interests of trade. Thus creditors whose rights are secured on moveables, can prevent their security from vanishing only by retaining possession of the property.[k]

Justinian enacted that a third party in possession of hypothecated property should not be sued by the creditor until after he had sued the debtor and his sureties.[l]

The various species of pledges or securities on property for the payment of debts must now be briefly explained. And in the first place, under the general name of *pignus*, or pledge, is included hypothec, as well as pawn or pledge strictly so called. The nature of both is the same,[m] but *pignus* is constituted with a delivery of the pledged property to the creditor, and *hypotheca* is completed by contract alone without delivery.[n]

As *pignus* or pawn requires delivery, it cannot arise *ipso jure*; but the law is otherwise with regard to hypothec, which may be conventional, that is to say, expressly constituted by contract; or legal, that is, arising *ipso jure* without any express contract constituting it. These two species of contracts may be either tacit or express.[o]

Thus the hypothec which the lessor has over the *invecta et illata*, or the moveables of the tenant which are on the premises, is a tacit con-

[i] Pand. lib. xx. tit. iii. Quæ Res Pignori vel Hypothecæ datæ obligari non possunt, L. 1, § 2, L. 9, § 1.

[k] Voet, Comm. ad Pand. lib. xx. tit. i. De Pignoribus et Hypothecis, num. 13.

[l] Novell 4, cap. 2.

[m] Pand. lib. xx. tit. i. De Pignoribus et Hypothecis, L. 5, § 1.

[n] Pand. lib. xiii. tit. vii. De Pignoratitia Actione, L. 9, § 2. Voet, Comm. ad Pand. lib. xx. tit. i. De Pignor. et Hypoth. num. 1. Instit. lib. iv. tit. vi. § 7.

[o] Voet, Comm. ad Pand. lib. xx. tit. ii. In Quibus Causis Pignus vel Hypotheca tacite Contrahatur, num. 1.

ventional hypothec. To enforce this security, the Servian action was devised. On the same principles, the fruits of rural tenements are hypothecated for the rent while they remain in the possession of the tenant.[p] And hence the remedy by distress for rent in the English Law is probably derived.

The hypothec which cities, churches, pious institutions, and wards have over the property of their administrators and guardians respectively, is an instance of a tacit legal hypothec.[q] As for express legal and conventional hypothecs, they do not require examples.

Such are the principal classes or species of hypothecs considered with reference to the mode whereby they are constituted. There are also judicial and Prætorian hypothecs, which are securities given by command of the magistrate, but they belong to the law of judicial proceedings or practice.

Every species of hypothec may be either general, including all the estate present and future of the debtor, or special, that is to say, comprising only certain things, or all the present estate of the debtor. Special hypothecs, however, include future accessories and fruits of the property.[r] There is an agreement called *pactum antichresios*, peculiar to the contract of pawn in the Roman Law. It is a paction providing that the creditor shall have the use or fruits of the pledged property by way of interest for the debt. *Mutuus pignoris usus pro credito.* But the emolument derived by the creditor must not exceed the legal rate of interest, unless it be uncertain and therefore involving a risk.[s]

The Emperor Constantine abolished as oppressive the *pactum commissorium*, or clause of forfeiture in pledges and hypothecs, whereby if the debt was not satisfied by a certain time, the property was absolutely forfeited to the creditor.[t]

Justinian regulated, on analogous principles, the mode whereby creditors may avail themselves of the power of selling which is essential to the very nature of pledge and hypothec.[u] The Emperor provides that unless the parties have expressly agreed as to the mode of proceeding, the creditor may sell the property a year after notice given to the debtor. If there be no purchaser the creditor may call on the debtor to redeem within a specified time, and if the debtor should not appear, that time is to be settled by the judge. After the

[p] Voet, ubi supra, num. 2.

[q] Voet. ibid. num. 25, 11.

[r] Voet, Comm. ad Pand. lib. xx. tit. i. De Pignoribus et Hypothecis, num 5, 2. Cod. lib. viii. tit. xvii. Quæ Res Pignori obligari possunt, L. 9.

[s] Voet, Comm. ad Pand. ibid. num. 23. Cod. lib. iv. tit. xxxii. De Usuris, L. 14, 17.

[t] Cod. lib. viii. tit. xxxv. De Pactis Pignorum, L. 3.

[u] Pand. lib. xiii. tit. vii. De Pignoratitia Actione, L. 4

expiration of that time, the creditor must petition the Emperor that the property may be declared forfeited unless it be redeemed within two years.[x] But the modern civilians have rejected this mode of proceeding, and have adopted the older method, whereby the property is forfeited unless the debtor redeem within the year after notice given for that purpose.[y]

But as the only object of pawn and hypothec is to secure the debt, the creditor has an action against the debtor and his sureties to obtain what remains due after he has availed himself of his hypothecary right and remedy. And on the other hand, the creditor is bound and may be compelled by the *actio pignoratitia*, to restore to the debtor whatever he has received above the amount due to him. The reason is that the pledge or hypothec is intended only as a security, and not as a means of giving the creditor gain.[z]

And thus as the pawn or hypothec is only accessory to the principal debt, the extinction of that debt extinguishes the pawn or hypothec. *Sublato principali accessorium tollitur.*[a]

The *vinculum pignoris* may also be extinguished without the extinction of the principal debt, in the same manner as other obligations are extinguished by the tacit or express consent of the creditor, or by the thing pignorated perishing.[b]

And it may be dissolved by virtue of the rule *Resoluto jure dantis resolvitur jus accipientis;* for no man can transfer to another more right than he has, or has the disposal of himself.[c] No man can pledge or hypothecate property except so far as it is his. Therefore the rights of the hypothecary creditors or pawnees cannot prejudice the title of any one claiming against their debtor.

And on the same principles from which proceeds the rule *Qui prior est tempore potior est jure*, creditors rank as to their right of pawn or hypothec according to the priorities of their respective securities.[d]

We will now proceed from real to personal Prætorian actions; and first of the action *De Pecunia Constituta*, which is thus defined by Justinian.

[x] Cod. lib. viii. tit. xxxiv. De Jure Dominii impetrandi, L. 3.

[y] Vinnii Comm. ad Instit. lib. ii. tit. viii. Quibus licet vel non licet alienare, § 1, num. 2, 3

[z] Cod. lib. viii. tit. xxviii. De Distractione Pignorum, L. 3, 5. Pand. lib. xx. tit. v. De Distractione Pignorum vel Hypothecarum, L. 9, § 1, L. 6.

[a] Voet, Comm. ad Pand. lib. xx. tit. vi. Quibus Modis Pignus vel Hypoth. solvitur, num. 2.

[b] Voet, ibid. num. 4—7.

[c] Voet, Comm. ad Pand. lib. xx. tit. vi. Quibus Modis Pignus vel Hypotheca solvitur, num. viii. Pand. lib. l. tit. ult. L. 54.

[d] Vide Pand. lib. xx. tit. iv. et Cod. lib. viii. tit. xvii. Qui Potiores in Pignore vel Hypotheca habeantur.

The action De Constituta Pecunia, is competent against all those who bind themselves to pay anything due either on their own account or in the name of another, without the form of stipulation. For if the contract be by stipulation, it may be enforced by the Civil Law.[e]

This is a species of accessory obligation added to a former obligation and entered into only for the purpose of corroborating it. It is a Prætorian convention, that is to say, an agreement confirmed by the Prætor, whereby any one promises without the form of *stipulation* what he or some one else owes.[f] The contract called *Constitutum* or *Constituta Pecunia*, is a promise which the Roman Law holds good, though not clothed in the form of stipulation, because it is founded on the consideration of an obligation already subsisting, which it corroborates. But this is a subject of so technical a nature that any further explanations are not here desirable.

CHAPTER XLVIII.

OF ACTIONS.

Of Actions.—Instit. lib. iv. tit. vi. De Actionibus, § 13.—Definition of *Status.*—What are *Actiones Prejudiciales.* In what they differ from other Actions and why they conclude Third Parties.—Instit. lib. iv. tit. vii. *Quod cum eo qui in Aliena Potestate est Negotium Gestum dicitur.*—The *Actio Exercitoria* and *Actio Institoria* defined.—Power of the Person employed to bind his Employer.—Bottomry.—*Nauticum Fœnus.*—*Actio Institoria.* P. 298.

The actions for the determination of the *status* of persons remain to be explained. They are called *actiones prejudiciales.*

And in the first place the meaning of the word *status* must be defined. *Status est qualitas cujus ratione homines diverso jure utuntur.*[a] It is that quality of persons which renders them capable or incapable of certain legal rights and obligations.[b] Such is the quality of legitimate birth and the contrary, and of freedom or slavery. Actions having for their object the decision of these questions, which are called in the Civil Law *actiones prejudiciales,* are *in rem.*[c] The reason of this is that their end is to obtain certain rights

[e] Instit. lib. iv. tit. vi. § 9. Pand. lib. xiii. tit. v. De Constitutâ Pecuniâ, L. 1.

[f] Voet ad Pand. lib. xiii. tit. v. num. 1.

[a] Heineccii Elem. Jur. Civ. lib. i. tit. iii. § 76.

[b] Domat, Loix Civiles, liv. prélimin. tit. ii. and see Pand. lib. i. tit. iv. De Statu Hominum.

[c] Instit. lib. iv. tit. vi. § 13.

which the plaintiff claims as his, and not merely as due to him by virtue of an obligation;[d] though they differ from other *actions in rem*, whereby the parties contend for the dominion of a thing.[e]

These actions are called *prejudiciales*, because they prejudge and are intended to prejudge many others. They conclude with a judgment, being a declaration positive or negative, touching the status of a person, and thereby affect other actions by or against that person, which depend on that status.

That denomination is applied to them exclusively, because they are conclusive, not only between the parties, but against all men.

The general rule of the Civil Law is this: *Res inter alios judicata nullum inter alios prejudicium facit.*[f] But it is inapplicable to causes of status.[g] The reason of this may be deduced from the rule *Res judicata pro veritate accipitur.*[h] That rule applies (saving the right of appeal) to all causes so far as regards the parties. But the nature of the actions called *prejudiciales* is such, that unless they were taken *pro veritate*, not only as between the parties but with regard to all men, they would be of no effect, because the question decided therein would not be held *pro veritate.*

Thus, for instance, if it be decided that Titius is a slave, or that he is a freeman, he must be so to all the world, because the question decided by the court regards not the relative rights of the parties, but the positive and absolute right of Titius.

Thus if Sejus alleges himself to be the lawful son of Sempronius, he alleges what must be absolutely true or false with respect to all men. But if Sejus alleges a certain estate in the possession of Titius to be his, he only affirms his title to be superior to that of Titius, for there may be some other person who is the real owner, and the right of that person not being directly and lawfully decided upon by the court, as he is not a party to the cause (though it may be incidentally before the court) he is not concluded by the decree.

It follows that valid judgments deciding causes of status are conclusive and final against all men, while judgments in other causes are so only between the parties and touching their relative rights and obligations.

The plan of this treatise requires that we should now proceed

[d] Vide supra, chap. xlvi. Cujacii Op. tom. vii. col. 124, edit. Venet. Mutin.

[e] Vinnii Comm. ad Instit. lib. iv. tit. vi. § 13, num. 2.

[f] Pand. lib. xliv. tit. ii. De Exceptione Rei Judicatæ, L. 1. Pand. lib. xlii. tit. i. De Re Judicatâ, L. 63.

[g] Pand. lib. i. tit. v. De Statu Hominum, L. 25.

[h] Pand. lib. l. tit. ult. L. 207. Cod. lib. vii. tit. l. Sententiam rescindi non posse, L. 3; lib. vii. tit. lxvii. De his qui propter Metum Judicis non appellaverunt, L. 1.

(passing over several paragraphs) to the seventh title of the sixth book of the Institutes, which treats of actions on contracts entered into with persons in legal bondage, which bind their fathers and masters.[i] And two of these must be here explained, namely, *Actio exercitoria*, and *Actio institoria*.

Actio exercitoria is where any one places his slave as master of his ship, and any transactions are entered into by third parties with him touching the business with which he is entrusted. The person who has the profits from the ship is called *exercitor*. The *actio institoria* lies where any one has placed his slave at the head of a shop or any other trade or commercial business, and the slave has entered into engagements in that business. It is called *institoria*, because those who are so employed are called *institores*. The persons who deal with exercitors and institors do so on the credit of their employers, against whom therefore the Prætor gives an action. And the Prætor for the same reason gave an action where the person employed was a freeman.[k]

The *exercitor* of a ship who appoints a master to whom its management is entrusted, is responsible for the acts of that agent and for the effects of his incapacity. The *exercitor* is the person who derives the profit from the employment of the ship, whether he be the owner or only the lessee or charterer.[l] And whoever appoints the master must be held to give him authority to bind his principal whom he represents as agent, so far as regards the duties and business with the discharge of which he is entrusted.[m]

Upon these principles the modern Civil Law allows the master to hypothecate the ship for necessary expenses when he is out of reach of assistance from his employers, and to take up for that purpose money at high interest, placing the money at the risk of the lender in the event of the loss of the ship. This is called *Bottomry*.[n] And it in some respects resembles *nauticum fœnus*, which is an agreement for the payment of a high rate of interest, where money or other merchandise is carried across the sea at the risk of the creditor, so that he loses the debt if the voyage be not safely performed.[o] And from this contract the modern contract of insurance was probably in part derived.

[i] Instit. lib. iv. tit. vii. Quod cum eo qui in Alienâ Potestate est Negotium Gestum dicitur.

[k] Instit. lib. iv. tit. vii. § 2. Heineccii Antiquit. lib. iv. tit. vi.

[l] Pand. lib. xiv. tit. i. De Exercitoriâ Actione, L. 1, § 15.

[m] Voet, Comm. ad Pand. lib. xiv. tit. i. num. 3. Pand. ibid. L. 1, § 2, 5.

[n] Voet, Comm. ad. Pand. ibid. num. 3.

[o] Voet, Comm. ad Pand. lib. xxii. tit. ii. De Nautico Fœnere, num. 1. These contracts were restrained by Stat. 19 Geo. II c. 37.

The exercitor is however liable for those acts only of the master which relate to the matters committed to him.[p] It follows therefore that those who deal with the master, or indeed with any agent, should endeavour to acquaint themselves with the nature and extent of his power. *Qui cum alio contrahit vel est vel debet esse non ignarus conditionis ejus.*[q] And so persons lending money to the master are bound to examine into the necessity and use of the loan, though they need not see to the application of the money.[r]

But it follows from the principles explained above that if the master deceive the person dealing with him in matters within the natural limits of his business and notwithstanding the inquiries of that person, the exercitor is liable.[s]

Where there are several exercitors, the Roman Law allows the *actio exercitoria* to be brought against any one of them for the whole debt, and that exercitor having paid the whole has an action to compel the others to bear their share. Gajus says that this is allowed *ne qui cum uno contraxit in plures adversarios distringatur.*[t] But Grotius holds that according to equity each should be liable only to the extent of his share.[u]

We come now to the *actio institoria*, which is similar in its general rules to the *actio exercitoria.*

The equitable grounds of this are the same as those of the former action. *Is qui contrahit videtur fidem sequi ejus qui præposuit institorem.*[x] Dealings are entered into with the institor on the credit of his principal, who is therefore liable. And as the principal derives advantage from the services of the institor, it is just that the former should be liable for the acts of the latter in the business for which he is employed.[y]

But the liability of the principal for the acts of the agent is subject to the same rules as that of the exercitor for the act of the master. *Conditio præpositionis servanda est:* and on the other hand, *Non debent decipi contrahentes.*[z]

From the latter rule depends the principle that those who deal with the agent *bonâ fide* and being justly ignorant of the cessation or modification of his power as agent are not to suffer prejudice thereby.[a]

[p] Pand. lib. xiv. tit. i. De Exercitoria Actione, L. 1, § 7, L. 1, § 12.

[q] Pand. lib. l. tit. ult. L. 19.

[r] Pand. lib. xiv. tit. i. De Exercitoria Actione, L. 7.

[s] See the explanation of the Contract of Mandate, chap. xxxix.

[t] Pand. ubi supra, L. 1, L. 3, L. 2.

[u] Grot. Droit de la Guerre, liv. ii. chap. xi. § 13.

[x] Instit. lib. iv. tit. vii. § 1, 2.

[y] Pand. lib. xiv. tit. iii. De Institoria Actione, L. 1. Pand. lib. l. tit. ult. L. 149. Pand. lib. xiv. tit. iii. De Institoria Actione, L. 11, § 5. Voet ad Pand. lib. xiv. tit. iii. num. 3.

CHAPTER XLIX.

THE LAW OF ACTIONS.—OF THE EXTINCTION AND PERPETUATION OF RIGHTS OF ACTION.

Of the Extinction and Perpetuation of Rights of Action.—Instit. lib. iv. tit. xii. De Perpetuis et Temporalibus Actionibus et quæ ad Heredes et in Heredes transeunt.—General Rules given by Justinian.—Explanation of the word *Heirs.*—Principles as to Action *in Rem.*—Principles as to Actions *ex Contractu.*—Principles as to Actions *ex Delicto.*—Penal Actions.—Rule of the Canon Law making Heirs liable in Actions *ex Delicto* for Wrongs done by the Deceased.—Perpetuation of Actions by *Litiscontestation.* P. 302.

Certain actions may be prosecuted by and against the heirs of the original parties, while other actions expire with the person in whom they are first vested, and can be brought only against the party originally liable to them. And on this subject Justinian lays down the following rules.

Not all actions competent to any one, either by the Civil Law or under the edict of the Prætor, lie against the heir, or are given by the Prætor against the heir. It is an undoubted rule of law that penal actions touching maleficia are not competent against the heir of the person who has committed the maleficium, as, for instance, actions of theft, rapine, injury, and injurious damage. But these actions are competent to the heir of the injured person, excepting the action of injury,[a] *and those of a like nature. But in some cases an action ex contractu is not competent against the heir, as, for instance, where the deceased was guilty of fraud (dolum) and the heir derived no profit from that fraud. The penal actions, however, which we have enumerated above, are competent to and against heirs, if the original parties have come to litiscontestation on them.*[b]

It is necessary here to call to mind that in the Roman Law the term *heirs* embraces testamentary as well as legal heirs; and that the heir is *una eademque persona cum defuncto;* and that the deceased is represented by the heir of his heir. *Heres heredis heres est.*[c] Some actions are competent to and against heirs; some to, but not against heirs, and others neither to nor against heirs.

[a] *De Injuriis,* vide Instit. lib. iv. tit. iv. princip.

[b] Instit. lib. iv. tit. xii. § 1.

[c] Pand. lib. l. tit. penult. L. 170, 65, tit. ult. L. 59, 120, 62, 194.

Actions *in rem* are competent against heirs, if they possess the thing the dominion over which is asserted by the action; though they are liable rather as possessors than as heirs. And actions *in rem* are competent to heirs because they represent the deceased in his rights of property,[d] provided the duration of such rights be not restricted to the life of the deceased.

Actions *ex contractu* (which are *in personam*) are competent to heirs, because men stipulate not only for themselves but for their heirs.[e] And they are competent against heirs also, so far as they are *rei persecutoræ*,—to obtain something, by not obtaining which the estate of the deceased would suffer diminution. Thus an action for money lent can be brought against the heir of the borrower, because that money is part of the estate of the plaintiff—*res abest* out of the estate.[f] And the action lies as well against the heir of the borrower as against the borrower himself, for the heir received the inheritance subject to the obligations of the deceased, as no man can transfer to another more right than he himself has.[g]

Upon the same principles, where an action *ex contractu* is to obtain satisfaction for the *dolum* of the defendant—there as that dole binds the party guilty of it, because it defeats the rights of the other—the liability for dole descends on the heir, who would otherwise be freed by the dole of the deceased from the hereditary obligation. Thus if a deposit perish through the dole of the deceased depositary, his heir would be freed from the obligation of the contract, unless he were liable for that dole as heir, and thus the depositor would suffer a loss of his property.[h] It follows from the same doctrines, that where the action is not *rei persecutoria*, that is to say, not to obtain something, but wholly of a penal nature, though it be for breach of a contract, the liability to the action does not descend on the heir. *Pœnâ ex delicto defuncti heres teneri non debet.*[i] But as no man shall profit by his own wrong, so neither shall he profit by the wrong of those who he represents. Consequently if the heir derive any gain from the wrong of the deceased, he must be liable so far as that gain extend .[k] *Turpia lucra heredibus quoque extorqueri constitutum est, licet crimina extinguantur.* Thus if the deceased received anything as a reward for a breach of the law, or by any other crime, the heir is liable so far as the lucre came to

[d] Pand. lib. vi. tit. i. De Rei Vindicatione, L. 42. Pand. lib. xliv. tit. vii. De Obligationibus et Actionibus, L. 28.

[e] Pothier, Des Obligations, num. 673.

[f] Pand. lib. l. tit. penult. lib. xlix.

[g] Pand. lib. l. tit. ult. L. 54, 120.

[h] Pand. lib. xv. tit. iii. Depositi vel Contra, L. 7, § 3. Pand. lib. l. tit. ult. L. 157, § 2, L. 152, § 3.

[i] Pand. lib. l. tit. ult. L. 38.

[k] Pand. ibid. et L. 44, 127.

him.[l] And this is so though the form of the action be of a penal nature. But strictly penal actions, which are intended to punish the offender for the purpose of example, do not lie against his heir.[m]

Actions on obligations *ex delicto*, which are not penal, but *rei persecutoriæ*, that is to say, for a remedy, are competent to and against heirs on the same principles which apply to actions arising from obligations *ex contractu*.

Thus these actions are as extensive in their operation with regard to the heir as with regard to the wrong-doer himself, and the heir is bound *in solidum*, and not merely so far as he has profited by the wrong.[n]

Except so far as the heir has profited by the delict of the deceased, he is not liable by the Civil Law to a penal action, though it be in part for the recovery of compensation for the injury suffered by the delict of the deceased.[o]

But the Canon Law improved on the Civil Law, by giving an action against the heir wherever the deceased has injured any one by delict, though the heir has received no emolument thereby; and this equitable provision has been adopted by the modern civilians.[p] And it is just that the heir should be liable, on the same principle on which the heir is liable for the dole of the deceased in an action *ex contractu*. The plaintiff in both species of cases seeks to recover something *quod ei abest*, and which is due to him by virtue of the obligation of the deceased. But the heir is not liable beyond the value of the inheritance.

Penal actions are in general competent to the heir of the person injured, because the inheritance is impaired by the damage done, and the heir therefore inherits less than he would have inherited if the injury had not been committed.[q]

On that principle the right of action for personal insults and outrages does not pass to the heir of the injured person, because the wrong is personal and does not affect the inheritance, and therefore if the heir were to bring the action, he would assert the right of another person and not his own right. *De suo, non de alieno jure quemque agere oportet.*[r] And so it is in all actions of a similar nature where the heir

[l] Pand. lib. iii. tit. vi. De Calumniatoribus, L. 5.

[m] Cod. lib. ix. tit. xlvii. De Pœnis, L. 22.

[n] Vinnii Comment. ad Instit. lib. iv. tit. xii. num. 7.

[o] Instit. lib. iv. tit. xxii. § 1.

[p] Vinnii Comm. ad Instit. lib. iv. tit. xii. § 1, num. 7.

[q] Instit. lib. iv. tit. vi. § penult.

[r] Pand. lib. xlvii. tit. x. De Injuriis et Famosis Libellis, L. 13. Pand lib. vii. tit. vi. Si Ususfructus petatur, L. 5.

has nothing to claim, because he has suffered no loss by the wrong done to the deceased.

All temporary actions,—that is to say, all actions which expire by the death of a party, or even by lapse of time, —have this in common, that they become perpetual by being *inclusæ judicio*, that is to say, by litiscontestation.[s]

Litiscontestation is when the plaintiff has brought in his libel, and the defendant has pleaded to it.[t] And by the Imperial Constitutions penal actions become perpetual by the defendant being summoned.[u]

The doctrine with respect to the perpetuation of actions by litiscontestation is that, by pleading, the defendant enters into an engagement to submit to the judgment, and the obligation arising therefrom passes to his heirs, as the right does to the heirs of the plaintiff. As for perpetuation by summons and before contestation, it is founded on the principle that the obligation to plead attaches on the defendant, and has the same effect as if contestation had been made.

CHAPTER L.

THE LAW OF ACTIONS.—OF EXCEPTIONS AND REPLICATIONS.

Of Exceptions and Replications.—Instit. lib. iv. tit. xiii. De Exceptionibus.—Confession.—Its Effect in Civil and in Criminal Proceedings.—Simple Denial.—Rule as to the *Onus Probandi*.—Nature of an Exception.—Exceptions of Law and of Fact.—Examples of Exceptions given by Justinian.—The Exception *quod Metus Causa* explained.—Effect of Fear and Force.—*Exceptio Doli Mali*.—Effect of Dole.—Exception *in Factum*.—Effect of Error.—*Exceptio Rei Judicatæ*. Peremptory Exceptions and Dilatory Exceptions.—Replications.—Subsequent Steps of Pleading.—Effect of Exceptions as to Fidejussors and Heirs. P. 311.

Having given the rudiments of the Law of Actions, Justinian proceeds to show the mode whereby the defendant may contest the demand made upon him.

When the plaintiff has brought in his libel, the defendant must choose out of three courses of proceeding, namely, *confession*, *denial*, and *exception*.

If he confess, the judgment of the court for the plaintiff necessarily

[s] Pand. lib. l. tit. ult. L. 139. Pand. lib. xliv. tit. vii. De Obligationibus et Actionibus, L. 58. [t] Voet, Comm. ad Pand. lib. v. tit. i. num. 144.

[u] Pand. lib. xliv. tit. vii. De Obligationibus et Actionibus, L. 33.

follows, for Paulus says, *Confessus pro judicato est, qui quodammodo sua sententia damnatur.*[a]

This rule, however, exclusively applies to civil proceedings; and in criminal accusations, the Civil Law allows no man to be condemned on his own confession alone,[b] because there have been instances where an innocent man has confessed himself guilty from insanity, enthusiasm or secret motives.[c] And herein the Civil Law seems more humane than the Law of England, which holds a confession to be conclusive in criminal as in civil cases.[d]

If the defendant simply deny the demand contained in the action, he puts the plaintiff to the proof of the allegations of fact necessary to support it. *Ei incumbit probatio qui dicit, non qui negat.*[e] Hence the common maxim, *Actore non probante reus absolvitur.*

This rule, however, which casts the burthen of proof on the party asserting, and confines the judge to deciding on what is alleged and proved (*allegata et probata*), does not apply to questions of law, for the law is in the breast of the judge.[f]

If the defendant oppose the demand of the plaintiff not by a simple denial, but by the allegation of some new matter incompatible with the action, for the purpose of defeating it wholly or in part, that defence is an *exception.*[g]

Every exception must contain an admission, for if the defendant admit nothing, his defence is a simple denial and not an exception, which admits that the action would be good, but for the new matter which the defendant propounds. And thus if the defendant deny that the action lies in point of law, he admits the truth of the facts, but relies on their insufficiency in law. This is called an *exception of law.*[h] So if the defendant plead a set-off or compensation, or the payment of the debt demanded in the action, or a release or discharge, he admits that the demand would be good but for the new fact which he thus propounds. This is an *exception of fact.*[i]

On the principle that he who asserts must prove, and not he who

[a] Pand. lib. xlii. tit. ii. De Confessis, L. 1, and the Comment of Voet on that title.

[b] Pand. lib. xlviii. tit. xviii. De Quæstionibus, L. 1, § 17. Carmignani Instit. Jur. Crimin. tit. De Confessis.

[c] And see Boehmerus, Element. Jur. Crim. sect. i. § 206, &c.

[d] Blackst. Comm. book iv. chap. xxv. p. 329.

[e] Pand. lib. xxii. tit. iii. De Probationibus et Præsumptionibus, L. 2.

[f] Cod. lib. ii. tit. xi. Ut quæ desunt Advocatis Partium Judex suppleat, L. unic.

[g] Instit. lib. iv. tit. xiii. princip. Pand. lib. xliv. tit. i. De Exceptionibus, L. 2, L. 22.

[h] Vinnii Comm. ad Instit. lib. iv. tit. xiii. paratit. Donelli Com. lib. xii. cap. i. § 3, note 3, Hilligeri.

[i] Voet, Comm. ad Pand. lib. xliv. tit. i. § 4.

denies, the *reus*, or defendant, must prove the new matter of fact alleged in his exception. Thus, Ulpian says, *Reus in exceptione actor est.*[k]

We will now proceed to the examples of exceptions given in Justinian's Institutes. And first of the exceptions, *Quod metus causa, de dolo, et in factum.*

If compelled by fear or induced by dole, or through error you promised by stipulation with Titius that which you were not bound to promise, you are technically bound in law, and an action lies alleging that you are bound to give what you promised. But it would be unjust that you should be defeated in that action. Therefore you have the exception quod metus causa, or doli mali, or in factum to impugn the action.[l]

The meaning of this paragraph is that where consent has been extorted by fear, obtained by fraud, or given through error, the consent is a fact which by itself gives ground for an action, but the exception brings before the court the efficient cause of that consent which renders it ineffectual and not binding.

And first we will briefly examine the exception, *quod metus causa.* Ulpian says, *Nihil consensui tam contrarium est quam vis et metus, quem comprobare contra bonos mores est.*[m] And the same principles are applicable whether consent be extorted by force or by fear.

Intimidation and force render void those acts which they have caused. They affect the validity of the act only so far as they are the efficient cause of consent which would not have been given but for such fear or force, and this principle governs all other legal vices of acts rendering null or excluding the consent of the party, such as error, or fraud.

Force and fear do not annul any act unless they be *contra bonos mores*, and it is for this reason that Justinian says: *If compelled by fear, or induced by dole, or through error you promised that which you were not bound to promise.*[n]

Where a man is compelled by lawful authority to do that which he ought to do, that compulsion does not affect the validity of this act, because the obligation does not spring from his free will and consent. Thus Ulpian decides that lawful compulsion employed by the magistrate is not included in the words of the Prætor, promising relief

k Pand. lib. xliv. tit. i. De Exceptionibus, L. 1. Pand. lib. xxii. tit. iii. De Probationibus, L. 19.

l Instit. lib. iv. tit. xiii. § 1.

m Pand. lib. l. tit. ult. L. 116. Pand. lib. iv. tit. ii. Quod Metus Causa, L. 1, 2. Pufendorf, Droit de la Nature et des Gens, liv. iii. chap. vi. § 10.

n Pand. lib. l. tit. ult. L. 116. Instit. lib. iv. tit. xiii. § 1. Domat, Loix Civiles, liv. i. tit. xviii. § 2, *De la Force* against whatever has been done on compulsion: but that it is otherwise if the magistrate compelled any one to do that which the law did not require him to do and which the magistrate therefore had no right to require.[o]

On this principle, as the rules of public law have established among nations that every war lawfully made on either side by authority of the sovereign, shall be reputed to be just so far as regards its external effects, it is also a maxim of the law of nations, that the force or fear whereby any one has been compelled to do any act in the course of such war shall be held to be legal, and not to be avoided on the ground that compulsion has been used.[p]

But it is contrary to internal public law for any man to employ any means not permitted by Municipal Law, for the purpose of compelling any one to do even that which he ought to do; for no man ought to take the law into his own hands.[q]

Fear or force do not vitiate an act unless they be such as could affect a man of ordinary firmness. Celsus says, *Vani timoris justa excusatio non est.*[r] But this rule applies only to persons not more than usually weak, for it is the duty of the judge to take into consideration the nature of the means of coercion used, having regard to the circumstances of the party, such as age, sex, and constitution.[s]

Compulsion is never presumed. It must therefore be proved, especially where the party complaining of or alleging it could have appealed to the law for protection.[t] And the modern Civil Law has provided a remedy where any one has reason to apprehend evil from another: for the former can apply to the magistrate, that the latter may be bound, giving security or fidejussors for his good behaviour.[u] This, which is called *cautio de non offendendo,* resembles the proceeding in the English Law, by binding persons to keep the peace, which Blackstone appears to consider peculiar to this country.[x]

We will now proceed to the *exceptio doli mali*, or *de dolo.* Dole is any deceit or cunning used with intent to deceive any one, and it is evidently contrary to free consent.[y] The antients say, *dolum malum,*

[o] Pand. lib. iv. tit. ii. Quod Metus Causa, L. 3, § 1. Pufendorf, Droit de la Nature et des Gens, liv. iii. chap. vi. § 11.

[p] Grotius, Droit de la Guerre, liv. ii. chap. xvii. § 19. Vattel, Droit des Gens, liv. iii. chap. xiii. § 197.

[q] Pand. lib. iv. tit. ii. Quod Metus Causa, L. 13. Pand. lib. l. tit. ult. L. 176.

[r] Pand. lib. l. tit. ult. L. 184.

[s] Pand. lib. iv. tit. ii. Quod Metus Causa, L. 6 L. 5. Voet, Comm. ad Pand. ibid .lib. iv. tit. ii. num. 11.

[t] Pand. ibid. L. 32.

[u] Voet, Comm. ad Pand. lib. iv. tit. ii. num. 13.

[x] Blackst. Comm. book iv. chap. xviii. parag. 1.

Pand. lib. iv. tit. iii. De Dolo Malo, L. 1, § 2, 3.

because there may be *dolum bonum*, or justifiable or not unlawful deception, which does not affect the validity of acts to which it attaches,[z] and thus stratagems and *ruses de guerre* are lawful among belligerents provided they do not involve treachery or direct falsehood.[a]

Paulus writes that this exception was provided by the Prætor, that no man might profit by his own fraud.[b]

Dole does not render an act void unless it be the cause of such act; that is to say, unless the act would not have been done but for the dole.[c]

If, however, the party with whom the person dealt, who was deceived, did not participate in, and was not cognizant of the dole, the former is not prejudiced thereby, but the person on whom the dole was practised has his remedy by *actio doli mali* against the deceiver.[d]

In this respect the *exceptio doli mali* differs from the exception *quod metus causa*, which is competent even when the wrong proceeded from a third party without any participation of the plaintiff.[e] This diversity is grounded on the inconvenience which would result from permitting debtors to allege the fraud of third parties to avoid contracts, and on the reason that if the parties are themselves honest they may easily defeat the fraud of others. But the Civil Law, for the protection of society, renders invalid all obligations contracted through violence or, which is the same thing, fear of violence or other injury.[f]

Grotius, however, holds the obligation contracted by reason of fear without the participation of the obligor, to be invalid only by Civil Law, but valid by Natural Law, because the consent of the party was in fact given, though under circumstances of perturbation of mind. *Coacta voluntas, voluntas est.*[g]

But Pufendorf and Barbeyrac hold the better opinion,—that though consent given under compulsion is so far valid that it renders the party consenting to or doing the act guilty, if the act be contrary to law, yet it is not such a consent as to produce a valid obligation even towards a party not participating in the coercion, because as the Natural Law leaves to our free choice whatever is permitted, it fol-

[z] Pand. ubi sup. Grotius, Droit de la Guerre, liv. iii. chap. i. § 9, &c.

[a] Grotius, ibid. § 6. Pand. lib. xlix. tit. xv. De Captivis et Postliminio, L. 26.

[b] Pand lib. xliv. tit. iv. De Doli Mali et Metus Exceptione, L. 1, § 1.

[c] Pothier, Des Obligations, num. 31. Domat, Loix Civiles, liv. i. tit. xviii.

[d] Pothier, Des Obligations, num. 32. Voet, Comm. ad Pand. lib. iv. tit. iii. De Dolo Malo, num. 32.

[e] Pothier, ibid. num. 23. Pand. lib. iv. tit. ii. Quod Metus Causa, L. 9, § 1, et L. 14, § 3.

[f] Pothier, ubi sup. Pand. lib. l tit. ult. L. 116. Pand. lib. iv. tit. ii. Quod Metus Causa, L. 13.

[g] Grotius, Droit de la Guerre, liv. ii. chap. xi. § 7, and note.

lows that we can be bound only by our free choice towards another to do or to give to him what we are not otherwise bound to do or to give.[h]

There is one case in which, by the Civil Law, the fraud of a third party may invalidate a contract of sale, though there be no participation of the obligee in the fraud. It is where either party to the contract is injured beyond half the value of that which is the subject of the contract. There the law holds the contract to be intrinsically tainted with fraud. *Res in se dolum habet.*[i] This gross disproportion between the price and the value of the things sold is called by the Civil Law *enormous lesion*, and it is a sufficient ground in itself to rescind a sale, unless the party injured be compensated by the other.[k]

The *exceptio in factum* remains for consideration, whereby error is specifically pleaded as the cause of the apparent consent which is the ground of the action.

Ulpian says, *Non videntur qui errant consentire.*[l] He who is in error consents to that which he believes to be true, but not to that which is true. His consent therefore is not real.[m]

An error touching the quality of the subject of the contract does not invalidate the transaction, unless that error fall upon the quality which the parties had principally in view, and the same rule applies to error touching the person with whom a contract is made. In such cases it is presumed that the contract would not have been concluded but for the error.[m] If, however, the error attaches not to the subject of the contract, but only to the reason or motive inducing the party to enter into it, that error does not affect the validity of the contract.[n]

There is this difference between error touching the identity of the thing, or the very substance of the contract, and error respecting the essential qualities of the thing. In the former case there is no agreement at all, because the parties are not of one mind; but in the latter, there is an agreement which however was caused by an erroneous belief. In the former case (strictly speaking) the transaction is void *ipso jure*, and in the latter it is voidable on plea *per exceptionem.* But in practice this distinction is not material so far as regards the

[h] Pufendorf, Droit de la Nature et des Gens, liv. iii. chap. vi. § 9.

[i] Cod. lib. iv. tit. xliv. De Rescindenda Venditione, L. 2. Pand. lib. l. tit. penult. L. 26. Pand. lib. xlv. tit. i. De Verborum Obligationibus, L. 36.

[k] Voet, Comm. ad Pand. lib. xviii. tit. v. De Rescindenda Venditione, num. 3, 5.

[l] Pand. lib. l. tit. ult. L. 116, § 2.

[m] Pothier, Des Obligations, num. 17, &c. Domat, Loix Civiles, liv. i. tit. xviii. § 1.

[n] Pothier, Des Obligations, num. 20.

remedy, for in both cases the defendant must plead the error by exception.[o]

The next plea explained by Justinian is the *exceptio non numeratæ pecuniæ. It is the same if any one contracted with you that you should pay money to him on account of a supposed loan, and did not in fact lend you the money. For he may sue you for the money, as you are bound by the contract to pay it to him. But it would be unjust for you to be condemned in the action, and therefore you may defend yourself by the exception non numeratæ pecuniæ.*[p]

The meaning of this paragraph is, that when the contract is proved, the supposed debtor has the onus cast upon him of proving that the money was not in fact paid to him; and therefore, but for the exception *non numeratæ pecuniæ*, he is liable on the contract.

We will next proceed to the *exceptio rei judicatæ*, which consists in pleading a former judicial decision of the cause which is the subject of the action.

If you have been sued in a real or personal action, the obligation nevertheless remains; and therefore in strict law you may again be sued in the same cause: but in case of a second suit you may be relieved by pleading that the cause has already been adjudged.[q]

The exception here sketched out by Justinian is founded on the maxim of Ulpian, *Res judicata pro veritate accipitur.*[r] And it is for the public good that every legal controversy should be decided in one action, in order that litigation may not be indefinitely multiplied, and to avoid the confusion which would arise from conflicting decisions upon the same matter.[s]

But on the other hand, as no man can be condemned unheard, the rule obtains, *Res inter alios judicatæ nullum aliis prejudicium faciunt.*[t]

It follows from these principles, that the same claims must not be adjudicated upon more than once between the same parties, except on appeal. Such is the object of the plea called *exceptio rei judicatæ*.

The general rule is, that this exception is a good defence when the same question and between the same parties is again litigated (other-

[o] Vinnii Comm. ad Instit. lib. iv. tit. xiii. § 1. Voet, Comm. ad Pand. lib. xliv. tit. i. num. 4. Vinnius, ibid. paratit. (Introduction ad eundem, tit. xiii. Pand. lib. l. tit. ult. L. 112.

[p] Instit. lib. iv. tit. xiii. § 2.

[q] Instit. ibid. § 5.

[r] Pand. lib. l. tit. ult. L. 207.

[s] Pand. lib. xliv. tit. ii. De Exceptione Rei Judicatæ, L. 6. Pand. lib. xlii. tit. i. De Re Judicata, L. 1.

[t] Pand. lib. xliv. tit. ii. De Except. Rei Jud. L. 1. Pand. lib. xlii. tit. i. De Re Judic. L. 63.

wise than on appeal) after having been judicially decided.[u] This exception is not competent unless the same litigation be renewed; that is to say, between the same parties, touching the same thing, and upon the same *causa petendi* or title.[x]

Exceptions are divided by the Civil and by the Canon Law into two classes; namely, perpetual or peremptory exceptions, and temporary or dilatory exceptions.[y]

Perpetual or peremptory exceptions are those always competent against the plaintiff, and which always repel the action. Such are the exceptions doli mali et quod metus causa factum est, and the exception pacti conventi where the plaintiff has agreed not to sue the defendant.[z]

Gajus thus neatly defines this species of plea: *Perpetuæ et peremptoriæ exceptiones sunt quæ semper locum habent nec evitari possunt.*[a] They may be pleaded at any period of the proceedings until the judgment.[b]

We come now to Justinian's description of dilatory exceptions.

Temporary or dilatory exceptions are those competent only for a time, and which only produce delay. Such is the exceptio pacti conventi, where the plaintiff promised not to make the demand during a certain time, for after that time has expired the plaintiff is no longer hindered from pursuing his action. Therefore these exceptions are called dilatory.[c]

There are also dilatory exceptions ex persona, or with reference to the person of the plaintiff, as for instance, the exceptio procuratoria, which is competent where a plaintiff sues by a soldier or a woman, or any other person legally incapacitated from the office of proctor.[d]

Dilatory exceptions are those whereby an action is opposed which is legally competent, but improperly brought; that is to say, at an improper time or in an improper manner.

Some dilatory exceptions are directed against the action itself, as when it is brought at a wrong time contrary to a *pactum conventum*. Others are directed against the person of the judge, or the person of the plaintiff, or of his procurator. There are exceptions to the mode of the action. *Dilatoriæ et temporales exceptiones sunt quæ non semper locum habent, et evitari possunt.*[e] Thus the exception to the juris-

[u] Pand. lib. xliv. tit. ii. De Except. Rei Judic. L. 3.

[x] Voet, ad Pand. ibid. num. 3. Pand. eod. tit. L. 12, 13, 14. And see Pothier, Des Obligations, part 4, num. 851, &c.

[y] Instit. lib. iv. tit. xiii. § 8. Lancelotti Instit. Jur. Canon. lib. iii. tit. viii. princip.

[z] Instit. ibid. § 9.

[a] Pand. lib. xliv. tit. i. De Exceptionibus, L. 3. And see Voet, Comment. on that title, num. 4.

[b] Voet, Comm. ibid. num

[c] Instit. lib. iv. tit. xiii. § 10.

[d] Insti

[e] Pand. lib. xliv. tit. i. De Exceptionibus, L. 3.

diction of the court, which is called in the Canon Law the *declinatory* exception, is a temporary or dilatory exception.[f] Dilatory exceptions must be pleaded at the earliest stage of the pleadings at which the party has an opportunity of doing so, otherwise they are waived.[g]

After having explained exceptions, Justinian proceeds to the next stage of the pleading, that is to say, *replications*. A replication is the exception of the plaintiff to the exception of the defendant. The use of this part of the pleadings is thus shown by the Emperor.

Sometimes it happens that the exception which primâ facie seems just, is nevertheless unjust. In such cases another allegation is requisite to assist the plaintiff, and it is called a replication. For instance, if a man bound himself towards his debtor not to demand payment, and they afterwards entered into a contrary agreement, that is to say, that the creditor should be at liberty to demand payment. In this case, if the debtor be sued, and he except, admitting that but for the first agreement he must have judgment against him, and resting his defence on the agreement, there the exception is an answer to the action, for the agreement was in fact made. It remains a fact, though a contrary agreement was afterwards concluded. But as it would be unjust that he should be concluded by the exception, he may plead the second agreement in a replication.[h]

Thus it appears that the great object of the mutual allegations of the parties is, that the whole matter in dispute may be before the court, and that by each party making his exceptions to the allegation immediately preceding, the points in dispute may be narrowed until something is asserted on one side and denied on the other, and upon the question thus raised the court is to decide.

If the plaintiff deny the allegation of fact contained in the exception, or the legal inference arising thereon, the court must decide on the exception. The result of that decision is different according as the exception is dilatory or peremptory. Where a dilatory exception is held good by the court, a new action must be brought, at such time or in such manner as not to be liable to the exception,—or the objection to the action contained in the exception may be remedied. Thus, if the exception be to the jurisdiction of the court, another and a right court may be resorted to; or if it be to the person of the procurator, a new procurator must be appointed. But if the exception be held not good, the defendant must then plead to the action itself by a peremptory exception. As for peremptory exceptions, they are to

[f] Lancelotti, Inst. Jur. Canon. lib. III. tit. VIII.
[g] Vinnii Comm. ad Instit. lib. iv. tit. XIII. § 11.
[h] Instit. lib. IV. tit. XIV. De Replicationibus, princip.

the action itself, and a final judgment is given on them. For this reason, the defendant may plead several different exceptions to the same action, provided they be not repugnant to each other.[i] An exception may be met with a simple general denial, or by the allegation of some new matter avoiding it, and the latter pleading is a replication.

The defendant in his turn may except to the replication, that is to say, admit that if it were as alleged by the plaintiff he would be entitled to judgment, but state some new matter to defeat the replication. This new plea is called a *duplication*.[k]

The duplication may then be denied generally or excepted to, and this new exception is called a triplication, and so on multiplying the names of the allegations.[l]

But the practice of the Civil Law does not permit the parties to proceed in their allegations beyond the duplication, except upon cause shown to the court.[m] In the whole course of the pleadings, the party who asserts must prove.

Exceptions competent to a debtor benefit his fidejussors (sureties), and may be pleaded by them, unless the cause of the exception be one of the risks against which the fidejussor is intended to secure the creditor; and exceptions descend to the heirs of those to whom they were originally competent, upon the same principles on which rights of action descend to heirs.[n]

[i] Pand. lib. xliv. tit. i. De Exceptionibus, L. 5, L. 8. Sext. Decretal, Bonifacius VIII.) tit. ult. De Regulis Juris, Reg. 20.

[k] Instit. lib. iv. tit. xiv. § 1.

[l] Instit. ibid. § 2, 3. Pand. lib. xliv. tit. i. De Exceptionibus, L. 2, § 3.

[m] Vinnii Comm. ad Instit. lib. iv. tit. xiv. § 3. Voet, Comm. ad Pand. lib. xliv. tit. i. num. 10.

[n] Instit. lib. iv. tit. xiv. § 4. And see the Comment. of Vinnius.

CHAPTER LI.

THE LAW OF ACTIONS.—OF INTERDICTS.

Of Interdicts.—Instit. lib. iv. tit. xv. De Interdictis.—Definition of Interdicta.—Their Use.—First Division of Interdicta into Prohibitory, Restitutory, and Exhibitory.—The Interdict *De Libero Homine Exhibendo.*—The Writ of *Habeas Corpus.*—Second Classification of Interdicta,—to obtain Possession, to retain Possession, and to recover Possession —Interdicta to obtain Possession. Prætorian Heirs Interdicta to retain Possession.—*Uti Possidetis et Utrubi.*—In the Modern Civil Law the Possession and the *Dominium* are claimed together.—Privileges of Possessors.—Presumption of Law. General Legal Principles respecting Possession. Interdict to recover Possession.—Lex Julia de Vi. P. 318.

After explaining the elements of the law of ordinary actions, and the mutual allegations of the parties whereby they are prepared for adjudication, Justinian proceeds to sketch out the nature of certain extraordinary actions called *Interdicta*, which so far as regards their general purpose resemble others, but differ from them in form though included under the same generic appellation.[a]

And first the Emperor thus defines interdicta or *extraordinariæ actiones.*

We have yet to examine the subject of interdicta, or the actions which are brought to serve the purpose of interdicta. Interdicts were formulæ of words whereby the Prætor ordered that something should be done, or forbade something to be done, and this proceeding was most frequently resorted to when there was a disputed question of possession or quasi possession.[b]

It was part of the jurisdiction of the Prætor to grant interdicta, (from whence injunctions in the English Law are supposed to be derived) forbidding or commanding something; and by means of these interdicta questions touching the right of possession were raised and brought to adjudication. But under Justinian, the preliminary proceeding of suing for a formula of action (resembling the original writs of the English Law)[c] was no longer requisite, and thus possessory causes were decided in possessory actions in the nature, and bearing

[a] Pand. lib. xliv. tit. vii. De Obligationibus et Actionibus, L. 37

[b] Instit. lib. iv. tit. xv. princip.

[c] Blackst. Comm. book iii. chap. viii. p. 116, 117.

the name of interdicta without any actual grant of a formula of interdict by the Prætor.[d]

Interdicta are used most particularly in questions involving the possession of corporeal things and the *quasi* possession of incorporeal things, because it is expedient for the peace of society to set such questions at rest speedily, without prejudice to the question of dominion or of ownership.[e] And thus the law holds the maxim *Spoliatus ante omnia restituendus est.* In some cases, however, the Prætor decided the question of *dominium*, or of *quasi dominium* (a term applied to the holding of sacred things which are *res nullius*), as well as that of possession, and in those cases the interdict was not preparatory, but a final remedy.[f]

Justinian subjects interdicta to three successive classifications, two of which require to be separately considered.

The principal division of interdicta is as follows. They are prohibitory, or restitutory, or exhibitive.

Prohibitory interdicta are those whereby the Prætor forbids something to be done: as, for instance, where he forbids the forcible disturbance of a person in possession without legal vice, or the burial of a dead body where it ought not to be buried, or the erection of buildings on sacred ground, or in a public river, to the injury of the navigation of the stream.

Restitutory interdicta are those whereby the Prætor orders the restitution of something: as, for instance, the restitution of anything to a person forcibly dispossessed.

Exhibitory interdicta are those whereby he commands the production of a person or a thing: as, for instance, of a man concerning whose liberty there is a dispute, or of children to their parent in whose legal power they are.

Some persons hold that interdicta strictly speaking are those which are prohibitory, because interdicere is the same as prohibere, and that restitutory and exhibitory interdicta are more properly to be called decreta. But it is customary to call all equally interdicta.[g]

Justinian here shows (as it is laid down in the Pandects by Ulpian) that interdicta are applicable as well to public as to private, and both to sacred and human or secular things.[h] Ulpian also decides that the exhibitory interdict is competent for the production in court of a free

[d] Heineccii Antiquitates, lib. iv. tit. xv. princip. Instit. lib. iv. tit. xv. § 9. And the Comment. of Vinnius on that paragraph.

[e] Vinnii Comm. ad Instit. lib. iv. tit. xv. princip.

[f] Voet, Comm. ad Pand. lib. xliii. tit. i. De Interdictis, num. 20.

[g] Instit. lib. iv. tit. xv. § 1.

[h] Pand. lib. xliii. tit. i. De Interdictis seu Extraordinariis Actionibus, L. 1.

man who is confined as a slave, that it may be inquired whether he be a slave or no. *Hoc interdictum proponitur tuendæ libertatis causa; videlicet ne homines liberi retineantur a quodam.*[i] And this interdict may be sued for or resorted to, not by the person only who seeks to recover his liberty but by any one, *Nemo enim prohibendus est libertati favere.*[k]

The same remedy is given by the Civil Law to parents for the recovery of their children, and to a husband for the recovery of his wife.[l] From this part of the Civil Law the writ of *habeas corpus* was probably derived.

The second classification of interdicta is as follows:—

The next division of interdicta is thus Some are to obtain possession, others to retain possession, and others to recover possession.[m]

Interdicta to obtain possession are called Quorum bonorum, and are competent to those who obtain possession of an inheritance by the Prætorian Law, and to bonâ fide possessors of an inheritance for the purpose of obtaining possession of things which belong to the inheritance.[n]

These interdicta were first competent to Prætorian heirs, that is to say to those persons who by the strictness of the antient Civil Law could not inherit, and to whom the Prætor, in the exercise of an equitable jurisdiction, gave *bonorum possessio*, which was a species of equitable inheritance. But these remedies were afterwards extended to mere *bonâ fide* heirs, to enable them to obtain possession of detached portions of the inheritance without prejudice to the title of the rightful heir.

We come next to *interdicta retinendæ possessionis.*

Interdicta to retain possession are the interdicta uti possidetis and utrubi, which are provided for cases where there is a dispute touching the property of something. And it is first to be inquired which of the litigating parties has the right of possession as against the other. For unless it be first decided which has the possession, the action on the right of property cannot be instituted; for both legal principle and reason require that one party should possess, and that the other should sue the possessor. And as it is far more advantageous to possess than to demand, so there is usually much contention as to the right of possession. The advantage of possession consists in this: even if the

[i] Pand. lib. xliii. tit. i. De Interdictis seu Extraordinariis Actionibus, L. 1. Pand. lib. xliii. tit. xxix. De Libero Homine Exhibendo, L. 1, § 1.

[k] Ibid L. 3, § 9.

[l] Pand. lib. xliii. tit. xxx. De Liberis Exhibendis et Ducendis, L. 1.

[m] Instit. lib. iv. tit. xv. § 2. Pand. lib. xliii. tit. i. De Interdictis seu Extraordinariis Actionibus, L. 2, § 3.

[n] Instit. ubi sup. § 3.

thing be not the property of the possessor, yet if the claimant cannot prove it to be his, the possessor retains possession; and consequently when the rights of both parties are doubtful, the question is decided against the demandant. The interdict uti possidetis is intended for the purpose of disputing the possession of immoveables, such as a house and an estate: and the interdict utrubi regards moveables. These interdicta formerly differed in their effects, but this is no longer so, for he is successful, whether the dispute be regarding moveables or immoveables, who possesses at the time of litiscontestation, not by force, nor by stealth or concealment, nor by a precarious title derived from the other party.[o]

Heineccius observes that some have fallen into the error of giving the name of *uti possidetis* to the trial of the mere fact of possession or *status quo*, when it is clear from this paragraph that the interdict *uti possidetis* regards the legal nature and quality, and not the mere fact of possession.[p]

The interdict *uti possidetis*, the name of which has superseded that of *utrubi* (the two remedies having been assimilated), is grounded on two celebrated maxims of law: 1st. *In pari causa possessor potior est:* and 2nd, *Adversus extraneos etiam vitiosa possessio prodest.* The law presumes in favour of possession, and requires the demandant to prevail by the strength of his own title and not by the weakness of that of the possessor.[q] Therefore the law puts the demandant to the proof of his title, which he must show to be better than that of the possessor, otherwise the latter prevails. Thus Justinian says, *Longe commodius est possidere quam petere:* because *cum obscura sunt utriusque jura, contra petitorem judicari solet.*[r]

By the modern Civil Law the right of possession and the *dominium* or right of property may be demanded together; and on the demandant proving his superior right to the possession, and consequently the wrongfulness of the possession of the defendant as against him, the possessor is put to the proof of his title to the dominion. Therefore possessory remedies separate from those which vindicate the right of ownership or dominion are not necessary.[s]

The presumption of law is in favour of the possessor, and when his title to the possession is subverted by the demandant showing a better title to the possession, then it is in favour of the latter. Thus the

[o] Instit. lib. iv. tit. xv. § 4.

[p] See an instance of this error in Wheaton, Elem. of Nat. Law, vol. ii. p. 288, in margin.

[q] Pand. lib. xliii. tit. xvii. Uti Possidetis, L. 1, § 9; L. 2; L 3, princip.

[r] Instit. ibid. Pufendorf, Droit de la Nature et des Gens, liv. v. chap. xiii. § 6.

[s] Voet, Comm. ad Pand. lib. xliii. tit. i. num 5.

onus probandi is thrown on the possessor after the subversion of his possession, because a legal presumption casts the burthen of proof on him against whom it militates. And unless the defeated possessor then show a title to the dominion which the demandant cannot subvert by showing a better title, the latter prevails.[t]

By the Civil Law the interdict *uti possidetis* brings in question the possession at the time of litiscontestation. But by the Canon Law that party prevails whose possession is the most antient as well as the most just, and this principle is followed by the modern civilians.[u]

Justinian, after thus describing the legal remedies by *uti possidetis*, gives the following general principles respecting possession.

A man is held to possess, not only where he actually himself possesses but where another is in possession in his name, such as a tenant or a farmer. A depositor and a lender also possess through the instrumentality of the depositary and borrower. And in this sense it is said that one person retains possession by means of another, who is in possession in his name. But possession may be retained by intention only (solo animo): that is to say, though a person be not in possession himself, and though no one be in possession in his name, still if he left the thing without an intention of relinquishing the possession, he is held to retain the possession. We have already explained in the second book by means of what persons possession may be acquired. But there is no doubt that possession cannot be acquired by intention alone (solo animo).[x]

The law of possession has already been explained, but a few observations on this important paragraph of the Institutes are here required.

The antients distinguish between *possidere*, to possess, and *in possessionem esse*, to be in possession. The former expression signifies possession *pro suo*, that is to say as proprietor; and the latter means possession not *pro suo*, but by a right, which is a part of, and included in the dominion or right of ownership of the proprietor, or possession as a mere trustee or keeper.[y]

Thus if Titius lease his house to Sempronius for a term of years, the right of Sempronius the lessee is a part of and included in the right of Titius the lessor, and the former is in possession by virtue of the right of ownership or dominion of the latter; for if the house

[t] Pand. lib. l. tit. ult. L. 12. Instit. lib. iv. tit. xv. § 4.

[u] Voet, Comm. ad Pand. lib. xliii. tit. xvii. num. 5.

[x] Instit. lib. iv. tit. xv. § 5.

[y] See the distinction in the above paragraph of the Institutes; and see Pand. lib. xli. tit. ii. De Acquirenda vel Omittenda Possessione, L. 10, § 1, which chiefly relates to an inferior sort of holding, *custodiæ causa*.

be not the property of the lessor, it follows that as no man can transfer more right than he has,[z] the subversion of his title subverts that of the lessee which it includes. *Resoluto jure dantis resolvitur jus accipientis.*

On this principle, the possession of a tenant and of others *in possession* is held in the eye of the law to be the possession of the lessor or other person on whose title their possession depends and in whose name they hold.[a]

There is also a mere detention or possession in fact only. Such is the possession acquired and held *jure gentium* by invasion, and it extends in law no further than the actual possession in fact.[b]

Possession may be retained by the mere will of possessing, *solo animo*, because that which is ours cannot without our act be transferred to others, and therefore we retain our rights of property unless we relinquish them. Consequently the mere fact that property is not in the actual power and detention of the owner does not entitle another to take it for his own.[c]

Thus the Emperor Constantine distinguishes between corporeal or physical apprehension or detention, and possession in right which is retained, unless it be relinquished or alienated.[d] Thus one who leaves his property, with the intention of returning and again taking it, retains his right of possession, or possession in law, though he does not hold the property in his power.

Justinian, in the above paragraph of the Institutes, refers to the antient Roman Law, whereby persons acquired through the instrumentality of those who were under their bondage, and to two constitutions; one of Severus and Antoninus, and the other of Diocletian and Maximian, establishing, contrary to the subtilty of the antient Jurisconsulti, that possession might be acquired through the instrumentality of a procurator, and with that possession either the *dominium*, or the power of acquiring it by usucapion, as the case might be.[e]

Justinian concludes the paragraph with the rule, *Solo animo adepisci possessionem nemo potest*, which is founded on the general

[z] Pand. lib. l. tit. ult. L. 54.

[a] Pand. lib. xli. tit. ii. De Adquirenda vel Omittenda Possessione, L. 21, § 1.

[b] Pand. ibid. L. 18, § 4 . . . . *eam tantummodo partem quam intravit exercitus) obtinet.* And see Bynkershoek, Questiones Juris Publici.

[c] Pand. lib. l. tit. ult. L. 11. Cod. lib. vii. tit. xxxii. De Acquirenda et Retinenda Possessione, L. 4.

[d] Cod. lib. vii. tit. xxxii. De Acquirenda et Retinenda Possessione, L. 10.

[e] Cod. ibid. L. 1, L. 8. Instit. lib. ii. tit. ix. Per quas Personas cuique Adquiritur, § 6. Cod. lib. ii. tit. xix. De Negotiis Gestis, L. 39.

principle that a mere act of the mind not manifested by an outward act has no effect in law.[f]

The next paragraph of the Institutes regards the interdict *recuperandæ possessionis*, and the remedies analogous thereto. A sketch of its contents will suffice here.

So great is the care of the Roman Law to discourage all violence, even for the vindication of right, as unbecoming a well-governed and civilized state, that if any one be turned out of possession of immoveable property, he may obtain immediate restitution by the interdict *unde vi*, though his possession was wrongful as against him who expelled him.[g] And it is provided by the Emperors Constantine and Valentinian, Theodosius and Arcadius, that any one placing himself forcibly in possession of that which is his, shall forfeit the property; and that if it be not his, he shall pay the value, and restore the land to the person wronged.[h] And persons so offending are also liable to the *Lex Julia de Vi;* and are held guilty of *vis privata* if unarmed, and of *vis publica* if they use any other means or weapons of offence besides their own bodies.[i]

But a man attacked while in possession may defend himself, because *vim vi repellere naturaliter licet*, and having been actually turned out of possession, he may immediately expel the usurper. But he must do this immediately. *Confestim, non ex intervallo*, because during the interval he ought to appeal to the authority of the law.[k]

[f] Pand. lib. xli. tit. ii. De Acquirenda vel Omittenda Possessione, L. 1, § 3. Grotius, Droit de la Guerre, liv. ii. chap. iv. § 3, num. 2.

[g] Instit. lib. iv. tit. xv. § 6.

[h] Cod. lib. viii. tit. iv Unde Vi, L. 5, 7.

[i] Instit. lib. iv. tit. xv. § 6. Pand. lib. l. tit. penult. L. 9.

[k] Pand. lib. xliii. tit. xvi. De Vi et Vi Armata, L. 3, § 9.

CHAPTER LII.

THE LAW OF ACTIONS.—OF THE OFFICE OF THE JUDGE.—OF PARTITIONS AND BOUNDARIES.

Of the Office of the Judge. Of Partitions and Boundaries.—Instit. lib. iv. tit. xvii. De Officio Judicis.—The Judge must decide according to Law.—The Remedy by Appeal.—Acts performed by an Authority *de Facto*, but secretly defective. —Case of Barbarius Philippus.—General Rules of Judicial Conduct given by Callistratus.—The Requisites of a Final Judgment or Decree.—Interlocutory Judgments.—Distinction between Questions of Law and Fact, with reference to the Power of the Judge. *Judicium Familiæ Erciscundæ.—Judicium Communi Dividundo. — Judicium Finium Regundorum.* Evidence of Boundaries. — Effect of Adjudications in these Proceedings. P. 324.

Justinian thus lays down the first duty of the judge:—

We have yet to examine touching the duty of the judge. And his first care must be not to judge otherwise than according to the laws and constitutions.[a]

The Roman Law gives the remedy of appeal, by which, as Ulpian says, bad or erroneous judgments are rectified, though it sometimes happens that they are altered for the worse;[b] and also renders absolutely void judgments which are directly contrary to law, or otherwise intrinsically illegal.[c]

Thus a judgment is void without appeal, if its very object be contrary to law; as, for instance, if it be contrary to a former judgment in the same matter and between the same parties, or if its execution be impossible, or if it be *coram non judice*. In such cases the judgment is of no effect, or the judge may himself rectify or set it aside.[d] So if there be an error in arithmetical reckoning apparent on the face of a decree, it may be rectified by the judge without appeal. But if the judge be a delegate, the remedy must proceed from him who delegated him.[e]

The modern civilians, however, have rejected the distinction between void judgments and judgments which may be reversed on appeal,

[a] Instit. lib. iv. tit. xvii. princip.

[b] Pand. lib. xlix. tit. i. De Appellationibus et Relationibus, L. 1.

[c] Pand. lib. xlix. tit. viii. Quæ Sententiæ sine Appellatione rescindantur.

[d] Pand. ibid. L. 3. Voet, Comm. ad Pand. lib. xlix. tit. viii. num. 1.

[e] Pand. ibid. L. 1, § 1. Cod. lib. ii. tit. v. De Errore Calculi, L. unic.

because it is too subtle and nice for convenient application.[f] Therefore a decree can only be reversed on appeal unless the judge was without jurisdiction in the cause, or for want of a citation, or because of the nullity of a procuration.[g]

And a pretended judgment, pronounced without any colour of authority, and therefore absolutely *coram non judice*, is a mere nullity, and thence not the subject of an appeal. But it is otherwise where an act of jurisdiction is performed by an authority lawfully derived and apparently lawful, but yet void by reason of a concealed legal defect. In such a case as this, by the Roman Law, the acts of that authority *de facto* shall not be avoided, but remain good. This important doctrine of public law is established by the case of Barbarius Philippus, contained in a law of Ulpian.[h] Barbarius Philippus, though a fugitive slave and therefore incapable of holding any office, was elected Prætor, his condition being unknown. Ulpian proposes the question whether if his status had remained concealed, and he had exercised the Prætorian functions, his edicts and decrees and other acts of authority would have been void. And Ulpian holds that those acts of jurisdiction would have been valid, for this is the most convenient and liberal solution of the difficulty, because the authority of Barbarius sprang from the lawful source—the Roman people, who could have remedied the defect of capacity of their magistrate.[i] This celebrated law presents an instance of the application of the rule *Fieri non debuit, sed factum valet*, which is founded on an enlarged view of what is most for the public benefit in the particular case. That rule is especially followed in matters of Ecclesiastical Law, where everything is considered equitably, *ut res magis valeat quam pereat;* because the Ecclesiastical Law regards internal effect rather than external form, and prefers rather to punish irregularities or violations of discipline than to annul acts affecting the welfare of the church or its individual members.

The Pandects contain may valuable rules respecting the duty of the judge in administering justice. And the following law of Callistratus (who lived under Alexander Severus) deserves to be given at length here. *Observandum est jus reddenti, ut in adeundo quidem facilem se præbeat; sed contemni non patiatur. Ex conversatione æquali contemptus dignitatis nascitur. Sed et in cognoscendo neque excandescere adversus eos quos malos putat, neque præcibus calamitosorum inlacry-*

[f] Voet, Comm. ad Pand. lib. xlix. tit. viii. num. 3. [g] Voet, ibid. num. 3.

[h] Pand. lib. i. tit. xiv. De Officio Prætoris, L. 3.

[i] Vide Gothofredi de Electione Magistratus inhabilis per errorem facta Dissertatio. Inter opusc. 1654.

mari oportet: id enim non est constantis et recti judicis, cujus animi motum vultus detegit. Et summatim ita jus reddet ut auctoritatem dignitatis ingenio suo augeat.[k]

In the remainder of the title of the Institutes *De Officio Judicis*, Justinian lays down rules touching the points on which, and the mode whereby judgments should be given in cases of different descriptions.

The general rule as to the effect which a judgment ought to have, to be valid, is that it ought to conclude the matter at issue in the cause by condemning the defendant, or dismissing him.[l]

This rule shows the difference between a final and an interlocutory judgment, the latter of which is a decision on an incident in the commencement or in the subsequent part, but before the termination of the cause, and which does not, or does not fully, determine the cause.[m]

It follows from these principles that when the judge has given final judgment he is *functus officio* as to that particular cause, and can change nothing therein; but he may change or rescind his own interlocutory judgments until he has given his final judgment.[n] And the same principle is applied to animinal proceedings by Diocletian and Maximian, and it is sanctioned generally by those Emperors and by Gordian and Constantine.[o]

And so it is with arbitrators. *Arbiter etsi erraverit in sententia dicenda, corrigere eam non potest;* but he may alter or rescind his interlocutory decisions [p]

The extent of the power of the judge, respecting the materials whereof he is to form his judgment, is different with regard to law and as to matters of fact.

It is decided by the Emperors Diocletian and Maximian that the judge must decide upon his own knowledge of the law, though it be not relied on or alleged by the parties.[q] Vinnias holds that the same principle applies to questions of fact.[r] But the better and more received doctrine in the Civil Law is, that as to questions of fact the

[k] Pand. lib. i. tit. xviii. De Officio Præsidis, L. 19.

[l] Pand. lib. xlii. tit. i. De Re Judicata, L. 1. Pand. lib. iv. tit. viii. De Receptis qui Arbitrium recipiunt, L. 19. Pufendorf, Droit de la Nature et des Gens, liv. v. chap. xiii. § 6.

[m] Voet, Comm. ad Pand. lib. xlii. tit. i. De Re Judicata, num. 4.

[n] Pand. lib. xlii. tit. i. De Re Judicata, L. 14, 42, 55.

[o] Cod. lib. ix. tit. xlvii. De Pœnis, L. 15. And see Cod. lib. vii. tit. l. Sententiam Rescindi non posse.

[p] Pand. lib. iv. tit. viii. De Receptis et qui Arbitrium recipiunt, L. 20, L 19.

[q] Cod. lib. ii. tit. xi. Ut quæ desunt Advocatis Partium Judex suppleat, L. unic.

[r] Vinnii Comm. ad Instit lib. iv. tit. xvii. princip.

judge must decide not on his own private knowledge, but *secundum allegata et probata.*[s] So the rule of Accursius the Glossator prevails, *De facto supplere vel proferre non debet judex.* It is indeed impossible to hold a contrary doctrine without confounding the functions of the judge with those of the witness. If the judge has extrajudicial knowledge of any matter of fact relevant to the questions at issue in the cause, he should abdicate his judicial functions, and give his evidence as a witness.[t]

Three important paragraphs of this title of the Institutes remain for consideration, wherein the Emperor shows the duty of the judge in adjudicating on three actions, namely: *Familiæ erciscundæ; communi dividundo; and Finirin regundorum.*

The judge must, in the action familiæ erciscundæ (for the partition of an inheritance), *adjudicate the several things forming the inheritance to each of the heirs respectively; and if the adjudication produce an unequal result, he who is favoured in the distribution must be decreed to pay a proportionate sum of money to his co-heir. And each is to be decreed to pay to his co heir the value of whatever exclusive benefit he has derived from the inheritance beyond his share, and of whatever he has spoiled or consumed. The same rules are observed where there are more than two co-heirs.*[u]

The same proceeding is followed where several things, belonging in common to several persons, are to be divided among them by the judicial proceeding called communi dividundo. Where a single thing is to be divided, if it can be conveniently partitioned into shares, one of those shares should be adjudicated to each of the parties; and if the share of one preponderate, he must be decreed to pay a proportionate sum of money to the other. But if the property cannot be divided conveniently, or be incapable of division, it must be adjudicated to one of the parties, who must be decreed to indemnify the other by a payment in money.[x]

The maxim of the Civil Law, *Nemo invitus compellitur ad communionem,* requires that any co-heir or other joint-owner should be at liberty to demand a division of the common property, so far as his own share is concerned.[y]

Ulpian lays down the general rule, that the judge must make the division in the mode most advantageous to all parties, or that to which they agree; and this is consonant with the principle of Proculus with

[s] Voet, Comm. ad Pand. lib. xlii. tit. 1 De Re Judicata, num. 50.
[t] Voet, ibid. [u] Instit. lib. iv. tit. xvii. § 4. [x] Instit. ibid. § 5.
[y] Pand. lib. xii. tit. vi. De Condictione Indebiti, L. 26, § 4; and see above, p. 221, 241-2.

regard to partnership, that the common advantage of the association should be preferred to that of an individual partner.[z]

Where the parties cannot agree among themselves which of them should have a specific thing in the division, it must, by a constitution of the Emperor Antoninus, be sold by auction amongst the co-proprietors, and adjudged to the highest bidder, giving him credit for a portion of the price equal to his share.[a]

We will now proceed to the action *Finium regundorum*, or to determine boundaries of lands obliterated, forgotten, or otherwise disputed. This action is derived from the Law of the Twelve Tables, which entrusted the assignment of boundaries to three commissioners, whose number was reduced to one by the Manilian Law.[b]

In the action Finium regundorum the judge must inquire whether an adjudication of boundaries be necessary. It is so in one case, namely, where it is expedient that the lands be bounded by clearer limits than those formerly existing. In such case, part of the land of one man must be adjudicated to the neighbouring landowner, and therefore it is just that the latter must pay an equivalent (as nearly as possible) in money to the former.[c] *And whoever has done anything fraudulent respecting the boundaries: as, for instance, by moving boundary stones, or cutting boundary trees, he is liable in these proceedings. And any of the parties may be condemned for contumacy: as, for instance, if he would not permit the land to be measured according to the command of the judge.*[d]

The first object of inquiry in this action is to ascertain the boundaries of the lands, and if this cannot be effected, or if it be matter of extreme difficulty, the judge has power to assign and trace new boundaries according to the mode here prescribed.[e]

The judge should restore the boundaries which appear in the title of the proprietors, unless it be proved that those boundaries were subsequently changed.[f] And if a boundary be proved to have existed at any time it must be restored, unless it be shown to have been altered or that a different boundary existed subsequently. Hence the common maxim of Baldus, *Non presumuntur fines antiqui mutati nisi probetur.* It follows, therefore, that the most recent boundary prevails over one more remote.[g]

[z] Pand. lib. x. tit. iii. Communi Dividundo, L. 21. Pand. lib. xvii. tit. ii. Pro Socio, L. 65, § 5.

[a] Cod. lib. iii. tit. xxxvii. L. 1, 3.

[b] Voet, Comm. ad Pand. lib. x. tit. i. Finium Regundorum, num. 1.

[c] Pand. lib. x. tit. i. Finibus Regundis, L. 8, § 1.

[d] Instit. lib. iv. tit. xvii. § 6.

[e] See something similar in the Hindu Law, Manou, Instit. lib. viii. § 245, 265

[f] Voet, Comm. ad Pand. lib. x. tit. i. Finium Regundorum, num. 10.

[g] Pand. lib. x. tit. i. Finium Regundorum, L. 11.

The instruments of the land tax, and records of a public nature, are of great authority in questions of boundary;[h] provided they were made before the question was mooted *ante litem inchoatam*;[i] because, after the parties have commenced the dispute, they are likely to have it in view in their transactions with the public revenue.

Testimonial evidence may also be resorted to, and even hearsay evidence or tradition, of the existence of certain boundaries.[k] The evidence of the former owner of both estates also deserves weight.[l] And ocular inspection of the ground, by an *agrimensor* or surveyor, is prescribed by a constitution of the Emperor Constantine, and recommended by a law of Ulpian.[m]

With regard to the power of the judge to punish contumacy in this action,[n] it is worth observation that a general power of fining for contempt is by the Civil Law incident only to the jurisdiction of the judges of superior courts, as by the English Law it belongs to the courts of record.[o]

The action *Finibus regundis* is excluded when boundaries have existed without dispute for thirty years.[p]

Whatever is adjudicated to any one in these proceedings Familiæ erciscundæ, Communi dividundo, and Finibus regundis, immediately becomes the property of the person to whom it is adjudicated.[q]

Justinian here decides that the judgment or decree of adjudication actually transfers dominion. The adjudication is made to carry into effect an obligation for the benefit of the parties and of the public.

We have now reached the end of the third and last part of the Institutes, namely, that which regards actions,—and also the conclusion of these Commentaries.

[h] Pand. lib. x. tit. i. Finium Regundorum, L. 10. [i] Pand. ibid. L. 11.

[k] Voet, Comm. ad Pand. ubi supra, num. 9. Pand. lib. xxxix. tit. iii. de Aqua, L. 2, § 8. [l] Pand. lib. x. tit. i. Finium Regundorum, L. 12.

[m] Cod. lib. iii. tit. xxxix. Finium Regundorum, L. 3. Pand. ubi supra, L. 8, § 1.

[n] Pand. ibid. L. 4, § 3.

[o] Pand. lib. v. tit. i. De Judiciis, L. 2, § 8. Pand. lib. l. tit. penult. De Verborum Signif. L. 131, § 1.

[p] Voet, Comm. ad Pand. lib. x. tit. i. num. 11.

[q] Instit. lib. iv. tit. xvii. § 7.

Printed in Dunstable, United Kingdom

91220005R00198